The Men of Madina
(Volume One)

Muhammad Ibn Sa'd

translated by
Aisha Bewley

Ta-Ha Publishers
1 Wynne Road
London SW9 0BB

© 1418 / 1997 Aisha Bewley

Published by

Ta-Ha Publishers Ltd.
1 Wynne Road
London SW9 0BB
website:http://www.taha.co.uk/
email   :sales@taha.co.uk

Editing and typesetting by Bookwork, Norwich

Translated by Aisha Bewley

All rights reserved. No part of this publication may be reproduced, stored in a retrieval system, or transmitted, in any form or by any means, electronic, mechanical, photocopying, recording or otherwise, without the written permission of the publishers.

British Library Cataloguing in Publication Data

Ibn Sa'd, Muhammad
The Men of Madina - Volume One
1. Islam
I. Title

ISBN 1 897940 62 9 Paperback
ISBN 1 897940 68 8 Hardback

Printed and Bound by Deluxe Printers, London.
website:http://www.de-luxe.com
email   :naresh@aapi.co.uk

Contents

Introduction   v

Map   xxvii

Chapter One: The Companions of the Prophet Muhammad in Basra   1
    The First Generation (Tabi'un)   55
    The Second Generation   91
    The Third Generation   143
    The Fourth Generation   153
    The Fifth Generation   170
    The Sixth Generation   177
    The Seventh Generation   184
    The Eighth Generation   189

The *Fuqaha'* and *Hadith* Scholars in Wasit   191

The Companions in Mada'in   195
    The *Fuqaha'* and *Hadith* Scholars in Mada'in   196

The *Fuqaha'* and *Hadith* Scholars in Baghdad   198

The Companions in Khurasan   227

Those in Khurasan after them   228

The *Fuqaha'* and *Hadith* Scholars in Rayy   235

The *Fuqaha'* in Hamadan   236

The *Hadith* Scholars in Anbar   236

Chapter Two: The Companions of the Messenger of Allah in Syria — 237

   The First Generation (Tabi'un) — 273
   The Second Generation — 278
   The Third Generation — 281
   The Fourth Generation — 285
   The Fifth Generation — 288
   The Sixth Generation — 290
   The Seventh Generation — 292
   The Eighth Generation — 294
  The Companions in Mesopotamia — 295
  The *Fuqaha'* and *Hadith* Scholars in Mesopotamia — 296
  Those at the Frontiers — 302

Chapter Three: The Companions of the Messenger of Allah in Egypt — 305

   The First Generation (Tabi'un) — 316
   The Second Generation — 316
   The Third Generation — 318
   The Fourth Generation — 319
   The Fifth Generation — 320
   The Sixth Generation — 321

  Other Locations — 322

Glossary — 325

Index — 332

بسم الله الرحمن الرحيم

Introduction

The *Kitab at-Tabaqat* by Abu 'Abdullah Muhammad ibn Sa'd is one of the earliest collections of biographical details of the early Muslims, extending from the Prophet, may Allah bless him and grant him peace, to Ibn Sa'd's own time (he lived from 148/764 to 230/845 or 236/770). Volume 8, which deals exclusively with women, was published as *The Women of Madina*. This present translation covers Volume 7, which deals with the Companions, Tabi'un and subsequent generations of the people of knowledge in Basra, Baghdad, Khurasan, Syria and Egypt. The people of Kufa are found in Volume 6 and the people of Madina in Volume 5, as yet untranslated.

The Companions are mentioned first in each locality, and then the next generation, the Tabi'un, and then the following generations. The scope of Ibn Sa'd covers the time of the Rashidun khalifs, the Umayyads and the 'Abbasids, and so some brief comments about Islamic history are necessary in order to put the events and individuals mentioned into perspective, and to make the events and comments described more comprehensible, particularly in view of the fact that not much material is available on the Umayyad period!

Books on Islam tend to concentrate on either the Prophet, peace be upon him, and the major Companions, or to deal with the problems of modern times. Why, it might be asked, is it so important to learn about the lives of the Muslims during the first two centuries after the Prophet's death, a period of history which is so often ignored?

Perhaps the most important lesson we can take from this early period is the attitude and action of the Companions and the Tabi'un when confronted by that most dangerous of trials - *fitna* or civil war. In Arabic, *fitna* means 'civil strife, discord, sedition, temptation, trial'. It is used to refer to those disagreements in the community which develop into factions and then into outright armed conflict. This is extremely important because we continue to be constantly confronted by *fitna* wherever we turn. We can learn a great deal from how the early Muslims dealt with it.

v

Introduction

In this period of history, various *fitnas*, both major and minor, reared their heads:

- the Great *Fitna*, stemming from the murder of 'Uthman ibn 'Affan in 35/656, leading to the Battle of the Camel (36/656) between 'Ali and 'A'isha, Talha and az-Zubayr, and to the Battle of Siffin between Mu'awiya and 'Ali (37/657), and finally to the assassination of 'Ali in 40/661.

  This *Fitna*, the first inter-Muslim fight, resulted in the deaths of all the Companions who had been at the Battle of Badr and moved the capital of the Muslims away from Madina. It also resulted in the emergence of the Kharijites, which means 'those who revolt, or go out from the community'. They will be discussed in more detail later.

- the Second *Fitna* War between the Umayyads (Marwan and 'Abdu'l-Majid) and 'Abdullah ibn az-Zubayr which began after the death of Yazid I, preceded by the tragedy of the killing of the grandson of the Prophet, Husayn, at Karbala' in 61/680, and ending in the defeat and death of 'Abdullah ibn az-Zubayr in 73/692. The Ka'ba was destroyed in the course of it. This consolidated various sectarian positions, particularly those of the Shi'a and the Kharijites, which in turn resulted in greater centralisation of the government and made it more autocratic. It also marked the end of the influence of the Ansar and opened the way to various non-Islamic influences.

- Various other smaller *fitnas* - like the rebellion of Ibn al-Ash'ath in Iraq which ended in the Battle of Dayr al-Jamajim in 82/701, and that of Yazid ibn al-Muhallab which really marks an intensification of tribal factionalism in 101/720. An analogy could be made with the effects of nationalism today.

- The third Civil war, beginning with the rebellion against al-Walid II in 126/744 which ended with control being re-established by Marwan II in 129/747, but almost immediately followed by Abbasid revolt, culminating in the Battle of the Greater Zab in 132/750. This put an end to the Umayyad dynasty, quite literally as the Abbasids massacred every

Introduction

Umayyad they could lay their hands on, and moved the khalifate to Iraq. The only surviving member of the family, 'Abdu'r-Rahman ad-Dakhil, escaped to Andalusia.

In *Sahih al-Bukhari*, Sa'id ibn Al-Musayyab is reported as saying, "When the first civil strife (in Islam) took place because of the murder of 'Uthman, it left none of the Badr warriors alive. When the second civil strife, that is the battle of al-Harra,[1] took place, it left none of the Hudaybiyya treaty Companions alive. Then the third civil strife took place and it did not subside till it had exhausted all the strength of the people."

We can grasp the gravity of *fitna* from the comments made by the men mentioned in the *Tabaqat*. Mutarrif said, "When *fitna* comes, it does not come to guide, but to contend with the believer for his own self." The real insidious and seductive nature of *fitna* is that everyone is convinced that they are in the right and, indeed, the group which initiates the strife often has a legitimate grievance and are convinced that they are putting things right. Abu Hurayra reported that the Prophet, peace and blessings be upon him, said, "You people will be keen to have the authority of government, which will be a thing of regret for you on the Day of Resurrection. What an excellent wet-nurse it is, yet what a bad means of weaning it is!" It is very easy to think that you will be able to change things once you are in charge, and usually very difficult to do so!

After the event, when the damage is done and the bodies of Muslims slain by one another litter the battlefield, it is easy to see the mistake:

> Al-Hasan al-Basri said, "When this *fitna* first came, every man of knowledge recognised it; and when it retreated, every ignorant man recognised it."

One of the men mentioned in this book, Abu'l-'Aliyya ar-Riyahi, was very eager at first to go out and fight alongside 'Ali at Siffin, but when he got there, he realised the ramifications of what was happening:

---

1. Al-Harra is a stony tract of black volcanic rock east of Madina where a terrible battle took place in 63 AH (26 August 683) between the forces of Yazid I and 'Abdullah ibn az-Zubayr which ended in Madina being sacked and plundered.

Introduction

"In the time of the conflict between 'Ali and Mu'awiya, I was young and eager and preferred fighting to good food. So I made excellent provisions in order to join the army. At Siffin, the ends of the two armies could not be seen because each side was so large. If one side were destroyed, the other side would be destroyed as well. I thought to myself, 'Which of the two groups will I consider to be unbelievers? Which will I consider to be believers? Who can force me to take part in this?' I continued to reflect on it until I went back and left them."

May Allah give us such insight in times of unrest and dispute!

Ibn al-Ash'ath

One of the major *fitnas* mentioned in this period is that of Ibn al-Ash'ath who revolted in 80/699. This uprising was partially a reaction against the authoritarian and arbitrary actions of al-Hajjaj, the Umayyad governor in Iraq, and also an assertion of tribal pride of the *ashraf*, the local nobles, and their feeling of having been slighted and bypassed. Al-Hajjaj, in turn, believed that he was doing what was necessary to quell the constant unrest in Iraq caused by the Kharijites, even though his actions clearly exceeded the proper bounds laid down by the *Shari'a* – a manifestation of the conviction that the ends justify the means.

'Abdal-Malik ibn Marwan had come to power in 65/685 after the death of Marwan ibn al-Hakam in the middle of the civil war with 'Abdullah ibn az-Zubayr. It took him ten years of war – which involved the sack of Madina and the destruction of the Ka'ba – before he defeated Ibn az-Zubayr. Then he had to put down the Berbers of North Africa who taken advantage of the Civil War in Arabia, Syria, and Iraq to revolt.

At this point, Iraq was largely ungovernable, thanks mainly to the Kharijites. Things were further muddled by the Shi'ite rebellion led by al-Mukhtar in the name of Muhammad ibn al-Hanafiyya, the son of 'Ali ibn Abi Talib, which began in 66/683. Thus in Iraq, the civil war was a three-sided affair (or four-sided if you include the

Introduction

Kharijites who were still active). There were the Umayyad forces, the forces of Ibn az-Zubayr, led by his brother, Mus'ab, and the forces of al-Mukhtar and the Kharijites – all fighting one another. At this point, a brief summary of the events in the second *fitna* might help to make things clearer:

Death of Mu'awiya		60/680
Death of Husayn at Karbala'		61/680
Battle of al-Harra	summer	63/683
Death of Yazid I	autumn	63/683
Marwan becomes khalif		64/684
Battle of Marj Rahit, Umayyad control of Syria assured		64/683
'Abdal-Malik becomes khalif		65/685
Shi'ite rebellion of Mukhtar in Kufa		66/686
Battle of Sillabra (defeat of Kharijites)	May	66/686
Battle of Khazir (Umayyads defeated by Mukhtar)	August	67/686
Mukhtar crushed by Zubayrids	April	67/687
Kharijites control Yemen & Hadramaut		68/687
Defeat of Zubayrids in Iraq		72/691
Fall of Makka & death of Ibn az-Zubayr		73/692

Thus the situation in Iraq during this period was extremely turbulent and nowhere was there any security. While pro-Shi'ite elements predominated in Kufa, Basra was constantly threatened by the Kharijites. Indeed, in 64/683, the governor of Basra, Mas'ud ibn 'Amr, had been killed by Kharijites while he was preaching on the minbar in the mosque. The unsettled situation there was not resolved by the elimination of the Zubayrids. Given the fact that the *ashraf* had supported the Zubayrids (and many of them had been involved in the revolt against 'Uthman ibn 'Affan), their loyalty to the Umayyads was somewhat questionable, to say the least. This fact was not lost on 'Abdal-Malik.

'Abdal-Malik's first governor in Iraq was his brother, Bishr ibn Marwan, who had no effect on the turbulent situation whatsoever. The Iraqis refused to help to subdue the Kharijites and did not even want to pay the Syrian troops who were doing the actual fighting to

Introduction

re-establish order. They had come to feel that they were entitled to their stipends simply because they were Arabs and did not need to participate in the armies.

It is also possible that an underlying tension left over from pre-Islamic times and the long-standing animosity between the Byzantines and the Sasasians was re-surfacing, which was equated as 'Syria versus Iraq'. You often find the Iraqis referring to fighting 'the people of Syria'. There were several factors which probably reinforced this division. Customs taxes continued to be collected at the old Byzantine-Sasasian border at the Euphrates. Up until the time when 'Abdal-Malik made Arabic the official language in 78/697, government business continued to be conducted in Greek, Coptic and Persian. Al-Hajjaj played a key role in the implementation of the use of Arabic. This did not take place overnight. It was not until the very end of the Umayyad period that Arabic was used for administration in Khurasan. Thus the language of administration in the two provinces remained the same. Up until the time when 'Abdal-Malik and Hajjaj minted their own coins, the old Sasanian and Byzantine coins continued to be used.

To a certain extent, for the Iraqis, especially the Kufans, the Shi'ite cause represented the lost glory of the homeland, and the idea of a charismatic family who inherits authority was something they could grasp. The idea of an elected ruler was not something the native population found comprehensible. For them, rule was hereditary and had a divine sanction. The family of the Prophet, blessings and peace be upon him, represented such a charismatic family for the Iraqis – which more extreme groups continued to endow with more and more powers, often much to the distaste of the individuals so glorified. Al-Mukhtar had a chair which was purported to have once belonged to 'Ali covered in silk and brocade and carried into battle. Ibn al-Ash'ath was a descendant of the forner kings of Hira and so he had a kind of charisma as well.

In contrast, the situation in Basra tended to be more a re-assertion of tribal independence and individualism, as we will see when we discuss the Kharijites. While the Kufans tended towards charismatic movements, the Basrans tended towards individualist democratic ones. In Basra there was also an underlying factionalism, to no small extent based on tribal affiliations.

Introduction

Arab-Sasanian coin, 25 AH

'Abdullah ibn az-Zubayr 65 AH

Hajjaji dirham, 79 AH

One side has Surat al-Ikhlas
Reverse has: "la ilaha illa'llah wahdahu la sharika lah"

Introduction

To sort out this intractable situation, in 75/695 'Abdal-Malik sent them the most severe and effective governor possible – al-Hajjaj ibn Yusuf, who had personally defeated Ibn az-Zubayr in the Hijaz. Initially he forced the people to go on expeditions against the Kharijites – and there were two separate Kharijite risings which were taking place at the time, one threatening Basra and one threatening Kufa. If anyone refused to go, they were beheaded. He reduced the stipends which had been increased by the Zubayrids. There were several more Kharijite revolts – taxes were one of the central injustices to be decried by the Kharijites.

Al-Hajjaj then decided to reduce the power of the tribal chiefs (*ashraf*) and raised a large army which he sent against Zabulistan (modern Afghanistan). He put it under the leadership of Ibn al-Ash'ath, the grandson of the leader of the Ridda (Apostasy), al-Ash'ath. This was known as the 'Army of the Peacocks'.

Eventually when they realised that al-Hajjaj did not intend for them to return, but to remain in the east for a rather long time, perhaps indefinitely, Ibn al-Ash'ath and his people revolted and were joined by many devout Muslims demanding the dismissal of al-Hajjaj because of his brutal behaviour which exceeded the bounds of the *Shari'a*. Eventually 'Abda'l-Malik agreed to this and said that he would dismiss his governor.

At this point, pride reared its head and the rebels decided that 'Abdal-Malik himself must be overthrown, thus exceeding their legitimate grievance and putting themselves in the wrong. It is not clear whom they wanted to replace him with, if anyone. They were all killed in the Battle of Dayr al-Jamajim in 82/701. This led, in fact, to an even more authoritarian governorship, as the cycle of reaction and counter-reaction inevitably does. It also ended the role of the *ashraf* as middlemen between the government and its subjects. They were replaced by government officials whose loyalty could be relied on, and a standing army was formed.

The rebellion of Ibn al-Ash'ath is referred to frequently in the *Tabaqat*. It posed a terrible dilemma – what is the proper position to take in such a situation? It divided families as the Kharijite movement did - al-Hasan al-Basri refused to take part while his brother, Sa'id ibn Abi'-Hasan supported it, seeing it as a struggle against injustice. Al-Hasan's position is described thus:

Introduction

"During the uprising of al-Ash'ath, when he rose against al-Hajjaj ibn Yusuf, 'Ubqa ibn 'Abdu'l-Ghafir, Abu'l-Jawza' and 'Abdullah ibn Ghalib went with a group of their peers to visit al-Hasan. They asked, 'Abu Sa'id, what do you say about fighting these tyrants who shed inviolate blood and take inviolate property and abandon the prayer and do this and that?' They mentioned the things which al-Hajjaj had done. Al-Hasan replied, 'I think that you should not fight him. If it is a punishment from Allah, then you will not repel the punishment of Allah by your swords. If it is affliction, *"Be steadfast until Allah judges between us. He is the best of judges."* (7:87).' They left him saying, 'Why should we obey this non-Arab?' They were Arabs. They went out to fight with al-Ash'ath and were all killed.'

Al-Hasan said, "If people are tested by their ruler and are patient, they will receive relief. But if they resort to the sword and rely on it, by Allah, they will never bring about good."

After the event, it is easy to see the mistakes involved during the event:

Ayyub mentioned the *qurra'* who went out with Ibn al-Ash'ath and he said, "I do not know any of them who was killed but that he disliked his end and was not saved. He was only killed regretting what he had done."

Abu Qilaba said that Muslim ibn Yasar accompanied him to Makka. He said, "He mentioned the *fitna* to me and said, 'I praise Allah to you that I did not shoot an arrow nor thrust with a spear nor strike with a sword during it.' I said to him, 'Abu 'Abdullah, what about the one who saw you standing in the row and said, "This is Muslim ibn Yasar. By Allah, he would not take this position unless it were the truth!" Then he advanced and fought until he was killed.' He wept and wept until I wished that I had not said anything to him."

Introduction

Clearly the proper position in such cases, is to stay well clear of them. During the first *fitna*, the qadi of Basra, Ka'b ibn Suwar, had himself sealed up in a hut with only a hole from which he received his food and drink. According to his son, Mutarrif, "He stayed well inside his house and did not go near to them on a *Jumu'a* or assembly until that ceased." As the Prophet, may Allah bless him and grant him peace, said regarding what to do in times of *fitna*, "Keep to your house, control your tongue, accept what you approve, abandon what you disapprove, attend to your own affairs, and leave alone the affairs of the generality."

Kharijites

As we have said, the first Kharijites were those who separated from the body of the Muslims in the Great *Fitna* in the wake of the Battle of Siffin, refusing to acknowledge 'Ali after he had agreed to arbitration. They broke away, hence their name, *'al-khawarij'*, and elected their own khalif. One of their characteristics is that they do not acknowledge the *jama'a*, the Muslim community as a whole. In their view, only utterly sincere and devout Muslims who do not commit wrong actions or harbour incorrect beliefs are part of the community.

Once they had broken away, they promptly started killing any Muslim who did not agree with their position, holding that even a trivial wrong action puts a person – along with his wives and children who were also killed – outside the *deen*. At the same time, they were renowned for their piety and were extremely tolerant of non-Muslims. They were militant, self-righteous, homicidal and suicidal. An example of this intolerance and fanaticism is the sack and massacre of the Muslims in Mada'in in 67/687, and at Sabat they killed a woman while she was reciting the Qur'an.

This sort of attitude was foretold by the Prophet at Ji'rana, when a man criticised the Prophet's distribution of the booty and 'Umar wanted to kill him. He said:

> "Leave him. There will come forth from among you people who are so zealous in praying and fasting that your praying and fasting will seem trivial to you. They will plunge so

deeply into religion that they will come out again on the other side, just as a sharp arrow passes through a deer without a trace of blood or gore."

The Kharijites became a focus for dissidents who were hostile to the government and disliked paying taxes. A factor in the success of this form of intolerant factionalism in this region may well have been because it reflected an already existing factionalism in the Nestorian Church where there was a struggle, which continued well into 'Abbasid times, between the monastic branch with their militant asceticism, and the aristocratic clerical branch, who were closer to the government authorities. A number of the Kharijites had come from tribes with a Christian tradition and their bases were often found in areas with monasteries. They were certainly noticed by the monks and the Kharijite leader, Shabib, is one of the few Muslim figures to be noted in Christian chronicles. Some groups went so far as to put Christians and Jews on a par with Muslims – provided that they acknowledged that Muhammad was a Prophet.

Another theme among the Kharijites was their democratic view of leadership. If they disagreed with a leader, they would displace him or break away and start yet another group – their personal views being more important than the cohesion of the community. The idea that anyone could be the khalif was most appealing and a good number of *mawali* (freed slaves) joined the movement for this reason.

A lot of these attitudes were crystallised in the second *fitna*. Some of the Basran Kharijties (Nafi' ibn al-Azraq of the Azariqa Kharijites and Najda ibn 'Amir) initially joined Ibn az-Zubayr. When they discovered that he disagreed with their opinion that 'Uthman and 'Ali were unbelievers, they returned to Basra and split into two groups, Nafi' saying that those who did not take up arms were unbelievers along with their wives and children. The bloodshed and terror they left in their depradations goes some way towards explaining the ferocity which al-Hajjaj directed at the situation in Iraq and the people who had caused it.

Introduction

Murji'ites

The Murji'ites were the opponents of the Kharijites. They held that it is faith and not actions which is important. So whereas the Kharijites held that a Muslim who commits a wrong action ceases to be a believer, the Murji'ites held that wrong actions had no effect on belief. There was also a political position resulting from this position which suspends judgement on a person guilty of major sins and hence leads to quietism.

There were several criticisms of their position. One was that their position did not object to the unjust shedding of Muslim blood and hence legalises injustice. Another was that it did not allow for any assessment of character in respect of leaders. Yet another, and more important, was that they were imposing their own rationale and opinion upon the *deen* without reference to the early community. In other words, they made themselves arbiters of what is acceptable or not. However, the intensity of their denunciation in the time seems somewhat surprising and may well be due to other factors which are no longer apparent to us. They are decried as doubters (*shukkak*) and one of them (Mis'ar ibn Kidam) is reported as saying that he doubted everything except his faith. They are extremely rationalist in their approach. It is also possible that they took their position from an existing and now lost school of Empiricism left in Iraq – which would account for the intensity of people's dislike of them. However, there is no way to ascertain whether this is true or not.

Qadar

There is also the question of *Qadar,* which is frequently mentioned. The Qadariyya insisted that human beings had free will – in their opinion, any given situation was not the result of divine decree, but rather a result of man's choice and subject to change. Thus rebellion against the existing political authority was justified. Some of the more extreme Qadarites went so far as to deny that Allah's knowledge exists before a man's actions occur, thus denying divine Ominiscience. It was a view espoused by opponents of the government – both the Kharijites and the Shi'a. It has both theological and political aspects.

In referring to the doctrine of *Qadar*, Ibn 'Abbas stated, "This is the first act of *shirk* (associating others with Allah) on the part of the community. By Allah, their evil opinion will lead them to exclude Allah from the determination of good, just as they have excluded Him from the determination of evil." He also considered it to be a denial of Divine Unity. This is the reason for the objections that people made to those who espoused this position. This point of view was later incorporated into Mu'tazilism under the 'Abbasids after it was developed in a more sophisticated manner philosophically.

Mu'tazilites

The Mu'tazilites were characterised by rationalism and severe criticism of unquestioning adherence to traditions. They employed Greek concepts of substance and accident in their analysis, looking to Aristotle for their methodology. Mu'tazilism became the official theology of the early Abbasids, and the khalif al-Ma'mun instituted a proclamation in 212/827 that the Qur'an was created and was not the uncreated Word of Allah. Thus the khalif was the one who could interpret it. He set up the Mihna, or Inquisition, to enforce this dogma. The Kharijites also had a kind of inquisition to which they subjected people - the *imtihan*. If you failed to give the proper answers, you were killed. If you were not in accord with the official position in the Mihna, you were dismissed, imprisoned, beaten and possibly killed. Obviously intolerance seems to go hand in glove with this position.

There were a lot of breakaway groups in Iraq at this time, some political and some doctrinal. This was inevitable, given the cultural mix of the native populace of Iraq. The population included Kurds, Syrians, Greeks, Turks, Indians and Africans, as well as Aramaeans, Persians, native Arabs and immigrant Arabs. There were Magians, of course, since Zoroastrianism had been the state religion of the Sasanian empire, and they, in turn, had their own sects. There were a large number of Jews, including Messianic groups. There were Nestorian and Monophysite Christians. There were a large number of pagans and gnostic sects. There were Manichaeans, Zurvanites, Mazdaeans, and Mandaeans. There seems to have been just about

Introduction

every sort of sect or belief you could imagine. Thus we find the men of knowledge in the *Tabaqat* strongly criticising people whose ideas had been tainted by some of the pre-existing tenets in Iraq, which had resulted in the plethora of sects in Iraq:

> Abu Qilaba said, "Do not sit with the people of sects and do not argue with them. I do not feel safe that they will not cause you to plunge into their misguidance or make you befuddled about what you know."

> Al-Hasan and Muhammad said, "Do not sit with the people of sects and do not argue with them, and do not listen to them."'

> Abu Qilaba said, "The people of sects are the people of misguidance, and I only think that their ultimate destination will be the Fire. It pulls them on. There is none of them who takes up a banner and or takes a position whose affair stops before he ends up taking up the sword. There are various types of hypocrisy." Then he recited, *"Among them there were some who contracted with Allah,"* (9:70) *"Among them are some who insult the Prophet,"* (9:61), and *"Among them there are some who find fault with you concerning the collected* sadaqa." (9:58)' He added, "So their position varies but they are united in doubt and denial. Their positions vary but they agree on resorting to the sword, and I think that their ultimate destination is only the fire."

Transmission

Given the emergence of such grave misunderstandings and differences of opinion concerning the original pure teachings brought by the Prophet, may Allah bless him and grant him peace, and established by him and his Companions, may Allah be pleased with all of them, it was inevitable that the science of establishing the authenticity of transmitted knowledge should develop.

This was reflected in the troubles brought about by the various fitnas. Ibn Sirin (d. 110/725) said:

They did not ask about the *isnad,* but when the *Fitna* broke out, they said, "Name your men for us.' They accepted the traditions of those who belonged to the *Ahl as-Sunna* and ignored those of those who were innovators.

Thus we see that the outbreak of sectarianism and partisanship led to spurious *hadiths* and, in response to this, people wanted to know the exact source so as to be able to ascertain their reliability. For those interested in a detailed analysis of this subject, I recommend *Studies in Early Hadith Literature* by M.M. Azami as a starting point.

Clientage

Clientage was important in the early days of Islam. A *mawla* (plural *mawali*) could either be connected to a person through having once been a slave set free by them, or it derived from men attaching themselves to important tribes or families to seek their protection. The word came to be used to apply to all non-Arab Muslims, whether they had ties to a tribe or not. The Arabs regarded them as being inferior to them because they were not Arabs. Under the Abbasids the term fell into disuse.

A brief historical summary of important events which occurred during the first two centuries after the Prophet's death follows:

During the Prophet's Lifetime (570 -10/632)

The Prophet's Hijra from Makka to Madina	622
Battle of Badr	2 /624
Battle of Uhud	3 /625
Battle of the Ditch	5 / 627
Treaty of al-Hudaybiyya	6 /628
Conquest of Makka	8 /630
Battle of Hunayn	8 /630
Expedition to Tabuk	9 /631

Final Hajj of the Prophet 10/632
Death of the Prophet 10/632

Rashidun Khalifs

Abu Bakr 10-13 (632-634)

Ridda (War of Apostasy)	11/632
Battle of Yamama against Musaylima of Banu Hanifa	11/632
Ayn at-Tamr taken (now Shitata)	12/633
Khalid goes to Syria from Iraq	Safar 13/634
Battle of Ajnadayn (Byzantine army defeated by the Muslims)	Jumada II 13/634

'Umar 13-23 (634-644)[1]

Battle of the Bridge in Iraq (Muslim defeat by Persians)	Sha'ban 13/634
Battle of Fihl in Syria	Dhu'l-Qa'da 13/635
Capture of Damascus	Rajab 14/635
Battle of Yarmuk (decisive battle against Byzantines)	Rajab 15/636
Battle of Qadisiyya in Iraq	Sha'ban 15/636
Jerusalem surrenders	16/637
Occupation of Mada'in (Ctesiphon)	Safar 16/637
Muslim calendar introduced	17/637
Basra and Kufa founded	17-18/638
Year of the Ashes (drought in Hijaz) ('Amwas plague in Syria, 20,000 die)	18/639
Conquest of Egypt led by 'Amr b.al-'As	19-20/640-641
Diwans for stipends set up	20/641
Battle of Nihawand (final defeat of Persians)	21 or 22/641-642
Fustat (Cairo) founded	22/642
Assassination of 'Umar	23/644

---

1. Several of these dates are disputed, with different sources giving different dates.

'Uthman 23-35 (644-656)

Conquest of North Africa	26/647
Cyprus occupied	28/649
'Uthman's recension of the Qur'an	30/651
Initial Conquest of Khurasan	31/651
Muslim Naval victory of Alexandria	32/652
Assassination of 'Uthman	35/656

'Ali 35-40 (656-661)

Battle of the Camel	36/December 656
Battle of Siffin	37/July 657
Kharijites break away from 'Ali	37/657
Battle of Nahrawan (Kharijites defeated by 'Ali)	38/658
Assassination of 'Ali	40/January 661
Hasan ibn 'Ali khalif for five months before ceding his title to Mu'awiya	40/661

Umayyads

Mu'awiya ibn Abi Sufyan 40-60 (661-680)

'Year of the Community'	40/661
Attack on Constantinople	49/669
Hasan ibn 'Ali dies	50/670
Foundation of Qayrawan	50/670
Rhodes conquered	53/673
'A'isha dies	58/678
Definitive defeat of Kharijites	59/679

Yazid b. Mu'awiya 60-63 (680-684)

Battle of Karbala (in which Husayn ibn 'Ali is killed by Yazid's troops)   10 Muharram 61/10 Oct 680

Introduction

Ibn az-Zubayr proclaims himself khalif   61/680
Battle of Harra (after which Madina is sacked
    and plundered)   63/August 26 683

Mu'awiya II 63 (684)
Marwan b. al-Hakam 64-65 (685)

Battle of Marj Rahit between Marwan
    and 'Abdullah ibn az-Zubayr (Umayyad victory) 64/683
Ka'ba destroyed during siege of Makka
    and rebuilt by Ibn az-Zubayr   65/684

'Abdu'l-Malik ibn Marwan 65-86 (685-705)

Shi'ite rebellion of Mukhtar in Kufa	66/686
Al-Jarif Plague, a terrible plague in Iraq:	69/689
Dome of the Rock and al-Aqsa' Mosque built in Jerusalem	72/691
Death of 'Abdullah ibn az-Zubayr	73/October 692
Azraqite Kharijite rebellion begins in Iraq	74/693
Al-Hajjaj appointed governor of Iraq	75/695
Arabic made official language	78/697
Muslim coins minted in Syria and Iraq replacing old coinage	*circa* 79/698
Ibn al-Ash'ath Revolt against al-Hajjaj	80/699
Battle of Dayr al-Jamajim	82/701
Wasit built by al-Hajjaj	83/702

Al-Walid ibn 'Abdu'l-Malik 86-96 (705-715)

Plague in Basra	87/706
Bukhara falls	90/709
Conquest of Spain; Muslims reach the East Indies	92/711-712
Capture of Kashgar, Multan	95/713

Sulayman ibn 'Abdu'l-Malik 96-99 (715-717)

Unsuccessful siege of Constantinople
  by the Muslims   97-98/716-718

'Umar ibn 'Abdu'l-'Aziz 99-101 (717-720)

Narbonne and other parts of southern France
captured by the Muslims   100/719

Yazid ibn 'Abdu'l-Malik 101-105 (720-724)

Rebellion of Yazid ibn al-Muhallab	101/720
Last Companion dies	101/720

Hisham ibn 'Abdu'l-Malik 105-125 (724-743)

Turgesh tribes and Soghdians in Transoxiania defeat Muslims in 'Day of Thirst'	106/724
South of France overrun by Muslims	107/725
Battle of Poitiers (Muslim invasion of Europe stopped)	114/732
Kharijite outbreaks in Iraq	118-119/736-737
Balkh made capital of Central Asia	118/736
Defeat of Khazars in north Armenia	119/737
Shi'ite revolt of Zayd ibn 'Ali in Kufa	122/740
Abu Muslim incites revolt in Khurasan	128/746

Walid II 125-125 (743-744)
Yazid III 126 (744)
Ibrahim 126 (744)
Marwan II 127 - 132 (744-750)

Abbasid Black Banner raised in Khurasan	129/748
Battle of Qudayd (Kharijites occupy Madina)	130/748
Year of the Plague	131/749

Introduction

Battle of the the Greater Zab
(Marwan II defeated by Abu'l-'Abbas as-Saffah)
11 Jumada II 132 /25 Jan. 750
Muslims defeat Chinese   133/751

'Abbasids

Abu'l-'Abbas as-Saffah 132-136 (750-754)
Abu Ja'far al-Mansur 136-158 (754-775)

'Abdu'r-Rahman ad-Dakhil becomes Umayyad
  Amir of Spain   136/755
Kharijites in control of western Maghrib   140/758
Narbonne falls to the Christians   142/759
Shi'ite revolt of Muhammad an-Nafs az-Zakiyya
  and Ibrahim, grandsons of al-Hasan   145/762
Foundation of Baghdad by the 'Abbasids   146/763
Birth of Muhammad ibn Sa'd, author of
  Kitab at-Tabaqat   148/764
Death of Ja'far as-Sadiq   148/765
Death of Abu Hanifa   150/767

Muhammad Al-Mahdi 158-169 (775-785)
Musa Al-Hadi 169-170 (785-786)
Harun ar-Rashid 170-193 (786-809)

Death of Malik ibn Anas   179/795
Moroccan city of Fez founded   192/808

Muhammad al-Amin 193-198 (809-813)

Civil war between the brothers al-Amin and al-Ma'mun

'Abdullah al-Ma'mun 198-218 (813-833)

Al-Ma'mun leaves Marw	202/818
Al-Ma'mun enters Baghdad	204/819
Death of ash-Shafi'i	205/820
Crete conquered by Muslims	210/825
Al-Ma'mun adopts Mu'tazilite beliefs	212/827
Mihna or inquisition about the Qur'an begins	218/833

Muhammad al-Mu'tasim 218-227 (833-842)

Reliance on Turkish troops begins

Harun al-Wathiq 227-232 (842-847)

Death of Muhammad ibn Sa'd, author of *Kitab at-Tabaqat*	230/845
Muslims raid Rome	231/846

al-Mutawakkil 232-247 (847-861)

End of *Mihna*	234/847
Death of Ibn Hanbal	241/855
Al-Mutawakkil murdered by his Turkish troops	247/861

*****

To conclude, it is clear that many of the underlying ideological and behavioural patterns which helped shape these events have continued to manifest themselves and shape events again and again throughout Muslim history, up to, and including the present day. Thus in his preface to *Root Islamic Education*, Shaykh Abdalqadir al-Murabit writes:

Introduction

Historically, the Mu'tazila come out of the Khawarij. The Khawarij make takfir of the main body of believers. Then they in turn split from their original allegiance and set up a further, more extreme 'correctness'. At that instant they become Mu'tazili, and indeed, it was from their ranks that the movement emerged.

So, by their nature these two impulses to deviation and sectarianism are forced to cross-connect one with the other in a doomed dialectic, one which is rarely if ever recognised by its practitioners, lacking as they do the furqan of full Islam.

It is hoped that for the sincere Muslim, living in the present age so fraught with difficulty and teeming with sectarianism and partisanship, who wishes to avoid these pitfalls and to truly follow in the steps of the Prophet Muhammad and his Community, may the blessings and peace of Allah be upon him and his family and Companions and on his Followers until the Last Day - will find some benefit in the pages which follow in clarifying what happened then and what to do now.

Aisha Bewley
Norwich 1996

xxvii

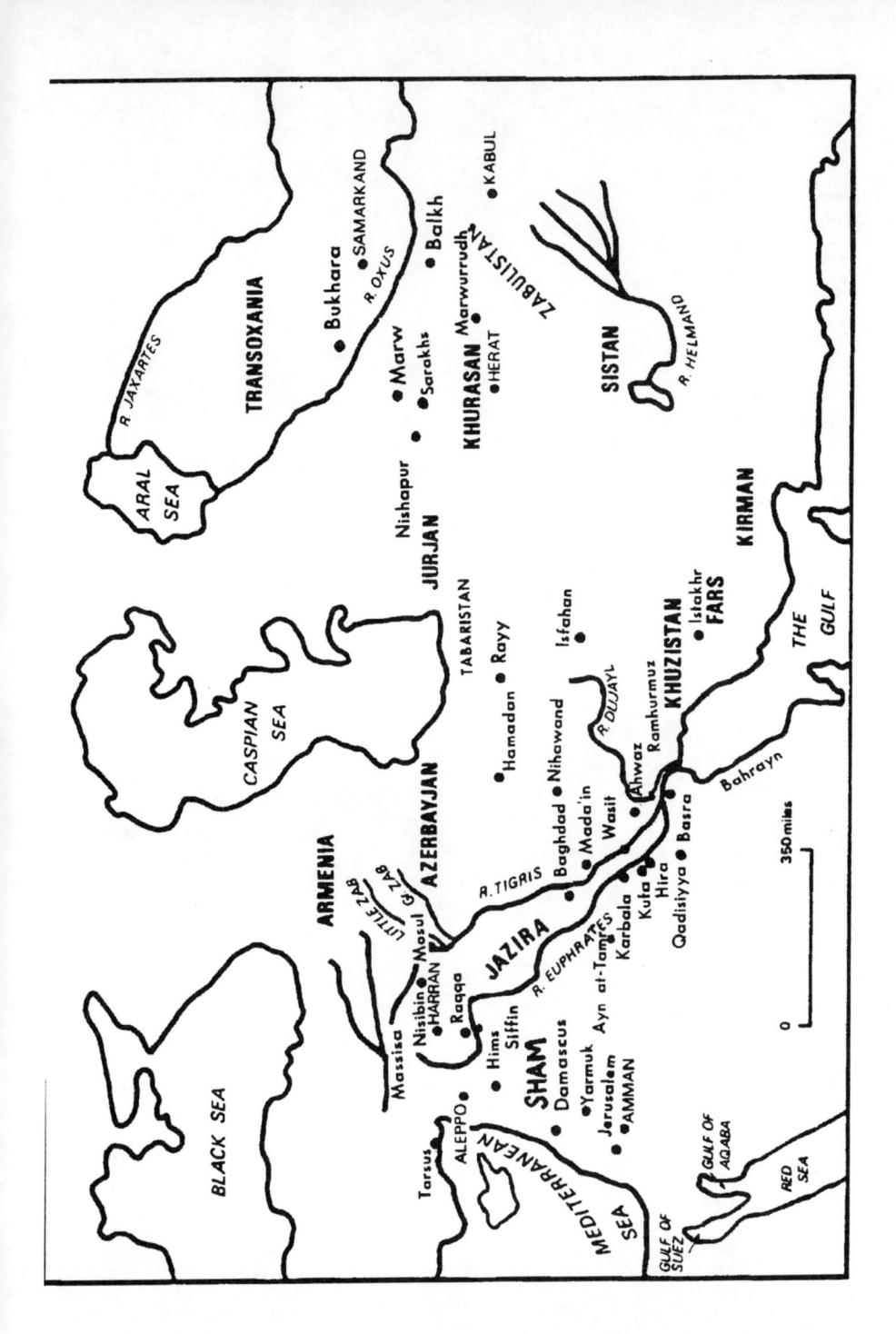

Chapter One:
The Companions of the Prophet Muhammad who settled in Basra, and the Tabi'un and people of knowledge and *fiqh* there after them

'Utba ibn Ghazwan

His *kunya* was Abu 'Abdullah. Ibn Sa'd said, "I heard some people say that his *kunya* was 'Abu Ghazwan'. He was a very tall man and became Muslim very early on. He emigrated to Abyssinia and was present at the Battle of Badr."

'Umar ibn al-Khattab put 'Utba ibn Ghazwan in charge of Basra. He was the one who conquered that area and gave it the name Basra and first settled there. Before that it had been called Ubulla. He built the mosque of Basra at Qasab when there were no houses there.

It is related that 'Utba ibn Ghazwan was with Sa'd ibn Abi Waqqas at the Battle of al-Qadisiyya, and then he sent him to Basra when he received 'Umar ibn al-Khattab's letter commanding him to do that.

Muhammad ibn Sharahbil said, "'Utba ibn Ghazwan was with Sa'd ibn Abi Waqqas when he defeated the Persians. 'Umar ibn al-Khattab wrote to Sa'd ibn Abi Waqqas instructing him to base his troops in Kufa and to send 'Utba ibn Ghazwan to the land of 'Hind'. 'Utba had some prestige in Islam. He had been present at the Battle of Badr. At that time Basra was called the 'land of Hind'. So Sa'd established his troops at Kufa and adopted it as a residence for the Muslims.

"Then Sa'd ibn Abi Waqqas summoned 'Utba ibn Ghazwan and told him about 'Umar's letter, so 'Utba set out from Kufa with 800 men and went to Basra. Basra was given its name because there are black stones (*basra*) there. When 'Utba ibn Ghazwan arrived there, he established a base for his troops. The Muslims erected their tents and shelters there. 'Utba ibn Ghazwan erected his tent which was made of cloth, and then 'Umar ibn al-Khattab sent more men there. When there were a large number of them, a group of them built seven brick villages there: two in al-Khurayba, one in Zabuqa, two in the Banu Tamim, and two in Azd. Then 'Utba went to the Euphrates region of Basra, conquered it, and returned to Basra. The people of Basra used to make raids into the adjacent mountains of Persia [Khuzistan]. 'Umar ibn al-Khattab sent a letter to 'Utba ibn Ghazwan ordering him to attack the enemy nearby [as a diversion].

"'Utba addressed the people in the first *khutba* in Basra. He said, 'Praise belongs to Allah. I praise Him and seek His help. I believe in Him and trust in Him. I testify that there is no god but Allah and Muhammad is His slave and His Messenger. O people! This world has turned in retreat and bade farewell to its people. Whatever is left of it is like the dregs in the bottom of the vessel. You must leave it, so leave it with the best you have. It is extraordinary that a large stone will be thrown from the edge of Jahannam and will fall in it for seventy years before reaching its bottom. By Allah, it will be filled. It is extraordinary that the Garden has seven gates and the width between the two sides of a gate is a distance of fifty years. By Allah, a time will come for them when they will be crammed because of crowding.

'I can recall myself with the Messenger of Allah ﷺ when I was one of seven and the only food we had to eat were some balsam leaves and tragacanth thorns until we had blisters on the corners of our mouths. One day I found a cloak and I divided it with Sa'd ibn Abi Waqqas. Later there was not one of us seven, O company, who was not a commander over one of the garrisons. There is no prophethood which is not followed by kingdom. I seek refuge with Allah from thinking myself important while I am inconsequential in the eyes of people. You will experience commanders after me. Some you will like and some you will dislike.'

"While 'Utba was giving his *khutba*, a man of Thaqif brought a letter from 'Umar to 'Utba ibn Ghazwan which said, 'Abu 'Abdullah ath-Thaqafi has mentioned to me that he purchased some horses in Basra at a time when no one purchased them. When this letter reaches you, be a good neighbour to Abu 'Abdullah and assist him when he asks for your help.'" Abu 'Abdullah was the first to depend on and make use of horses in Basra.

Then 'Utba went to Maysan and Abazqubadh and conquered them. The *marzban*, the commander of Madhar, went out to meet him with a large army and 'Utba fought and defeated him. So Allah defeated the *marzban* who was captured and beheaded. His coat and belt studded with gold and jewels were sent to 'Umar ibn al-Khattab.

When the booty of the *marzban* reached Madina, the people inquired about the state of the people. The newcomer said, "O company of Muslims! About what are you asking? By Allah, I left the people piling up gold and silver." He excited the people and 'Umar sent about 150 men as reinforcements to 'Utba in Basra. Sa'd, who was his governor, used to write to 'Utba. 'Utba was upset at that and asked 'Umar's permission to come to Madina to speak directly to him. He gave him permission and delegated al-Mughira ibn Shu'ba in his place.

'Utba went to 'Umar and complained to him about Sa'd's authority over him. 'Umar remained silent and 'Utba repeated his complaint several times. When it was too much for 'Umar, he said, "'Utba, why do you worry about affirming the command of a man of Quraysh who was a Companion of the Messenger of Allah ﷺ and a man of honour?" 'Utba said to him, "Am I not one of Quraysh? The Messenger of Allah ﷺ said, 'The ally of a people is one of them.' And I was a long-standing Companion of the Messenger of Allah ﷺ which is not denied or refuted." 'Umar said, "That is not denied to be part of your excellence." 'Utba said, "If command is given to this one, by Allah, I will never return to it!" 'Umar refused to do anything except restore him to it and so 'Utba returned, but died on the way back to Basra.

He was in charge of Basra for six months. He fell ill with an intestinal complaint and died at Ma'din Bani Sulaym. His slave Suwayd took his goods and legacy to 'Umar ibn al-Khattab. That was in 17 AH. 'Utba ibn Ghazwan was 57 when he died.

Burayda ibn al-Husayb al-Aslami

Burayda's *kunya* was Abu 'Abdullah. He became Muslim when the Prophet ﷺ passed by him on the *Hijra* but he remained in his people's land and was not present at the Battle of Badr. Then he emigrated to Madina and remained there with the Messenger of Allah ﷺ and went on his subsequent expeditions with him until the death of the Messenger of Allah ﷺ. When Basra was made into a garrison, he moved there and built a house there. Then he left there to go on an expedition to Khurasan during the khalifate of 'Uthman ibn 'Affan and remained there until he died at Marw while Yazid ibn Mu'awiya was khalif. His son also remained there and then some of his son's people came and settled in Baghdad where they died.

Abu Ya'qub ad-Dabbi said that he was told that Burayda al-Aslami was heard to say while he was beyond the river of Balkh, "There is no life except in the transport of horses!"

Muwarriq said, "Burayda al-Aslami commanded that two palm leaves be placed in his grave.[1] He died in the nearer part of Khorasan. They could only be found in the saddle-bags of the donkeys. Burayda ibn al-Husayb died in Khurasan in 63 AH."

Abu Barza al-Aslami

Muhammad ibn 'Umar and some of the sons of Abu Barza told us that his name was 'Abdullah ibn Nadla. Hisham ibn Muhammad al-Kalbi and other people of knowledge said that his name was Nadla ibn 'Abdullah. Others say that it was Nadla ibn 'Ubaydullah.

Abu Barza became Muslim early on and was present with the Messenger of Allah ﷺ at the conquest of Makka. He continued to go on expeditions with the Messenger of Allah ﷺ until the death of the Messenger of Allah ﷺ. Then he moved to Basra and settled there when the Muslims settled there and he built a house there. He had descendants there. Then he went on an expedition to Khurasan and died in Marw.

Sayyar ibn Salama said, "I saw Abu Barza when he had white hair and a beard."

Umayya ibn 'Abdu'r-Rahman reported from his mother that Abu Barza and Abu Bakra had a bond of brotherhood.

---

1. The Prophet once placed two palm leaves on the grave of two people who were suffering punishment in the grave, saying that they would have relief from their torment until the leaves had withered.

'Imran ibn al-Husayn ibn 'Ubayd

He became Muslim early on with his father and brother and went on expeditions with the Messenger of Allah ﷺ. He remained in his people's land and visited Madina frequently until the Prophet died. When Basra was established, he moved there and remained there until his death. He had descendants there. They included Khalid ibn Taliq ibn Muhammad ibn 'Imran, who became qadi of Basra.

Abu'l-Aswad ad-Du'ali said, "I came to Basra when Abu'n-Nujayd 'Imran ibn al-Husayn was there. 'Umar ibn al-Khattab had sent him to teach *fiqh* to the people of Basra."

'Ata' reported that 'Imran ibn al-Husayn gave judgement against a man in a case and the man exclaimed, "By Allah, you have given judgement against me unjustly although I have not been remiss." He said, "How is that?" He said, "There was false testimony against me." 'Imran said, "What I judged against you will come out of from my own property, and by Allah, I will never sit here ever again!"

'Ata', 'Imran ibn al-Husayn's client, said, "'Imran ibn al-Husayn's seal had a man wearing a sword engraved on it." His son Ibrahim said, "I saw a ring of ours in the mud in our house, and my father said, 'This is the signet ring of 'Imran ibn al-Husayn.'"

Abu Raja' al-'Utaridi said, "'Imran ibn al-Husayn came out to us wearing a robe of rough silk which we never saw on him before or after. He said that the Messenger of Allah ﷺ said, 'When Allah bestows a blessing on His servant, He likes the mark of His blessing to be seen on His servant.'"

Hilal ibn Yasaf said, "I came to Madina and entered the mosque. There was an old man with white hair and a beard, leaning against a column speaking to a circle. I asked who it was and was told that it was 'Imran ibn al-Husayn."

Mutarrif said, "I told 'Imran ibn Husayn, 'All that prevented me from visiting you when you were ill was what I saw of your state.' He said, 'Do not do it. That which is most beloved to Allah is most beloved to me.'"

Ibn Sirin said, "'Imran ibn al-Husayn suffered from dropsy for thirty years. Cauterisation was suggested to him but he refused to be cauterised until he finally agreed and it was done about two years before his death."

Companions

Lahiq ibn Humayd said, "'Imran ibn al-Husayn forbade cauterisation. He became ill and was cauterised. He used to shout, 'I have been cauterised with a brand of fire! I was not freed of the pain nor cured of the illness!'"

Mutarrif said, "'Imran ibn al-Husayn said to me, 'Are you aware that [the angels] used to greet me, but when I was cauterised, the greeting stopped?' I asked, 'Did the greeting come to you from above your head or from your feet?' He replied, 'It came from above my head.' I said, 'I do not think that you will die until that recurs.' Then after that, he said to me, 'Are you aware that the greeting has returned to me?'" He said, "It was only a short time until he died."

Al-Hasan said, "'Imran ibn Husayn left instructions, 'When I die, take me out and walk swiftly and do not proceed slowly with me as the Jews and Christians do.[1] Do not let fire or noise follow me.'" He said, "He left some bequests to the *umm walads* he had. He said, 'Any woman among you who cries out for me will receive no bequest.'"

'Ata ibn Abi Maymuna, the client of the family of 'Imran ibn Husayn, said that 'Imran ibn Husayn told his family that when he died, no sound should follow him and cursed whoever made such noise (wailing). He said that they should make his grave square and elevate it about four fingers high.

'Imran ibn al-Husayn's daughter said that when he was near death, he said, "When I am dead, bind my bed about me with my turban, and when you come back, slaughter an animal and feed people."

Muhammad ibn 'Umar and others said that his *kunya* was Abu'n-Nujayd. He related from Abu Bakr and 'Uthman, and died in Basra a year before Ziyad ibn Abi Sufyan. Ziyad died in 53 AH while Mu'awiya ibn Abi Sufyan was khalif.

Mihjan ibn al-Adra' al-Aslami

Muhammad ibn 'Umar said that he became Muslim early on and that he laid out the mosque of the people of Basra. The Messenger of Allah صلعم had passed by him when he was shooting with some peo-

---

1. The Muslims thought it very important to avoid assimilating the various non-Muslim customs prevailing in Iraq.

ple, and said, "Shoot, and I am with the son of al-Adra'!" Then he returned from Basra to Madina and died while Mu'awiya was khalif.

Umayya ibn Makhshi al-Khuza'i

Jabir ibn Subh said, "I accompanied al-Muthanna ibn 'Abdu'r-Rahman al-Khuza'i to Wasit. He would say the *basmala* when he began to eat and with the last morsel he would say, 'In the Name of Allah, the first of it and the last of it.' I remarked, 'You said the *basmala* when you started to eat, so why do you say with the last morsel, "In the Name of Allah, the first of it and the last of it"?' He replied, 'I heard my grandfather Umayya ibn Makhshi, who was one of the Companions of the Prophet ﷺ, say, "The Messenger of Allah ﷺ saw a man who was eating without saying the *basmala*. When he got to the last morsel of the food, he said, 'In the Name of Allah, the first of it and the last of it.' The Messenger of Allah ﷺ said, 'Shaytan continued to eat with him. Then when he said, "In the Name of Allah, the first of it and the last of it," he vomited everything in his stomach.'"'"

'Abdullah ibn al-Mughaffal al-Muzani

Yahya ibn Ma'in said, "'Abdullah ibn al-Mughaffal's *kunya* was Abu Ziyad." He said, "I mentioned that to a man among his children and he said, "His *kunya* was Abu's-Sa'id and he was one of the Weepers.[1] He was one of those who gave allegiance to the Messenger of Allah ﷺ under the tree on the Day of al-Hudaybiyya. He remained in Madina and then moved to Basra and remained there until his death."

Ziyad, the grandson of 'Abdullah ibn al-Mughaffal said, "In his final illness, 'Abdullah ibn al-Mughaffal told his family, "Only my companions should be near me, and [the governor, 'Ubaydullah] Ibn Ziyad is not to pray over me." When he died, they sent for Abu Barza al-Aslami and 'A'idh ibn 'Amr and some of the Companions of the Messenger of Allah ﷺ in Basra, and they washed and shrouded him. They rolled up their shirt sleeves and tucked their shirts in their

---

1. "The Weepers" were those Muslims who wanted to go on the expedition to Tabuk with the Prophet but lacked the means to go due to poverty. They wept in sorrow when they were unable to go.

Companions

waistbands. Then they washed and shrouded him. Then people only did *wudu'*. When they brought him out of the house, Ibn Ziyad was waiting at the door with his retinue. He was told that Ibn Mughaffal had left instructions that he should not pray over him. So he accompanied them until he was near al-Bayda' and then he went on to al-Bayda' and left him.

'Abdullah ibn al-Mughaffal left instructions that he should not be followed with fire in the funeral procession.

Muhammad ibn 'Umar said, "He died near the end of Mu'awiya's khalifate . He built a house in Basra and was one of the group whom 'Umar ibn al-Khattab sent to the people of Basra to teach them *fiqh*.

Ma'qil ibn Yasar al-Muzani, Abu 'Abdullah

He was responsible for the canal of Ma'qil. 'Umar ibn al-Khattab commanded him to excavate it and he did that and then he moved to Basra, stayed there and built a house there. He died there during the khalifate of Mu'awiya ibn Abi Sufyan while 'Ubaydullah ibn Ziyad was governor.

Al-Harith ibn Nawfal ibn al-Harith

He moved to Basra and laid out a house there and settled there while 'Abdullah ibn 'Amir ibn Kurayz was governor. He died in Basra at the end of the khalifate of 'Uthman ibn 'Affan and had descendants there. He related a *hadith* about the prayer over the dead from the Prophet ﷺ.

'Abdu'r-Rahman ibn Samura

He moved to Basra and settled there and died there. He related from the Messenger of Allah ﷺ.

'Abdu'r-Rahman ibn Jawshan said, "I saw Abu Bakra riding his mule in the funeral procession of 'Abdu'r-Rahman ibn Samura.

Abu Bakra, who is Nufay' ibn Masruq

Some *hadiths* give his name as Masruh. His mother was Sumayya, and he was the brother of Ziyad ibn Abi Sufyan by the same mother. He was a slave in Ta'if. When the Messenger of Allah besieged the people of Ta'if, he announced, "Any free man who comes down to us is safe and any slave who comes down to us is free." So a number of the slaves of Ta'if went down to him. Abu Bakra was one of them. The Messenger of Allah ﷺ set him free. Abu Bakra let himself down to them by the sheaf of a pulley (*bakra*), which is why he was called 'Abu Bakra'. He used to say, "I am the client of the Messenger of Allah ﷺ."

It is reported from Khalid ibn Sumayr that Thaqif [the people of Ta'if] wanted to lay claim to the clientage of Abu Bakra. He retorted, "I am Masruh, the client of the Messenger of Allah ﷺ."

Shabbak said that a man of Thaqif said, "While the Messenger of Allah ﷺ was besieging Thaqif, we asked him to return Abu Bakra to us. He was our slave. He refused to return him to us. He said, 'He is freed by Allah and freed by His Messenger.'"

Ibrahim al-Asadi said that when Abu Bakra was dying, he said to his daughter, "Appoint Ibn Masruh al-Habashi as my executor." He was a righteous scrupulous man. He was among those who had testified against al-Mughira ibn Shu'ba and had been flogged with the *hadd*-punishment.[1] That incident caused Abu Bakra to be displeased with his brother Ziyad. When Mu'awiya claimed Ziyad as his brother, Abu Bakra forbade him to acquiesce in that.[2] Ziyad refused. Abu Bakra swore that he would never speak to him, and he died without speaking to him. Ziyad brought the children of Abu Bakra close to him, honoured them, gave them a land grant and appointed them to offices. They became very important and claimed to be Arabs and to be descendants of Nufay' ibn al-Harith ath-Thaqafi. Abu Bakra died in Basra in the khalifate of Mu'awiya ibn Abi Sufyan while Ziyad was governor.

Al-Bara' ibn Malik ibn an-Nadr

He was an Ansar from the Banu'n-Najjar. He was present with the Messenger of Allah ﷺ at the Battles of Uhud and the Ditch and the

---

1. For slander. They accused al-Mughira of fornication, but then Ziyad, who was one of the four witnesses, said that he was not sure about what he had witnessed. Therefore they were flogged for slander.

2. Abu Sufyan had stated that he was Ziyad's father, although at the time his mother, Sumayya, belonged to a man in Ta'if.

subsequent battles. He was courageous in war, inflicting much slaughter.

Ibn Sirin said, "'Umar ibn al-Khattab wrote that they should not appoint al-Bara' ibn Malik over the armies of the Muslims. He might well lead them into destruction."

Anas ibn Malik said, "I visited al-Bara' ibn Malik when he was singing and twanging his bow. I said to him, 'How long will you do this?' He replied, 'Anas, do you think I am going to die in bed? By Allah, I have killed about ninety able-bodied idolaters.'"

Anas ibn Malik said, "On the day of al-'Aqaba in Persia the people were in a tight corner and al-Bara' ibn Malik mounted his horse which was prancing about, calling out to his companions, 'Evil is what your peers call you to!' He attacked the enemy and Allah gave victory to the Muslims by him. He was martyred on that day, may Allah have mercy on him."

Muhammad ibn 'Umar said, "He was martyred in the battle for Tustar. That entire region was held by the Persians."

Anas ibn Malik ibn an-Nadr

He was one of the Banu'n-Najjar. His mother was Umm Sulaym bint Milhan, who was also the mother of his brother, al-Bara' ibn Malik.

Al-'Ala' ath-Thaqafi said, "I heard Anas ibn Malik say, 'I served the Messenger of Allah ﷺ when I was eight years old.'"

Anas ibn Malik said, "I served the Messenger of Allah ﷺ for ten years. He never criticised me for something he commanded which I was lax in doing or for anything I did. If any of his family criticised me, he would say, 'Leave him. If it had been decreed to be, it would have been.'"

Musa ibn Anas said, "If we were not among the Azd, we would not be among the Arabs." This means that they were from the Azd.

Abu Ghalib al-Bahili said that he followed the bier of 'Abdullah ibn Umayr al-Laythi. He said, "There was a man on a large Persian horse wearing a thin black cloak and a cloth over his head to protect it from the sun. There were two bits of cotton to protect his eyes. I asked, 'Who is this landowner?' They replied, 'It is Anas ibn Malik.' So I pushed through the people in order to get near him. When the

Basra

bier was put down, Anas stood at his head and prayed over him. He said four *takbirs* which were neither long nor quick."

Salama ibn Wardan said, "I saw Anas wearing a black turban which hung down behind him, without a tall cap."

'Abdu's-Salam ibn Shaddad said, "I saw Anas wearing a turban of rough silk."

Humayd said that Anas ibn Malik said, "'Umar ibn al-Khattab forbade that any Arabic be inscribed on signet rings. Anas's ring had a wolf or a fox on it." Muhammad said that Anas's ring had a reclining lion engraved on it.

Yahya ibn Abi Kathir said, "I saw Anas ibn Malik enter the Masjid al-Haram and he laid out something on which he prayed."

Qatada said, "Anas ibn Malik was unable to fast about a year before he died. He did not fast and fed thirty poor people instead."

Ibn 'Awn said, "When Anas ibn Malik was near death, he commanded that he be washed and prayed over by Muhammad ibn Sirin. Muhammad was in prison at that time. So they went to the governor, who was a man of the Banu Asad, and he gave permission for him to attend. Ibn Sirin went and washed and shrouded him and prayed over him in the fortress of Anas in at-Taff. Then he returned to prison without visiting his family."

'Abdu'l-'Aziz ibn Suhayb said that Anas ibn Malik said, "When the Messenger of Allah ﷺ came to Madina, Abu Talha took my hand and brought me to the Messenger of Allah ﷺ and said, 'Messenger of Allah, Anas is a clever boy. Let him serve you.' So I served him at home and on journeys. By Allah, he never said to me about something I had done, 'Why did you do it like that?' nor about something I had not done, 'Why didn't you do it?'"

Humayd at-Tawil said that Anas said, "Umm Sulaym took my hand when the Prophet ﷺ arrived and brought me to the Messenger of Allah ﷺ and said, 'Messenger of Allah, this is my son and he is a boy who can write.'" Anas said, "I served him for nine years, and he never said about something I had done, 'You did it badly,' or 'What you have done is bad.'"

Sinan ibn Rabi'a said, "I heard Anas ibn Malik say, 'My mother took me to the Messenger of Allah ﷺ and said, "Messenger of Allah, make supplication to Allah for your little servant!" and he said, "O Allah, give him abundant wealth and many children and

11

Companions

make his life long, and forgive him his wrong actions.'" Anas said, 'I have buried 98 (or 102) of my children, and my fruits are harvested twice a year. And I have lived so long that I am weary of life, and I still hope to be restored to good health.'"

'Abdu'l-'Aziz ibn Abi Jamila reported that Anas ibn Malik said, "I recognise the supplication of the Messenger of Allah ﷺ in myself and my property and my children."

Al-Ja'd ibn Abi 'Uthman reported that the Prophet ﷺ had called Anas "My son."

Anas ibn Malik said, "No one is left who prayed to both *qiblas* except me."

The Messenger of Allah ﷺ gave Anas a *kunya* when he was still a boy.

Az-Zuhri reported that Anas ibn Malik said, "The Messenger of Allah ﷺ arrived in Madina when I was ten years old and he died when I was twenty. My mother took me to serve him. He entered our house one day and we milked a tame sheep we had for him, and he drank water from a well in the house. Abu Bakr was at his left and a bedouin at his right and 'Umar was beside him. The Messenger of Allah ﷺ drank and 'Umar said, 'Give it to Abu Bakr, Messenger of Allah.' But he handed it to the bedouin and said, 'The right first and then the next one on the right.'"

Al-Muthanna ibn Sa'id reported that he heard Anas ibn Malik say, "There is no night in which I have not seen my beloved," and he wept.

Thabit reported that Abu Hurayra said, "I have not seen anyone whose prayer more resembled the Messenger of Allah ﷺ than the son of Umm Sulaym," meaning Anas ibn Malik.

Muhammad said, "When Anas reported from the Messenger of Allah ﷺ he would say, 'Or as the Messenger of Allah ﷺ said...'"

Humayd mentioned that Anas ibn Malik reported a *hadith* from the Messenger of Allah ﷺ and a man said to him, "You heard it from the Messenger of Allah ﷺ?" Anas became very angry and said, "No, by Allah, not all we report to you did we hear from the Messenger of Allah ﷺ, but we do not accuse one another!"

Anas ibn Malik said, "I went to Madina when Abu Bakr had died and 'Umar had been made khalif. I said to 'Umar, 'Lift your hand

and I will give allegiance to you on the basis that I gave allegiance to your companion before you, to hear and obey as much as I am able.'"

Thumama ibn 'Abdullah said, "The ploughman in charge of his fields came to Anas in the summer to complain of lack of water. He called for water, did *wudu'* and prayed. Then he said, 'Have you seen anything?' He said, 'I haven't seen anything.' So he went in and prayed, and then the third or fourth time, he said, 'Look again.' He said, 'I saw something like the wisp of a cloud.' He began to pray and make supplication until the caretaker entered and said, 'The sky has clouded over and it has rained.' He said. 'Mount the horse which Bishr ibn Shaghaf sent and see how far the rain has reached.' He investigated and the rain had not gone beyond the fortresses of al-Musayyirin nor the fortress of Ghadaban."

Abu Ghalib said, "I did not see anyone more sparing in words than Anas ibn Malik."

'Ata' al-Wasiti reported that Anas ibn Malik said, "No one has fear of Allah until he grieves over what issues from his tongue."

Al-Juwayri said, "Anas ibn Malik put on *ihram* from Dhat 'Irq. We did not hear him speak except to mention Allah until he was out of *ihram*. He said to him, 'Nephew, that is how *ihram* is.'"

Thumama ibn 'Abdullah reported that Anas ibn Malik said to his sons, "My sons, confine knowledge to the Book."

Thabit al-Bunani reported that the sons of Anas ibn Malik asked their father, "Father, why do you not relate *hadith* to us as you do to others?" He replied, "My sons, whoever is given too much abandons some."

Az-Zuhri reported that Anas ibn Malik had engraved on his ring, "Muhammad is the Messenger of Allah." Whenever he entered the lavatory, he would remove it.

'Isa ibn Tahman said, "I saw Anas ibn Malik visit al-Hajjaj wearing a black turban and his beard was dyed yellow."

'Imran ibn Muslim said, "I saw Anas ibn Malik wearing a yellow waist-wrapper and I saw him put one of his feet over the other."

Ibn 'Awn said, "I saw Anas ibn Malik wearing a cloak of rough silk and a turban of rough silk and a jubbah of rough silk. Its warp was cotton."

Isma'il ibn Abi Khalid said, "I saw Anas ibn Malik wearing a Yemeni garment and a turban."

Companions

Badr ibn 'Uthman said, "I saw Anas ibn Malik wearing a black turban."

Abu 'Ubayd ibn Muhammad said, "I visited Anas ibn Malik and he was wrapped up, i.e. in a garment of rough silk."

'Abdu's-Salam ibn Shaddad said, "I saw Anas wearing a turban of coarse silk and a jubbah of coarse silk and a cloak of coarse silk. They said to him, 'Why do you forbid us silk and wear it yourself?' He said, 'Our amirs gave it to us and we wanted them to see it on us.'"

Yazid ibn Salih said, "I saw Anas wearing that which we call rough silk, red and yellow."

Abu Ka'b said, "I saw Anas ibn Malik with a green silk cloak with a border."

'Imran ibn Muslim said, "I saw Anas with a red waist-wrapper."

'Imran ibn Anas said that he saw Anas with two red garments.

Rashid ibn Ma'bad ath-Thaqafi said, "I saw that the sleeves of Anas ibn Malik had wide wrists and large sleeves."

'Abbad ibn Abi Sulayman said, "I saw Anas ibn Malik wearing a tall white cap."

Ibn Abi Khalid said, "I saw Anas ibn Malik with a red beard and I saw his turban was loose behind him."

It is reported from some of Anas's family that in the year he died Anas ibn Malik could not fast and he fed thirty poor people with bread and meat with more than one or two bowls.

Humayd at-Tawil said, "I asked 'Umar, Anas's son, 'What did Anas do? How did he act?' He said, 'He was too weak to fast for a year before he died. He told us to prepare bowls and feed a poor person for every day. So he fed that number and more.'"

Muhammad said that when Anas ibn Malik died, Muhammad ibn Sirin was in prison on account of a debt he owed. Anas left a will that Muhammad should wash him. So 'Umar ibn Yazid spoke on his behalf and he was allowed out of prison and washed him. Then Muhammad returned to prison. Muhammad ibn Sirin continued to be grateful to the family of 'Umar ibn Yazid until he died.

Humayd at-Tawil reported that Anas said, "A bundle of musk was put in his perfume as well as a hair of the Messenger of Allah ﷺ."

Muhammad ibn 'Umar said, "I asked Muhammad ibn 'Abdullah al-Ansari, the Qadi, how old Anas ibn Malik was when he died and he said that he was 107."

'Abdullah ibn Yazid al-Hudhali said that Anas ibn Malik died in Basra in 92 AH during the khalifate of al-Walid I.

Al-Hasan said, "Anas ibn Malik was the last of the Companions of the Prophet صلعم to die in Basra."

Al-Fudayl ibn Dukayn said that Anas ibn Malik died in 93 AH.

Muhammad said, "Anas related from Abu Bakr, 'Umar, 'Uthman and 'Abdullah ibn Mas'ud."

Hisham ibn 'Amir

He was one of the Banu'n-Najjar, but his mother was from Bahra'. His father, 'Amir ibn Umayya, was present at Badr and Uhud, and was killed as a martyr that day. Hisham was a Companion of the Prophet صلعم and people related from him in Basra. He died there without leaving descendants.

Al-Hasan reported that Hisham ibn 'Amir said that he went to the Prophet صلعم who asked, "What is your name?" He replied, "Shihab." He said, "Rather you are Hisham."

Humayd ibn Hilal said, "Some men of the area ignored Hisham ibn 'Amir in favour of 'Imran ibn al-Husayn and other Companions of the Messenger of Allah صلعم. He said, "You ignore me for men who were not present with the Messenger of Allah more than I was and who did not memorise more *hadiths* than I did. I heard the Messenger of Allah صلعم say, 'There will be no more terrible trial between Adam and the Final Hour than the Dajjal.'"

Thabit ibn Zayd ibn Qays al-Khazraji, Abu Zayd

Sa'id ibn Aws said, "Thabit ibn Zayd was my grandfather. He was present at Uhud and he was one of the six who collected the Qur'an during the lifetime of the Messenger of Allah صلعم. He settled in Basra and built a house there. Then he came to Madina and died there while 'Umar ibn al-Khattab was khalif. 'Umar stood at his grave and said, "May Allah have mercy on you, Abu Zayd. Today the most trustworthy of the people of the earth has been buried."

His son, Bushayr ibn Abi Zayd

He was killed in the Battle of al-Harra and his descendants still live in Basra.

Al-Hasan said, "I and another man went to the General Mosque and we went to Abu Zayd al-Ansari. His foot had been wounded at Uhud. When the prayer came, he gave the *adhan* sitting and the *iqama* sitting, and then he said to a man, "Go forward and lead us in the prayer."

'Amr ibn Akhtab al-Ansari

He is Abu Zayd, and he was the grandfather of 'Azra ibn Thabit.

Tamim ibn Huways said that he heard Abu Zayd say, "I fought thirteen battles alongside the Messenger of Allah صلعم."

Anas ibn Sirin said that Abu Zayd ibn Akhtab said, "The Messenger of Allah صلعم said to me, 'May Allah make you beautiful.'" Anas said, "He was a handsome man with grey hair. I heard some of the people of Basra say that 'Amr ibn Akhtab was the grandfather of 'Azra ibn Thabit." He has a mosque named after him in Basra.

Al-Hakam ibn 'Amr ibn Mujadda'

He was a companion of the Prophet صلعم. When the Prophet died, he moved to Basra and settled there. Ziyad ibn Abi Sufyan appointed him over Khurasan and he went there.

Al-Hasan reported that Ziyad sent al-Hakam ibn 'Amr to Khurasan and Allah gave the Muslims victory and they took great booty. Ziyad wrote to him, "The Amir al-Mu'minin has written to me to select the gold and silver for him. Do not distribute any gold or silver." He wrote back to him: "Peace be upon you. You wrote to me mentioning the letter of the Amir al-Mu'minin. I find the Book of Allah before the letter of the Amir al-Mu'minin. By Allah, if the heavens and the earth had been stitched into a single mass against a person and he feared Allah, Allah would make a way out of that for him. Peace be upon you." Then he said to the people, "Go to your booty and divide it."

'Ali ibn Muhammad al-Qurashi said, "Al-Hakam ibn 'Amr remained in charge of Khurasan until he died there in 50 AH while Mu'awiya ibn Abi Sufyan was khalif."

Rafi' ibn 'Amr al-Ghifari

Al-Hakam's brother. He was a Companion of the Prophet صلعم. 'Amr ibn Sulaym and others related from him.

Rafi' ibn 'Amr al-Ghifari said, "When I was a boy I used to throw stones at palm trees. The Prophet صلعم was told, 'There is a boy who throws stones at our palm trees.' So I was brought to the Prophet صلعم and he said, 'Boy, why do you throw stones at the palm trees?' I replied, 'To eat.' He said, 'Do not throw stones at the trees, but eat whatever falls below them.'" Then he stroked his head and said, "O Allah, fill his stomach."

'Abdullah ibn as-Samit reported from Abu Dharr that the Messenger of Allah صلعم said, "After me there will be some people of my community who recite the Qur'an and it will not go beyond their throats. They will come out of the *deen* as the arrow passes through its target and they will not return to it. They are the worst of creatures." 'Abdullah ibn As-Samit said, "I met Rafi' ibn 'Amr al-Ghifari, the brother of al-Hakam ibn 'Amr and asked, 'What is this *hadith* which I heard Abu Dharr say?' and I mentioned the *hadith*. He said, 'What surprises you about this? I heard it from the Messenger of Allah صلعم as well.'"

Mujashi' ibn Mas'ud as-Sulami

Mujashi' ibn Mas'ud said, "I came to the Prophet صلعم with my brother to give our allegiance to him on the basis of emigration. He said, 'Emigration is finished.' We said, 'On what basis shall we give you allegiance then?' He said, 'On Islam and *jihad* in the way of Allah.' So we gave him our allegiance." The narrator said that he met Mujashi's brother and he confirmed what Mujashi' had told him.

His brother, Mujalid ibn Mas'ud as-Sulami

Abu 'Uthman reported that Mujashi' said, "Messenger of Allah, this is Mujalid ibn Mas'ud. Take his allegiance with mine on the basis of emigration." He said, "There is no emigration after the conquest of Makka, but I will take his allegiance in Islam."

Al-Hasan said that Mujalid ibn Mas'ud had a slight limp.

Companions

'A'idh ibn 'Amr al-Muzani

Al-Hasan said, "He was one of the best of the Companions of the Messenger of Allah صلعم."
Qatada said that 'A'idh ibn 'Amr used to wear rough silk.
Qurra said, "A Kharijite arose in the time of the Companions of the Messenger of Allah صلعم and a group of the Companions of the Messenger of Allah went out against him with swords, including 'A'idh ibn 'Amr."
It is reported that 'A'idh ibn 'Amr left instructions that Abu Bazra should pray over him. 'Ubaydullah ibn Ziyad set out in order to pray over him. When he reached Muslim's house, he was informed that 'A'idh had left instructions that Abu Bazra was to pray over him. So Ibn Ziyad turned back.

'Abdullah ibn 'Amr al-Muzani

He was the father of Bakr ibn 'Abdullah and was a Companion of the Messenger of Allah صلعم. He settled in Basra and has descendants there.
Bakr ibn 'Abdullah al-Muzani said, "'Alqama ibn 'Abdullah al-Muzani told me that four of the Companions of the Messenger of Allah صلعم washed our father. They did not do more than roll up their sleeves and tuck their shirts in their waistbands. When they had finished washing him, they did *wudu'* as they would do it for the prayer."

Qurra ibn Iyas

He was the father of Mu'awiya ibn Qurra.
Mu'awiya ibn Qurra reported that his father said that he went to the Prophet صلعم who milked his goat for his family. He said, "He stroked my head and made supplication for me."
Mu'awiya ibn Qurra said, "I killed my father's killer in the Battle of Ibn 'Ubays." Qurra had been murdered.

The brother of Qurra ibn Iyas

Mu'awiya ibn Qurra reported from his uncle that he used to go to the Prophet صلعم with his son. He had him sit in front of him and the

Prophet ﷺ asked him, "Do you love him?" He said, "Yes, very much." Then the boy died and the Prophet ﷺ said, "It seems that you are grieved over him." He replied, "Yes, Messenger of Allah." He said, "Are you not happy that when Allah admits you to the Garden you will find him at one of its gates which he will open for you?" He said, "'Yes." He said, "It will be like that, Allah willing."

Hamal ibn Malik al-Hudhali

He became Muslim and then returned to his people's land. Then he moved to Basra, settled there and built a house there among the Hudhayl. Then his house later became the property of 'Amr ibn Mihran, the scribe.

Al-'Abbas ibn Mirdas ibn Abi 'Amir as-Sulami

He became Muslim before the conquest of Makka and came to the Messenger of Allah ﷺ in a group of nine of his people mounted on horses and armed with spears ready to participate in the conquest of Makka. He went on expeditions with the Messenger of Allah ﷺ and then returned to his people's land. He settled in the valley of Basra. He used to visit Basra often. The Basrans related from him. His descendants are located in the desert of Basra and some of his people are settled in Basra.

Jahima ibn al-'Abbas ibn Mirdas

He became Muslim and was a Companion of the Prophet ﷺ and reported *hadiths* from him.

It is reported that Jahima went to the Messenger of Allah ﷺ and said, "Messenger of Allah, I want to go on expeditions and I have come to you to seek your advice." He asked, "Do you have a mother?" He replied, "Yes." He said "Stay with her. The Garden is at her feet." He gave him this reply on the second and third occasions when he made the same request.

'Abdullah ibn ash-Shikhkhir

He was the father of Mutarrif and Yazid ibn 'Abdullah.

Companions

He was a Companion of the Prophet ﷺ and related from him and settled in Basra and his descendants are still there.

Mutarrif reported that his father said, "We came to the Messenger of Allah ﷺ in a delegation from the Banu 'Amir. He asked, 'Shall I provide you with mounts?' We said, 'We found some unattended camels on the road.' The Messenger of Allah ﷺ said, 'The stray animals of the Muslim can be a cause of the burning in the Fire.'"

Yazid said, "My father was in the delegation of the Banu 'Amir to the Messenger of Allah ﷺ. They said, 'Messenger of Allah, you are our master and possess kindness for us.' He said, 'No no! Speak properly and do not let Shaytan make you bold! The Master is Allah. The Master is Allah. The Master is Allah.'"

Mu'awiya ibn Hayda

He came to the Messenger of Allah ﷺ and became Muslim and kept his company. He asked him about things and related *hadiths* from him. He was the grandfather of Bahz ibn Hakim.

His brother, Malik ibn Hayda

He became Muslim and he was the one who asked his brother Mu'awiya to go with him to the Messenger of Allah ﷺ telling him that his neighbours had become Muslims.

Qabisa ibn al-Mukhariq

He came to the Messenger of Allah ﷺ and became Muslim and related *hadiths* from him. He settled in Basra and still has descendants of some note there, including Muhammad ibn Harb who was in charge of the police of Ja'far ibn Sulayman in Madina and also in charge of the police of Basra.

Qabisa said, "I heard the Messenger of Allah ﷺ say, "Techniques of divination are part of idolatry."

'Iyad ibn Hammad at-Tamimi

He came in a delegation to the Prophet ﷺ before becoming Muslim. He had a fine camel with him as a gift for the Messenger of Allah ﷺ. The Prophet asked, "Have you become Muslim?" He replied, "No." He said, "Allah has forbidden us to accept the scum of the idolaters." He became Muslim and the Messenger of Allah صلعم accepted the gift. He said, "O Prophet of Allah! A man of my people beneath me insults me – should I help myself against him?" He said, "Two people who abuse one another are two devils calling one another liars." Other things are related from him. He settled in Basra and the Basrans transmitted from him.

Qays ibn 'Asim

Qays had forbidden himself to drink wine in the *Jahiliyya*. Then he came to the Messenger of Allah صلعم with the delegation of the Banu Tamim and became Muslim. The Prophet صلعم said, "This is the master of the people of desert, and he is a generous master."

Khalifa ibn al-Husayn reported that Qays ibn 'Asim became Muslim and went to the Prophet صلعم and he commanded him to bathe with water and lote leaves.

Hakim ibn Qays said, "When he was dying, Qays ibn 'Asim told his sons, 'My sons! Let the eldest of you be your leader. When the people are led by the eldest of them, they follow their father. When they are led by the youngest of them, they are belittled. You must have wealth and produce it. It is the splendour of the generous man and will protect him against critics. Beware of begging from people. It is the last resort for a man's earnings. Do not mourn for me. The Prophet of Allah صلعم was not mourned for. Do not bury me where the Bakr ibn Wa'il will know. I used to raid them in the *Jahiliyya*.'"

Az-Zibriqan ibn Badr ibn Imru'l-Qays

Az-Zibriqan's name was Husayn. He was an excellent poet and was called 'the moon of Najd'. He was in the delegation of the Banu Tamim who came to the Messenger of Allah صلعم. He became Muslim and the Messenger of Allah صلعم put him in charge of the *zakat* of the people of the Banu Sa'd. The Messenger of Allah صلعم died while he was in charge of it. Then the Arabs apostatised and refused to pay *zakat*. Az-Zibriqan ibn Badr remained firm in Islam and took the *zakat* from his people and sent it to Abu Bakr as-Siddiq. He settled in the land of the Banu Tamim in the desert of Basra and used to visit Basra often.

Al-Aqra' ibn Habis

He was in the delegation of the Banu Tamim which came to the Messenger of Allah ﷺ. He became Muslim and settled in the land of the Banu Tamim in the desert of Basra.

'Amr ibn al-Ahtam

He was in the delegation of the Banu Tamim who came to the Messenger of Allah ﷺ. He was the youngest of them and remained with their baggage. He became Muslim. He was a poet. He settled in the land of the Banu Tamim in the desert of Basra.

Muhammad ibn az-Zubayr said, "The Messenger of Allah ﷺ said to 'Amr ibn al-Ahtam, 'Tell me about az-Zibriqan ibn Badr.' He said, 'He is obeyed in his gathering and defends those behind him.' Az-Zibriqan said, 'Messenger of Allah, he knows that I am better than what he says, but he envies me!' 'Amr said, 'You! A person with little manliness, narrow-minded, with a stupid father and a blameworthy uncle!' Then he said, 'Messenger of Allah, I did not lie in the first or the last. I am satisfied with him and said the best of what I know of him. Then he made me angry and I said what I do not know about him.' The Messenger of Allah ﷺ said, 'Eloquent speech is a form of magic.'"

Sa'sa'a ibn Najiyya

One of the Banu Tamim. He came to the Prophet ﷺ and became Muslim. His grandchildren included the poet al-Farazdaq ibn Ghalib ibn Sa'sa'a. Sa'sa'a transmitted from the Prophet ﷺ and he and his children settled at Basra.

Sa'sa'a ibn Mu'awiya

It is reported that Sa'sa'a ibn Mu'awiya, the uncle of the poet al-Farazdaq, went to the Prophet ﷺ who recited to him: *"And anyone who did the smallest atom's weight of good will see it. And anyone who did the smallest atom's weight of evil will see it."* (99:7-8) He said, "That's enough for me. I don't care if I hear nothing else." Sa'sa'a reported from Abu Dharr.

An-Namir ibn Tawlab ibn Uqaysh

He was a poet. He came to the Messenger of Allah صعلم and became Muslim. He settled in Basra after that and the Prophet صعلم wrote a letter for him.

Yazid ibn 'Abdullah ibn ash-Shikhkir said, "A man of 'Ukl brought us a letter from the Messenger of Allah صلعم on a piece of hide on which was written: 'From Muhammad, the Messenger of Allah, to the Banu Zuhayr ibn Uqaysh.' The man was an-Namir ibn Tawlab the poet." Banu Zuhayr is a sub-tribe of 'Ukl.

'Uthman ibn Abi'l-'As

'Uthman ibn Abi'l-'As was part of the delegation of Thaqif who came to the Messenger of Allah صلعم in Madina. They became Muslim and he eventually reached an agreement with them. 'Uthman was the youngest of them. He went to the Prophet صلعم before them and became Muslim. He had him learn to recite the Qur'an and he stayed close to Ubayy ibn Ka'b who recited to him.

When the delegation of Thaqif wanted to return to Ta'if, they said, "Messenger of Allah, put someone in charge of us," and he put 'Uthman ibn Abi'l-'As over them. He was clever and had learned the Qur'an by heart. They said, "We will not change someone whom the Messenger of Allah صلعم has put in charge." He used to lead them in the prayer in Ta'if and recite the Qur'an to them.

In the time of 'Umar ibn al-Khattab, Basra was laid out and the Muslims settled there. 'Umar wanted to appoint over them a man of intelligence, rectitude and skill. They said, "You must have 'Uthman ibn Abi'l-'As." He said, "That is the one whom the Messenger of Allah صلعم put in charge in at-Ta'if. I will not remove him." They said to him, "Write to him to appoint a successor in at-Ta'if and then to come to you." He said, "This is good." So he wrote to him about that and he appointed his brother al-Hakam ibn Abi'l-'As ath-Thaqafi over Ta'if. He came to 'Umar and he sent him to Basra and he built a house there and there he extracted wealth, including the Shatt 'Uthman which was ascribed to him opposite Ubulla and its land. His descendants are still there and are honoured. They have much revenue and property and are very numerous.

Companions

Musa ibn Talha said, "The Messenger of Allah صلعم sent 'Uthman ibn Abi'l-'As to Ta'if and said, 'Lead them in the prayer according to their weakest one and do not employ your *mu'adhdhin* for a wage.'"

Mutarrif said that his *kunya* was Abu 'Abdullah.

His brother, al-Hakam ibn Abi'l-'As ath-Thaqafi

We mentioned him in the story of his brother. We have not heard that he was in the delegation of Thaqif. He also has noble descendants, including the poet Yazid ibn al-Hakam.

Their brother, the poet Hafs ibn Abi'l-'As

We have not heard that he was a Companion of the Messenger of Allah or that he saw him. He reported from him, and we record him with his brothers to make his position clear. He also has noble descendants in Basra. Al-Hasan al-Basri related from Hafs ibn Abi'l-'As.

Malik ibn 'Amr al-'Uqayli, then al-Qushayri

Malik ibn 'Amr al-Qushayri said, "I heard the Messenger of Allah صلعم say, 'If anyone sets free a Muslim slave, he will be his ransom from the Fire, each bone of the freed person for each of his bones. May Allah alienate anyone who has his parents reach old age and is not forgiven! The Garden is mandatory for anyone who takes in an orphan of two Muslim parents to share in his food and drink until Allah makes him self-sufficient.'"

Al-Aswad ibn Sari'

He was a Qadi. Al-Hasan reported that Al-Aswad ibn Sari' said, "I went to the Messenger of Allah صلعم and went on an expedition with him."

Al-Hasan reported from al-Aswad ibn Sari' and he was a poet and was the first to relate edifying stories in this mosque. He said, "I went on four expeditions with the Messenger of Allah صلعم."

Al-Hasan said that al-Aswad ibn Sari' was a poet. He said, "Messenger of Allah, shall I let you hear some praises with which I have praised my Lord?" The Messenger of Allah صلعم said, "Your Lord loves praise," or he said, "There is nothing He loves more than praise of Allah."

Al-Hasan said that al-Aswad ibn Sari' used to relate things to remind people in the back of the mosque.

At-Talib ibn Zayd

He related *hadiths* about emancipation and other things from the Messenger of Allah صلعم.

At-Talib reported that he came to the Prophet صلعم and said, "Messenger of Allah, ask forgiveness for me!" He said to me, "When I have spoken to you," or, "When you have heard." So he waited until he had finished and then he prayed for him and touched his face with his hand and said, "O Allah, forgive at-Talib and have mercy on him," three times. At-Talib was in the delegation of Banu Tamim who called to the Messenger of Allah صلعم from outside the apartments.

Qatada ibn Milhan as-Sadusi

'Abdu'l-Malik ibn Qatada reported from his father that the Messenger of Allah صلعم commanded them to fast the nights of the full moon, which is like a perpetual fast.

Sulaym ibn Jabir al-Hujaymi

His *kunya* was Abu Jurayy. Some of them call him 'Jabir ibn Sulaym al-Hujaymi'.

Muhammad ibn Sirin said that Sulayman ibn Jabir said, "I went to the Messenger of Allah صلعم with a group of my people."

Sulaym ibn Jabir said, "I came to the Messenger of Allah صلعم when he was sitting with his knees up and a cloak wrapped around him whose hem came over his feet. I asked, 'Which of you is Muhammad or the Messenger of Allah?' He pointed to himself. I said, 'Messenger of Allah, I am a man from the people of the desert and I have their rough manners. Advise me.' He said, 'Do not consider any act of kindness insignificant.'"

Malik ibn al-Huwayrith al-Laythi, Abu Sulayman

Abu Qilaba reported that Malik ibn al-Huwayrith said, "We went to the Messenger of Allah ﷺ and we were a group of young men. We stayed with him for about twenty days and the Prophet was merciful. He said, 'When you return to your land, teach them and instruct them, and pray when the prayer time comes.'"

Usama ibn 'Umayr al-Hudhali

He is the father of Abu'l-Malih al-Hudhali from whom Ayyub and others related.

Abu'l-Malih reported that his father was with the Messenger of Allah ﷺ in the Battle of Hunayn and it rained on them and the Messenger of Allah ﷺ commanded a caller to announce that they should pray standing.

'Arfaja ibn As'ad al-'Utaridi

One of the Banu Tamim. It is reported that 'Arfaja ibn As'ad had received a nose wound in the Battle of Kilab during the *Jahiliyya* and had a nose made of silver but he became allergic to it. He mentioned it to the Prophet ﷺ and he told him to use a gold one.

Anas ibn Malik

A man of the Banu 'Abdullah ibn Ka'b, then one of the Banu'l-Harish.

Anas ibn Malik said, "Some cavalry of the Messenger of Allah ﷺ attacked us, and I went to the Messenger of Allah ﷺ while he was eating. He said, 'Come and eat.' I said, 'I am fasting.' He said, 'Sit. I will tell you about fasting.' He said, 'Allah has remitted the fast for the traveller, the pregnant woman and the nursing woman.' By Allah, the Prophet ﷺ said both of them or one of them. I still regret that I did not eat from the food of the Messenger of Allah!"

Kahmas al-Hilali

Kahmas al-Hilali said, "I became Muslim and went to the Prophet ﷺ and I got to him and told him about my Islam and then I left him and stayed away for a year. Then I came to him and greeted him. He looked up and then down. I said, 'Messenger of Allah, it seems you do not remember me.' He said, 'Yes, who are you?' I said, 'I am Kahmas al-Hilali who came to you a year ago.' I had become very emaciated. The Messenger of Allah ﷺ said, 'What has brought you to this state?' I said. 'I have not broken the fast in the day since I left you nor slept at night.' The Messenger of Allah ﷺ said, 'Who told you to torture yourself? Fast the month of patience and then a day every month.' I said, 'Messenger of Allah, let me do more.' He said, 'Two days.' I said, 'Messenger of Allah, I am strong. Let me do more.' He said, 'Three days a month.'"

Ma'iz al-Bukka'i

'Abdullah ibn Ma'iz reported that Ma'iz went to the Prophet ﷺ and he wrote him a letter stating that Ma'iz was the last of his people to become Muslim and that he had could only offer him his own hand and he received his allegiance on that basis.

Qurra ibn Du'mus an-Namiri

Jarir ibn Hazim said, "In Ayyub's place I saw a bedouin man wearing a wool jubbah. When he heard the people relating *hadith*, he said, 'My master Qurra ibn Du'mus told me, "I went to Madina and there was the Prophet ﷺ with his Companions around him. I wanted to go near him but could not. So I said, 'Messenger of Allah, ask forgiveness for the Namiri boy!' He said, 'May Allah forgive you!'" He said, "The Messenger of Allah ﷺ had sent ad-Dahhak to collect *zakat* and he had brought large camels. The Prophet ﷺ said to him, 'Go back to Hilal ibn 'Amir, Namir ibn 'Amir, and 'Amir ibn Rabi'a. You have taken the large camels from their property.' He said, 'Messenger of Allah, I heard you mention the expedition and I wanted to bring you camels to ride and to carry your Companions.' He said, 'You have left what I prefer for what you have brought. Go and return to them and take their *zakat* from the sides of their property [meaning, not selecting the best].'"

Al-Khashkhash ibn al-Harith al-'Anbari

Al-Khashkhash al-'Anbari said, "I went to the Prophet ﷺ with a son of mine, and he asked, 'Your son?' I said, 'Yes.' He said, 'He should not harm you, nor you him.'"

Ahmar ibn Jaz' as-Sadusi

Ahmar, a Companion of the Messenger of Allah ﷺ said, "When the Messenger of Allah ﷺ prostrated, he put his arms out far away from his sides."

Sawada ibn Rabi'a al-Jarmi

Sawada ibn Rabi'a al-Jarmi said, "I went to the Messenger of Allah ﷺ with my mother, and he ordered some sheep for us and told her, 'Tell your sons to cut their nails lest they cause pain or harm the udders of the sheep. Command your sons to feed their flocks well.'"

'Ulatha ibn Shajjar as-Saliti

One of the Banu Tamim. Al-Hasan reported that he heard the Messenger of Allah ﷺ say, "The Muslim is a brother of the Muslim." He said, "I went to the Prophet ﷺ when he was in a group of people."

'Uqba ibn Malik al-Laythi

'Uqba ibn Malik al-Laythi said, "The Messenger of Allah ﷺ sent an expedition against some people. A man began to run away and a man from the expedition followed him with his sword drawn. The man cried, 'I am a Muslim!' but he did not pay any attention to what he said and struck him down with his sword and killed him. The news reached the Messenger of Allah ﷺ and he said something harsh about it which the killer heard. While the Messenger of Allah ﷺ was giving a speech, the killer said, 'Messenger of Allah, he only said what he said to save himself from being killed!' The Messenger of Allah ﷺ turned away from him and those people before him and continued speaking. When he could not endure it any more, he said for the third time, 'Messenger of Allah, he only said what he said to save himself from being killed!' The Messenger of Allah ﷺ turned to him and the displeasure could be seen in his face. He said, 'Allah refuses my acceptance to the one who kills a believer.' He said it three times."

Khuzayma ibn Jaz' al-Asadi

Hibban ibn Jaz' reported that his brother Khuzayma said, "I asked the Messenger of Allah ﷺ about eating foxes. He asked, 'Does anyone eat a fox?' I asked him about wolves and he said, 'Does anyone with any good in him eat a wolf?' I asked him about hyenas and he said, 'Does anyone eat a hyena?'"

Khuzayma said, "I asked the Prophet ﷺ about lizards and he said, 'I neither eat them nor forbid them.'"

Samura ibn Jundub

He was a Companion of the Prophet ﷺ and went on expeditions with him. He was an ally of the Ansar. His mother was married to Murayy ibn Sinan, the uncle of Abu Sa'id al-Khudri. They relate that Samura was among those present at the Battle of Uhud. He later settled in Basra and then he moved to Kufa and purchased some houses there among the Banu Asad at Kunasa. He built there and settled there and died there. He has descendants. He related many *hadiths* from the Messenger of Allah ﷺ. Ziyad left him in charge of Basra when he went to Kufa.

Abu Yazid al-Madani said, "When Samura ibn Jundub was in his final illness, he felt terribly cold and a fire was kindled for him and a stove placed before him, a stove behind him, and one at his right and one at his left. That did not help. He said, 'What can I do about what is inside me?' He remained like that until he died."

Harmala al-'Anbari

Harmala said, "I came to the Messenger of Allah ﷺ and prayed the dawn prayer with him. When we finished the prayer, I looked towards the faces of the people and I could barely make out their faces after I had finished the prayer. When I was about to go, I said,

'Messenger of Allah, advise me!' He said, 'You must have fear of Allah. When you stay with a people, and hear them saying what you like, go to it. When you hear them saying what you dislike, leave it.'"

Nubaysha al-Hudhali

He was called Nubaysha al-Khayr.

Al-Mu'alla ibn Rashid al-Hudhali said that his grandmother, Umm 'Asim, spoke about a man of Hudhayl called Nubaysha al-Khayr. She said, "Nubaysha came in while we were eating from a bowl and said to us, 'The Messenger of Allah ﷺ told us that whoever eats from a bowl and then licks it will be forgiven.'"

Talha ibn 'Abdullah an-Nadri

He was one of the Banu Layth from Kinana. Some called him Talha ibn 'Amr. He was one of the *Ahl as-Suffa*.

Abu Harb ibn Abi'l-Aswad reported that Talha al-Laythi, one of the Companions of the Messenger of Allah ﷺ told him, "I came to Madina and had no home, and so I stayed in the Suffa."

Al-'Adda' ibn Khalid

He came to the Prophet ﷺ who made him a grant of some waters which belonged to the Banu 'Amr ibn 'Amir.

'Abdu'l-Majid ibn Abi Yazid said, "In the time of Yazid ibn al-Muhallab, Hujr ibn Abi Basr and I went to Makka. We passed by some water called al-Rukhaykh and they told us, 'Here is a man who saw the Messenger of Allah ﷺ.' So we went to a very old man and asked, 'Did you see the Messenger of Allah ﷺ?' He replied, 'Yes, and he wrote a letter guaranteeing these waters for me.' He brought out a skin on which was the letter of the Messenger of Allah ﷺ. We asked, 'What is your name?' He replied, 'Al-'Adda' ibn Khalid.' We asked, 'Did you hear anything from the Messenger of Allah ﷺ?' He said, 'On the Day of 'Arafa I was under his camel while it was chewing its cud. He said, "O people! What is this day? What is this month? What is this land?" We said, "Allah and His Messenger know best." He said, "Is it not a sacred month? And a sacred land? And a sacred day?" We said, "Allah and His Messenger know best." He said, "Your blood and property and honour are sacred for you as the sacredness of this day of yours in this month of yours in this land of yours until the day when you meet your Lord. O Allah, Have I conveyed it? O Allah, bear witness!"'"

'Abdu'l-Majid said, "Al-'Adda' ibn Khalid produced a letter for me and said, 'This is what the Prophet ﷺ wrote for me.' Written on it was, 'In the Name of Allah, the Merciful, the Compassionate. This is what al-'Adda' ibn Khalid ibn Hawdha has purchased from Muhammad, the Messenger of Allah. He has purchased from him a slave, or slavegirl, with no disease or wickedness or maliciousness. The sale of one Muslim to another Muslim.'"

A'sha ibn Mazin

One of the Banu Tamim. A'sha ibn Mazin said, "I went to the Prophet ﷺ and said:

> 'O master of the people and judge of the Arabs!
> I married one of the sharp-tongued women!
> I went to seek food for her in Rajab
> and she left me with strife and war.
> Women are the worst conquerors for the one who is conquered.'

The Messenger of Allah ﷺ began to repeat, 'Women are the worst conquerors for the one who is conquered. Women are the worst conquerors for the one who is conquered.'"

Nadla reported that a man of theirs was called A'sha. His real name was 'Abdullah ibn al-A'war. He was married to a woman called Mu'adha. He went away in the month of Rajab to seek provision for his family and his wife ran away and deserted him and sought refuge with a man of theirs called Mutarrif ibn Buhsul. He lodged her out of his sight. When A'sha came back, he did not find her in his house and was told that she had deserted him and had sought refuge with Mutarrif ibn Buhsul. He went to him and said, "Cousin! you have my wife Mu'adha with you! Send her to me." He said, "She is not with me, and even if she were with me, I would not send her to you." Mutarrif was stronger than him, so A'sha went to the Prophet ﷺ and sought his help and composed:

Companions

> "O master of the people and judge of the Arabs!
> > I complain to you of one of the sharp-tongued women
> Like the greedy grey she-wolf eyeing the flock.
> > I went out to seek food for her in Rajab,
> And she left me with strife and war
> > and broke the contract and committed wrong action.
> She wishes I were in the dense thicket.
> Women are the worst conquerors for the one who is conquered."

The Messenger of Allah ﷺ repeated, "Women are the worst conquerors for the one who is conquered!" He complained to him about his wife and what she had done to him and that she was with a man called Mutarrif ibn Buhsul. So the Messenger of Allah ﷺ wrote a letter to him, "See to the wife of this man, Mu'adha, and send her back to him." He took him the letter of the Prophet ﷺ and it was read to him. He said to her, "'Mu'adha, this is the letter of the Prophet ﷺ about you. I am going to return you to him." She said, "Take an undertaking on my behalf and the guarantee of his Prophet that he will not punish me for what I have done." He did that and Mutarrif returned her and then A'sha composed:

> By your life, my love for Mu'adha has not been changed
> > by denunciation nor long familiarity,
> Nor anything bad she has done,
> > when seductive men invited her away from me.

Abu Maryam as-Saluli

His name was Malik ibn Rabi'a. He is Abu Yazid ibn Maryam. He related from the Prophet ﷺ, "O Allah, forgive those who fall short."

'Abbad ibn Shurahbil al-Yaskhuri

It is related that 'Abbad ibn Shurahbil said, "I came to Madina in the time of the Messenger of Allah ﷺ and entered a garden and took some of its ears of corn. The owner of the garden came and beat me and took away my garment. I went to the Messenger of Allah ﷺ and the owner of the garden followed me. I mentioned all of that to him. The Messenger of Allah ﷺ said, 'By Allah, you did not teach him when he was ignorant nor feed him when he was hungry!' Then he commanded him to return my garment to me and ordered that I be given a *wasq,* or half a *wasq,* of dates."

Bashir ibn al-Khasasiyya

His name was Zahm ibn Ma'bad as-Sadusi.

Khalid ibn Sumayr said, "Zahm ibn Ma'bad emigrated to the Messenger of Allah ﷺ who asked him, 'What is your name?' He replied, 'Zahm ibn Ma'bad.' He said, 'Rather you are Bashir.'"

Qabisa ibn Waqqas

Qabisa ibn Waqqas reported that the Messenger of Allah ﷺ said, "After me there will be rulers in charge of you who will delay the prayer. It is to your credit and against them. So pray with them as long as they pray towards the *qibla.*"

Hisham at-Tayyalisi said that Qabisa was a Companion and he said, "This is the *hadith* of the congregation."

Jariya ibn Qudama as-Sa'di

Al-Ahnaf ibn Qays reported that a cousin of his called Jariyya ibn Qudama reported that he had asked the Messenger of Allah ﷺ, "Messenger of Allah, tell me something that will benefit me which is short so that I will remember it." The Messenger of Allah ﷺ said, "Do not get angry." He repeated the same question and he replied, "Do not get angry." This happened several times, and each time he said to him, "Do not get angry."

He said that Jariya ibn Qudama was one of those present when 'Umar ibn al-Khattab was murdered. He said, "We were among the last to go to him and we asked him for a final instruction and no one had asked him before us."

Jariya had historical reports and was present at various events. 'Ali ibn Abi Talib sent him to Basra when 'Abdullah ibn 'Amir al-Hadrami was there as the deputy of 'Abdullah ibn 'Amir ibn Kurayz. He laid siege to him in the house of Sanibil, a man of the Banu Tamim whom Mu'awiya had sent to Basra after he had given him his allegiance.

Sa'd ibn al-Atwal

It is related from Sa'd ibn al-Atwal that his brother died leaving a debt. He left 300 dirhams and also left dependants. Sa'd said, "I wanted to give it to his dependants and the Prophet ﷺ said, 'Your brother is imprisoned by his debt.' I said, 'Messenger of Allah, I have settled it except for two dinars claimed by a woman who does not have any proof.' He said, 'Give it to her. She is entitled.'"

'Abdullah, Sa'd's son, went out to his companions in Tustar and visited them and stayed for two days and left on the third. They asked, "Why don't you stay?" He said, "I heard my father say that the Messenger of Allah ﷺ forbade overstaying.[1] Whoever stays in a land subject to land tax [*kharaj*] for three days has overstayed. I do not want to stay."

Wasil ibn 'Abdullah said, "When Yazid ibn Mu'awiya died 'Ubaydullah ibn Ziyad feared that the people of Basra might harm him and he sent a message to Sa'd ibn at-Atwal, asking him to protect him from the people of Basra. He replied, 'My tribe is not in Basra. It is in Syria.'"

Hurayth ibn Hassan ash-Shaybani

He was the delegate of Bakr ibn Wa'il to the Messenger of Allah ﷺ. He is the one who escorted Qayla bint Makhrama when she went to the Messenger of Allah ﷺ. The two of them came to him and there were some words between him and her about the desert before the Messenger of Allah ﷺ which 'Affan ibn Muslim reported.

Harmala ibn 'Abdullah al-Ka'bi

He went to the Messenger of Allah ﷺ and stayed with him until he met him and questioned him and related from him.

'Abdullah ibn Sabra

'Abdullah ibn Sabra reported that he heard the Prophet of Allah ﷺ say, "Allah forbade us three things: too many questions, wasting property, and indulging in chit-chat."

---

1. Some of the Muslims who had participated in the Iraqi campaign would sometimes abuse the right of hospitality in the conquered lands.

'Abdullah ibn Sarjis

'Abdullah ibn Sarjis said, "I came to the Messenger of Allah ﷺ while he was sitting and I went behind his back and he recognised what I wanted and removed his cloak. I looked at the Seal at the top of his left shoulder-blade. It resembled a fist around which there were moles like warts. When I was in front of him I said, 'May Allah forgive you, Messenger of Allah,' and he said, 'And you.' People said to him, 'Can I ask forgiveness for you, Messenger of Allah?' He said, 'Yes, and for you.' Then he recited this verse: *'Ask forgiveness for your wrong actions and for the men and women who believe.'"* (47:19)

'Abdullah ibn Abi'l-Hamsa'

'Abdullah ibn Abi'l-Hamsa' said, "I did a business transaction with the Messenger of Allah ﷺ before the goods had been dispatched. I still owed him something and I promised to bring it to him where he was. Then I forgot that day and the next. Then I went to him on the third day and found him there. He said to me, 'Boy, you have been hard on me! I have been here for three days waiting for you!'"

'Abdullah ibn Abi'l-Jadh'a Al-'Abdi

Ibn Abi'l-Jadh'a said, "I said, 'Messenger of Allah, when were you a Prophet?' He said, 'When Adam was still between body and spirit.'"

Maysara al-Fajr

He was Abu Budayl ibn Maysara al-'Uqayli.

Maysara al-Fajr said, "I asked the Messenger of Allah ﷺ, 'When were you a Prophet?' He said, 'I was a Prophet when Adam was still between body and spirit.'"

Talq ibn Khushshaf al-Qaysi

Sawada ibn al-Aswad al-Qaysi said, "My father told me that they went to Talq ibn Khushshaf, one of the Companions of the Prophet, to visit him when he was ill. They began to make supplication for him. He said, 'O Allah, choose and resolve.'"

Abu Safiyya

The mother of Yunus ibn 'Ubayd said, "I saw Abu Safiyya, one of the Companions of the Messenger of Allah ﷺ. He was our neighbour here. He used to glorify Allah [counting using] with stones and date pits, and I never saw him without pebbles."

Abu 'Asib, the client of the Messenger of Allah

Some variants call him Abu 'Asim. It is the same man.

Abu 'Asib, the client of the Messenger of Allah ﷺ said that the Messenger of Allah ﷺ said, "Jibril, peace be upon him, came to me with the fever and the plague. I kept the fever for Madina and sent the plague to Syria. The plague is martyrdom for my community and a mercy for them and it is punishment for the unbelievers."

Hazim ibn al-Qasim said, "I saw Abu 'Asib drinking from a thick cup which was not carved. We said, 'Why don't you drink from these fine cups of ours?' He said, 'How could I not eat or drink from it when I saw the Prophet ﷺ drink from it?'"

Hazim ibn al-Qasim said, "I saw Abu 'Asib, the servant of the Messenger of Allah ﷺ, use yellow dye on his hair, beard and moustache. I heard Abu 'Asib say, 'Whoever is healthy and can go to *Jumu'a* should not abandon it. It is an obligation like that of the *hajj*.' We used to trim the ends of the moustache of Abu 'Asib and his nails."

Muslima bint Zabban al-Quray'iyya said that she heard Maymuna bint Abi 'Asib say, "Abu 'Asib used to always fast three days. He used to pray *Duha*[1] standing and then when he became too weak, he would pray it sitting. He used to fast the days when the moon is full." There was a bell by his bed. His voice became too weak to call her. When he shook it, she would come.

Numayr al-Khuza'i

Malik ibn Numayr al-Khuza'i, one of the people of Basra, reported that his father saw the Messenger of Allah ﷺ in the prayer with his right arm on his right thigh pointing with his index finger while moving it slightly."

---

1. The voluntary mid-morning prayer.

Qatada ibn al-A'war ibn Sa'ida

He was a Companion of the Prophet صلعم before the delegation (of Banu Tamim, his tribe) came. The Messenger of Allah صلعم wrote a letter granting him ash-Shabka, a place in the desert between al-Qana'a and al-'Arama.

Qays ibn al-Harith

He was also in the Banu Tamim's delegation to the Messenger of Allah صلعم. He later resided in Basra.

Al-Munaqqa' ibn al-Husayn

He was present at the Battle of al-Qadisiyya and then went to Basra and settled there. He had a horse called Janah which was with him at al-Qadisiyya. He said:

> When I saw the horses and the spearmen and archers
> make a breach in them, I reined in Janah.
> Then I pierced through when Allah sent down victory
> and Janah wished to finish it and rest.
> It seemed as if the swords of Hind flashing above its face
> were like shining scarves unfurled in Tihama.

Al-Munaqqa' transmitted *hadith* from the Messenger of Allah صلعم. It is related that al-Munaqqa' said, "I brought the Prophet صلعم the *zakat* of our camels, and said, 'This is the *zakat* of our camels.' The Messenger of Allah صلعم commanded that they be taken. I said, 'Among them are two she-camels which are a gift for you.' So I separated the gift from the *zakat* and stayed there for some days. People were saying that the Messenger of Allah صلعم was going to send Khalid ibn al-Walid to [the tribe of] Raqiq Mudar, or Mudar to take their *zakat*. I said, 'By Allah, that is our home and my family has no money. I will pay for them here before he goes to them!' I went to the Prophet صلعم while he was on his camel. There was a black man with him whose head was level with that of the Prophet. I had not seen anyone taller than him. When I approached, the man started to come down to me. The Prophet صلعم restrained him. I said, 'Messenger of Allah, the people are saying such-and-such.' The Prophet صلعم raised his arms until the white of his armpits could be seen and said, 'O Allah, it is not lawful for them to tell lies about me!'"

Al-Munaqqa' said, "I did not relate a *hadith* from the Prophet ﷺ except that which is in writing or on which there is a current *sunna*. If they lied about him during his life, what about after his death?"

Abu Ghassan said that he was from the Banu Tamim.

Al-Harith ibn 'Amr as-Sahmi

His grandson reported that al-Harith ibn 'Amr as-Sahmi met the Messenger of Allah ﷺ during the Farewell *Hajj* while he was on his camel al-'Adba'. He said, "I called out, 'Messenger of Allah, may my mother and father be your ransom! Ask forgiveness for me!' He said, 'May Allah forgive you.' Then I went to the other side hoping he would single me out again and I cried out, 'Ask forgiveness for me, Messenger of Allah!' He said, 'May Allah forgive you.' A man said, 'Messenger of Allah, what about the firstlings and the sheep?' He said, 'Whoever wishes can sacrifice a firstling or not do so. Whoever wishes to sacrifice a sheep can do so or not do so.' Then he said, 'Your blood and property are sacred among you as the sacredness of this day of yours in this land of yours.'"

'Abdu'r-Rahman ibn Khanbash

He related the *hadith* about Shaytan coming to the Prophet ﷺ with a brand of fire.

Sahl ibn Sakhr

Khalid as-Samti said, "My client, Sahl ibn Sakhr al-Laythi who was a Companion, spoke to me. He purchased or sold slaves. His wealth included many more slaves than his master had."

Abu 'Ubayd

Abu 'Ubayd said, "I cooked a pot of food for the Prophet ﷺ and he said, 'Give me a shoulder,' and so I gave him a shoulder. He said, 'Give me a shoulder.' So I gave him a shoulder. He said, 'Give me a shoulder.' I said, 'Messenger of Allah, how many shoulders does a sheep have?' He said, 'By the One Who has my soul in His hand, if you had remained silent, you would have given me however many shoulders I asked for.'"

Al-Asla', Maymun ibn Sinbadh

It is reported that a man called al-Asla' said, "I used to serve the Prophet ﷺ and saddle his camel for him. He said to me one night, 'Asla', get up and put on the saddle for me.' I said, 'Prophet of Allah! I am in *janaba*!' He was silent for a time and Jibril, peace be upon him, brought him the *ayat* of *tayammum*. So the Prophet ﷺ called me, and showed me how to do *tayammum*. So I did it and saddled for him and prayed. When we reached water, he said to me, 'Go and wash, Asla'.'"

Zayd, the client of the Messenger of Allah

Zayd said that he heard the Prophet ﷺ say, "Whoever says, 'I ask forgiveness of Allah. There is no god but Him. He is the Living, the Self-Subsistent, and I repent to Him,' will be forgiven, even if he has fled from the battlefield."

Abu Sud

Abu Sud reported that he heard the Prophet ﷺ say, "The false oath by which a man takes a Muslim's property causes barrenness."

Abu Hayya at-Tamimi

It is reported that Abu Hayya at-Tamimi heard the Prophet ﷺ say, "There is no liability when something collapses through inadvertence. The truest of omens is the good one."

Al-Harith ibn Uqaysh

He related from the Prophet ﷺ, "Whoever has three of his children die before him…" The Prophet ﷺ said, "A man of my community will intercede for the like of [the numbers of the tribes of] Rabi'a and Mudar."

'Abdullah ibn al-Aswad as-Sadusi

He went to the Prophet ﷺ in the delegation of the Banu Sadus.

Usayr, the Companion of the Messenger of Allah

Humayd ibn 'Abdu'r-Rahman said, "We visited Usayr, one of the Companions of the Messenger of Allah ﷺ, when Yazid ibn Mu'awiya was appointed khalif. He said, 'They say that Yazid is not the best of the community of Muhammad ﷺ nor the one who has the most *fiqh* nor the most honourable of them. I say that as well. But, by Allah, I prefer that the community of Muhammad ﷺ be in agreement than for it to be split. Do you think that if a door existed which would encompass the community of Muhammad ﷺ if they were to enter it, that a single man would be unable to enter it?' We replied, 'No.' He said, 'Do you think that if every man among the community of Muhammad ﷺ were to say that he would not shed the blood of his brother nor take his property that this would be enough for them?' We replied, 'Yes.' He said, 'That is what I say to you. Furthermore the Messenger of Allah ﷺ said, "Only good will come to you from forbearance."'"

Humayd said, "Then my companion said, 'The story of Luqman shows that some forbearance is weakness while some of it is respect for Allah.' The shaykh's hand shook and he said, 'Leave my room. Leave my house. I will not admit you to me!' I calmed him down. Then my companion and I left."

'Urwa ibn Samura al-'Anbari

'Urwa said, "We were waiting for the Prophet ﷺ to lead the prayer. He came out and his head was wet from *wudu'* or *ghusl*. He prayed and when he had finished the prayer, the people began to ask him, 'Messenger of Allah, is there any harm in us doing such-and-such?' The Messenger of Allah ﷺ said, 'O people! The *deen* of Allah is in ease.' He said it three times."

Abu Rifa'a al-'Adawi

His name was Tamim ibn Usayd of the Banu 'Adi. He was a Companion of the Prophet ﷺ and he settled in Basra.

Abu Rifa'a said, "During the *Jahiliyya*, I had a jinn who used to speak to me. After I became Muslim I missed him. While I was standing at 'Arafa, I heard his sound. He said, 'Are you aware that I became Muslim after you?' When he heard the people's voices raised, he said, 'You must have the strongest throat. Good does not come by the loudest voice.'"

Abu Rifa'a al-'Adawi used to say, "I have not forgotten *Surat al-Baqara* since the Messenger of Allah ﷺ taught it to me. In addition to it, I took what I took of the Qur'an and my back has never pained me when standing in the prayer at night."

Humayd ibn Hilal said, "When Abu Rifa'a prayed and finished his prayer and his supplication, the last supplication he made was, 'O Allah make me live as long as life is good for me. When I die, let it be a pure and good death for which my brother Muslims will envy me when they hear of its virtue, purity and excellence. Make my death being slain in Your path and outwit my self for me.' He went out in an army led by 'Abdu'r-Rahman ibn Samura. A detachment went out from this army most of which were from the Banu Hanifa. He said, 'I will go with this detachment,' Abu Qatada al-'Adawi said, 'None of your brother's tribe is in it and there is no one to look after you.' He said, 'This is something I am resolved on. I will go.' So he went with them and the detachment surrounded a fortress or a castle of the enemy at night. He spent the night in prayer until the end of the night and then used his shield as a pillow and fell asleep. His companions were looking to see where to make their attack. They forgot about him and left him there asleep. The enemy saw him and three Persians went down to him. He was asleep and they took his sword and killed him. His companions exclaimed, 'We forgot Abu Rifa'a!' They went back and found the Persians about to plunder him and drove them away from him so that they could remove him.' 'Abdu'r-Rahman ibn Samura said, 'The brother of the Banu 'Adi was not aware of martyrdom until it came to him.'"

Nafi' ibn al-Harith ibn Kalada

He was from Thaqif. His mother Sumayya was the mother of Abu Bakra and Ziyad. Al-Harith ibn Kalada claimed Nafi' and he was linked to him and his lineage from him was established. Nafi' is Abu 'Abdullah who was the first to pasture horses in Basra. He asked

Companions

'Umar ibn al-Khattab to give him a land grant in Basra and he wrote to Abu Musa al-Ash'ari to give him a grant of ten *jaribs* in which neither Muslim nor person with a treaty had a claim. He settled in Basra. Nafi' related *hadith* from the Messenger of Allah ﷺ.

A shaykh of Basra said that Nafi' stated that he had been with the Messenger of Allah ﷺ in a group of about four hundred men. He stopped with them where there was no water. It seemed to be difficult for the people when they saw that the Messenger of Allah ﷺ had stopped. So they made camp and then a goat came to the Messenger of Allah ﷺ with its horns decorated. The Messenger of Allah ﷺ milked it and he and the army quenched their thirst. Then he said, "Nafi'! Keep her, but I do not think that you will manage to keep her." Nafi' said, "When the Messenger of Allah ﷺ said to me, 'I do not think that you will manage to keep her,' I took a branch and fixed it in the earth and took a rope and firmly tied the sheep to it. The Messenger of Allah ﷺ slept and the people slept and I slept. In the morning, the rope was undone and there was no sheep. I went to the Messenger of Allah and told him. I said, 'The sheep has gone.' The Messenger of Allah ﷺ said to me, 'Did I not tell you that you would not manage to keep her? The one who brought her has taken her.'"

Hidhyam ibn Hanifa at-Tamimi

He related the *hadith* about the camels of *zakat* from the Messenger of Allah ﷺ.

Hanzala ibn Hidhyam said, "Hanifa said to his son Hidhyam, 'Gather your family together for me. I want to set forth my will.' So he gathered them together and said, 'I have gathered them, father.' He said, 'My first bequest is a hundred of the camels which we called 'al-Mutayyiba' in the *Jahiliyya* as *sadaqa* for this orphan who is in my care.' The name of the orphan was Dirs ibn Qati'a. Hidhyam said to his father, 'Father, I hear your family saying, "This boy is the apple of our father's eye. When he dies, we will divide the camels and give him the same share as one of us receives."' He asked, 'Did you hear them say this?' He replied, 'Yes.' He stated, 'The Messenger of Allah ﷺ must settle this between me and you.'

"So we went to the Prophet. He was sitting down and asked, 'Who are these people who are coming?' They replied, 'This is Hanifa of the Blessings, the man with the most camels in the desert.' He asked, 'Who are these two with him?' They said, 'The one on his right is his eldest son Hidhyam, but we do not know the one on his left.'

"When they reached the Prophet Hanifa greeted the Messenger of Allah and then Hidhyam greeted him. The Prophet صلعم inquired, 'What has brought you to me, Abu Hidhyam?' He replied, 'This is what has brought me,' and he struck Hidhyam's thigh. He said, 'Isn't this Hidhyam?' He replied, 'Yes.' He said, 'Messenger of Allah, I am a man with a lot of property. I have more than a thousand camels and forty horses, not to mention my property in my houses. I fear that Allah may decree an expected death for me, so I wanted to make a will and I made a bequest of a hundred camels of those called 'al-Mutayyiba' in the *Jahiliyya* as *sadaqa* to this orphan who is in my care.'"

He said, "I saw anger in the face of the Messenger of Allah صلعم until he knelt down. There he said, 'There is no god but Allah. *Sadaqa* is five, or ten, or fifteen, or twenty, or twenty-five, or thirty, and if more, then forty.' Then Hanifa spoke up, 'Messenger of Allah, I implore you that it be forty of the camels which we called 'al-Mutayyiba' in the *Jahiliyya*.' Hanifa took his leave and the Prophet صلعم asked, 'Where is your orphan, Abu Hidhyam?' He replied, 'He is that one over there asleep.' He seemed to be someone who had nearly reached puberty. The Prophet صلعم said, 'What a great cudgel of a boy this orphan is!' Then Hanifa and his sons went back to their camels. "

Adh-Dhayyal said, "Hidhyam said, 'Messenger of Allah, I have many sons and some of them have beards and some are younger than that.' (Hanzala interjected, "I was the youngest of them.") He said, 'Ask for blessing for him, Messenger of Allah!' He said, 'Come near, boy.' So he went up to him and he placed his hand on his head and said, 'May Allah bless you!'"

Adh-Dhayyal continued, "I saw a man brought to Hanzala whose face was swollen and a sheep whose udders were swollen. He spat in his palm and placed it on his black head and said, 'In the Name of Allah on the trace of the Messenger of Allah صلعم,' and then he wiped the swelling and it vanished."

'Umara ibn Ahmar al-Mazini

'Umara ibn Ahmar al-Mazini said, "During the *Jahiliyya* I was tending my camels when the cavalry of the Messenger of Allah صلعم

43

attacked us. I collected my camels and mounted a stallion, but the girth made it start to urinate. So I got off it and mounted a she-camel and I escaped on her. They drove off the camels. So I went to the Messenger of Allah ﷺ and became Muslim and he returned them to me. They had not yet divided them."

Jawwab ibn 'Umara said, "My brother and I got the she-camel which 'Umara rode that day to the Messenger of Allah ﷺ."

Asmar ibn Mudarris

His daughter 'Aqila reported that Asmar ibn Mudarris said, "I went to the Prophet ﷺ. The Prophet ﷺ said, 'If anyone comes to a water source to which a Muslim has not come before him, it is his.' People went out competing with one another."

'Amr ibn 'Umayr

He was a Companion of the Prophet ﷺ. 'Amr ibn 'Umayr reported that the Messenger of Allah ﷺ once stayed away from his Companions for three days during which they only saw him in the prayer. They said to him, "Why have we not seen you except for the prayer for three days?" He said, "My Lord promised me that 70,000 of the people of my community would enter the Garden without reckoning." They asked, "Who are they?" He said, "Those who do not use talismans nor seek omens or brands, and who put their trust in their Lord. I said, 'O Lord, give me more!' He said, 'You have 70,000 for each of the 70,000.' I said, 'O Lord, give me more! What if they are not enough?' He said, 'Then they will be completed from the Arabs.'"

'Ikrash ibn Dhu'ayb

He was a Companion of the Prophet ﷺ and listened to him.

'Ikrash ibn Dhu'ayb said, "My tribe, Murra ibn 'Ubayd, sent me to the Messenger of Allah ﷺ with the *zakat* of their property. I arrived in Madina and found him sitting with the Muhajirun and Ansar. I presented the camels to him in an offhand way. He asked, 'Who is this man?' I said, 'I am 'Ikrash ibn Dhu'ayb.' He said, 'A bit more of your lineage.' I said, 'Ibn Hurqus ibn Ja'da ibn 'Amr ibn Nazzal ibn Murra ibn 'Ubayd. This is the *zakat* of the Banu Murra ibn 'Ubayd.'

The Messenger of Allah ﷺ smiled and then said, 'These are the camels of my people. These are the *zakat* of my people.' Then the Messenger of Allah ﷺ commanded them to be marked with the brand of the *zakat* camels and added to the other *zakat* camels.

"Then he took my hand and brought me to the house of one of his wives and asked, 'Is there any food?' We were brought a platter with a large amount of *tharid* with pieces of meat. We began to eat and I put my hand in all directions. The Messenger of Allah ﷺ grabbed my right hand with his left hand and said, "Ikrash, eat from one place. It is all one kind of food.' Then we were brought a plate with dates, and I began to eat from in front of me and his hand went around the plate. Then he said, "Ikrash, eat where you wish. It is not one kind.' Then water was brought to us and the Messenger of Allah ﷺ washed his hands and wiped his face and forearms and head with the moisture of his palms. He said, "Ikrash, this *wudu'* is on account of what has been altered by fire.'"

Abu Raja' al-'Utaridi

His name was Abu Raja' 'Utarid ibn Barz.

'Abdu's-Salam Abu'l-Khalil said, "We visited Abu Raja' al-'Utaridi and he said, 'I was a bedouin and I am a man. We heard about the Prophet ﷺ and we left our homes until we could find reassurance. Then we heard that his affair was true and so we returned to our homes. My father and a group from the area went to the Messenger of Allah ﷺ and listened to him. They said, 'No harm. He calls you to Allah. We have become Muslim.'"

Qutba ibn Qatada as-Sadusi

Qutba ibn Qatada as-Sadusi is reported to have said, "I said, 'Messenger of Allah, give me your hand and I will give you my allegiance and that of my daughter al-Harmala. If I lie against Allah, then I have betrayed you.'"

Qutba said, "Khalid ibn al-Walid attacked us with his cavalry and we said, 'We are Muslims.' So he left us alone and we attacked Ubulla with him. And we completely destroyed it and filled our hands until our dogs were licking gold and silver plates."

Companions

Al-Hakam ibn al-Harith as-Sulami

Al-Hakam ibn al-Harith as-Sulami said, "The Prophet of Allah ﷺ said, 'If anyone wrongs someone else even to the extent of a piece of land measuring a hand's width, his neck will be encircled with it from the seven earths.'"

He said, "I went on seven expeditions with the Prophet ﷺ the last of which was Hunayn. I was in the vanguard of the Prophet ﷺ when my camel knelt and would not move. The Messenger of Allah ﷺ passed me while I was hitting it. He said, 'Stop.' He scolded it and it got up."

Al-'Abbas as-Sulami (*not* Ibn Mirdas)

It is reported that al-'Abbas went to the Messenger of Allah ﷺ and asked him for a grant of a well at ad-Dathina and he gave it to him provided that he only had what was beyond the needs of travellers. Abu'l-Azhar said, "Na'il ibn Mutarrif ibn al-'Abbas as-Sulami was at ad-Dathina and was their amir. He brought out for me a container which contained a piece of red skin on which his land grant was written."

Bashir ibn Zayd ad-Duba'i

Bashir ibn Zayd ad-Duba'i reported that the Messenger of Allah ﷺ said on the Day of Dhu Qar,[1] "Today the Arabs have diminished the kingdom of the Persians."

'Alqama ibn al-Huwayrith al-Ghifari

He was a Companion of the Prophet. He said that the Messenger of Allah ﷺ said, "The fornication of the eyes consists of the look."

'Abdullah ibn Mu'arrid al-Bahili

'Abdullah ibn Mu'arrid reported that he came to the Messenger of Allah ﷺ in a delegation and he stipulated a share to be taken from their camels. A she-camel, whether they were few or numerous, was to be taken from them.

---

1. A short-lived victory of Arab tribes (Banu Shayban) over a Sasanid army led by Hurmuzan around the turn of the seventh century.

'Abdu'r-Rahman ibn Khabbab as-Sulami

'Abdu'r-Rahman ibn Khabbab as-Sulami said, "I saw the Messenger of Allah ﷺ when he was encouraging people to support the Army of Hardship [to Tabuk]. 'Uthman said, 'Prophet of Allah, I have a hundred camels with their blankets and saddles for the Way of Allah.' Then he continued to ask and 'Uthman said, 'Two hundred camels.' He continued and he said, 'Three hundred camels.' I saw the Messenger of Allah ﷺ descend from the *minbar* saying twice, "Uthman does not have to do anything more after this.'"

'Asim, Abu Nasr ibn 'Asim al-Laythi

'Asim al-Laythi said, "I went into the mosque of the Messenger of Allah ﷺ and the Companions of the Prophet were saying, 'We seek refuge with Allah from the anger of Allah and the anger of His Messenger!' I said, 'What is it?' They said, 'Mu'awiya took his father's hand while the Messenger of Allah ﷺ was on the minbar and they left the mosque, and the Messenger of Allah, said something to them.'"

Asrim

The Messenger of Allah ﷺ named him Zur'a. He was a man of the Banu Shaqira.

Usama ibn Ukhdari said that a man of the Banu Shaqira called Asrim was in a group who went to the Messenger of Allah ﷺ. He brought him an Abyssinian boy whom he had purchased. He said, "Messenger of Allah, I purchased this lad and I want you to name him and pray for blessing for him." He asked, "And what is your name?" He replied, "Asrim." He said, "Rather you are Zur'a. What do you want of him?" He said, "I want him to be a herdsman." He said, "He is 'Asim," and clasped his hand.

Jurmuz al-Hujaymi

Jurmuz al-Hujaymi said that he had gone to the Prophet ﷺ and asked, "What do you forbid me?" He replied, "I forbid you to be a curser." He never cursed anyone for the rest of his life.

Companions

Suwayd ibn Hubayra

Suwayd ibn Hubayra said, "I heard the Prophet ﷺ say, 'The best property a man can have is a prolific filly or a row of fertile palm-trees.'"

Fadala al-Laythi

Fadala al-Laythi said, "I went to the Prophet ﷺ and became Muslim and he taught me the five prayers at their times. I said, 'These are times when I am busy, so command me to do them all together.' He said, 'Do not be distracted from the two ends.' I said, 'What are the two ends?' He said, 'The dawn prayer and the *'Asr* prayer.'"

Uhban ibn Sayfi al-Ghifari

His *kunya* was Abu Muslim. He left a will that he be shrouded in two garments but he was shrouded in three garments. In the morning they found the third garment on the clothes rack.

Khidash

Bahriyya said, "My uncle Khidash asked the Messenger of Allah ﷺ for the gift of a bowl from which he saw him eat. We kept it with us. 'Umar used to say, 'Bring it out,' and we would fill it with Zamzam water and bring it to him and he would drink from it and pour it on his face and head. Then a thief burgled us and stole it with some things of ours. 'Umar came to us after it had been stolen and asked for us to bring it out and we said, 'Amir al-Mu'minun, it was stolen along with some other things of ours.' He exclaimed, 'May his father go to Allah! He stole the dish of the Messenger of Allah ﷺ!' By Allah, he did not curse or abuse him."

Abu Salama

'Abdu'l-Hamid ibn Salama related from his grandfather that two men took a dispute regarding his paternity to the Prophet ﷺ. One of them was a Muslim and the other an unbeliever. So he gave him a choice about which was his father. He turned towards the unbeliever, and the Prophet said, "O Allah, guide him!" and he turned to the Muslim and chose him.

The uncle of 'Abdu'r-Rahman ibn Salama al-Khuza'i

The uncle of 'Abdu'r-Rahman ibn Salama said, "We went to the Messenger of Allah ﷺ on the Day of 'Ashura' when we had already eaten. He said, 'Did you fast today?' We said, 'We had lunch.' He said, 'Fast the rest of today.'"

Qays ibn al-Asla' al-Ansari

Nafi', the client of Hatma, related that his uncles complained to the Prophet ﷺ that he was wasting his property.

'Ubada ibn Qurs al-'Abasi

He is also called Laythi and is called Ibn Qurt.
'Ubada ibn Qurt said, "You do things which seem to you smaller than a hair which we used to consider to be grave wrong actions in the time of the Messenger of Allah ﷺ."

The father or uncle of Mujiba al-Bahiliyya

He related from the Prophet ﷺ.
A woman of Bahila called Mujiba related that her father or uncle said, "I went to the Prophet ﷺ for something I needed and he asked, 'Who are you?' I said, 'Don't you recognise me, Messenger of Allah? I am the Bahili man who came to you last year.' He said, 'When you came to me your complexion, body and appearance were good and now I see that you are in a bad way.' I said, 'Since I left you I have only broken the fast on one day.' He asked, 'Who commanded you to torture yourself? Fast the month of Ramadan.' I said, 'Messenger of Allah, I am strong. Let me do more.' He said, 'Fast the month of steadfastness and then two days every month.' I said, 'Messenger of Allah, give me more. I feel strong.' He said, 'Why do you want more than two days beyond the month of steadfastness?' I said, 'Messenger of Allah, give me more. I feel strong.' He said, 'Fast the month of steadfastness and three days of every month only and break the fast.' He made a gesture with his hand."

Companions

Muhammad ibn Sa'd said, "We wrote this *hadith* in our book originating from Kahmas al-Hilali and that *hadith* is similar to what is from Mujiba al-Bahiliyya from her father or uncle. Allah knows best."

The uncle of Abu's-Sawwar al-'Adawi

Abu's-Sawwar reported that his uncle said, "I saw the Messenger of Allah ﷺ when some people were following him. So I followed him with them. Suddenly some people ran to me and held me, and the Messenger of Allah ﷺ came to me and hit me lightly with a palm branch, stalk or stick or something he had with him. By Allah, he did not hurt me at all. I spent the night saying, 'The Messenger of Allah ﷺ only hit me because of something Allah has told him about me.' I told myself that I would go to the Messenger of Allah ﷺ in the morning. Jibril, peace be upon him, descended on the Prophet ﷺ and said, 'You are a shepherd. Do not break the horns of your flock.' He said, 'By Allah, I did not hit you on account of any disobedience or opposition.' When we had prayed the morning prayer, the Messenger of Allah ﷺ said, 'Some people followed me and I did not want them to follow after me. O Allah, if I hit or abuse anyone, make it an expiation and reward for him,' or he said, 'forgiveness and mercy,' or words to that effect."

The uncle of Hasna' bint Mu'awiya as-Suraymiyya

Hasna' bint Mu'awiya as-Suraymiyya related that her uncle said, "I asked the Prophet ﷺ, 'Who will be in the Garden?' He replied, 'The Prophet will be in the Garden. The martyr will be in the Garden. The oppressed will be in the Garden.'"

The uncle of Abu Hurra ar-Raqqashi

He said, "I was holding the bridle of the she-camel of the Messenger of Allah ﷺ in the middle of the Days of *Tashriq* when he bade farewell to the people." Then he mentioned the Prophet's *khutba*.

Ashajj 'Abdu'l-Qays

They disagree about his name.

Ashajj said, "The Messenger of Allah ﷺ said to me, 'You have two qualities which Allah and His Messenger love.' I asked, 'What are they?' He replied, 'Forbearance and modesty.' I said, 'Are they inherent in me or new?' He said, 'They are long-standing.' I said, 'Praise belongs to Allah who made me naturally formed with two qualities which Allah loves!'"

Muhammad ibn Bishr said, "I asked our Shaykh al-Buhtari about al-Ashajj's name. He said, 'His name was al-Mundhir ibn 'A'idh. He was in the delegation of 'Abdu'l-Qays who came to the Messenger of Allah ﷺ from al-Bahrayn. Then he later settled in Basra.'"

Al-Jarud

His name was Bishr ibn 'Amr. His *kunya* was Abu'l-Mundhir and his mother was Darmaka bint Ru'aym, the sister of Yazid ibn Ru'aym ash-Shaybani. Al-Jarud was a noble in the *Jahiliyya*. He was a Christian. He came to the Messenger of Allah ﷺ in the delegation [of 'Abdu'l-Qays] and the Messenger of Allah ﷺ invited him to become Muslim. Al-Jarud said, "I have a debt. If I leave my *deen* for your *deen*, will you guarantee my debt?" The Messenger of Allah ﷺ said, "I am your guarantor. Allah has guided you to better than what you have of it."

Then al-Jarud became a good Muslim and was not censured. He wanted to return to his people's land and asked the Prophet ﷺ for some mounts. He said, "I do not have any animals available for you to ride." He said, "Messenger of Allah, there are some stray camels between me and my land. Can I ride them?" The Messenger of Allah ﷺ said, "They are flames of the Fire! Do not go near them."

Al-Jarud lived until the time of the Ridda. When some of his people apostatised with al-Gharur ibn al-Mundhir, al-Jarud testified to the truth and called the people to Islam. He said, "O people! I testify that there is no god but Allah and that Muhammad is His slave and His Messenger, and I reject those who do not so testify!" Then he said:

> We are pleased with the *deen* of Allah in every event,
> and we are pleased with Allah, the All-Merciful as a Lord.

After that al-Jarud settled in Basra and had sons there who were nobles and al-Hakam ibn Abi'l-'As sent al-Jarud to the Battle of

Companions

Suhrak and he was killed as a martyr at 'Aqaba at-Tin in 20 AH. It became known as 'Aqaba al-Jarud.

Al-Mundhir ibn al-Jarud was a generous chief and 'Ali ibn Abi Talib, may Allah be pleased with him, put him in charge of Istakhr. No one came but he gave them a gift. Then 'Ubaydullah ibn Ziyad appointed him over the Indian frontier, and he died there in 61 or the beginning of 62 AH. He was 60 years old.

Suhar ibn 'Abbas al-'Abdi

One of the Banu Murra ibn Zafar. His *kunya* was Abu 'Abdu'r-Rahman. He was in the delegation of 'Abdu'l-Qays.

Khalda bint Talq said, "My father said to us, 'We were sitting with the Messenger of Allah ﷺ when Suhar ibn 'Abdu'l-Qays came and asked, "Messenger of Allah, what do you think about a drink which we make from our dates?" The Prophet ﷺ turned away from him until he had asked three times. Then he led us in the prayer. When he had finished the prayer, he said, "Who is the one who asked about the intoxicant? You asked me about the intoxicant. Do not drink it. Do not give it to your brother to drink. By the One Who has the soul of Muhammad in His hand, any man who drinks it seeking the pleasure of intoxication will be forced to drink the wine of the Day of Rising.'" He said, 'Suhar was one of those who sought revenge for the blood of 'Uthman.'"

Abu Khayra as-Subbahi of 'Abdu'l-Qays

Abu Khayra as-Subbahi said, "I was in the delegation which came to the Messenger of Allah ﷺ from Abdu'l-Qays. He provisioned us with arak wood to use for *siwak* and we said, 'Messenger of Allah, we have palm branches, but we will accept your generosity and gift.' The Messenger of Allah ﷺ said, 'O Allah, forgive 'Abdu'l-Qays since they have become Muslim voluntarily without compulsion, for some people only become Muslim when they are shamed and seeking blood money.'"

Aban al-Muharibi of 'Abdu'l-Qays

It is reported from Aban al-Muharibi, who was among the delegation which came to the Messenger of Allah ﷺ from Abdu'l-Qays that the Messenger of Allah ﷺ said, "There is no Muslim who says in the morning, 'Praise be to Allah, my Lord. I do not associate anything with Him and I testify that there is no god but Allah,' but that his wrong actions continue to be forgiven until evening. If he says it in the evening, his wrong actions continue to be forgiven until morning.'"

Az-Zari' ibn al-Wazi' al-'Abdi

He was in the delegation of 'Abdu'l-Qays. Then he settled in Basra.

Jabir ibn 'Abdullah al-'Abdi

They were in the delegation of 'Abdu'l-Qays. Then they later settled after that in Basra.

Salama al-Jarmi

He is the father of 'Amr ibn Salama.

Salama said, "We went to the Messenger of Allah ﷺ and said, 'Messenger of Allah, who should lead us in the prayer?' He replied, 'You should be led in prayer by the one who knows the most Qur'an.'" 'Amr, Salama's son said, "My father used to lead them in the prayer in their mosque and he led their funeral prayers and no one contended with him for that until his death."

'Amr ibn Salama said, "My father and some of his people went in a delegation to the Prophet ﷺ. When the people became Muslim and learned the Qur'an and satisfied their needs, they said to him, 'Who should lead us in the prayer?' He replied, 'The one who knows the most Qur'an should lead you in the prayer.'" He said, "So they went to their people and asked them about it and did not find anyone with more Qur'an than I had. At that time I was a lad with but one sheet to cover me. So they put me forward and I led them in the prayer. Since then I have never been present with a group of Jarm but that I have been their Imam, right up until today."

'Amr ibn Salama al-Jarmi said, "We lived by water by which people passed. We used to ask them, 'What is this business?' They replied, 'There is a man who claims to be a Prophet and that Allah has sent him and that Allah has revealed to him such-and-such.' Everything that I heard I memorised as if it stuck firmly in my breast until I had amassed a lot of the Qur'an.

"The Arabs were temporising about embracing Islam up until the Conquest of Makka. They were saying, 'Wait and see. If he defeats them, then he is telling the truth and he is a Prophet.' When the news of the Conquest came, every tribe hastened to become Muslim. My father went to tell the Prophet that we had become Muslim and he stayed with the Messenger of Allah صلى الله عليه وسلم for as long as Allah wished for him to stay.

"Then he came back. When he approached, we met him and when we saw him, he said, 'By Allah, I have brought you the truth from the Messenger of Allah صلى الله عليه وسلم. He commands you such-and-such and forbids you such-and-such. You should pray such-and-such a prayer at such-and-such a time, and such-and-such a prayer at such-and-such a time. When the prayer-time comes, one of you should give the *adhan* and the one of you with the most Qur'an should lead you.' The people of our tribe looked and they did not find anyone with more Qur'an than me because of the Qur'an I had memorised from the travellers. They put me in front of them and I used to lead them in the prayer and I was only six years old. I was wearing a cloak and when I prostrated, it rode up on me. A woman of the tribe said, 'Why don't you cover the buttocks of your reciter from us!' So they cut me a shirt with knots from Bahrayn. I was never so happy about anything as I was about that shirt."

'Amr ibn Salama al-Jarmi said, "I used to meet riders and they would recite *ayats* to me, and so I led the prayer in the time of the Messenger of Allah صلى الله عليه وسلم."

✼✼✼✼✼

Other Companions mentioned by Muhammad ibn Sa'd are: 'Abdullah al-Muzani, Qatada ibn Awfa ibn Mawala, "Amr ibn Taghlib an-Namri, Ubayy ibn Malik, al-Fakih ibn Sa'd, Abu 'Azza al-Hudhali, Zuhayr ibn 'Amr, Habis at-Tamimi, Abu Buhaysha, the father of Abu'l-'Ushayra ad-Darimi, Sulayman ibn 'Amir ad-Dabbi, Muddaris ibn Asmar, and Salama ibn al-Muhabiqq.

✼✼✼✼✼

The First Generation
The *fuqaha'*, *hadith* transmitters, and *Tabi'un* of the people of Basra among the companions of 'Umar ibn al-Khattab

Abu Maryam al-Hanafi

His name was Iyas ibn Dubayh. He was one of the people of Yaman and was one of the followers of Musaylima. He killed Zayd ibn al-Khattab in the Battle of Yamama. Then he repented and became Muslim and was a good Muslim. He was appointed qadi of Basra after 'Imran ibn al-Husayn in the time of 'Umar ibn al-Khattab.

Abu Maryam al-Hanafi said that 'Umar ibn al-Khattab entered a chamber of his and then came out and began to recite the Qur'an. Abu Maryam said to him, "Amir al-Mu'minin, you have left the lavatory!" He said, "Did Musaylima give you this *fatwa*?" They say that Abu Maryam died at Sanbil, part of Ahwaz. He has few *hadiths*.

Ka'b ibn Suwar

Ash-Sha'bi said, "A woman came to 'Umar ibn al-Khattab and said, 'I complain to you of the best of the people of this world unless some man has done it before him or done the like of what he does. He stands in prayer for the entire night until morning, and fasts the day until evening.' Then modesty and embarrassment overcame her and she said, 'Dismiss me, Amir al-Mu'minin.' He said, 'May Allah repay you well. Excellent is the praise you have uttered. I have dismissed you.' When she had gone away, Ka'b ibn Suwar said, 'Amir al-Mu'minin, she has been eloquent in her complaint.' He asked, 'What was she complaining about?' He replied, 'Her husband.' He said, 'I owe the woman a response.' He told Ka'b, 'Judge between them.' He said, 'Me judge when you are present?' He said 'You grasped what I did not grasp.' Ka'b said, 'Allah says, *"Marry other permissible women, two, three or four."* (4:3) Therefore fast three days and break the fast for a day on one day. Stand in prayer for three nights and spend one night with her.' 'Umar said, 'This is more wondrous to me than the first!' So he sent him as a qadi to the people of Basra."

Ash-Sha'bi said that 'Umar ibn al-Khattab sent Ka'b ibn Suwar as qadi of Basra.

Al-Ahnaf ibn Qays said, "When the two groups met on the Day of the Camel, Ka'b went out holding an open Qur'an in his hand, admonishing both parties until an arrow struck and killed him."

Some of the people of knowledge say that when Talha, az-Zubayr and 'A'isha came to Basra, Ka'b ibn Suwar went into a house and had it covered with clay, leaving only a hole from which to receive his food and drink. This was in order to withdraw from the *fitna*. 'A'isha was told, "If Ka'b ibn Suwar comes out with you, none of Azd [his tribe] will hold back." So she rode to him and called to him and spoke to him, but he did not answer her. She said, "Ka'b! Am I not your mother and do I not have a right from you?" So he spoke to her. She said, "I want to make peace between the people!" That was when he came out and took the Qur'an and opened it and walked between the rows calling them to what it contained. An arrow came from an unknown source and killed him. He was known for virtue and righteousness but does not have any *hadith*.

Al-Ahnaf ibn Qays

One of the Banu Sa'd of Banu Tamim. His mother was from the Banu Qarad of Bahila. When she gave birth to him, he had a foot deformity (*ahnaf*). She recited:

O Allah, were it not for a deformity of his foot,
 there would not be a lad like him in the tribe.

Al-Ahnaf's *kunya* was Abu Bahr. He was reliable and trustworthy with few *hadiths*. He related from 'Umar ibn al-Khattab, 'Ali ibn Abi Talib and Abu Dharr.

Al-Ahnaf ibn Qays said, "While I was doing *tawaf* of the House when 'Uthman was khalif, a man of the Banu Layth met me and took my hand. He said, 'Shall I give you good news?' I replied, 'Certainly.' He said, 'You remember when the Messenger of Allah sent me to your people, the Banu Sa'd, and I began to offer Islam to them and call them to it and you said, "You call to virtue and I have only heard good"?' He went on, 'I mentioned that to the Messenger of Allah صلعم and he said, "O Allah, forgive al-Ahnaf!"' Al-Ahnaf said, 'There is nothing I hope for more than that.'"

Muhammad said, "I have been informed that 'Umar mentioned the Banu Tamim and censured them. Al-Ahnaf said, 'Amir al-Mu'minin, let me speak.' He said, 'Speak.' He said, 'You mentioned the Banu Tamim and covered them with blame. They are people. Some of them are righteous and some are wicked.' He said, 'You have spoken the truth.' He said something good instead. Then al-Hutat, who was hostile to him, stood up and said, 'Amir al-Mu'minin, let me speak.' He said, 'Your master al-Ahnaf has spared you.'"

Al-Hasan reported that al-Ahnaf said, "I came to 'Umar ibn al-Khattab and he kept me with him for a year. He said, 'Ahnaf, I have tested you and learned about you and I have only seen good. I have seen that your public part is good, and I hope that your secret is like what you make public. We were told that this community would be destroyed by every knowledgeable hypocrite. But you are not one of them, Allah willing.' 'Umar wrote to Abu Musa al-Ash'ari, 'Bring al-Ahnaf ibn Qays close to you, consult him and listen to him.'"

Abu'l-Asfar said that al-Ahnaf was appointed over Khurasan. When he reached Persia, he found himself in *janaba* on a cold night. He said, "He did not wake up any of his slaves or his army. He went out to look for water. He pushed on through thorns and trees until his feet bled until he finally found some snow. He broke it up and performed *ghusl*. He got up and found two new sandals side by side on top of his garments. He put them on. In the morning he told his companions and they said, 'By Allah, we did not know about you.'"

Al-Hasan said, "I did not see any noble of his people better than al-Ahnaf."

Al-Ahnaf ibn Qays said, "Fear of the reply keeps me from speaking a lot."

Al-Hasan said, "People mentioned something in the presence of Mu'awiya. They spoke but al-Ahnaf remained silent. Mu'awiya said, 'Speak, Abu Bahr!' He said, 'I fear Allah if I lie and I fear you if I speak the truth.'"

Al-Hasan said that al-Ahnaf said, "I am not actually forbearing, but I strive to be forbearing."

The client of al-Ahnaf said, "Al-Ahnaf was rarely alone but that he called for a copy of the Qur'an." Yunus said, "Studying copies of the Qur'an was a characteristic of the early ones."

A slave of al-Ahnaf's who had been bought by Abu Mansur said, "Usually al-Ahnaf prayed at night. He would place the Qur'an close to him and would place his finger on the Qur'an and say, 'Excellent.' Then he would say, 'Ahnaf, what led you to do such-and-such on such-and-such a day!'"

Zayd said, "It was said to al-Ahnaf, 'You are an old man and the fast debilitates you.' He replied, 'I prepare with it against a great evil.'"

Marwan al-Asfar said that he heard al-Ahnaf ibn Qays say, "O Allah, if You forgive me, You are worthy of that. If you punish me, I deserve that."

Abu'l-Mukhayyash said, "I was sitting with al-Ahnaf ibn Qays when a letter came from 'Abdu'l-Malik summoning him to come to him. He said, 'He is calling me to the rule of the people of Syria. I wish that there was a mountain of fire between me and them that would burn any of them who came to us and burn any of us who went to them.'"

It was said to al-Ahnaf, "Abu Bahr, you have great deliberateness in you." He said, "I recognise haste in myself in three matters: in my prayer when it is time to pray it, the funeral until the body disappears into the earth, and in giving my daughter in marriage when her equal asks for her hand."

Al-Azraq ibn Qays said that al-Ahnaf ibn Qays disliked praying in the *maqsura*. He also said that al-Ahnaf ibn Qays disliked stepping across the necks of the people before the Imam came out on Friday.

Isma'il ibn Abi Khalid said that he saw al-Ahnaf ibn Qays wearing a silk-wool shawl and a cut garment made of Yemeni cloth and a silk-wool turban while he was on a mule. Al-Ahnaf was a friend of Mus'ab ibn az-Zubayr. He visited him in Kufa when Mus'ab ibn az-Zubayr was its governor. Al-Ahnaf died in Kufa. Mus'ab was seen walking in his funeral procession without a cloak.

Abu 'Uthman an-Nahdi

It is related that his name was 'Abdu'r-Rahman ibn Mull.

Al-Hajjaj ibn Abi Zaynab said, "I heard Abu 'Uthman an-Nahdi saying, 'In the *Jahiliyya* we used to worship a stone. Then we heard someone calling to us, "O people of ar-Rijal! Your Lord has been destroyed, so seek him." We searched high and low. While we were seeking we heard a call, "We have found your Lord or one like him!" We went and it was a stone. We made a sacrifice on it.'"

'Asim al-Ahwal said, "I asked Abu 'Uthman, 'Did you actually see the Prophet ﷺ?' He replied, 'No.' I said, 'Did you see Abu Bakr?' He replied, 'No, but I followed 'Umar when he was in power and our *zakat* went to the Prophet ﷺ three times.'"

Abu 'Uthman said, "I accompanied Salman for twelve years."

Humayd reported that Abu 'Uthman an-Nahdi said, "I have lived 130 years and there is nothing about me which I do not object to you except for my hope and I find it just as it was.'"

Thabit al-Bunani reported that Abu 'Uthman an-Nahdi said, "I know when Allah remembers me." He was asked, "How do you know?" He replied, "Allah Almighty says, *'Remember me and I will remember you'* (2:152). When I remember Allah, He remembers me." He said, "When we made supplication, he said, 'Allah has answered us.' He then quoted, *'Call on me and I will answer you.'"* (40:60)

Abu Talut ibn Shaddad said "I saw Abu 'Uthman an-Nahdi when he was a sergeant (*'arif*). He came and took from the people of arms."

Malik ibn Isma'il an-Nahdi said, "Abu 'Uthman an-Nahdi was one of the inhabitants of Kufa although the Banu Nahd did not have any houses there. When al-Husayn ibn 'Ali was killed, he moved and settled in Basra. He said, 'I will not live in a town in which the grandson of the Messenger of Allah ﷺ was killed.' He was alive in the time of the Messenger of Allah ﷺ but did not see him. He was reliable. He related from 'Umar, 'Abdullah ibn Mas'ud, Abu Musa al-Ash'ari, Salman, Usama, and Abu Hurayra. He died in Basra at the beginning of the governorship of al-Hajjaj ibn Yusuf over Iraq."

Abu'l-Aswad ad-Du'ali

His name was Dhalim ibn 'Amr. He was a partisan poet of the Shi'a. He was reliable in *hadith*, Allah willing. When 'Abdullah ibn

'Abbas resigned as governor and left Basra, he delegated Abu'l-Aswad ad-Du'ali in charge of it and 'Ali ibn Abi Talib confirmed him.

Qatada reported that Abu'l-Aswad ad-Du'ali said, "The most hateful of people to me is the jumping to conclusions by every sharp-tongued foolhardy one."

Ziyad ibn Abi Sufyan ibn Harb

His mother was Sumayya, the slavegirl of al-Harith ibn Kalada ath-Thaqafi. Some call him "Ziyad ibn Abihi (son of his father)" and some say "Ziyad the amir." He was governor of Basra for Mu'awiya after he claimed him as his brother and he later added Kufa to his jurisdiction. He spent the winter in Basra and the summer in Kufa. He left 'Amr ibn Hurayth in charge of Kufa when he left it, and Samura ibn Jundub over Basra when he left it. Ziyad was neither a reciter nor a *faqih*, but he was well-known and a scribe for Abu Musa al-Ash'ari. He related from 'Umar.

Muhammad said that Ziyad's signet ring had a peacock on it.

A man of Quraysh called Muhammad al-Harith said that Murra went to 'Abdu'r-Rahman ibn Abi Bakr as-Siddiq whose client he was and asked him to write to Ziyad about something he needed. He wrote, "From 'Abdu'r-Rahman to Ziyad," without ascribing him to Abu Sufyan. He said, "I will not take this letter of yours so that he harms me." So he went to 'A'isha and she wrote for him, "From 'A'isha, Mother of the Believers, to Ziyad ibn Abi Sufyan." When he brought the letter, he said, "Come tomorrow with your letter." The people gathered and he said, "Boy, read it." He said, "From 'A'isha, Mother of the Believers, to Ziyad ibn Abi Sufyan." He granted him his request.

'Amir said, "Ziyad was approached about a man who had died leaving a paternal aunt and a maternal aunt. He said, 'Do you know what 'Umar ibn al-Khattab judged about them? By Allah, I am the person with the most knowledge of 'Umar's decision about her. He put the maternal aunt in the position of the sister and the paternal aunt in the position of the brother. He gave the paternal aunt two-thirds and the maternal aunt one-third.'"

'Amir reported that Ziyad ibn Abi Sufyan was born in Ta'if in the Year of the Conquest of Makka and died in Kufa while he was governor there for Mu'awiya ibn Abi Sufyan in 53 AH.

'Abdullah ibn al-Harith ibn Nawfal

His *kunya* was Abu Muhammad. He was from the Banu Hashim. His mother was Hind bint Abi Sufyan ibn Harb. He was born in the time of the Prophet صلعم and listened to 'Umar ibn al-Khattab's speech at al-Jabiyya [in Syria], and he listened to 'Uthman ibn Abi 'Affan, Ubayy ibn Ka'b, Hudhayfa ibn al-Yaman, 'Abdullah ibn 'Abbas and his father al-Harith ibn Nawfal.

'Abdullah ibn al-Harith moved to Basra with his father and built a house there. While Mas'ud ibn 'Amr was governor, 'Ubaydullah ibn Ziyad left Basra and people disagreed with one another. The tribes and clans summoned one another and agreed to appoint 'Abdullah ibn al-Harith to lead their prayer and be in charge of their booty. They wrote to 'Abdullah ibn az-Zubayr, "We are pleased with him," and so 'Abdullah ibn az-Zubayr confirmed him over Basra.[1] 'Abdullah ibn Harith mounted the *minbar* and took the allegiance of people on behalf of 'Abdullah ibn az-Zubayr until he was exhausted. Then he continued to take their allegiance while he was asleep with his hand outstretched. Suhaym ibn Wuthayl al-Yarbu'i said:

> I gave allegiance to those awake and I fulfilled my allegiance.
> I gave allegiance to him while he was asleep.

'Abdullah ibn al-Harith remained governor of Basra for 'Abdullah ibn az-Zubayr until he was dismissed and al-Harith ibn 'Abdullah al-Makhzumi appointed. 'Abdullah ibn al-Harith left for Oman where he died.

Abu Sufra al-'Ataki

His name was Zalim ibn Sarraq. He was from the tribe of Azd from Daba' which is between Oman and Bahrayn.

His tribe became Muslims and their delegation went to the Messenger of Allah صلعم to affirm their Islam. He sent a *zakat* collector to them called Hudhayfa ibn al-Yaman al-Azdi, one of the people of Daba'. He wrote out for him the obligations of *zakat* and instructed him to collect the *zakat* of their property and to give it to their poor.

---

1. This is during the civil war between 'Abdullah ibn az-Zubayr and the Umayyads while Ibn az-Zubayr was in control of Iraq.

When the Messenger of Allah died, they apostatised and refused to pay *zakat*.

Hudhayfa wrote to Abu Bakr about that and Abu Bakr sent 'Ikrima ibn Abi Jahl to him and they fought them. Then Allah gave 'Ikrima victory over them, and Allah defeated them and inflicted much killing among them. Their remnants took refuge in the fortress of Daba' and then fortified themselves there. The Muslims laid siege to them in their fortress. They eventually surrendered to the judgement of Hudhayfa ibn al-Yaman al-Azdi. He killed a hundred of their nobles and took their children captive and sent them to Abu Bakr in Madina. They included Abu Sufra, a lad who had not yet reached puberty. Abu Bakr wanted to kill him, but 'Umar said, "Khalif of the Messenger of Allah, some people are miserly about their property." Abu Bakr refused to let them go. They remained in the house of Ramla bint al-Harith until Abu Bakr died and 'Umar ibn al-Khattab was appointed. He summoned them and said, "This business has come to me. So go to whatever land you wish. You are free people and owe no ransom." So they left and went to Basra and some returned to their land. Abu Sufra, who was Abu'l-Muhallab, was one of those who settled in Basra and he and his children were honoured there.

Some of those who related from 'Umar ibn al-Khattab but had few *hadiths* include:

Abu'l-'Ajfa' (Harim) as-Sulami
As-Sa'ib ibn al-Aqra' ath-Thaqafi
Hujayr ibn ar-Rabi' al-'Adawi
His brother, Hurayth ibn ar-Rabi' al-'Adawi
Dabba ibn Muhsin al-'Anazi

Al-Aqra', the *mu'adhdhin* of 'Umar

He related from 'Umar that he called the Bishop and said, "Do you find that it says in your book..."

'Amir ibn 'Abdullah ibn 'Abdu Qays al-'Anbari

His *kunya* was Abu 'Amr or Abu 'Abdullah. He was one of the Banu Tamim. He related from 'Umar.

'Amir ibn 'Abdullah said that he received his stipend of 2000 dirhams from 'Umar. No beggar came but that he gave him something. Then he went to his family and gave it to them and they counted it and found that it had not decreased at all.

Ibn Sirin said, "'Amir's stipend was issued and he commanded a man to divide it. He counted it and said, 'It is more.' He said, 'This had been increased. I think that the amir knows what you do and so he gave you more.' He said, 'Do you think he is more capable (or entitled) than the amir?'

"He was told, 'So-and-so is your wife in the Garden.' So he went to look for her, and she turned out to be a girl who belonged to some vile desert Arabs. She herded sheep for them. When she came, they abused her and were harsh to her and tossed her a couple of loaves. She took one of them to the people of a house and gave it to them. When she wanted to eat, they threw her two loaves. She took them to the people of a house and gave them both to them. When she was fasting, she broke the fast on a loaf.

"He followed her and she went to a suitable place and left her sheep there and stood to pray. He said, 'Tell me, do you need anything?' She replied, 'No.' When he pressed her about it, she said, 'I would like to have two white garments for my shroud.' He asked, 'Why do they abuse you?' She said, 'I hope for a reward for this.' He returned to them and asked, 'Why do you abuse your slave-girl?' They said, 'We fear that she may become spoiled for us.' They had another slave-girl not like her whom they did not abuse. He asked, 'Will you sell her?' They said, 'Even if you gave us such-and-such, we would not sell her.' He went and brought two garments and continued to meet her until her death. He said, 'Let me deal with her,' and they said, 'All right.' So he buried her and prayed over her."

It is reported that 'Amir passed through a public square and saw a *dhimmi* being maltreated. 'Amir cast off his cloak and then said, "Am I to see the protection (*dhimma*) of Allah being violated while I am alive?" And he rescued him.

Muhammad said, "The first that Ma'qil ibn Yasir learned of 'Amir was when he was mentioned regarding something that happened in a public square. He was told that 'Amir had passed by a man of the people of *dhimma* who had been seized. He rebuked them about their treatment of him but they refused to relent. Then he spoke to them about him again and they still refused to relent. He said, 'You lie. By Allah, you will not wrong the *dhimma* of Allah (or the *dhimma* of the Messenger of Allah) today while I am present.' He dismounted and rescued the man from them. People were saying, "Amir does not eat meat or ghee. He does not pray in mosques or marry women. His skin does not touch anyone else's skin and he says, "I am like Ibrahim."' So he went to visit him and found him wearing a burnoose. He said, 'People claim that you do not eat meat.' He replied, 'When we want it, we command that a sheep be slaughtered and we eat its meat. Those people are saying something which I know nothing about. As for ghee, I eat what comes from here,' and he gestured towards the desert, 'but I do not eat what comes from there (meaning the mountains). As for the statement that I do not pray in the mosques, on Friday I pray with the people. After that I prefer to pray here. As for their statement that I do not marry women, I have but one self, and I fear that it will overpower me. As for their statement that I say that I am like Ibrahim, that is not the case. I said, "I hope that Allah will put me with *'the Prophets, the men of truth, the martyrs, the righteous. And such people are the best of company!'* (4:69)"'"

Abu 'Abda al-'Anazi said, "A man of the tribe who was truthful said, 'I accompanied 'Amir on an expedition and we camped near a thicket. He collected his gear and put his horse on a long rope and released it. Then he entered the thicket and I said, "I will see what he does in the night." So he went to a hill and began to pray until morning was near and then made supplication. Part of his supplication was: "O Allah, I have asked you for three and You have given me two and denied me the third. O Allah, give it to me so that I can worship You as I desire."

'Morning broke and he saw me and said, "If I had known that you were observing me in the night, I would have dealt with you!" He raised his voice to me but I was insistent and I said, "Stop this! By Allah, you will tell me about the three things for which you asked your Lord or I will tell people what you were doing in the night." He said, "Bother you! Do not do it!" I said, "I will do what I tell you." When he saw my resolve, he said, "Do not speak about it while I am alive." I said, "You have that promise from me." He said, "I asked my Lord to remove love of women from me as there is nothing which makes me more fearful for my *deen* than them. By Allah, I do not care whether I see a woman or a wall. I asked my Lord that I would not fear anyone but Him. By Allah, I have not feared anyone except Him. I asked my Lord to remove sleep from me so that I could worship Him night and day as I wish, but He has denied me that.""

Qatada said, "'Amir ibn 'Abdullah asked his Lord to make purification easy for him in the winter, and he used to be brought water which was steaming. He asked his Lord to remove the desire for women from his heart, and he did not care whether he met a male or female. He asked his Lord to come between Shaytan and his heart when he was praying so that he would have no power against him. When he was on an expedition, he was told, 'We are afraid of this forest because there is lion in it.' He said, 'I am too ashamed before my Lord to fear other than Him.'"

'Amir said, "I prefer one message in the Book of Allah which He gave to all of this world." He was asked, "What is that, Abu 'Amr?" He replied, "That Allah makes me among the godfearing. He says, *'Allah only accepts from the Godfearing.'* (5:27)"

'Amir said, "By Allah, if I were able, I would gather all my concerns into one." Al-Hasan remarked, "By Allah, he did it."

It was said to 'Amir ibn 'Abdullah, "You have harmed yourself." He took hold of the skin of his arms and said, "By Allah, if I am able, the earth will only obtain a little of its fat!"

Sukayn al-Hajari said, "When 'Amir ibn 'Abdullah passed by fruit he would say, 'failing, restricted.'" [referring to Qur'an 56:32-33: *"And fruits in abundance, never failing, unrestricted."*]

Malik ibn Dinar said, "Someone saw 'Amir call for oil and pour it in his hand. He wiped his hands together and said, *'A tree springing forth from Mount Sinai yielding oil and seasoning to those who eat it.'* (23:20). He oiled his head and beard."

Muhammad said, "There was a dispute between 'Amir ibn 'Abdullah al-'Anbari and a man. 'Amir insulted him in a way that reflected on his mother. Then later people said to him, 'We do not think you acted well in this.' He said, 'There are many things which you think I do not do well which I know even more than you are not good.'"

Sahm ibn Shaqiq said, "I went to 'Amir ibn 'Abdullah and sat at his door. He came out and he had done a *ghusl*. I said, 'I see you like *ghusl*.' He said, 'I often have a *ghusl*.' He went on, 'What do you need?' I replied, '*Hadith*.' He said, 'Do you know that I love *hadith*?'"

Muhammad ibn Sirin said, "'Amir ibn 'Abdullah was asked, 'Why don't you marry?' He said, 'I do not have energy and I do not have property. So I would not care to tempt a Muslim woman.'"

Abu Qilaba said that a man met 'Amir and said to him, "What is this you have done? Did not Allah say, '*We sent Messengers before you and gave them wives and children too.*' (13:38)?" He retorted, "And did not Allah say. '*I only created jinn and men to worship Me*'?" (51:56)

Maymun ibn Mihran said that the governor of Basra sent a messenger to 'Amir who said, "The Amir al-Mu'minun has commanded me to ask you why you do not marry women." He replied, "I have not left them, but have proposed in vain." He asked, "Why don't you eat cheese?" He replied, "I am in a land where there are fire-worshippers. If a Muslim witness were to state that it does not contain carrion, I would eat it." He said, "What prevents you from going to the rulers?" He replied, "At your doors are those who seek needs, so satisfy their needs and leave alone those who do not have any needs to request."

Bilal ibn Sa'd said that 'Amir was denounced to Ibn 'Amir. He was told, "There is a man to whom it was said, 'Ibrahim was not better than you,' and yet he remained silent. Furthermore he has abandoned women." He wrote about him to 'Uthman and he wrote back saying that he should deport him to Syria. When the letter arrived, he sent for 'Amir and said, "You are the one to whom it was said that Ibrahim was not better than you and yet you remained silent." He replied, "By Allah, my silence was only due to astonishment. I wish that I would be the dust on his feet when he enters the Garden." He asked, "Why have you abandoned women?" He replied, "I have only abandoned them because I know that if I had a wife she might have a child and the child might cause this world to accumulate in my heart and I want to avoid that." So he sent him by camel to Syria.

Basra

When he arrived, Mu'awiya lodged him with him in his castle at al-Khadra' and sent a slavegirl to him and commanded her to ask him about his circumstances. He went out at dawn and she did not see him until well after dark. Mu'awiya sent food to him and he did not take any of it. He had a chunk of bread with him which he would put in water, and then he would eat the bread and drink from that water. Then he would get up to pray. He continued like that until he heard the *adhan* and then he went out and she did not see him until dark again.

So Mu'awiya wrote to 'Uthman and described him to him and he wrote back to him, telling him to make him the first to enter and last to leave and to give him ten slaves and ten riding animals. When the letter reached Mu'awiya, he sent for 'Amir and said, "The Amir al-Mu'minin has written to me to give you ten slaves." He said, "I have a shaytan and he has overcome me, so how shall I deal with ten?" He said, "And he has commanded ten riding animals for you." He said, "I have one mule and I am afraid that Allah will ask me about excess mounts on the Day of Rising!" He said, "And he commands me to make you the first to enter and last to leave." He exclaimed, "I have no need of that!"

Bilal ibn Sa'd reported that he was seen in the land of the Greeks riding his mule and encouraging the fighters. When he wanted to attack, he would stop and inspect the forces, and when he saw a suitable group he would say, "I want to accompany you provided that you grant me three things." They asked, "What are they?" He said, "That I will be your servant and none of you will contend with me about serving; and that I will be the *mu'adhdhin* and none of you will contend with me to give the *adhan*; and that I will spend on you according to my ability." If they agreed, he joined them. If any of them disagreed with any of it, he went to someone else.

'Ubaydullah ibn al-Hasan al-'Anbari the Qadi said, "I came to Syria and I asked about 'Amir. I was told that he had taken refuge with an old woman there. I went and asked her and she said, 'He is on top of that mountain praying night and day.' I went to him and came upon him at the time of his fast-breaking. I went to him and greeted him and he asked me about a man I had met the day before, but he did not ask me about his people or who had died and who was still alive. He did not invite me to supper. I said to 'Amir, 'I have seen something extraordinary from you!' He asked, 'What is that?' I said, 'You have been absent from us for such a long time and yet you ask me about a man I met yesterday!' He said, 'I saw that you were righteous. So what could I ask you about your condition?' I said, 'You did not ask me about your people and who has died and who is still alive and yet you know my position with them.' He said, 'I did not ask you about the people because whoever is dead is dead, and whoever is not dead will die.' I said, 'You did not invite me to supper.' He replied, 'I know that you eat the food of the amirs and my food is coarse.'"

He said, "Later I entered the mosque, and he was sitting beside Ka'b and between them were volumes of the Torah which Ka'b was reading. Whenever he passed by something he liked, he explained it to him. He came to something which looked like a *ra'* or a *zayy*. He said, 'Abu 'Abdullah, do you know what this means?' He replied, 'No.' He said, 'Dishonesty about the Book of Allah obliterates sight and seals the heart.'"

Malik ibn Dinar said, "When Ka'b saw 'Amir in Syria, he asked, 'Who is this?' They said, "Amir ibn 'Abdu Qays al-'Anbari al-Basri.' He said, 'This is the monk of this community.'"

Ayyub as-Sakhtiyati said, "When that group was brought to Syria, they included Madh'ur, 'Amir ibn 'Abdu Qays and Sa'sa'a ibn Sawhan.[1] When some of them were acquitted, he commanded them to go, and some of them went and some remained. Among those who remained were Madh'ur and 'Amir. Sa'sa'a ibn Sawhan was one of those restrained.

Wasil was heard to mention that 'Amir went on an expedition with some people. The Muslims dismounted to camp and 'Amir went into a church and told a man, "Mind the door of the church for me and do not let anyone come in to me." The man came and said, "The amir asks permission." He said, "Give him permission." When he entered and came near, 'Amir said to him, "I ask you by Allah for Allah to remind you that you either want to make me love this world or to make me forsake the Next world."

Asma' ibn 'Ubayd said, "Once when 'Amir al-'Anbari was in an army they captured a slave girl belonging to an important man of the enemy. She was described to 'Amir and he said to his companions,

---

1. Those suspected of being involved in stirring up sedition against 'Uthman.

'Give her to me. I am a man like men.' They did that and were happy about it. They brought her and he said, 'Go, you are free for the sake of Allah.' They said, "Amir, if you wished you could have freed such-and-such for her.' He said, 'I wish for the reward from my Lord.'"

Sa'id al-Juwayri said, "A man saw the Prophet صلعم in a dream and asked him, 'Ask forgiveness for me.' He said, "Amir asks forgiveness for you.' So he went to 'Amir and told him. He wept until I could hear his sobbing."

Mudarib ibn Hazn at-Tamimi said, "We asked Mu'awiya, 'How did you find those of our *qurra'* we sent to you?' He replied, 'They defame with bowed heads. They enter with lies and leave with fraud, except for one man. He is a true man.' We asked, 'Who is he, Amir al-Mu'minin?' He replied, "Amir ibn 'Abdu Qays.'"

Abu Musa said, "When 'Amir wanted to leave, he went to Mutarrif to greet him and knocked on the door. Mutarrif told the servant, 'Go and see who it is.' She said, "Amir.' So he went out to him and greeted him and then he left. When some of the night had passed, 'Amir returned and knocked on the door. Mutarrif told his servant, 'See who it is.' She said, "Amir.' He went out to him and asked, 'What has brought you back to my door, may my father and mother be your ransom!' He said, 'By Allah, only love for you has brought me back.' So he greeted him and bade him farewell and then left. When some more of the night had passed, he returned and knocked on the door. Mutarrif said to his servant, 'See who it is.' She called out, 'Who is it?' He replied, "Amir!' So Mutarrif went out to him and said the like of what he said before. That happened three times."

Qatada said that when 'Amir ibn 'Abdullah was dying, he began to weep and he was asked, "What is making you weep?" He said, "I am not weeping out of fear of death or desire for this world, but I am weeping on account of the thirst of the middays and for the standing in prayer in the cold winter nights."

Humayd ibn Hilal said, "'Amir said, 'This world has four qualities: sleep, property, women and food. I have abstained from two of them. I have no need of wealth; and as for women, I do not care whether I see a woman or a wall. I find no substitute for this food and sleep which I get. But by Allah, I have striven against them!'" He said, "He turned the night into day and stood in prayer; and when it was day, he turned it into night and fasted and slept."

Tabi'un

Abu'l-'Aliyya ar-Riyahi

His name was Rufay'. A woman of the Banu Riyah set him free.

Abu'l-'Aliyya said, "A woman bought me and then wanted to set me free. Her cousins said to her, 'If you free him he will go to Kufa and be cut off.'[1] So she took me to a place in the mosque. If you wish, I will show it to you. She said, 'You are free.'" Abu'l-'Aliyya left her all his property.

Abu'l-'Aliyya said, "Whatever I leave of gold or silver or property, a third is in the way of Allah, a third is for the family of the Prophet ﷺ and a third is for the poor Muslims, and give my wife her right." Abu Khulda said, "I said to him, 'This is enough for you. So where are your clients?' He replied, 'I will tell you my story. I was a slave of a bedouin woman of a masculine disposition. She met me on Friday and said, 'Where shall we go, slave?' I said, 'I am going to the mosque.' She asked 'Which mosque?' I said, 'The General Mosque.' She said, 'Go, slave.' So I followed her until she entered the mosque, and we found the Imam on the *minbar*. She took my hand and said, 'O Allah, keep him with You as a treasure. Bear witness, people of the mosque, that he is free for the sake of Allah and no one has any way to him except for a legitimate claim.' She left me and departed and never saw me again after that.'"

Abu'l-'Aliyya said, "We were slaves and some of us paid the duties (on our work) and some of us served our people. We used to recite the entire Qur'an every night. That was hard for us so we began to do it every two nights. That was still hard for us so we began to do it every three nights. That was still hard on us so that we complained to one another. We met the Companions of the Messenger of Allah ﷺ and they taught us to do it every week, or every seven days. So we prayed and slept, and it was not hard for us."

Abu'l-'Aliyya said, "I first read the *mufassal* part of the Qur'an ten years after the death of our Prophet ﷺ and Allah gave me two blessings and I do not know which of them is better: His guiding me to Islam or His not making me a Kharijite."

Abu'l-'Aliyya said, "I was a slave and served my people. I learned the Qur'an and Arabic writing."

---

1. Meaning that he might join the Kharijites or another dissident group.

Abu'l-'Aliyya said, "We used to listen to transmission in Basra which originated from the Companions of the Messenger of Allah صلعم but we were not content until we went to Madina and heard it from their own mouths."

Abu'l-'Aliyya said, "The greatest thing I heard from 'Umar was when he said, 'O Allah, protect us and pardon us!'"

Abu Khulda said, "Abu'l-'Aliyya freed a slave of his and wrote, 'This is a young lad which a man of the Muslims has freed for the sake of Allah. No one has any way to him except for some legitimate claim.'"

Abu'l-'Aliyya said, "I have not touched my penis with my right hand for sixty or seventy years."

Abu'l-'Aliyya said, "In the time of the conflict between 'Ali and Mu'awiya, I was young and eager and preferred fighting to good food. So I made excellent provisions in order to join the army. At Siffin, the ends of the two armies could not be seen because each side was so large. If one side were destroyed, the other side would be destroyed as well. I thought to myself, 'Which of the two groups will I consider to be unbelievers? Which will I consider to be believers? Who can force me to take part in this?' I continued to reflect on it until I went back and left them."

Abu'l-'Aliyya said, "I went to Ibn 'Abbas when he was the Amir of Basra and he took me by the hand until I was level with him on the seat. A man of the Banu Tamim exclaimed, 'But he is only a client!' I was wearing a shirt, cloak and turban worth only twelve dirhams." Abu Khulda asked, "What did you do?" He said, "I used to buy coarse cotton for twelve dirhams and make a shirt and turban from it. I was satisfied with a wrapper for three dirhams which I wore under the shirt although I had a good cloak which was worth 20 or 30."

Abu Khulda said, "I saw Abu'l-'Aliyya wearing trousers. I said, 'Why are you wearing trousers in the house?' He replied, 'They are men's clothes and they are a good covering.'"

Abu'l-'Aliyya was heard to say, "When I pass by the door of a money-changer or tax-collector, I will not drink from his water."

Shu'ayb ibn al-Habhab said, "Abu'l-'Aliyya used to come and say, 'Feed me from the food in the house and do not trouble yourselves to buy me anything.'"

Abu'l-'Aliyya was heard to say, "Abu Umayya 'Abdu'l-Karim visited me wearing a wool garment. I said to him, 'This is the garment of the monks. When the Muslims visit, they make themselves look smart.'"

Abu'l-'Aliyya said, "I prayed the beginning of the day when al-Hajjaj did what he did at the end of the *Jumu'a* prayer,[1] sitting directly in front of him, and Allah made him blind to me. I prayed behind him until I feared Allah and I stopped praying behind him when I feared Allah."

Abu'l-'Aliyya was heard to say, "When you hear a man say, 'I love for Allah and hate for Allah,' do not emulate him."

Abu Khulda said, "I was sitting with Abu'l-'Aliyya when a slave of his brought a sealed kerchief of sugar cane. He broke the seal and gave him ten sweets. He said, 'If he has cheated me, it was not for more than this. We are commanded to end dealings with a messenger and servant in such a way that they will not think ill of us.'"

Abu Khulda said, "I purchased a slave for Abu'l-'Aliyya and he did not buy him until Abu'l-'Aliyya had imposed a condition that he would increase the impost on his work by two dirhams and he did so."

Abu'l-'Aliyya said, "We used to think that the greatest of sins was for a man to learn the Qur'an and then sleep until he forgot it and did not recite any of it."

Abu Khulda said, "I visited Abu'l-'Aliyya and he brought some food to me which included onions. He said, 'Eat. These are not onions from which we fear anything. This was sent by my brother Anas ibn Malik from his garden.' I inquired, 'What is it about onions?' He said, 'Onions can be grown in a foul manner – don't you know?' I said, 'What is that?' He replied, 'In excrement, urine, and blood.'"

Abu Khulda said, "Abu'l-'Aliyya set free a slavegirl of his and then married her. I asked her how Abu'l-'Aliyya paid his *zakat al-fitr*. She said, 'He gives a *qafiz* for himself and two cups for each of us.'"

Abu Khulda said, "Abu 'Aliyya used to send his *zakat* to Madina and give it to the people of the House of the Prophet ﷺ and they would distribute it."

---

1. He ordered people out to either join the army or be killed.

Abu Khulda said, "Abu'l-'Aliyya's shroud was with Bakr ibn 'Abdullah. It was a shirt with a hem and buttons, and he used to wear it every 24 days, and at the beginning of Ramadan, and then he would return it to him."

Abu Khulda said, "I saw Abu'l-'Aliyya prostrate on a pillow while sitting on a rug when he was ill."

Abu Khulda said, "I saw Abu'l-'Aliyya make a will in his illness. He had some dirhams with a man called al-Hasan. He said, 'Buy a small animal for slaughter with it. I dislike to leave it as dirhams.'"

Abu Khulda said, "Abu'l-'Aliyya made his will seventeen times when he was healthy. He set a term for the will. When the term ended he carried out what he had willed or otherwise retracted it."

Shu'ayb ibn al-Habhab said, "Abu'l-'Aliyya had a round cap lined with fox-skin. When he prayed, he put it inside his sleeve."

'Asim al-Ahwal reported that Abu'l-'Aliyya left instructions for Muwarriq al-'Ijli that he was to put two palm branches in his grave. Muwarriq said, "Burayda al-Aslami left a will that two palm branches be placed in his grave and he died near Khurasan and they were only found in the baggage of a donkey. When they put him in his grave they also put them in his grave."

Abu Khulda reported that Abu'l-'Aliyya died on a Monday in Shawwal in 90 AH.

Shu'ba said, "Rufay' met 'Ali but did not listen to him. Another said that he listened to 'Umar, Ubayy ibn Ka'b and other Companions of the Prophet ﷺ. He was reliable and had many *hadiths*."

Abu Umayya, the client of 'Umar ibn al-Khattab

He was a *mukatab*. His name was 'Abdu'r-Rahman. He was the grandfather of al-Mubarak ibn Fadala ibn Abi Umayya.

Abu Umayya, who was a slave of 'Umar, said, "'Umar ibn al-Khattab gave me a *kitaba*-contract for some *uqiyyas* which he stipulated and arranged for it to be paid in instalments. When the scribe had finished writing it out, he sent to Hafsa and borrowed 200 dirhams from her. Then he gave them to me and I said to him, 'Take it from my instalments.' He refused. When 60, or 30, remained, I brought him a hair-cloth and said, 'Use this as a bed,' but he refused. He said, 'Use it to help with your instalments.' I asked him to write for me to his governor and he refused. He said, 'Go. You are permit-

Tabi'un

ted what the people are permitted.' I went and spoke to 'Ikrima about this and he said, 'This, by Allah, is what Allah says in His Book: *"Give them some of the wealth Allah has given you."* (24:33)'"

Abu Umayya said, "I asked 'Umar ibn al-Khattab for a *kitaba* contract and he said to me, 'How much are you offering?' I replied, 'A hundred *uqiyyas*.' He did not ask for more, and he wrote me a kitaba on that basis. He wanted to give me some money. On that day he did not have any money to hand so he sent to Hafsa, Umm al-Mu'minin, 'I have given a *kitaba* contract to my slave and I want to advance him some of my property. Send me 200 dirhams until we get some money.' She sent them to him. 'Umar ibn al-Khattab took them with his right hand and then he recited this *ayat: 'If any slaves you own desire to make a contract to free themselves, write it for them if you know of good in them and give them some of the wealth Allah has given you.'* (24:33) He said, 'Take it. May Allah bless you in it!' Allah did bless me in it and I freed myself with it and received much wealth from it.

"I asked him to give me permission to go to Iraq and he said, 'Since I have given you a *kitaba,* you may go where you wish.' Some people whose clients had given them a *kitaba* said to me, 'Speak on our behalf to the Amir al-Mu'minin and ask him to write a letter for us to the governor of Iraq so he will be generous to us.' I knew that would be unacceptable to him but I was embarrassed before my companions. So I spoke to him, 'O Amir al-Mu'minin, write a letter for us to your governor in Iraq so as he will be generous to us.' He became angry and scolded me, 'No, by Allah!' and he never had insulted me or scolded me at all before that. He exclaimed, 'Do you want to wrong people?' I said, 'No.' He said, 'You are a man of the Muslims. You are permitted what they are permitted.'"

He said, "I went to Iraq and got some property and realised a great profit on it. I gave him a velvet-like carpet and a rug. He began to joke with me and say, 'This is fine.' I said, 'Amir al-Mu'minin, it is a gift which I give you!' He said, 'You still owe some of your *kitaba*. Sell it and use it to help your *kitaba*.' He refused to accept it."

Sirin, the client of Anas ibn Malik al-Ansari

He related from 'Umar ibn al-Khattab. Muhammad ibn Sirin said that Sirin's *kunya* was Abu 'Amra.

Basra

Anas ibn Malik said, "Sirin wanted me to give him a *kitaba* but I refused. He went to 'Umar ibn al-Khattab and mentioned that and I was brought to 'Umar and he told me, 'Give him a *kitaba*,' and so I did."

Qatada said, "Sirin asked Anas ibn Malik for a *kitaba* but he refused, and 'Umar ibn al-Khattab raised his whip to him and quoted [the Qur'an], *'Write it for them,'* (24:33), and so he gave it to him."

Muhammad ibn Sirin said, "Anas ibn Malik gave a *kitaba* to my father for 40,000 dirhams which he paid."

Anas's grandson, 'Ubaydullah, said, "We have the *kitaba* contract of Sirin in our possession: 'This is a *kitaba* which Anas ibn Malik has given to his slave Sirin for so many thousand and two lads to do his work.' He was a blacksmith."

Bakkar ibn Muhammad said, "The *kitaba* of Anas ibn Malik to Sirin was a contract on a red page which is in our possession: 'This is a *kitaba* which Anas ibn Malik has given to his slave Sirin for 10,000 dirhams and 10 servants – each year 1000 dirhams and a servant.'" He added, "The clay on it is the seal in the middle of the page and the *kitaba* is around it."

Sirin said, "Anas ibn Malik gave me a *kitaba* for 20,000 dirhams. I was at the conquest of Tustar and I bought some old clothes and realised a profit and brought Anas all of my *kitaba* but he refused to accept it except in instalments. So I went to 'Umar ibn al-Khattab and mentioned that to him: He said, 'You are him?' He had seen me with the garments and prayed for blessing for me. I said, 'Yes. Anas wants the inheritance.' Then he wrote for me to Anas to accept it and he accepted it."

Muhammad said, "Sirin wrote to Anas ibn Malik that he was lame and had three wives. Anas ibn Malik wrote to him that he should come to him in Madina so that he could marry him to the daughter of his brother, al-Bara' ibn Malik, who was in his care. Sirin asked his daughter, Hafsa, 'Daughter, what do you think about what this man has written?' She said, 'Father, you should accept. Allah will increase you with honour on top of your honour.' Her mother was sitting there. Her mother slapped her and said to her, 'May Allah not make you young! You say this to your father?'"

Umm Hafsa said, "When Sirin married me, he invited the people of Madina to feast for seven days. Among those he invited was

Tabi'un

Ubayy ibn Ka'b. He came although he was fasting. He made supplication for the people."

Muhammad ibn Sirin said that his father Sirin gave a wedding feast in Madina for seven days and he invited the Companions of the Prophet ﷺ and invited Ubayy ibn Ka'b who was fasting, and he faced them and prayed for blessing for them.

Muhammad ibn Sirin said, "Sirin had 23 children from various *umm walads*."

Muhammad ibn Sa'd asked Muhammad ibn 'Abdullah al-Ansari about the origins of Muhammad ibn Sirin. He replied, "He was one of those captured at 'Ayn at-Tamr. He was the client of Anas ibn Malik." Ibn Sa'd said, "I heard someone say that he was from the people of Jarjaraya, and I think that the one who said that was incorrect. They did have some land in Jarjaraya."

Muhammad reported that Sirin bought this land at Rustaq Jarjaraya and it came into the possession of Muhammad and his brother Yahya. He took it for its *kharaj*-tax. There were some vines on it and they wanted to press them. Muhammad said, "Do not press them. Sell them fresh." They said, "It will not cover our expenses." He said, "Make them into raisins." They said, "No raisins are produced from them." So he cut down the vines and threw them in the water and they floated away.

Bakkar ibn Muhammad said, "I saw the assembly platform of Sirin which he had built with palm trunks. I bought forty palm trunks from it, each for a dinar."

Artaban

He was the client of 'Abdullah ibn Durra al-Muzani. He related from 'Umar ibn al-Khattab.

Artaban said, "When I was freed, I earned some money and took my *zakat* to 'Umar ibn al-Khattab. He asked me, 'What is this?' I replied, 'The *zakat* on my property.' He asked, 'You have property?' I replied, 'Yes.' He said, 'May Allah bless you in your property!' I said, 'Amir al-Mu'minin, and in my children!' He asked, 'You have children?' I said, 'I may have.' He said, 'May Allah bless you in your property and your children!'"

Abu Rafi' as-Sa'igh

He was one of the people of Madina who moved to Basra. Its people related from him but the people of Madina did not relate from him because he left them early on. He related from 'Umar ibn al-Khattab and others and was reliable.

Al-Hasan reported that Abu Rafi' said, "I prayed with 'Umar ibn al-Khattab for two years and I did the *qunut* with them after the first *rak'at*."

Muhammad ibn Abi Bakr al-'Anazi said, "While I was in the Masjid al-Haram, an old man wearing a white turban passed by leaning on a staff which I think was from galbanum root. The people of the mosque said, 'This is Abu Rafi' al-Madini.' So I joined him and said, 'Abu Rafi'! Relate to me some of the *hadiths* which you relate!' He said, "A'isha said that the Messenger of Allah ﷺ said, "Allah accepts the breaking of the fast of Ramadan for those of my community who are ill or travelling.""

Abu Firas

He said, "'Umar ibn al-Khattab reported to us and said, 'We used to be made acquainted with you when the Prophet ﷺ was among us and the revelation was coming down on us." Abu Firas was an old man with few *hadiths*.

Ghunaym ibn Qays al-Ka'bi

One of the Banu Tamim. His *kunya* was Abu'l-'Anbar.

Abu Kinana al-Qurashi reported about Abu Musa al-Ash'ari coming to Basra after al-Mughira ibn Shu'ba. He said, "Not two months had passed before seven of us had recited the entire Qur'an. One of them was Ghunaym ibn Qays. So al-Ash'ari sent them to 'Umar ibn al-Khattab. When they came to him, he allotted them two thousand dirhams each."

Ghunaym ibn Qays said, "I memorised some words which my father said about the Prophet ﷺ:

'I have regret regarding Muhammad.
    I sat apart during my life.
I slept the night feeling secure about the morrow.'"

Tabi'un

He said that he was reliable but with very *hadiths*.

Sinan ibn Salama ibn al-Muhabbiq al-Hudhali

He related from 'Umar.

Harun ibn Rithab al-Usaydi said, "Sinan ibn Salama, who was governor of Bahrayn, told us, 'We were some lads in Madina among the roots of the palm trees picking up the dates we call *khalal*. 'Umar ibn al-Khattab came out to us with a whip and the boys scattered but I remained were I was. When he was standing over me, I said, "Amir al-Mu'minun, these are windfalls." He said, "Let me look and do not conceal them from me." He looked in my lap and said, "You spoke the truth." I said, "Amir al-Mu'minin, you see those boys now? By Allah, if I go, they will attack me and take what I have." So he walked with me until he conveyed me to where I was safe.'"

'Umayr ibn 'Atiyya al-Laythi

'Umayr ibn 'Atiyya al-Laythi said, "I went to 'Umar ibn al-Khattab and said, 'Amir al-Mu'minin, raise your hand. Allah has elevated it. I will give you allegiance based on the *sunna* of Allah and the *sunna* of His Messenger. He raised his hand and laughed, saying, 'It is for you against us and against you for us.'"

'Abbad al-'Asari

'Asar is a subtribe of 'Abdu'l-Qays. 'Abbad related from 'Umar.

'Abbad al-'Anbari said, "'Umar ibn al-Khattab stopped with us on the Day of 'Arafa when we were at 'Arafat, and he said, 'Whose tents are these?' They said, "Abdu'l-Qays.' He prayed for forgiveness for them and then said, 'This is the Day of the Greatest *Hajj*. No one should fast on it.'"

Husayn ibn Abi'l-Hurr

He was one of the Banu Tamim. 'Amr ibn 'Asim al-Kilabi said, "Husayn ibn Abi'l-Hurr was the governor for 'Umar ibn al-Khattab over Maysan and he remained there until al-Hajjaj came. He was brought to him and wanted to kill him. Then he was told, 'Do not give him prominence by killing, but put him in prison until he dies.'

So he imprisoned him until he died. Husayn ibn Abi'l-Hurr was qadi of the people of Basra."

Abu'l-Muhallab al-Jarmi

His name was 'Abdu'r-Rahman ibn Mu'awiya and he was the uncle of Abu Qilaba al-Jarmi. He related from 'Umar and 'Uthman, and was reliable with few *hadiths*.

Ghadira ibn 'Urwa ibn Samura al-'Anbari

He was one of the Banu 'Adi. He related from 'Umar.

Hammad ibn Zayd said, "I saw in one of the books of Abu Qilaba, 'From 'Umar ibn al-Khattab to Abu Musa: I have sent papers to you with Ghadira ibn Samura al-'Anbari. When he comes to you for such-and-such, then give him 200 dirhams. If he comes to you after that, do not give him anything and write to me on any day that he comes to you.'"

'Abdullah ibn Shaqiq al-'Uqayli

He related from 'Umar ibn al-Khattab. He said, "We were sitting at the door of 'Umar with Abu Dharr. He said, 'I am fasting.' Then 'Umar gave him permission to come in and brought him supper and he ate."

Abu Qilaba mentioned 'Abdullah ibn Shaqiq and said, "What a man were it not that he pretended to be Arab!"

Bishr ibn Kathir al-Asadi said, "I saw 'Abdullah ibn Shaqiq wearing a shawl of rough silk." They said that 'Abdullah ibn Shaqiq was an 'Uthmani partisan and was reliable in *hadith*. He related sound *hadiths*. He died while al-Hajjaj ibn Yusuf was governor of Iraq.

Al-Musayyab ibn Darim

He related from 'Umar ibn al-Khattab and the Basrans related from him.

Al-Musayyab ibn Darim said, "I saw 'Umar with a whip in his hand and he struck at the head of a slavegirl until the veil fell off her head. He said, 'Why does a slavegirl make herself resemble a free woman?'"

Tabi'un

Al-Musayyab ibn Darim said, "I saw 'Umar ibn al-Khattab strike a camel driver and say, 'Why do you load your camel with what it cannot bear?'"

Shuways ibn Jabbash, Abu'r-Raqqad al-'Adawi

One of the Banu 'Adi. He related from 'Umar and went on expeditions while 'Umar was khalif.

Shuways al-'Adawi said, "We used to pray *Dhuhr* with 'Umar ibn al-Khattab and then we would go to our mounts and have a nap."

Shuways Abu'r-Raqqad al-'Adawi said, "I went on an expedition against Maysan in 'Umar's time and received two thousand dirhams. I captured a slave girl and had intercourse with her for a time until the letter of 'Umar arrived, 'Release any captives from Maysan.' So I sent her back with the others who were returned. By Allah, I did not know whether she was pregnant or not. By Allah, I do not know. I fear that there might be men and women who are descended from me in Maysan."

Shuways Abu'r-Raqqad said, "We used to be given a dirham or two in the time of 'Umar and would take them."

Sa'id al-Jurayri said, "I prayed the *'Asr* prayer in the mosque of the Banu 'Adi beside Shuways. He was one of those who received a stipend in the time of 'Umar ibn al-Khattab."

Husayn ibn Jurayr

He related from 'Umar ibn al-Khattab. Husayn had few *hadiths*.

Abu Sa'id, the client of Abu Usayd al-Ansari

He related from 'Umar and 'Ali.

Hittan ibn 'Abdullah ar-Raqqashi

He related from 'Umar and 'Ali. He died during the khalifate of 'Abdu'l-Malik ibn Marwan while Bishr ibn Marwan was governor of Iraq. He was reliable with few *hadiths*.

Iyas ibn Qatada ibn Awfa

His father, Qatada ibn Awfa, was a Companion. Iyas related from 'Umar, and he is reliable with few *hadiths*.

Jabir or Jubayr al-'Abdi

He related from 'Umar ibn al-Khattab and has few *hadiths*.

✲✲✲✲✲

Also among this generation:

This generation includes those who say that a letter reached them from 'Umar ibn al-Khattab and they related what he commanded in his letters to Abu Musa al-Ash'ari, al-Mughira ibn Shu'ba and others. Most of them went on expeditions in the time of 'Umar ibn al-Khattab.

Al-Fudayl ibn Zayd ar-Raqqashi

'Asim said, "Al-Fudayl ibn Zayd ar-Raqqashi went on seven expeditions while 'Umar was in command."

'Asim al-Ahwal reported that al-Fudayl ibn Zayd ar-Raqqashi said that he went on seven expeditions under 'Umar ibn al-Khattab. He used to say, "'Umar ibn al-Khattab wrote to us." He related from 'Abdullah ibn Mughaffal and others.

Al-Muhallab ibn Abi Sufra al-'Anaki

Abu Sufra's name was Zalim ibn Surraq and al-Muhallab's *kunya* was Abu Sa'id. He met 'Umar but did not relate anything from him. He related from Samura ibn Jundub and others. He was appointed over Khurasan and died in Marwurrudh in 83 AH while 'Abdu'l-Malik ibn Marwan was khalif. He appointed his son Yazid ibn al-Muhallab over Khorasan, and al-Hajjaj confirmed him.

Bajala ibn 'Abada

He was the scribe of Jaz' ibn Mu'awiya, the uncle of al-Ahnaf ibn Qays. He said, "'Umar's letter reached us instructing us to kill every sorcerer and sorceress, and his letter was about the Magians."

Abu Qatada al-'Adawi

His name was Tamim ibn Nadhir. He was reliable with few *hadiths*.

Abu'd-Dahma' al-'Adawi

His name was Qirfa ibn Bayhas. He was reliable with few *hadiths*. He reported from 'Imran ibn Husayn. In some *hadiths* his name is given as Malik ibn Sahm.

Abu Zaynab

'Asim said, "I heard Abu Zaynab, who went on expeditions in the time of 'Umar, say, 'We went on an expedition and Abu Bakra, Abu Barza and 'Abdu'r-Rahman ibn Samura were with us, and we used to eat dates.'"

Abu Kinana al-Qurashi

Abu Kinana al-Qurashi said, "'Umar sent a letter with al-Ash'ari to al-Mughira ibn Shu'ba, 'Something has reached me about you which is such that it would have been better if you had died before it.' 'Umar wrote to Abu Musa, 'Write to me regarding those who recite the Qur'an distinctly.'"

Qays ibn 'Ubad al-Qaysi

It is reported that Qays ibn 'Ubad al-Qaysi left instructions, "Shroud me wrapped in my cloak and wrap up my bed with my white garment in which I used to pray. When you place me in my grave, then make a hole in the part of the shroud next to my body so that the earth can reach my body." Wukay' said that he meant to make a slit in the shroud next to the earth. He said that Qays was reliable with few *hadiths*.

Harim ibn Hayyan al-'Abdi

He was reliable and was a man of virtue and much worship. Al-Hasan al-Basri related from him.

Al-Hasan said that he heard Harim ibn Hayyan say, "I seek refuge with Allah from a time in which their young are rebellious and their old people still have hankerings when their lives are near their ends." He was told, "Make a will." He said, "I commend to you the recitation of the final *ayats* of *Surat al-Baqara*."

Basra

Harim ibn Hayyan al-'Abdi said, "I came from Basra and I met Uways al-Qarani on the bank of the Euphrates. I said to him, 'How are you, my brother? How are you, Uways?' He said to me, 'And how are you, my brother?' I said, 'Relate to me.' He replied, 'I dislike to open this door for myself lest I be considered a *muhaddith*, or a qadi or a *mufti*.' Then he took my hand and wept. I said, 'Then recite to me.' He said, 'I seek refuge with the All-Hearing, the All-Knowing from the Accursed Shaytan: "*Ha Mim. By the Book which makes things clear. We sent it down on a blessed night. We are constantly giving warning.*' until he reached '*...He is the Almighty, the Most Merciful.*" (44:1-42)' He fainted and then came around and said, 'I prefer to be solitary.'"

Harim ibn Hayyan said, "I have not seen anything that someone should flee from worse than the Fire, nor anything that it is better to seek than the Garden."

Abu 'Imran al-Jawfi related that on a moonlight night Harim ibn Hayyan saw the master of his garden playing *kharaj* [a game similar to paper, rock, scissors]. He called him and said, "Fast tomorrow." He did that for three nights running. Then he said, "Go now and play *kharaj*." He said that Harim was the governor of 'Umar ibn al-Khattab.

Qatada reported that he heard that Harim ibn Hayyan was told to make a will. He said, "I do not know what instructions I should leave, but sell my armour and settle my debts with it. If it is not enough, then sell my horse and settle my debts for me. If it is not enough, then sell my slave. I commend to you the final *ayats* of Surat an-Nahl: '*Call to the way of your Lord with wisdom and fair admonition ... Allah is with those who are godfearing and with those who are good-doers.*' (16:125-128)"

Al-Hasan said, "When a man had to go to the lavatory while the Imam was giving the *khutba*, he would hold his nose and the Imam would indicate for him to go out. A man wanted to return to his family and stood up while Harim ibn Hayyan was giving the *khutba* and held his nose and Harim indicated to him to go out. He went to his family and stayed with them. Then he came and Harim asked him, 'Where were you?' He replied, 'With my family.' He said, 'Did you go with permission?' He replied, 'Yes, I stood up while you were speaking and held my nose and you indicated that I should go.' He said, 'This one is cunning,' or words to that effect. Then he said, 'O Allah, delay the men of evil to a time of evil.'"

Harim ibn Hayyan said, "Beware of the immoral scholar." That reached 'Umar ibn al-Khattab and he was concerned about what was meant by 'the immoral scholar'. Harim ibn Hayyan wrote to him, "By Allah, Amir al-Mu'minin, I only intended good by it. If an Imam speaks with knowledge and acts immorally, he will confuse people and they will be misled."

Malik ibn Dinar said, "Harim ibn Hayyan was appointed to office. He thought that his people might come to him and so he commanded fire to be kindled between him and those of his people who came to him. His people came and greeted him from afar. He said, 'Welcome to my people! Come near.' They said, 'By Allah, we cannot come near you: There is a fire between us and you.' He said, 'You want to meet me in a fire greater than it in Jahannam.' So they went back."

Al-Hasan said, "Harim ibn Hayyan died on an expedition on a hot summer day. When he was buried, a cloud came and covered the grave until it was moist and not one drop went beyond the grave. Then it departed."

Qatada said, "It rained on the grave of Harim ibn Hayyan the first day and plants grew from it on the first day."

Sila ibn Ashyam al-'Adawi

His *kunya* was Abu's-Sahba'. He was a reliable man of virtue and scrupulousness. 'Abdu'r-Rahman ibn Yazid ibn Jabir said that he heard that the Messenger of Allah ﷺ said, "There will be a man in my community called Sila by whose intercession so many people will enter the Garden."

Abu's-Salil al-Qaysi said, "I went to Sila al-'Adawi and said to him, 'Sila, teach me some of what Allah has taught you.' He replied, 'You are like me on the day I went to the Companions of the Messenger of Allah to learn from them and said, "Teach me some of what Allah has taught you."'

"Then he said, 'Follow the advice of the Qur'an and be faithful to the Muslims and make as much supplication to Allah as possible and do not be among those killed by the shaft of division, slain by the deluded arrogance of the *Jahiliyya*. I do not care whether I drag along a pigs' trotter or the foot of such a person. Beware of people who tell you, "We are believers," when they have no belief at all. They are the Kharijites,' and he repeated that three times."

Fudayl ibn Zayd said, "Sila ibn Ashyam visited me and said, 'People testify a lot. When you testify, testify with a testimony by which Allah and the people of knowledge will sanction you. I testify that Allah is One, Eternal, who did not beget and was not begotten, and there is no equal to Him.'"

Sila said, "I do not know which day gives me more joy: a day in which I hasten to remembrance of Allah, or a day in which I go out for some need and remembrance of Allah occurs to me."

Thabit al-Bunani said, "A lad who was trailing his garment passed by Sila ibn Ashyam and his companions, and his companions wanted to harshly rebuke him. Sila said, 'Leave him be. I will deal with him for you.' He said to him, 'Nephew, I need something from you.' He asked, 'What do you need?' He replied, 'I want you to raise your wrapper.' He said, 'Yes, and may your eye be blessed.' He raised his wrapper and Sila remarked to his companions, 'This is the same as what you wanted. If you had abused him and injured him, he would have vilified you.'"

Mu'adha al-Ansariyya related that Sila crossed the Hayy Bridge at Ramhurmuz and went beyond it. His provisions ran out and he became terribly hungry. He met a Persian carrying a bundle. He asked, "Do you have any food with you?" He replied, "Yes." He said, "Put down your bundle and let me eat." He said, "O slave of Allah! I am one of Farwandadh's men making for such-and-such a town and I only have enough for myself." He decided to leave him alone. Then he regretted that after he had let him pass. He said, "If I had taken it from him, it would have been lawful for me." He met another man carrying a bundle and asked, "Do you have any food with you?" He replied, "Yes." He said, "Put down your bundle and let me eat." He said something similar to him: "O slave of Allah! I am one of Farwandadh's men making for such-and-such a town and I only have enough for myself." He said, "What is lawful to me of this one is only what was lawful to me of the first one." So he left him. He met another man and said the like of that and felt he should leave him and said, "Only what was lawful to me from the first two is lawful to me from him." So he let him go.

While he was proceeding along a high narrow dyke completely open to both the right and left of him, he heard a sound from under his saddle when his camel rubbed against it. He turned around and saw a wrapped up cloth. He did not know what it was so he dismounted. He thought that if it had come from in front of him, he would have seen it because of the narrowness of the dyke. He got down and could not make his animal move because of the narrowness of the place so he took its head and brought it down to the animal's foot. He saw that there was a piece of cloth wrapped around a date basket containing fresh dates. He ate from them until he was full.

Then he continued until he stopped at a monk's place. The monk brought him some food but he refused to eat any of it. He said, "Slave of Allah! Why do you not accept my hospitality when I see that you have neither baggage nor food?" He said, "But I have received such-and-such." He asked, "Do you have any of it left?" He replied, "Yes." He asked, "Let me eat from it." So he gave him the basket and the monk said to him, "Slave of Allah, you have truly been fed. Do you not see that the palm trees are empty with no fruit on them? This is not the time for fresh dates." Mu'adha said, "He brought us that piece of cloth and it was with us for a time, but I do not know where it has gone now."

Abu's-Sahba' Sila ibn Ashyam said, "I sought this world being even suspicious of its lawful, and I began to only take necessary nourishment from it. I do not rely on it and it does not pass me by. When I saw that, I said, 'O self! consider your provision to be what is just adequate for you and then refrain.' It refrained and did not reassert itself."

Mu'adha said, "Abu's-Sahba' used to pray until he went to his bed crawling."

Thabit reported that a brother of Sila ibn Ashyam died and a man came to him while he was giving food. He said, "Abu's-Sahba'! Your brother has died." He said, "Come and eat. How preposterous! Someone coming to announce a death to us! Come near and eat. How preposterous! Someone coming to announce a death to us! Come near and eat." He said, "By Allah, has anyone come before me to inform you of his death?" He replied, "Allah Almighty says: *'You are dying and they are dying.'* (39:30)"

Basra

Sila's son, Humayd, reported that Sila ibn Ashyam said, "I dreamt that I was in a group and a man behind us had an unsheathed sword. Whenever he came to one of us, he struck off his head and then he put it back and it was as it had been. I began to wait for him to come and do that to me. Then he came to me and struck off my head and it was as if I was looking at my head when I picked it up and shook the dust from my hair. Then I put it back and it returned as it had been."

He said, "Sila ibn Ashyam went out in an army with his son and a desert Arab from the tribe. The desert Arab said, "Abu's-Sahba', I dreamt that you came to a shady tree and took three honeycombs from under it. You gave me one and kept two. I wondered why you did not divide the third.' Then they met the enemy and Sila said to his son, 'Advance!' He went forward and was killed and Sila was killed and the desert Arab was also killed."

Thabit reported that Sila ibn Ashyam was in an expedition with his son. He said, "My son, advance and fight until I expect to be rewarded for you." He attacked and was fought until he was killed. The women went to his wife, Mu'adha al-'Adawiyya, and she said, "Welcome to you if you have come to give me good news. If you have come with other than that, then go back." So they went back. They said, "Sila was killed as a martyr in one of the expeditions at the beginning of al-Hajjaj's governorship over Iraq."

Abu Raja' al-'Utaridi

One of the Banu Tamim. They disagree about his name. Yazid ibn Harun said that it is 'Imran ibn Taym. Someone else said: 'Imran ibn Milhan. Yet another said: 'Utarid ibn Barz.

Abu Raja' al-'Utaridi said, "In the time of the Prophet صلعم I was a beardless youth."

Abu Khulda said, "I asked Abu Raja', 'What were you doing when the Prophet صلعم was sent?' He replied, 'I was herding camels for my people.' I asked him, 'What made you run away from him?' He replied, 'We were told that a man of the Arabs had been sent to kill the people except for those who obeyed him. We did not know what was meant by obeying him. So we fled across the sands of the Banu Sa'd.'"

Abu Raja' al-'Utaridi said, "When we heard about the Prophet صلعم we were at a water source called Sanad, and we fled towards the

87

trees with our families. We were told that he drank blood and that when he was asked what it was like, he had replied, 'Sweet.'"

Abu Raja' was heard to say, "The Messenger of Allah ﷺ was sent while I was herding for my people. I was competent for that task. When we heard about the Messenger of Allah ﷺ we fled. We came to a wilderness and whenever we spent the night in such a place, our chief would say, 'We seek refuge with the Mighty one of this valley from the jinn of the night,' and we repeated that." Then he gave a long account at the end of which he said, "We were informed that the path of this man consisted of the testimony: 'There is no god but Allah and Muhammad is His slave and Messenger,' and that the blood and property of anyone who states that is safe. We returned and entered Islam." Jarir ibn Hazim said, "It may be that Abu Raja' said, 'I think that this *ayat* was sent down about me and my companions: '*Certain men among mankind used to seek refuge with certain men among the jinn and they increased them in wickedness.*' (72:6)"

Jarir ibn Hazim said, "I saw Abu Raja' when he had white hair and a beard."

Abu Khulda said, "I saw Abu Raja' dye his beard yellow."

Abu'l-Ashhath said that Abu Raja' used to recite the entire Qur'an in the month of Ramadan every ten nights. They said that Abu Raja' related from 'Uthman, 'Ali and others. He was reliable in *hadith*. He had *riwaya* and knowledge of the Qur'an. He was the Imam of his people in their mosque for forty years. When he died, Abu'l-Ashhath Ja'far ibn Hayyan was their Imam for forty years. According to some accounts, Abu Raja' died in the khalifate of 'Umar ibn 'Abdu'l-'Aziz. Muhammad ibn 'Umar said that he died in 117 AH.

Abu Khulda said, "I saw al-Hasan pray at the funeral of Abu Raja' al-'Utaridi on his donkey while the Imam was saying the *takbirs*."

Abu Khulda told al-Fudayl ibn Dukayn, "I saw al-Hasan pray at the funeral of Abu Raja' while he was on a donkey holding his son." Al-Fudayl asked Abu Khulda, "Was he ill?" He replied, "No, he was old."

Bakkar ibn as-Saqr said, "I saw al-Hasan sitting at the grave of Abu Raja' al-'Utaridi opposite the grave, and there was a white garment spread out to mark the grave, and he did not move it or object to it until he was finished at the grave. Al-Farazdaq [the famous poet] was sitting before him. Al-Farazdaq asked, 'Abu Sa'id, do you know what those people are saying?' He said, 'No, what do they say, Abu

Firas?' He replied, 'They are saying, "Today the best of the people of Basra and the worst of the people of Basra are sitting at the grave."' He asked, 'Who do they mean by that?' He replied, 'They mean you and me.' Al-Hasan exclaimed, 'Abu Firas! I am not the best of the people of Basra and you are not the worst of them, but tell me what you have prepared for this final resting place.' He pointed to the grave. He replied, 'I have prepared abundant good, Abu Sa'id.' He asked, 'What is it?' He replied, 'The testimony that there is no god but Allah, for eighty years.' Al-Hasan said, 'You have prepared much good, Abu Firas.'"

Sa'id ibn 'Amir reported, "When Abu Raja' al-'Utaridi died, al-Farazdaq said:

'Do you not see that the great man of the people has died,
 one who was alive before Muhammad was sent?'"

Daghfal ibn Hanzala as-Sadusi

He was alive in the time of the Prophet صلعم but did not hear anything from him. Later he was a delegate to Mu'awiya ibn Abi Sufyan. He had knowledge and transmission of genealogy and its science.

Shihab al-'Anbari

He is Abu Habib ibn Shihab. Shihab said, "I was the first to set fire to the gate of Tustar."

Iyas ibn Qatada ibn Awfa

One of the Banu 'Abshams of Tamim. His mother was al-Fari'a bint Himyari. Qatada ibn Awfa was a Companion. Iyas was a leader among his people.

Salama ibn 'Alqama said, "Once Iyas ibn Qatada was putting on his turban intending to go to Bishr ibn Marwan. He looked in the mirror and saw a white hair on his chin. He said, 'Pluck it out, slavegirl.' She plucked it out and there was another white hair. He said, 'See which of your people are at the door.' They came into him and he said, 'Banu Tamim, I have given you my youth, so give me my old age. I see myself as the donkey who carries the burden of your needs, and death is approaching me.' Then he said, 'I will finish the

Tabi'un

turban.' He stopped calling his people to prayer and to worshipping their Lord and did not visit a ruler until he died."

Malih al-Jushmi said, "Iyas ibn Qatada left the mosque on Friday and they brought him a she-ass so that he could mount it. When he had his foot in the stirrup, he looked at a white hair and said, 'Welcome to you! Long have I been expecting you!' Then he went and lay down on his right side. He died during the khalifate of 'Abdu'l-Malik ibn Marwan."

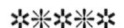

✲✲✲✲✲

The Second Generation
Those who related from 'Uthman, 'Ali, Talha, az-Zubayr, Ubayy, Abu Musa al-Ash'ari and others

Mutarrif ibn 'Abdullah ibn ash-Shikhkhir

His *kunya* was Abu 'Abdullah. He related from 'Uthman, 'Ali, Ubayy and Abu Dharr and his father. He was reliable with virtue, scrupulousness, *riwaya*, intellect and courteous behaviour.

Mutarrif said, "There is no widow sitting on the end of her skirt in greater need of the group than I am."

Mutarrif said, "The best of matters are their middle ones."

Mutarrif said, "I prefer the virtue of knowledge to the virtue of worship, and the best part of your *deen* is scrupulousness."

Mutarrif said, "When *fitna* comes, it does not come to guide, but to contend with the believer for himself."

Qatada said, "When there was *fitna*, Mutarrif proscribed it and fled. Al-Hasan proscribed it but did not leave. Mutarrif said, 'Al-Hasan is like a man who warns people about a flood but stays put where he is.'"

Thabit al-Bunani related that Mutarrif ibn 'Abdullah said, "I remained for nine or seven years during the *fitna* of Ibn az-Zubayr without reporting a single report or being asked to report a single report."

Mutarrif's son, 'Abdullah, was asked, "What did Mutarrif do when the people revolted?" He said, "He stayed well inside his house and did not go near to them for a *Jumu'a* prayer or an assembly until that ceased."

Mutarrif said, "I prefer to be faithful to contracts than to making demands," or he said, "I seek the virtue of *jihad* by imperilment."

Humayd ibn Hilal said, "In the time of Ibn al-Ash'ath, some people called on Mutarrif ibn 'Abdullah to fight al-Hajjaj. When they pressed him too much, he said, 'Do you think that what you are inviting me to will increase me in *jihad* in the way of Allah?' They replied, 'No.' He said, 'I will not put myself in danger of a destruction into which I may fall for a virtue which I might obtain.'"

Humayd ibn Hilal said, "The Kharijites came to Mutarrif ibn 'Abdullah inviting him to embrace their opinion. He said, 'People, if I had two souls, I would follow you with one of them and keep the other one. If what you say is guidance, I would follow it with the other. If it is misguidance, then one soul would be destroyed and I would still have a soul left. But it is only one soul and I dislike to endanger it.'"

Mutarrif said, "'Imran ibn Husayn said to me, 'Shall I tell you a *hadith* by which perhaps Allah will let you benefit the community? I see that you love the community.' I said 'I am more eager for the company than the widow, because when there is a community, I recognise my true bearing.'"

Mutarrif ibn 'Abdullah said, "No one has been given anything better than the intellect."

Mutarrif said, "People's intellects are according to their time."

Mutarrif said, "It is as if the hearts are not with us. It is as if the *hadith* is intended for other than us."

Mutarrif said, "I prefer to be thankful for well-being than to be tested and steadfast."

Mutarrif was heard to say, "If I had praised myself, I would have loathed people."

Qatada said, "Mutarrif visited Ziyad (or Ibn Ziyad) and he kept him waiting. He said, 'I have not got up since I parted from the amir but that Allah elevated me.'" He said that Mutarrif used to say, "Petitions contain scope for lying."

Yazid said, "Mutarrif used to go to the desert. On Friday he would come in to attend the *Jumu'a*. While he was travelling one night, there was a radiance which emerged from the top of his whip as a two-pronged light in the direction where morning was rising. He said to his son 'Abdullah who was behind him, 'O 'Abdullah, do you think that people would believe me if I told people about it?' When morning came, it departed."

Ghaylan said that Mutarrif used to share his saddle with people.

Ghaylan said that when the plague occurred, Mutarrif used to withdraw. He also said, "Mutarrif used to wear a burnous and wraps, and ride horses and visit the sultan, but when you went to him you went to delight."

Safiyya bint 'Abdullah, the client of Mutarrif, said, "I saw Mutarrif ibn 'Abdullah wearing a Qatari cloak and I saw him dye his hair and his beard with henna and indigo leaf, and I saw him do *wudu'* from a brass bowl about the size of a *makkuk* [which holds 1½ *sa's*] or a little less. He used to share his saddle."

Ghaylan reported that Mutarrif used to say, "Do not give your food to the one who does not desire it." Mahdi said, "It seems he was referring to *hadith*."

The wife of Mutarrif ibn 'Abdullah said that Mutarrif married her for 30,000 dirhams, a mule, a saddle cloth, a maid and a woman's saddle.

Hukayma bint Mas'uda, the client of Mutarrif, said, "My mother Durra, the client of Mutarrif, told me that Mutarrif used to share his saddle with people." He was afflicted by urine retention and he said, "Call my son." They called him and he recited to him an *ayat* of instruction. He said, *"The truth is from your Lord, so on no account be one of the doubters."* (2:147) His son went and brought a doctor. He said, "My son, what is this?" He replied, "A doctor." He said, "I forbid you to burden me with a charm or to puncture me." He told his sons, "Go and dig my grave." They went and dug it. Then he said, "Take me to my grave." So they took him to his grave. Then he made supplication over it and then they returned him to his family.

Yazid ibn 'Abdullah said that his brother, Mutarrif, instructed him not to announce his funeral to anyone.

Abu Khulda said, "I saw that Mutarrif dyed his beard yellow." They said that he died while al-Hajjaj ibn Yusuf was governor of Iraq after the devastating plague in 87 AH in the khalifate of al-Walid ibn 'Abdu'l-Malik.

It is reported that Thabit al-Bunani and another man visited Mutarrif ibn 'Abdullah when he was unconscious. Three lights shone from him: a light from his head, a light from his middle, and a light from his feet. He said, "That frightened us. He recovered consciousness and we said, 'How are you, Abu 'Abdullah?' He replied, 'Fine.' We said, 'We saw something which frightened us.' He asked, 'What was that?' We replied, 'Lights which shone from you.' He asked, 'You saw that?' We said, 'Yes.' He said, 'That is *"Alif Lam Mim, The Prostration"* (32). It is 29 *ayats*, the first of which shine from my head, the middle from my middle, and the end from my feet. It rises to intercede for me. These are blessings which protect me.'"

'Utayy ibn Zayd ibn Damra

One of the Banu Tamim. He was the cousin of al-Munaqqa' ibn al-Husayn and the nephew of Muslim ibn Nadhir. He was reliable with few *hadiths*. He related from Ubayy ibn Ka'b and others.

'Uqba ibn Suhban ar-Rasibi

Rasib is part of Azad. He died in the beginning of the governorship of al-Hajjaj. He was reliable and has transmission.

Humayd ibn 'Abdu'r-Rahman al-Himyari

He was reliable with *hadiths*. He related from 'Ali. Ibn Sirin said that Humayd ibn 'Abdu'r-Rahman had the greatest knowledge of *fiqh* among the people of Basra during the ten years before his death.

Safwan ibn Muhriz al-Mazini

One of the Banu Tamim. He was reliable, a man of virtue and scrupulousness. Al-Hasan said that Safwan ibn Muhriz had a small hut which he never left except for the prayer.

Ghaylan reported that Safwan ibn Muhriz and his brothers used to meet and relate *hadiths*. They did not see any tenderness in that. They said, "Safwan, relate to your companions." He said, "Praise belongs to Allah," and the people melted and their tears fell from them as if they were overflowing rain-gutters.

Al-Mu'alla ibn Ziyad said, "Safwan ibn Muhriz had a small hut in which he wept. He used to say, 'I would seek the place of martyrdom were it not that it was agreeable to my self.'"

Safwan ibn Muhriz said, "When I eat a loaf by which I strengthen my back, and drink a jug of water, it is effacement for this world and its people."

Thabit reported that Safwan ibn Muhriz had a special palm-trunk and the palm trunk broke. He was asked, "Will you mend it?" He said, "Leave it, I will die tomorrow."

Thabit said, "Al-Hasan and I went to visit Safwan ibn Muhriz while he was ill and his son came out to us and said, 'He has an intestinal problem. You cannot go into him.' Al-Hasan said, 'If your father has some of his flesh and blood wasted away by which Allah will expiate his errors, it is better for him than to enter his grave whole and have the earth consume him without him being repaid for it.'"

It is related that Safwan ibn Muhriz saw some people arguing in the mosque and stood up and shook his garment, and said, "You are war!"

It is related that Safwan ibn Muhriz said to his family when he was dying, "You know that part of what the Messenger of Allah صلعم said is: 'Anyone who wails, shaves off their hair and rends their garment is not one of us.'"

They said that he died in Basra while Bishr ibn Marwan was governor.

Humran ibn Aban, the client of 'Uthman ibn 'Abbas

He was one of those captured at 'Ayn at-Tamr whom Khalid ibn al-Walid sent to Madina. His son joined an-Namir ibn Qasit. Humran related from 'Uthman and others. The reason that he settled in Basra was that he acted dishonestly in an investigation for 'Uthman, and that reached 'Uthman and he said, "Do not live in the same town as me." So he travelled and settled in Basra and earned money there and had descendants.

Abu'l-Halal al-'Ataki

His name was Zurara ibn Rabi'a of Azd. He related from 'Uthman and he was reliable, Allah willing.

'Amira ibn Yathribi

He was qadi of Basra after Ka'b ibn Suwar al-Azdi. He was correct with few *hadiths*.

Khilas ibn 'Amr al-Hajari

He related from 'Ali and 'Ammar ibn Yasir. He had many *hadiths*. He had a paper from which he related.

It is reported that Khilas ibn 'Amr asked 'Ammar ibn Yasir, "When do you do the *witr*? At the beginning of the night, or at the end?" 'Ammar replied, "I do it at the beginning of the night and then I sleep. When I wake up, I pray pairs of *rak'ats* as Allah wills."

Al-Hayyaj ibn 'Imran al-Burjumi

One of the Banu Tamim, Al-Hasan al-Basri reported from him the *hadith* about the mutilated animal from 'Imran ibn Husayn. He had few *hadiths* and was reliable.

Zurara ibn Awfa al-Harshi

One of the Banu'l-Harish. His *kunya* was Abu Hajib. Qatada related that Zurara ibn Awfa was qadi of Basra.

'A'isha bint Damra reported that Zurara ibn Awfa used to pray *Dhuhr* and *'Asr* in his house but went to al-Hajjaj for the *Jumu'a*.

Abu Khulda said, "I saw that Zurara dyed his beard yellow."

Ayyub said, "I saw Muhammad at the funeral of Zurara ibn Awfa standing following the shade until he was placed in the grave." Ayyub said, "*Hadith* reached him in other than the correct manner." They said that Zurara ibn Awfa died suddenly in 93 AH [text has 73] in the khalifate of al-Walid I. He was reliable in *hadiths*.

Bahz ibn Hakim related that Zurara ibn Awfa led them in *Fajr* in the Banu Qushayr mosque, and recited until he reached, *"When the Trumpet is blown, that day will be a hard day for the unbelievers, not easy,"* (74:8-10) and fell down dead.

Bahz said, "I was one of those who carried him."

Hisham ibn Hubayra ad-Dabbi

He was the Qadi in Basra and he was correct with few *hadiths*.

'Amir said, "I read the letter of Hisham ibn Hubayra to Shurayh, "I have been appointed qadi in spite of my youth and lack of knowledge of much of it, so I cannot dispense with consulting the like of you." He said, "Hisham ibn Hubayra died at the beginning of the governorship of al-Hajjaj over Iraq during the khalifate of 'Abdu'l-Malik ibn Marwan.

Abu's-Sawwar al-'Adawi

He was reliable and related from 'Ali, 'Imran ibn Husayn and others. Qurra ibn Khalid said, "Abu's-Sawwar was a sergeant (*'arif*) in the time of al-Hajjaj."

Abu's-Sawwar said, "By Allah, I wish that my circle in my room had been in lieu of this position." Muslim ibn Ibrahim said, "He conducted a woman to the door of the amir and left her."

Abu Khulda said, "I saw Abu's-Sawwar wearing an iron ring," and he said, "I saw Abu's-Sawwar dye his beard yellow."

Abu Tamima al-Hujaymi

One of the Banu Tamim. His name is Tarif ibn Mujalid. He was reliable, Allah willing, and has *hadiths*. Muhammad ibn 'Amr said that he died in 97 AH in the khalifate of Sulayman ibn 'Abdu'l-Malik.

Qasama ibn Zuhayr al-Mazini

One of the Banu Tamim. He was reliable, Allah willing, and died while al-Hajjaj was governor of Iraq.

Al-Qasim in Rabi'a

Harun ibn Tamim related that when al-Hasan was asked about anything having to do with lineage, he would say, "You must ask al-Qasim ibn Rabi'a."

Maymun ibn Siyah

Kahmas ibn 'Abdullah said, "I listened Maymun ibn Siyah, who was older than al-Hasan and who met those whom al-Hasan did not meet. I heard him say, 'They mentioned one of those rulers in my presence and attacked him. I did not say ill or good of him. I returned to my house and lay down, and I dreamt that there was a dead foul-smelling putrid black corpse before me, and there was someone standing at my head, saying, "Slave of Allah! Why do you not eat?" He said, "Because so-and-so was slandered in your presence." I said, "But I did not mention either good or bad about him." He said to me, "But you were content to listen."'"

Abu Ghallab Yunus ibn Jubayr al-Bahili

He was reliable. He died before Anas ibn Malik and left instructions that Anas should pray over him.

'As'as ibn Salama

His *kunya* was Abu Sufra. He was from Banu'l-Harith ibn Ka'b.

A shaykh called Abu'l-Khalil said that 'As'as ibn Salama, a man of the Banu'l-Harith ibn Ka'b, went out one day and looked in the room and did not see any of his companions. He said, "I do not see my brothers. I prepared *Surat al-Waqi'a* for them." It was said to him, "Abu Sufra, are we not your brothers?" He said, "Yes, but some brothers are less than others."

Thabit al-Bunani reported that 'As'as ibn Salama said, "Come so that we can make this day a single tooth." He said, "The tooth is a single thing." [Meaning to devote it to one thing]

Thabit al-Bunani reported that 'As'as ibn Salama was at a grave and said, "I will utter a verse of poetry." He was asked, "Abu Sufra, will you recite poetry at the grave?" He said, "I will say it:

> 'If you are saved from it, you are saved from something terrible.
> Otherwise, I do not imagine you will have a rescuer.'"

Ziyad ibn Matar ibn Shurayh al-'Adawi

It is reported from Ziyad's son, al-'Ala', that his father left a will stating that if something should happen to him, they should see what the *fuqaha'* of the people of Basra commanded and do it. They asked, and they agreed on the fifth.

Walan ibn Qirfa al-'Adawi

He related from Hudhayfa ibn al-Yaman and Abu Hunayda al-'Adawi related from him.

'Abdullah ibn Abi 'Utba

He travelled with Abu'd-Darda', Abu Sa'id al-Khudri, Jabir ibn 'Abdullah and some of the Companions of the Prophet ﷺ.

'Uqba ibn Aws as-Sadusi

Muhammad ibn Sirin related from him. He was reliable with few *hadiths*.

'Amr ibn Wahb ath-Thaqafi

Muhammad ibn Sirin related from him. He was reliable with few *hadiths*.

Abu Shaykh al-Huna'i

He was from the tribe of Azd. His name was Khaywan ibn Khalid. He was reliable and had *hadiths*. He died before al-Hasan.

Muhammad ibn Sirin said that Ibn Ziyad was afflicted by forgetfulness and he told Abu Shaykh al-Huna'i to instruct him (meaning in the prayer).

'Imran ibn Hittan as-Sadusi

He was a poet and related from Abu Musa al-Ash'ari, 'A'isha and others.

Yazid ibn 'Abdullah ibn ash-Shikhkhir

His *kunya* was Abu'l-'Ala. Abu'l-'Ala' said, "I was ten years older than al-Hasan, and Mutarrif was ten years older than me."

It is reported that Yazid ibn 'Abdullah used to recite the Qur'an until he fainted.

Sa'd al-Jurayri said, "Abu'l-'Ala' Yazid ibn 'Abdullah used to recite from the Qur'an and he used to select and say, 'Let us have your copy of the Qur'an for the rest of the day.'"

Abu Khulda said, "I saw Abu'l-'Ala' dye his beard yellow."

Abu Hafs al-'Uqayli said, "Abu'l-Malih al-Hudhali passed by me while I was stitching the shroud of Yazid ibn 'Abdullah ibn ash-Shikhkhir, Abu'l-Ala'. He said, 'Make him a waist wrapper like the wrapper of the living.'"

Muhammad ibn 'Umar said that Abu'l-'Ala' died in Basra in 111 AH, but others said that he died while 'Umar ibn Hubayra was governor. He was reliable with sound *hadiths*.

✸✸✸✸✸

Those of the Second Generation who were younger and related from other Companions

Al-Hasan ibn Abi'l-Hasan

His name was Abu'l-Hasan Yasar. It is said that he was one of the captives of Maysan who were taken to Madina. Ar-Rubayya' bint an-Nadr, the aunt of Anas ibn Malik, bought him and freed him.

Al-Hasan mentioned that his parents belonged to a man of Banu'n-Najjar who married a woman from the Banu Salama of the Ansar. He brought them to her as part of her bride-price and she freed them.

It is said that al-Hasan's mother was a client of Umm Salama, the wife of the Prophet ﷺ and that al-Hasan was born in Madina two years before the end of the khalifate of 'Umar ibn al-Khattab. They mention that while his mother was away, he began to cry and Umm Salama nursed him to distract him until his mother came and gave him her breast and he drank. They think that his wisdom and eloquence was due to that blessing. Al-Hasan grew up in Wadi'l-Qura and was eloquent.

Al-Hasan said, "Al-Hajjaj asked me, 'When were you born, Hasan?' I replied, 'When two years were left of 'Umar's khalifate [21 AH].' He said, 'By Allah, your distinction is greater than your age.'"

Al-Hasan said, "I saw 'Uthman speaking while I was 15, both standing and sitting." He also said that he saw 'Uthman ibn 'Affan pour water on himself from a jug.

Abu Raja' reported that he asked al-Hasan, "When were you in Madina, Abu Sa'id?" He said, "During the time of Siffin [37 AH]." He asked, "When did you reach puberty?" He replied, "A year after Siffin." Muhammad ibn 'Umar said that he considers it established that he was fourteen on the day that 'Uthman ibn 'Affan was killed. He saw him, listened to him and related from him and from 'Imran ibn Husayn, Samura ibn Jundub, Abu Hurayra, Ibn 'Umar, Ibn 'Abbas, 'Amr ibn Taghlib, al-Aswad ibn Sari', Jundub ibn 'Abdullah, and Sa'sa'a ibn Mu'awiya. Sa'sa'a related from Abu Dharr.

Al-Hasan related that 'Abdu'r-Rahman ibn Samura went on an expedition with him to Kabul, Anduqan, Andaghan, and Zabulistan for three years. Yahya ibn Sa'id al-Qattab said about the *hadiths* of

Samura which al-Hasan related from him, "We heard that they were from a book."

They said, "Al-Hasan was comprehensive, a sublime and elevated scholar, a reliable *faqih*, trustworthy, worshipping, of great knowledge, excellent and refined eloquence. He gave an *isnad* for his *hadiths*, and he related from those he listened to and had good evidence. He did not consider *mursal hadith* to be evidence. He went to Makka and they sat him on a bench and people gathered to him and he related to them. He was among those to whom Mujahid, 'Ata', Ta'us, and 'Amr ibn Shu'ayb went. They said that they had not seen his equal.

Al-Hasan said, "If it had not been for the covenant which Allah took from the people of knowledge, I would not have related much of what you ask about."

Al-Hasan said, "I heard Abu Hurayra say, '*Wudu*' is done on account of what has been changed by fire.'" Al-Hasan said, "I never fail to do it."

Al-Hasan said, "Musa, the Prophet of Allah ﷺ only bathed when concealed." 'Abdullah ibn Burayda asked, "Abu Sa'id, from whom did you hear this?" He replied, "I heard it from Abu Hurayra."

Rabi'a ibn Kulthum said, "I heard a man say to al-Hasan, 'Abu Sa'id, the day of *Jumu'a* is damp, muddy and rainy.' Al-Hasan refused to allow him anything except *ghusl*. When he did so he said, 'Abu Hurayra reported to me, "The Messenger of Allah ﷺ charged me to do three things: a *ghusl* before *Jumu'a*, the *witr* before sleep, and to fast three days every month.""'

Some people allege that al-Hasan did not listen to Abu Hurayra.

Ibn 'Awn said, "Al-Hasan used to relate *hadiths* and meanings."

Jarir ibn Hazim said, "Al-Hasan used to relate *hadiths* to us and would vary. He would add and decrease the *hadith*, but the meaning remained the same."

Ghaylan ibn Jarir said, "I said to al-Hasan, 'Abu Sa'id, a man listens to *hadith* and relates them and does not care so there is increase and decrease in them.' He said, 'Who can do that?'"

Shu'ba said, "I asked Qatada from whom al-Hasan got the idea that the *khul'* separation was only permitted in the presence of the ruler? He replied, 'From Ziyad.'"

Yazid ar-Rishk said, "Al-Hasan was in charge of giving judgement."

'Umar ibn Abi Za'ida said, "I brought the letter of the Qadi of Kufa to Iyas ibn Mu'awiya. I brought it when he had been dismissed and al-Hasan had been made qadi. I gave him my letter and he accepted it and did not ask me for proof of it."

Qatada said, "Al-Hasan did not tell us that any of the people of Badr conveyed to him."

Shu'ba said, "I saw al-Hasan stand for the prayer and people crowded to him. He said, 'Those people must have a portion.' He used to sit at the old minaret at the end of the mosque."

Ibn 'Awn said, "There were lines on al-Hasan's signet-ring."

Muhammad ibn 'Amr said, "I saw al-Hasan's seal on his left hand. It was entirely made of silver."

'Abbas ibn Rashid said, "I saw al-Hasan pray in his sandals."

Sa'id ibn Abi 'Aruba and others said, "I saw al-Hasan dye his beard yellow."

Aban al-'Attar said, "I saw that al-Hasan did not shave off his moustache as some people do."

Salam ibn Miskin said, "I saw al-Hasan pray with his hands inside his shawl."

Mahdi ibn Maymun said, "I saw al-Hasan wearing a black turban."

Mubarak ibn Fadala said, "I saw al-Hasan put his shawl on his left side in the prayer."

Sufyan said, "I was informed that someone saw that al-Hasan's shirt came down to here," pointing to where shoelaces are tied.

'Isa ibn 'Abdu'r-Rahman said, "I saw al-Hasan al-Basri wearing a black turban hanging down at the back, and a shirt and yellow cloak in which he was wrapped."

Al-Hasan said, "I used to visit the houses of the wives of the Messenger of Allah ﷺ while 'Uthman ibn 'Affan was khalif. I could touch the ceiling of the rooms with my hand."

Humayd ibn Hilal said, "Abu Qatada said to us, 'You must have this shaykh,' meaning al-Hasan ibn Abi'l-Hasan. 'By Allah, I have not seen any man at all closer in opinion to 'Umar ibn al-Khattab than him.'"

'Ali ibn Zayd said, "I met 'Urwa ibn az-Zubayr, Yahya ibn Ja'da, and al-Qasim, and I did not see anyone among them like al-Hasan. If al-Hasan had been with the Companions of the Prophet, he is a man whose opinion they would have had need of."

'Uqba ibn Abi Thuwayb ar-Rasibi said, "Bilal ibn Abi Burda was visiting me when al-Hasan was mentioned. Bilal said to me, 'I heard Abu Burda say, "I have never seen a man who was not a Companion of the Prophet ﷺ who more resembled the Companions of the Messenger of Allah than this shaykh," meaning al-Hasan.'"

'Abdullah ibn 'Amir ash-Sha'bi said, "When Ibn Hubayra [Yazid ibn Hubayra, the last Umayyad governor of Iraq] sent for al-Hasan and ash-Sha'bi, they met. 'Amir ash-Sha'bi began to show his esteem for him and his son said to him, 'Father, I see you behaving with this shaykh in a manner which I do not see you have with anyone else.' He replied, 'My son, I have met seventy of the Companions of the Messenger of Allah, may Allah bless him and grant him peace, and I did not see anyone who resembled them more than this shaykh.'"

Mansur al-Ghudani said, "Ash-Sha'bi mentioned al-Hasan and said, 'I did not see any man of the people of this land better than him.'"

Yunus said, "Al-Hasan was a melancholy man. Ibn Sirin laughed and joked."

Humayd and Yunus ibn 'Abid said, "We have seen many *fuqaha'*, but we have not seen anyone more comprehensive than al-Hasan."

Yunus said, "Al-Hasan sought a reward for what he said and Muhammad (ibn Sirin) sought a reward for his silence."

'Amr ibn Murra said, "I envy the people of Basra for these two shaykhs: al-Hasan and Muhammad [ibn Sirin]."

Qatada said, "Al-Hasan had the most knowledge of the lawful and the unlawful."

Ibn 'Awn said, "I did not see anyone more generous than the two of them, meaning al-Hasan and Ibn Sirin, although al-Hasan was the more persistent of the two."

Yunus said, "By Allah, al-Hasan was one of the leaders of the scholars regarding seditions and homicide."

Ayyub said, "Ibn al-Ash'ath was told, 'If you wish for people to be killed around you as they were killed around the camel of 'A'isha, bring out al-Hasan.' So he sent for him and forced him to come."

Ibn 'Awn said, "In the time of Ibn al-Ash'ath people thought that things were going slowly and said to him, 'Bring out this shaykh,' (meaning al-Hasan)." Ibn 'Awn said, "I saw al-Hasan between the two bridges wearing a black turban. When they were distracted from him, he jumped into one of those rivers to save himself from them. He was almost killed on that day."

Sulayman ibn 'Ali ar-Rabi'i said, "During the uprising of al-Ash'ath when he rose against al-Hajjaj ibn Yusuf, 'Ubqa ibn 'Abdu'l-Ghafir, Abu'l-Jawza' and 'Abdullah ibn Ghalib went with a group of their peers to visit al-Hasan. They asked, 'Abu Sa'id, what do you say about fighting these tyrants who shed inviolate blood and take inviolate property and abandon the prayer and do this and that?' They mentioned the things which al-Hajjaj had done. Al-Hasan replied, 'I think that you should not fight him. If it is a punishment from Allah, then you will not repel the punishment of Allah by your swords. If it is affliction, *"Be steadfast until Allah judges between us. He is the best of judges."* (7:87).' They left him saying, 'Why should we obey this non-Arab?' They were Arabs. They went out to fight with al-Ash'ath and were all killed."

Salm ibn Abi'd-Dhayyal said, "While some people of Syria were listening, a man asked al-Hasan, 'Abu Sa'id! What do you say about the uprisings like those of Yazid ibn al-Muhallab and Ibn al-Ash'ath?' He replied, 'We are neither with these nor those.' A man of the people of Syria said, 'Nor with the Amir al-Mu'minin, Abu Sa'id?' He became angry and he made a gesture with his hand. Then he said, 'Nor with the Amir al-Mu'minin, Abu Sa'id?' He said, 'Yes, nor with the Amir al-Mu'minin.'"

Abu't-Tayyah said, "I saw al-Hasan and Sa'id ibn Abi'l-Hasan when Ibn al-Ash'ath revolted. Al-Hasan was forbidding people to go out against al-Hajjaj and commanding people to refrain. Sa'id ibn Abi'l-Hasan was encouraging them. Then Sa'id said, 'What do you think of the people of Syria when we meet them tomorrow?' We said, 'By Allah, we will not depose the Amir al-Mu'minin nor do we wish to depose him, but we will take revenge from him for appointing al-Hajjaj over us. He must remove him from authority over us.' When Sa'id finished speaking, al-Hasan spoke and praised Allah and then said, 'O people! Allah has only given al-Hajjaj power over you as a punishment. You cannot avert Allah's punishment with the sword. You must be calm and make supplication to Him. As for what you mentioned of my opinion of the people of Syria, my opinion of them is that if they were to come, and al-Hajjaj gave them his worldly goods, they would do whatever he urged them to do. This is my opinion of them.'"

Basra

Al-Hasan said, "If people are tested by their ruler and are patient, they will receive relief. But if they resort to the sword and rely on it, by Allah, they will never bring about good."

Ibn 'Awn said, "Muslim ibn Yasar was higher with the people of Basra than al-Hasan until he rushed to join Ibn al-Ash'ath. Al-Hasan refrained and continued to rise in their esteem while Ibn Yasar dropped."

Al-Hajjaj al-Aswad said, "A man made a wish and said, 'Would that I might have the asceticism of al-Hasan, the scrupulousness of Ibn Sirin, the worship of 'Amir ibn 'Abdu'l-Qays, and the *fiqh* of Sa'id ibn al-Musayyab.' He mentioned Mutarrif, but I forget what he said. They looked for that and found it all in al-Hasan."

Hatim ibn Wardan said, "While I was listening, a man asked Ayyub something and he replied, 'The *hadith* of al-Hasan.' The man laughed and Ayyub's face became red. He asked him, 'What made you laugh?' He said, 'Nothing.' He said, 'You are not to laugh at excellence. By Allah, your eyes have not seen a man with more *fiqh* than him at all!'"

Abu Salama ibn 'Abdu'r-Rahman asked Al-Hasan ibn Abi'l-Hasan, "What do you think about giving people a *fatwa* regarding some of what you have heard or your opinion (*ra'y*)?" Al-Hasan replied, 'No, by Allah, we will not give a *fatwa* about all that we have heard, but our opinion is better for them than their opinion for themselves.'"

Al-Hasan said, "When this *fitna* first came, every man of knowledge recognised it; and when it retreated, every ignorant man recognised it."

Thabit said, "We were sitting with al-Hasan on his roof when al-Hajjaj did what he did." [The narrator said, "He was expelling Muslims from Basra."] "Sa'id ibn Abi'l-Hasan came while we were sitting with al-Hasan and said, 'We accede to this because it is less than imprisonment.' Al-Hasan rejected that and disliked what he had said."

Al-'Ala' ibn Ziyad said, "I do not like to say 'Amen' to anyone's supplication when I hear it except for al-Hasan's."

Humayd and Yunus said, "We do not know of anyone with more extensive knowledge than al-Hasan."

Yunus ibn Muslim said, "A man said to al-Hasan, 'Abu Sa'id.' Al-Hasan asked him, 'Where were you brought up?' He replied, 'Ubulla.' He said, 'You have certainly come from there.'"

Tabi'un

Yunus stated that Sa'id ibn Abi'l-Hasan said, "I have the clearest Arabic of people." Al-Hasan said, "You?" He replied, "Yes. Can you criticise one word of mine?" He replied, "This word."

Al-Ash'ath said, "When we went to al-Hasan, we did not ask about any report nor did we report any events. We dealt with the matters of the Next World. We used to go to Muhammad ibn Sirin and he would ask us about news and poems."

Yazid ibn Ibrahim said, "I saw al-Hasan raise his hands in his stories in supplication so that you could see the backs of his hands."

Humayd said, "Al-Hasan used to buy half a dirham of meat every day." Both he and Ayyub said, "I did not ever smell a broth with a better aroma than the stew of al-Hasan."

Ayyub said, "I argued with al-Hasan about the *Qadar* [see introduction] more than once until the Sultan frightened him. He said, 'I will not speak about it again after today.'"

Ayyub said, "I do not know anyone who can fault al-Hasan except on account of it [*Qadar*]." Ayyub also said, "I met al-Hasan and, by Allah, he did not espouse it."

Abu Hilal said, "I heard Humayd and Ayyub talking and I heard Humayd say to Ayyub, 'I wish that the debt could be divided between us, and that al-Hasan would not say what he says about it.' Ayyub said that he meant the *Qadar*."

Mu'tamir said that his father used to say, "Al-Hasan was the shaykh of Basra and Bakr was the one who issued its *fatwas*."

Ghalib said, "Al-Hasan went out into the mosque and his donkey wandered off. So my donkey was brought and he mounted it. My donkey had a tendency to bite its rider on the leg and I was afraid for al-Hasan so I grabbed hold of its rein. He asked, 'Is this your donkey?' I replied that it was. He asked, 'Are there men walking behind it?' He went on, 'May you be fatherless! The sound of the sandals of these people does not spare the heart of a weak human. By Allah, if it were not that a Muslim [or a believer] could examine himself and know that he has nothing of consequence, this would swiftly corrupt his heart.'"

Yazid ibn Hazim said that he heard al-Hasan say, "The sound of sandals behind men rarely remains frivolous."

Al-Hasan said, "Hold this world in contempt. By Allah, I welcome what will come about when they hold it in contempt."

Ghalib al-Qattan said, "We were with al-Hasan when Iyas ibn Mu'awiya and Yazid ibn Abi Maryam were with him. When al-Hasan was asked about a question, Iyas would rush to answer. When al-Hasan was asked, we recognised the excellence of al-Hasan over others." He said, "Al-Hasan was asked about whether the *sa'* is satisfied by honey. Iyas said it was. Al-Hasan said, 'It may be satisfied or it may not be. A man may be kind and satisfy it, or awkward and not satisfy it.'" He added, "The excellence of al-Hasan over us is like the excellence of the falcon over sparrows."

Abu Shaddad, a shaykh of the Banu Mujashi', said, "I was with al-Hasan when those who wore wool were mentioned in his presence. He said three times, 'Why do they cause themselves loss! They conceal pride in their hearts while making a show of humility in their dress. By Allah, one of them takes more pride in his garment than the one with a fine cloak takes in his cloak.'"

Kulthum ibn Jawshan said, "A man visited al-Hasan and smelt the mouth-watering aroma of a pot. He said, 'Abu Sa'id, your pot smells delicious!' He said, 'Yes, because my loaf is Malik [ibn Anas] and its lid is Farqad.'"

Kulthum ibn Jawshan said, "Al-Hasan went out wearing a Yemeni jubbah and a Yemeni cloak and Farqad looked at him and said in Persian, 'A master should be like you.' Al-Hasan said, 'Son of Farqad's mother, do you not know that the majority of the people of the Fire are the people of fine garments?'"

Kulthum ibn Jawshan said, "A man asked al-Hasan to help him in some task, and he went out with him. He said, 'I asked for the help of Ibn Sirin and Farqad and they said, "After we have attended the funeral we will go out with you."'If they had gone with him, it would have been better."

'Utba ibn Yaqthan said, "We were sitting with al-Hasan while some youths were with him, not asking him about anything. They began to look at one another. He said, 'Why are they confused? Why are they confused? What do they pretend to miss?'"

Qurra said, "I heard al-Hasan say, 'Some people sit with us in this circle of ours who only desire this world by that.' I heard him say, 'May Allah have mercy on a person who does not attribute words to us which we did not say.'"

Tabi'un

Jarir ibn Hazim said, "We were with al-Hasan when more than half the day had passed. His son said, 'Give the shaykh a rest! You have been hard on him. He has not eaten nor drunk.' He said, 'Shoo!' rebuking him, 'Leave them be. By Allah, there is nothing more delightful to me than seeing them. A man of the Muslims visits his brothers and they talk and remind one another and praise their Lord until the midday nap prevents it.'"

Jarir ibn Hazim said, "We were with al-Hasan and whenever a man came and said, 'Peace be upon you,' al-Hasan would reply, 'And peace be upon you.'"

Ghalib said that al-Hasan said, "Preferring action to speech is honour. Preferring words to action is disgrace."

Al-Hasan said, "A believer's laughter is heedlessness in his heart."

Qatada said, "If I have four, I will not turn to others nor care about whoever opposes them: al-Hasan, Sa'id ibn al-Musayyab, Ibrahim and 'Ata'." He added, "These four are the Imams of the cities."

Hisham said that 'Ata' was asked about something and said, "I do not know." He was told, "Al-Hasan says such-and-such." He said, "By Allah, there is nothing inside me like the heart of al-Hasan."

Humayd said, "While we were in Makka ash-Sha'bi said to me, 'I wish that al-Hasan would go aside with me.' I told that to al-Hasan while I was with him in a room. He said, 'If he so wishes.' So ash-Sha'bi came while I was at the door. I said, 'Go to him. He is alone in the room.' He said, 'I would prefer that you go in with me.' So I went in and there was al-Hasan facing the *qibla*, saying, 'O son of Adam! You were not and then were given form. You asked and were given. You were asked for something and refused. Evil is what you have done!' Then he went out and came back and then said, 'O son of Adam. You were not and then were given form. You asked and were given. You were asked for something and refused. Evil is what you have done!' Then he went out and then came back again and then he said, 'O son of Adam! You were not and then were given form. You asked and were given. You were asked for something and refused. Evil is what you have done!' Then he went out. That happened several times. Ash-Sha'bi turned to me and said to me, 'I will go. This shaykh is in other than what we are in.'"

Yunus ibn 'Ubayd said, "Al-Hasan took his stipend and began to divide it. His family mentioned a need and he said to them, 'Beware of the rest of the stipend. There is no good in it unless this is done with it.'"

Humayd reported that al-Hasan said, "A lot of laughter is part of what kills the heart."

Muhammad ibn az-Zubayr said, "'Umar ibn 'Abdu'l-'Aziz asked me about al-Hasan and about his body, his food and his drink. He said, 'I have heard that he wears a black turban.' I replied, 'Yes.' He said, 'It is part of the clothing of the people.' He said, 'I think he is one of those against whom accusations are wrongfully made.' I said, 'Yes.' Then he asked me about his assembly and said, 'Have you seen him eat?' I said, 'Yes. One day he was brought a platter and took a peach and bit it and then put it back.'"

Abu Hurra said, "Al-Hasan would not accept a wage for judging."

Abu Malik said, "When al-Hasan was asked, 'Why do you not come out and change things?' he said, 'Allah changes by repentance. He does not change by the sword.'"

Al-Hasan and Muhammad said, "Do not sit with the people of sects, and do not argue with them, and do not listen to them.'"

Muhammad ibn az-Zubayr reported that al-Hasan's son came to him and he said to him, "Did you inquire about the man?" He replied, "Yes." It was regarding a man who had proposed to his daughter. He asked, "He is a client by emancipation?" He replied, "Yes." His companions objected to that. He said, "Go and carry out the marriage with him. How much did he offer you?" He replied, "Ten thousand." He said, "Ten thousand is the intimacy of an intimate.[1] When you take ten thousand from him, what will be left? Leave him 6000 and take 4000 of it." A man said to him, "Abu Sa'id, I have a hundred thousand." He exclaimed, "A hundred thousand!" He repeated, "A hundred thousand." He said, "No, by Allah, there is no good in this. Do not carry out a marriage with him." The girl's mother came and said, "Why will you forbid us provision which Allah has sent to us?" He said, "Go away, barbarian." She was a tall old woman.

Hisham ibn Hassan said, "Maslama ibn 'Abdu'l-Malik sent al-Hasan a jubbah and a blanket and he accepted them. I often saw him in the mosque with the blanket hanging over the jubbah."

---

1. A play on words: *'ishra* = intimacy and *'ashara* = ten; *ilf* = intimate and *alf* = thousand.

Jarir ibn Hazim said, "I saw al-Hasan pray wearing a blanket with many marks and he kept his hand under it when he prostrated."

Mahdi ibn Maymun said, "Al-Hasan did not remove his turban, summer or winter, when he went out to the people."

'Umara ibn Zadhan said, "I saw al-Hasan wearing a shirt of cotton, a square cloak, a robe, and a blue shawl."

Badr ibn 'Uthman said, "I saw al-Hasan ibn Abi'l-Hasan wearing a black turban."

Sulayman ibn al-Mughira said, "I saw al-Hasan wearing a Yemeni garment and shawls and turbans."

Muhammad ibn 'Amr al-Ansari said, "I saw al-Hasan wearing a ring on his left hand."

'Awf reported that a man asked al-Hasan, "Abu Sa'id, my house is very far away and it is hard on me to come frequently. I have some *hadiths*. Do you think that there is anything wrong in me reading to you?" He replied, "I do not mind if you read to me and I tell you, 'He reported to me' or 'I reported it to you'." He said, "Abu Sa'id, shall I say, 'Al-Hasan reported to me?'" He said, "Yes. Say, 'Al-Hasan reported to me.'" It is reported from Humayd that he took the books of al-Hasan and copied them and then returned them to him.

Abu Tariq as-Sa'di said, "I was with al-Hasan when he was making a will when he was dying. He told the scribe, 'Write: This is what al-Hasan ibn Abi'l-Hasan testifies: that there is no god but Allah and Muhammad is the Messenger of Allah. Whoever testifies to it truthfully at his death will enter the Garden.' It is related from Mu'adh ibn Jabal that he made that will when he died, relating that from the Messenger of Allah."

'Abdu'l-Wahid, the client of 'Urwa ibn az-Zubayr, said that a man said to Ibn Sirin, "I dreamt that a bird brought al-Hasan his pebbles in the mosque." Ibn Sirin said, "If you are speaking the truth, then al-Hasan will die." It was not long afterwards that he died.

Thabit said, "I visited al-Hasan when he was dying and his son let me understand what he said although what he said was inaudible to me. He said that he said: 'We belong to Allah and to Him we return.'"

Sallam ibn Miskin said, "We visited al-Hasan while he was ill and he glanced at us and said, 'If only the son of Adam could store up his health for the day when he is ill.'"

Abu Hilal said, "We were in Qatada's house when the news reached us that al-Hasan had died. I remarked, 'He dived deeply in knowledge.' Qatada rejoined, 'No, by Allah, but he was firm in it and retained it and let people drink of it. By Allah, only a Kharijite hates al-Hasan.'"

Sahl ibn Husayn al-Bahili said, "I sent to 'Abdullah, al-Hasan's son, asking him to send me his father's books. He sent word to me that when he was dying, he had told them to collect them for him. His son said, 'They were collected for him and, by Allah, I do not know what he did with them. I brought them to him and he told the servant, "Light the oven." Then he commanded that they be burned except for one page. He sent it to me and then I met him later and he recounted to me orally the like of what the messenger had told me.'"

Abu 'Ubayda said, "I heard a man ask al-Hasan, 'Abu Sa'id, have you ever gone on an expedition?' He replied, 'Yes, the expedition against Kabul with 'Abdu'r-Rahman ibn Samura.'"

Humayd said, "Al-Hasan only went on *hajj* twice: once at the beginning of his life and again at the end of his life."

'Umar, the client of Ghafara, said, "The people of *Qadar* lay claim to al-Hasan ibn Abi'l-Hasan but his words contradict them. He used to say, 'O son of Adam, do not please anyone by which you incur the wrath of Allah. Do not obey anyone in disobedience to Allah. Do not praise anyone for the bounty of Allah, and do not blame anyone because of what Allah has not given him. Allah created creation and creatures and they proceed according to that on which He created them. Whoever thinks that he can increase his provision by his zeal should increase his life by his zeal, or change his colour, or increase his constituents or his fingers.'"

Shu'ayb said, "I saw al-Hasan recite the Qur'an weeping until his tears made his beard wet."

Qatada said that al-Hasan did not make use of lights.[1]

Mahdi said, "I was at the door of al-Hasan when he went to his family and said, 'Peace be upon you.'"

Yahya ibn Sa'id, the nephew of al-Hasan said, "When I became skilled, I said, 'Uncle, the student desires something.' He said, 'They should not take anything.' Then he said, 'Give him five dirhams.' I kept at him until he said, 'Give him ten dirhams.'"

---

1. Because of their association with non-Muslim forms of worship.

Tabi'un

Qatada said, "We used to pray with al-Hasan on reed mats. Al-Hasan would shave his head every year on the Day of Sacrifice."

Abu Hilal said, "When al-Hasan finished his *hadith*, he would say, 'O Allah, you see our hearts full of idolatry, pride, hypocrisy, showing-off, reputation, doubt and uncertainty in your *deen*. O Turner of hearts, make our hearts firm in Your *deen* and make our *deen* Straight Islam!'"

It is related that Anas ibn Malik was asked about something and said, "You must have our master al-Hasan. Ask him." They said, "O Abu Hamza! We are asking you and you tell us to ask 'our master al-Hasan'?" He said, "We listened and he listened. He retained and we forgot."

'Umara ibn Mihran said that al-Hasan was asked, "Why do you not visit the rulers and command them to the correct and forbid them the incorrect?" He replied, "The believer should not waste himself. Their swords precede our tongues when we speak. They speak thus with their swords." And he made a striking gesture with his hand.

'Umara said, "I did not see anyone whose words are in harmony with his actions except al-Hasan."

'Umara said, "I was with al-Hasan when Farqad visited us while he was eating a sweet and al-Hasan said, 'Come and eat.' He said, 'I fear that I will not properly be thankful for it.' Al-Hasan said, 'Bother to you! You properly give thanks for cold water!'"

It is related that al-Hasan said, "When a young man is devout, we do not recognise him by his speech. We recognise him by his actions. That is beneficial knowledge."

'Umara said that al-Hasan told him that he disliked voices trilling when reciting the Qur'an.

Al-Hasan said, "Guard against having a bad opinion of people."

Ar-Rabi' ibn Subayh said, "Al-Hasan disliked being praised to his face. If invocation was made for him, that delighted him."

Ghalib al-Qattan said, "I brought al-Hasan a letter from 'Abdu'l-Malik ibn Abi Bashir and he said, 'Read it.' So I read it and there was a supplication in it. Al-Hasan said, 'Many a true brother of yours was not actually born of your mother.'"

It is related that 'Imran ibn Khalid al-Khuza'i said that a man told him, "Matar asked al-Hasan about a question and said, 'The *fuqaha*' oppose you.' He said, 'May your mother be bereaved, Matar! Do you see a *faqih* at all? Do you know what a *faqih* is? The scrupulous ascetic *faqih* is the one who does not care about who is above him nor mock the one below him, and who does not accept ephemeral rubbish in exchange for the knowledge which Allah has taught him.'"

It is related that when al-Hasan saw a funeral, he would say, "Praise belongs to Allah who has not made me part of that which is snatched away." He said, "He would not relate anything that day."

Muhammad ibn 'Umar said, "Al-Hasan died in 110." Isma'il ibn 'Ulayya said that it was in Rajab. There were a hundred days between the deaths of Muhammad ibn Sirin and him, al-Hasan dying first.

Hammad ibn Zayd said that al-Hasan died on Friday night. He said that Ayyub and Humayd at-Tawil washed him. He was brought out when the people left. He said, "My father took me with him," and Mu'adh ibn Mu'adh said, "Al-Hasan was ten years older than Muhammad."

Sa'id ibn Abi'l-Hasan

He was younger than al-Hasan and related and people related from him. Abu Khulda said that he saw Sa'id ibn Abi'l-Hasan dye his beard yellow.

Yunus ibn 'Ubayd said, "When Sa'id ibn Abi'l-Hasan died, al-Hasan was very sad indeed about him. He did not speak and people in his assembly and conversation noticed that. That was mentioned to him and he said, 'Praise belongs to Allah who did not make sorrow a disgrace for Ya'qub.' Then he said. 'Evil is a divided house!'"[1]

It is related that Mubarak ibn Fadala said, "We visited al-Hasan when we heard of his brother's death. He was weeping. Bakr ibn 'Abdullah visited him and consoled him. He said, 'Abu Sa'id, you teach people and they see you weeping. They will take this back to their clans and say, "We saw al-Hasan weep in an affliction," and they will criticise you about it to people.' He praised Allah and lauded Him. His words were choked. He said, 'Praise belongs to Allah Who has placed this mercy in the hearts of the believers so that by it they show mercy to one another. The eye weeps and the heart is sad, but that is not due to anguish. Anguish is what comes from the tongue or hand.' Then he said, 'Allah did not make Ya'qub's sorrow

---

1. Sa'id had supported Ibn al-Ash'ath while al-Hasan refused to take part.

a sin for him when he said, *"And then his eyes turned white from hidden grief."* (12:84) May Allah have mercy on Sa'id ibn Abi'l-Hasan.' He made much supplication for him. Then he said, 'I do not know in the earth of any intensity which befell me except that he wished that it had been him instead, and that he could protect me from it with himself.'"

Ibn 'Awn said, "Al-Hasan sent me an ornate burnous to sell. It had belonged to his brother Sa'id ibn Abi'l-Hasan who had died. Al-Hasan was very sad indeed. He said, 'I took it and was only offered 24 dirhams for it.' I said to him, 'Can I buy it?' He said, 'You know best, but I would not like to see you wearing it.' When I went to him, I did not wear it. I put it on and went to the mosque of the Banu 'Adi and prayed there, and a woman of the Banu 'Adi sent to me, 'Ibn 'Awn, do I see you wearing the like of this?' That caused some distress within me and I went to Muhammad ibn Sirin and mentioned that to him and he said, 'Give her my greetings and tell her that one of the Companions of the Prophet ﷺ purchased a robe for a thousand dirhams and wore it, but he only wore it for the prayer."

They say that Sa'id ibn Abi'l-Hasan died before 100 AH.

Jabir ibn Zayd al-Azdi

His *kunya* was Abu'sh-Sha'tha'. It is reported that Jabir ibn Zayd was blind.

Iyas said, "I went to Basra and its *mufti* was a man of the people of Oman, Jabir ibn Zayd."

'Amr said, "I did not see anyone with more knowledge than Abu'sh-Sha'tha'."

Ibn 'Abbas said, "If the people of Basra had settled for the words of Jabir ibn Zayd, he would have given them ample knowledge of what is in the Book of Allah."

Yahya ibn Sa'id al-Qattan said that Sulayman at-Taymi had more knowledge than him. He said, "Al-Hasan used to go on expeditions. The *mufti* of the people here was Jabir ibn Zayd. Then al-Hasan came and he gave *fatwa*."

Hammad ibn Zayd said, "One day Ayyub mentioned Jabir ibn Zayd and admired his *fiqh*."

Hammad ibn Zayd said, "Ayyub was asked whether he had seen Jabir. He said, 'Yes, he was intelligent, intelligent, intelligent.'"

Basra

Iyas ibn Mu'awiya said, "I went to Basra and they had no *mufti* to give them *fatwa* other than Jabir ibn Zayd."

Qatada said, "Jabir ibn Zayd was imprisoned and they sent to him to ask him for a *fatwa* about whether a hermaphrodite could inherit. He said, 'You imprison me and then ask for my *fatwa*?' Then he went on to tell them, 'See how he urinates and then let him inherit accordingly.'"

Hind said, "We fled from the plague to Iraq, and Jabir ibn Zayd came to us on a donkey saying, 'How near you are to what you seek!'"

Jabir ibn Zayd said, "Sixty years of my term has passed. In that period I have both suffered and been blessed. Now my sandals are dearer to me than all that except for the blessings which preceded them."

Yahya ibn 'Atiq said, "Jabir ibn Zayd was mentioned in the presence of Muhammad ibn Sirin who said, 'May Allah have mercy on Jabir. He was a true Muslim with the dirhams.'"

Al-Qasim ibn al-Fadl al-Huddani said, "I saw Jabir ibn Zayd with a white head and beard."

Abu Khulda said, "I saw Jabir ibn Zayd dye his beard yellow."

'Azra said, "I said to Jabir ibn Zayd, 'The Ibadiyya [Kharijites] claim that you are one of them.' He said, 'Before Allah I am innocent of them.'" He said that he said that to him when he was dying. Muhammad said, "He was innocent of what they say." 'Arim said that the Ibadiyya claimed him.

Thabit al-Bunani said, "I visited Jabir ibn Zayd when he was dying and asked him, 'What would you like?' He replied, 'A glance from al-Hasan.' I went to al-Hasan who was hiding in the house of Abu Khalifa and mentioned that to him. He said, 'Take us to him.' I said, 'I fear for you.' He said, 'Allah will avert their eyes from me.' So we went and visited him. Al-Hasan said to him, 'Abu'sh-Sha'tha'! Say: There is no god but Allah.' He said, *'On the day that one of the signs of your Lord does come'* (6:158), and so he recited this *ayat* to him. Al-Hasan said to him, 'The Ibadiyya lay claim to you.' He said, 'Before Allah, I am free of them.' He said, 'So what do you say about the people on the other side of the river?' He replied, 'Before Allah I am free of them.' We stayed with him until near dawn. When he feared the approach of morning and he had not yet died, he said four *takbirs* over him and made supplication for him and then left."

Jabir left instructions that his wife should wash him.

Muhammad ibn 'Umar and others said that Jabir ibn Zayd died in 103 AH. Abu Nu'aym said that Jabir died in 93 AH as well as Anas ibn Malik, on a Friday. Muhammad said, "This is a mistake. What Abu Nu'aym says about both of them is weak. It is agreed that Jabir ibn Zayd died in 103 AH. Anas died in 91 AH."

Abu Qilaba al-Jarmi

His name was 'Abdullah ibn Zayd. He was reliable with many *hadiths* and his *diwan* exists in Syria.

Ayyub reported that Abu Qilaba was asked, "Which person is the wealthiest?" He replied, "The one who is content with what he has been given." He was asked, "Which person has the most knowledge?" He replied, "The one who seeks provision from the knowledge of people to add to his knowledge."

Hammad ibn Zayd said, "I heard Ayyub mention Abu Qilaba, saying, 'By Allah, he was one of the *fuqaha'* with intelligence.'"

Ayyub said that Muslim ibn Yasar said, "If Abu Qilaba had been one of the non-Arabs, he would have been a *mobadh mobadhan*," meaning a chief judge.

Abu Qilaba said, "When people know more about a man than himself, that makes it more likely that he will be destroyed. If he has more knowledge of himself than people, that makes it more likely he will be saved."

Ayyub said, "I found the person with the most knowledge of judgement to be the strongest of them in avoiding it and the strongest of them in disliking to pass judgement, and I did not know in Basra of any man who had more judgement than Abu Qilaba."

Ayyub said, "Abu Qilaba was asked to be qadi so he fled to Syria and resided there for a time and then came back. I asked him, 'If you had taken the appointment as qadi and had been just between people, I hope that you would have received a reward for that.' He said to me, 'Ayyub, if a swimmer falls into the sea, how far can he swim?'"

Abu Khushayna said, "Abu Qilaba was mentioned in the presence of Muhammad ibn Sirin and he said, 'That man is truly my brother.'"

Basra

'Amr ibn Maymun said, "When Abu Qilaba came to 'Umar ibn 'Abdu'l-'Aziz, he said, 'Abu Qilaba, relate!' He replied, 'Amir al-Mu'minin, I dislike a lot of *hadith* and I dislike a lot of silence.'"

Abu Qilaba said, "When you inform a man about the *sunna* and he says, 'Do not bother us with this. Bring the Book of Allah,' know that he is misguided."

Abu Qilaba said, "No man innovates an innovation but that he will eventually regard the sword as lawful."

Abu Qilaba said, "Do not sit with the people of sects and do not argue with them. I do not feel safe that they will not cause you to plunge into their misguidance or make you befuddled about what you know."

Abu Qilaba said, "The people of sects are the people of misguidance, and I only think that their ultimate destination will be the Fire. It pulls them on. There is none of them who takes up a banner and or assumes a position whose affair does not stop until he ends up taking up the sword. There are various forms of hypocrisy." Then he recited, *"'Among them there were some who contracted with Allah'* (9:75); *'Among them are some who insult the Prophet'* (9:61); and, *'Among them there are some who find fault with you concerning the collected sadaqa.'* (9:58) So their position varies but they are united in doubt and denial. Their positions vary but they agree on resorting to the sword, and I think that their ultimate destination is only the Fire." Ayyub said, "By Allah, he was one of the *fuqaha'* with intelligence."

Abu Qilaba said, "I stayed for three [months?] in Madina, and I had no need except for a *hadith* which reached me from a man for whom I waited until he came and I asked him."

Khalid said, "We used to go to Abu Qilaba, and when he had related three *hadiths* to us, he would say, 'I have imparted a lot.'"

Ghaylan ibn Jarir said, "I wanted to go with Abu Qilaba to Makka and I asked permission to visit him, 'Can I enter?' He replied, 'Yes, if you are not a Kharijite.'"

Humayd said, "Abu Qilaba went to the silk merchants and said 'Write an agreement for me for a wrap of such-and-such a length and such-and-such a width and such-and-such a shape.' When it came to him, he bought it."

'Uqba ibn Abi's-Sahba' reported that Abu Qilaba used to use black hair dye.

Tabi'un

Ayyub said, "When Abu Qilaba became ill in Syria, 'Umar ibn 'Abdu'l-'Aziz went to visit him and said, 'Abu Qilaba, be strong. The hypocrites should not gloat over us."

Ayyub said that when Abu'l-'Aliyya visited Abu Qilaba, he said, "Be firm and do not allow the hypocrites to gloat over us.'"

Hammad ibn Zayd said, "Abu Qilaba said, 'Give my books to Ayyub if he is alive. Otherwise burn them.'"

Muhammad ibn 'Umar said, "Abu Qilaba died in Syria at Dayraya, and his library was in Syria. He died in 104 or 105 AH."

Muslim ibn Yasar

His *kunya* was Abu 'Abdullah. He was the client of Talha ibn 'Ubaydullah at-Taymi of Quraysh.

Humayd said that Muslim ibn Yasar was standing in prayer in his house and his garment caught fire and he was not aware of it until the fire was put out.

Ibn 'Awn said, "There was no one better than Muslim ibn Yasar in that time."

'Abdu'l-Hamid, the grandson of Muslim ibn Yasar, said, "My father informed me that when he entered the house, no noise was heard from them. While he prayed, they made a noise and laughed."

Ja'far ibn Hayyan said, "His lack of distraction in the prayer was mentioned to Muslim ibn Yasar and he said, 'What will inform you about where my heart is?'"

Ibn 'Awn said, "I saw Muslim ibn Yasar praying as if he was a pole, not turning towards anyone and his garment did not move."

Abu Qilaba said, "I asked Muslim ibn Yasar about humility in the prayer and he said, 'Lower your eye when you prostrate.'"

Thabit reported that Muslim ibn Yasar said, "I do not know what the reckoning will be for the belief of a slave who does not leave anything which Allah hates."

Muslim's son, 'Abdullah, reported that his father used to break his fast on dates, and that he had heard that the Messenger of Allah ﷺ used to break his fast on dates.

Thabit reported that Muslim ibn Yasar said, "There is none of my actions but that I fear that it will be sullied by what will corrupt it if it does not spring from love for Allah."

'Abdullah said that his father said, "It is not proper for a true person to be a curser. If I curse anything, I will not leave it in my house." He did not abuse anyone. The strongest thing that he said when he became angry was, 'Leave me!' When he said that, they knew that he could not be pressed any further."

'Abdullah, Muslim's son, said, "Muslim ibn Yasar was asked about praying sitting on a boat and he said, 'I dislike (or hate) it for Allah to see me praying sitting when I am not ill.'"

Muslim said, "I dislike to touch my private parts with my right hand since I hope to receive my book with it."

Muslim ibn Yasar said, "Beware of doubt. It is a moment when the knower is ignorant, and by it shaytan desires to make him slip." Muhammad said, "This disputation, this disputation!"

Habib ibn ash-Shahid said that one of his companions mentioned that Muslim ibn Yasar passed by a mosque when the *mu'adhdhin* gave the *adhan* and he went back. The *mu'adhdhin* said, "What made you come back?" He replied, "You made me come back."

Muslim's son, 'Abdullah, said, "My father had a slaveboy who did not pray, but he did not beat him. He said, 'I do not know what to do with him. He has overcome me.'"

Ayyub mentioned the *qurra'* who went out with Ibn al-Ash'ath and he said, "I do not know any of them who was killed but that he disliked his end and was not saved. He was only killed regretting what he had done."

Abu Qilaba said that Muslim ibn Yasar accompanied him to Makka. He said, "He mentioned the *fitna* to me and said, 'I praise Allah to you that I did not shoot an arrow nor thrust with a spear nor strike with a sword during it.' I said to him, 'Abu 'Abdullah, what about the one who saw you standing in the row and said, "This is Muslim ibn Yasar. By Allah, he would not take this position unless it were the truth!" Then he advanced and fought until he was killed.' He wept and wept until I wished that I had not said anything to him."

They said that Muslim was reliable and virtuous, a man of worship and scrupulousness. They held him in greater esteem than al-Hasan until he went out with 'Abdu'r-Rahman ibn Muhammad ibn al-Ash'ath and that lowered him in people's eyes and al-Hasan was raised above him.

They said that Muslim ibn Yasar died in the khalifate of 'Umar ibn 'Abdu'l-'Aziz in 100 or 101 AH.

Hayyan ibn 'Umayr al-Qaysi

His *kunya* was Abu'l-'Ala'. He was reliable with few *hadiths*. He related from Ibn 'Abbas and 'Abdullah ibn az-Zubayr and 'Abdu'r-Rahman ibn Samura.

Abu Madina as-Sadusi

His name was 'Abdullah ibn Husayn. He had few *hadiths*. He related from 'Abdullah ibn 'Abbas and 'Abdullah ibn az-Zubayr.

'Abdullah ibn Abi Bakra

His mother was a woman of the Banu Sa'd. 'Abdullah ibn Abi Bakra was born in Bahrayn and later settled in Basra. He was the oldest of the children of Abu Bakra and he was not appointed to any office. Abu Bakra died leaving forty children. His lineage extends from seven of them, one of whom was 'Abdullah ibn Abi Bakra.

'Ubaydullah ibn Abi Bakra

His mother was Hawla bint Ghalidh of the Banu 'Ijl. He had few *hadiths*. Abu Hamza said, "The first of those I saw doing this washing [in the lavatory] in Basra was 'Ubaydullah ibn Abi Bakr. We said, 'Look at this Abyssinian cleaning his bottom with water.'" 'Ubaydullah ibn Abi Bakr was appointed over Sijistan in the time of Ziyad ibn Abi Sufyan. 'Ubaydullah died, leaving descendants.

'Abdu'r-Rahman ibn Abi Bakra

He was the first Muslim child to be born in Basra. On that day they sacrificed an animal while they were at al-Khurayba and it fed the people of Basra and it was enough for all of them. He was reliable with *hadiths* and transmission. His mother was Hawla bint Ghalidh of the Banu 'Ijl. 'Abdu'r-Rahman died leaving descendants.

'Abdu'l-'Aziz ibn Abi Bakra

His mother was a *umm walad*. People relate from him, and he has *hadiths*, and he died leaving descendants.

Muslim ibn Abi Bakra

People relate from him and he died leaving descendants.

Abu Bakra's sons included: Rawwas ibn Abi Bakra, Yazid ibn Abi Bakra, Yazid ibn Abi Bakar, and 'Utba ibn Abi Bakra.

An-Nadr ibn Anas ibn Malik

His mother was an *umm walad*. He was reliable and has *hadiths*. People relate from him. He died before al-Hasan.

Maymun al-Ansari said, "Muhammad ibn Sirin was washing an-Nadr ibn Anas's corpse while al-Hasan was present and I was handing things to them. Muhammad said to me, 'Bring a rug.' I brought a red rug. Muhammad said, 'Abu Sa'd, this is the adornment of Qarun'[1]. Al-Hasan said to him, 'Yes, it is.' Muhammad told me to bring another. So I brought another rug which was green and he wrapped him in it."

Al-Aswad ibn Shayban said, "Al-Hasan ibn Abi'l-Hasan was at the funeral of an-Nadr ibn Anas, and al-Ash'ath ibn Aslam al-'Ijli was with them. He said, 'Abu Sa'id, I am amazed that I do not hear a sound at the funeral.' Al-Hasan said, 'It is good for the family. Good for the family.' Musa ibn Anas prayed the *'Asr* prayer on that day by the grave of an-Nadr ibn Anas." It was a remote, wide grave according to al-Aswad ibn Shayban.

Al-Aswad ibn Shayban said, "I saw Musa ibn Anas on that day pray at an-Nadr's grave wearing a red coat without any cloak."

'Abdullah ibn Anas ibn Malik

His mother was al-Qari'a bint al-Muthanna ash-Shaybaniyya. He was reliable with few *hadiths*.

Musa ibn Malik ibn an-Nadr

His mother was one of the people of Yemen. He was reliable with few *hadiths*.

---

1. Qarun was an immensely wealthy Israelite who was extremely arrogant because of his immense wealth. Allah caused the earth to swallow him up.

Malik ibn Anas ibn Malik

Muhammad said, "We were in Bahrayn and Malik ibn Anas and Anas ibn Sirin were with us. I fell ill and remained unconscious for six days and nights. Malik ibn Anas sent me every doctor in Bahrayn while I was completely comatose. They began to examine me and say, 'We will shave his head and cauterise him.' (The narrator mentioned that he had beautiful hair.) Malik said, 'I will not have him treated with fire and I will only bury him in a handsome state.'" He did not mention that Malik ibn Anas visited Muhammad when he was ill.

Muhammad ibn Sirin

His *kunya* was Abu Bakr. He was the client of Anas ibn Malik. He was reliable and trustworthy, virtuous and eminent, a *faqih* and an Imam with much knowledge and scrupulousness. He was somewhat deaf. He said, "I asked Muhammad ibn 'Abdullah al-Ansari, 'From where did Muhammad ibn Sirin originate?' He replied, 'He was one of the captives of 'Ayn at-Tamr. He was the client of Anas ibn Malik.'"

Anas ibn Sirin said, "Muhammad ibn Sirin was born in the second last year of 'Uthman's khalifate. I was born in the last year of his khalifate."

Muhammad reported that Muhammad ibn Sirin's mother was Safiyya, a client of Abu Bakr. Three of the wives of the Prophet, may Allah bless him and grant him peace, perfumed her. Her marriage was attended by eighteen of the people of Badr, including, Ubayy ibn Ka'b. He made supplication and they said "Amen." Bakkar ibn Muhammad said that Muhammad ibn Sirin had thirty children from one wife, but none of them survived except for 'Abdullah ibn Muhammad.

Anas ibn Sirin said, "Zayd ibn Thabit visited us. We were six brothers, Muhammad being one of them. He said, 'If you like, I will tell you which brother belongs to his mother. This and this have the same mother, and him and him have the same mother, and him and him have the same mother.' He did not err at all."

Shu'ba said, "My mother asked Hisham ibn Hasan, 'From which of the Companions of the Messenger of Allah صلعم did Muhammad relate?' He replied, 'From Ibn 'Umar and Abu Hurayra.' She asked, 'Did he actually listen to them?' He said, 'Yes.'"

Ibn 'Awn said, "Muhammad only had three *hadiths* from Abu Hurayra which went back to the Prophet: that the Prophet ﷺ prayed one of the two evening prayers, his words, 'The people of Yemen have come,'" and he forgot the third.

Muhammad said, "I used to listen to *hadiths* which had the same meaning while the words might vary slightly."

Ibn 'Awn said, "Muhammad used to report *hadiths* letter for letter."

Muhammad said, "We were informed by Ibn 'Abbas that he heard it from 'Ikrima whom he met in the time of al-Mukhtar[1] in Kufa." They said that Muhammad also related from Zayd ibn Thabit, Anas ibn Malik, Yahya ibn al-Jazzar, Shurayh and others.

As-Sari ibn Yahya said, "I heard Ibn Sirin say, 'May Allah have mercy on Shurayh. He used to come to my gathering.'"

Ibn 'Awn reported that Muhammad ibn Sirin used to say, "This knowledge is the *deen*. Investigate carefully the one from whom you take it."

Ibn 'Awn said that when Muhammad ibn Sirin related something, it seemed as if he was fearful and cautious about something.

Muhammad ibn Sirin said, "Beware of books. Those before you were befuddled," or, "Those before you were mislead by books." Bakkar ibn Muhammad said, "There is no book by my grandfather or my father or Ibn 'Awn which contains a complete *hadith*."

Ibn 'Awn said, "I heard Muhammad say, 'If I were to have a book, I would have the letters of the Prophet, may Allah bless him and grant him peace.'"

It is related from Yahya ibn 'Atiq that Muhammad ibn Sirin did not see any harm in writing down *hadiths*. Then when he had memorised them, he erased them.

Shu'ayb said, "Ash-Sha'bi said to us, 'You must have this deaf one,' meaning Muhammad ibn Sirin."

Ghalib al-Qattan said, "Imitate the forbearance of Muhammad but do not imitate the anger of al-Hasan."

Muhammad ibn 'Amr Abu Sahl al-Ansari said, "I heard Muhammad ibn Sirin object to people writing the *ba'* and then extending it to the *mim* until the *sin* was written [بِسم]. He said, 'Look at what I write: *bismillah* [بِسم],' and then he said something severe about it."

---

1. Leader of the Shi'ite rebellion in Kufa in 66 /686.

Tabi'un

Muhammad ibn 'Amr also said that he heard Muhammad ibn Sirin disliked people writing: "In the Name of Allah, the Merciful, the Compassionate, to so-and-so." He said "Write: 'In the Name of Allah, the Merciful, the Compassionate. From so-and-so to so-and-so.'"

Yahya ibn 'Atiq said, "Muhammad saw a man writing with his spit on his sandals, and he said, 'Are you happy to eat your sandal?' and he knocked it from his hand."

Yunus said, "Al-Hasan spoke seeking a reward [from Allah] and Muhammad was silent seeking the reward."

Al-Ash'ath said, "We used to sit with Muhammad ibn Sirin and speak to him and he would speak to us and laugh and ask about events. When he was asked about something of *fiqh* and the lawful and the unlawful, his face changed and altered so that he seemed to be a completely different person."

Mahdi ibn Maymun said, "I listened to Muhammad. When a man saw him doing something, Muhammad would say to him, 'I may know what you want and perceive the argument in you, but I do not want to argue with you.'"

Muwarriq al-'Ijli said, "I did not see a man with more *fiqh* in his scrupulousness, nor more scrupulousness in his *fiqh*, than Muhammad."

Abu Qilaba said, "Say what you wish about him, but you will find him the most scrupulous and the most self-controlled among you."

Jarir ibn Hazim said, "I heard Muhammad ibn Sirin relate to a man and he said, 'I did not see the black man.' Then he said, 'I ask Allah's forgiveness. I think I may have slandered the man.'"

Talq ibn Wahb at-Taji said, "I visited Muhammad ibn Sirin when I was ill. He said, 'Go to so-and-so and consult him. He has excellent knowledge of medicine.' Then he said, 'Rather go to so-and-so. He has more knowledge than him.' Then he said, 'I ask Allah's forgiveness. I think that I must have slandered him.'"

Muhammad said, "I have never envied anyone for anything at all, either pious or impious."

'Uthman al-Batti said "No one in this period has more knowledge of judgement than Muhammad ibn Sirin."

Ibn 'Awn said, "Muhammad said of something about which I consulted him: 'I did not say that there was nothing wrong with it. I said that I do not know of anything wrong in it.'"

Basra

Bakkar ibn Muhammad said, "More than one person whom I consider trustworthy and truthful related from Sawwar ibn 'Abdullah that Muhammad and al-Hasan were the masters of the people of this city, both Arabs and clients."

Ibn 'Awn said that Muhammad said, "If the one who speaks had known that his words would be written down, he would say little."

Hisham ibn Hassan reported that one of his family said, "He never found anything doubtful but that he abandoned it, since he grew up," meaning Muhammad ibn Sirin.

Yahya ibn 'Atiq said that a bedouin visited Ibn Sirin and began to ask him about things concerning his *deen* and he answered him. Then Ibn Qutayba gave the greeting and the man said, "Ask him what he says about *Qadar*." He said, "Abu Bakr, what do you say about *Qadar*?" He replied, "What people told you this?" Then he was silent for a time. Then Muhammad said, "Shaytan has no power over anyone, but he destroys whoever obeys him."

Ibn 'Awn said, "A man came to Muhammad and mentioned something about *Qadar* to him. Muhammad said, *'Allah commands to justice and doing good and giving to relatives. And He forbids indecency and doing wrong and tyranny. He warns you so that perhaps you will remember.'* (16:90) He placed his fingers in his ears and said, 'Either you leave me or I leave you!' The man left. Muhammad said, 'My heart is not in my hand, and I fear that something might be spat into my heart and I might not be able to bring it out of it. So I prefer not to listen to his words.'"

Anas ibn Sirin said, "When two *hadiths* were conveyed to Muhammad and one was stronger than the other, he took the stronger of them without seeing any harm in the other. He was capable of that."

Abu Qilaba said, "Which of you is capable of what Muhammad was capable? Muhammad used to proceed like the edge of a spear."

Hafsa bint Sirin said, "His mother was a woman of the Hijaz. She liked dyes. When Muhammad bought her a garment, it would be the softest he could find. Every *'Id* day he would dye her clothes for her." She said, "I did not see him ever raise his voice to her, and when he spoke to her, he spoke like someone attentively listening for something from her."

Ibn 'Awn said that if a man saw Muhammad when he was with his mother, he would not have recognised him and would have supposed that he was ill because of how much he lowered his voice to her. He said, "I asked Muhammad ibn 'Abdullah al-Ansari about the reason for the debt which Muhammad ibn Sirin had when he was imprisoned. He replied, 'He bought some food for 40,000 dirhams, and then learned something about the source of the food which he disliked, and he either left it or gave it away as *sadaqa* and so he still owed some money. So he was jailed for it by a woman. The one who had him imprisoned was Malik ibn Dinar.'"

It is related that Muhammad ibn Sirin sold a slavegirl to Umm Muhammad bint 'Abdullah. The girl went back to Muhammad and complained that the woman tortured her, and so Muhammad took her back when he had already spent the money. This woman was the one who imprisoned him, and she is the one whom Salam ibn Ziyad married and took to Khurasan. Her father had the nickname 'Kirkira'.

Qatada said, "I visited Ibn Sirin in prison when he was dictating a poem to a man."

Muhammad ibn Sirin said, "I certainly was made notorious."

Thabit al-Bunani said, "Muhammad ibn Sirin said to me, 'O Abu Muhammad, nothing prevented me from sitting with you except fear of notoriety. My affliction continued until I was seized by the beard and I was made to stand on the bench and it was said, "This is Muhammad ibn Sirin who consumes people's property."'" He owed a debt.

Ibn Sirin said that he purchased some food in a deferred sale, anticipating a profit of 80,000 dirhams from it. Then something about it occurred to his heart and he left it. Hisham said, "By Allah, it was not usury."

Abu Khalif ibn 'Uqba said, "Ibn Sirin used to glorify Allah on his own."

'Uthman al-Batti said, "I visited Ibn Sirin and he asked, "Uthman, what do people say about the *Qadar*?' I replied, 'Some affirm it and some say what you have heard.' He said, 'Why do you bring the *Qadar* to me? If Allah wills good for someone, he will give him success in obeying Him and will make him love good actions. If He wills other than that for him, He will punish him without being unjust.'"

Khalid al-Hadhdha' said, "Muhammad ibn Sirin used to fast every other day. When his fast coincided with the day which is not fasted because of the uncertainty about whether it is part of Sha'ban or part of Ramadan, he would fast it."

Anas ibn Sirin said, "Muhammad used to recite the Qur'an in sevenths, and if he missed anything at night, he would recite it in the day."

Ibn 'Awn reported that Muhammad used to have a bath every day.

Ayyub reported that Muhammad said, "My self made me do things which I wish it had not made me do."

Ibn 'Awn reported that Muhammad said, "I am in extreme affliction, yearning to be full but not full and desiring to be quenched but not quenched."

Ibn 'Awn reported that when Muhammad recited the *ayat*, *"And so that Allah can purge those who believe and wipe out the rejectors,"* (3:141), he would say, "O Allah, purge us and do not make us rejectors."

Ibn 'Awn said, "When they mentioned something bad about a man in Muhammad's presence, Muhammad would say the best that he knew about him."

Ibn 'Awn said, "Some people came to Muhammad and said, 'We have harmed you, so put us in the lawful.' He retorted, 'Nothing is lawful for you which Allah has made unlawful.'"

Ibn 'Awn said, "When Muhammad slept, he took account of himself." He said, "Sometimes he lay on his back."

Ibn 'Awn said, "We did not come to Muhammad on an *'Id* day but that he fed us a hotchpotch or *faludhaj* sweet on it, and he did not go out on the day of the *'Id al-Fitr* until he had commanded the *zakat* of Ramadan to be brought, put on perfume, and sent it to the general mosque. Then he went to the *'Id*."

Ibn 'Awn said, "Muhammad disliked reciting the Qur'an other than how it had been revealed. He disliked to recite it and then stop to comment and then return to reciting."

When Muhammad bade farewell to a man, he said, "Fear Allah and seek what has been decreed for you of the lawful. If you take it from the unlawful, you will not get any more than what has been decreed for you."

Hisham reported that Muhammad said, "They used to say that the Muslim is the one who is Muslim with the dirham."

Ibn 'Awn said, "Muhammad ibn Sirin used to bring me to the shop and men would come and he would show them the goods. Muhammad would say to them, 'If you like, I will take it to your house.' He took it to their house for them."

Tabi'un

Ibn 'Awn reported that when Muhammad ibn Sirin borrowed money, he weighed it against something and sealed it. When he paid it, he weighed it by that weight and then paid it back. Muhammad said, 'Measure can be less or more.'" He said, "When Ibn Sirin received any counterfeit or dud dirhams, he would not spend them. On the day he died he had five hundred dud and counterfeit coins."

Maymun ibn Mihran said, "I came to Kufa intending to buy clothes and I went to Muhammad ibn Sirin who was in Kufa that day and bargained with him. When he sold me a type of clothes, he asked, 'Are you satisfied?' I replied, 'Yes.' He repeated that to me three times. Then he summoned two men and made them witnesses to our transaction. Then he said, 'I will convey your goods.' He would not buy or sell with Hajjaji dirhams.[1] When I saw his scrupulousness, I bought everything I needed which I found with him, even striped garments."

Abu Hilal said, "I saw Muhammad ibn Sirin go out and he was wearing a loose garment tied at his neck and he sat in the mosque."

Muhammad said, "Sa'id ibn Jubayr was afraid that he would do what he did and then went to Makka to give *fatwas* to people."

Yahya ibn 'Atiq reported that Muhammad used to dislike making an agreement with the *Qassam* (the one who divides the inheritance). He said that he destested bribes for judgement, saying, "A judgement for which they take a wage."

Ibn 'Awn said that 'Umar ibn 'Abdu'l-'Aziz sent for al-Hasan and he accepted, and he sent for Ibn Sirin and he did not accept.

Hammad ibn Zayd said, "Hisham ibn Hassan circumcised his son and invited those in error from the family of al-Muhallab.[2] Muhammad was asked, 'Do you see what Abu 'Abdullah has done?' He replied, 'Do not reproach Abu 'Abdullah. Do not reproach Abu 'Abdullah.'"

Ghalib said, "I went to Muhammad and mentioned his state of health and asked him about Hisham. He replied, 'He passed away yesterday. Don't you know?' I said, *'To Allah We belong and to Him is our return'* (2:156), and he laughed."

---

1. Although the Hajjaji silver dirhams were held, even by the Abbasids, to be the purest coins in terms of silver content, many people objected to their use because they had an *ayat* of Qur'an on them and might either be touched by people who were impure or fall into the hands of unbelievers.

2. The family of Muhallab were headed by the governor in Khurasan, Yazid ibn al-Muhallab, who was on bad terms with al-Hajjaj. They formed two factions between whom there was great rivalry. Eventually he led a rebellion in Basra, in which he called for *jihad* against the Syrians, in 101/720. He was killed in battle.

Basra

Mahdi ibn Maymun said, "I saw Muhammad doing *wudu'*. His washing of his feet for *wudu'* reached his leg muscles."

Qurra ibn Khalid said, "I saw Muhammad sweep the mosque with his garment."

Qurra and Hisham said that engraved on the ring of Muhammad ibn Sirin was his *kunya*, 'Abu Bakr'.

Mahdi ibn Maymun said, "I saw Ibn Sirin wearing a silver ring on his left hand."

Ibn 'Awn said, "I set out with Ibn Sirin when he went to 'Umar ibn Hubayra [the governor]. When the prayer time came, he said to me, 'Go forward and lead us in the prayer.' So I led the prayer. I thought to him, 'Did you not say that no one is advanced except for one who knows all the Qur'an? Why then did you advance me?' Then I said, 'I have done something which Muhammad disliked to do himself.' I mentioned that to him and he said, 'I dislike to put myself forward so that people say, "This is Muhammad who sets himself in front of the people."'"

Muhammad said, "They disliked stepping over people's necks on *Jumu'a*." He said, "They say that Ibn Sirin steps over people's necks. I do not step over people's necks, but I come and a man will recognise me and make room for me so I will pass. Then another will recognise me and make room for me and I will pass."

Bakkar ibn Muhammad said, "I went to the mosque of Muhammad ibn Sirin, the mosque of Anas, and the mosque of Hafsa at al-'Aranis al-Mu'arra in Sirin's house which neither child nor anyone else entered."

Thabit al-Bunani said, "One of al-Hasan's daughters died and I went to him and he said, "Do this. Do that." I hoped that he would tell me to pray over her. He said, 'When you bring her out, tell Muhammad ibn Sirin to pray over her.'"

Muhammad ibn 'Amr said, "I heard Muhammad ibn Sirin say, 'I became abstemious after being a man of affluence.'"

Mahdi ibn Maymun said, "I saw Ibn Sirin wearing a shawl, and he wore a white outer wrapper in the winter and a white turban and fur."

Sulayman ibn al-Mughira said, "I saw Muhammad ibn Sirin wearing Yemeni garments and shawls and turbans."

Abu Khulda said, "I saw Muhammad ibn Sirin wearing an untwisted white turban whose end hung down behind."

Abu'l-Ashhab said, "I saw Ibn Sirin wearing cotton garments."

Muhammad ibn Sirin mentioned that Anas ibn Malik said, "I asked about the use of hair-dye by the Messenger of Allah ﷺ." He said, "The Messenger of Allah ﷺ did not reach the age for that, but Abu Bakr dyed his hair with henna and privet." Ibn Sirin added, "I use henna and privet dye today."

Abu Khulda said, "Muhammad ibn Sirin used to say to the tailor when he sewed leather socks for him, 'Do not moisten the thread with your spit.'"

Muhammad ibn 'Amr said, "I saw that Ibn Sirin did not overclip his moustache as some people do."

Muhammad ibn Sirin commanded Suwayd to make him a robe in which he would be shrouded.

Ibn 'Awn said, "The will of Ibn Sirin stated: 'Muhammad ibn Abi 'Amra commands his sons and his family to fear Allah, put right their mutual relations, and to obey Allah and His Messenger if they are believers. He commends to them what Ibrahim commended to his sons and Ya'qub: *"My sons! Allah has chosen this deen for you, so do not die except as Muslims who submit."* (2:132) He commends to them not to fail to be brothers of the Ansar and their clients in the *deen*. Chasteness and truthfulness are better and more lasting and more honourable than fornication and lies.'"

Muhammad ibn Sirin's son, 'Abdullah, said, "When I acted as guarantor for my father's debts, he said to me, 'Faithfully?' I replied, 'Faithfully.' So he prayed for good for me."

Bakkar ibn Muhammad said that 'Abdullah ibn Muhammad ibn Sirin settled debts of 30,000 dirhams his father owed. 'Abdullah ibn Muhammad did not die until we had assessed his property to be worth about 300,000 dirhams.

Ayyub reported that Muhammad used to command that buttons and hems be sewn on the shirt of the deceased.

Hisham reported that Muhammad said, "Give it buttons but do not button it up." Ayyub said, "I put on buttons for Muhammad."

Hammad ibn Zayd said, "Muhammad died on Friday and Ayyub and Ibn 'Awn washed him. I do not know who was with them."

Muhammad ibn Sa'd said that Mansur said, "Muhammad ibn Sirin died a hundred days after al-Hasan. That was in 110 AH." Bakkar ibn Muhammad said, "Muhammad ibn Sirin died at about the age of 80."

Ma'bad ibn Sirin

He was older than Muhammad ibn Sirin, being the eldest of the brothers. He was reliable. He related *hadiths* and listened to the son of Abu Sa'id al-Khudri.

Muhammad said, "Ma'bad and Anas ibn Sirin, 'Amra bint Sirin, and Sawda bint Sirin were children of the *umm walad* of Anas ibn Malik who relinquished her in favour of him and married her to him. Anas ibn Malik had two children by her, Ma'bad and Umm Hiram.

Yahya ibn Sirin

He was the half brother of Muhammad ibn Sirin on the mother's side. Their mother was Safiyya.

Bakkar ibn Muhammad said, "I heard that Sirin sent his sons to Abu Hurayra. When they arrived, his son Yahya took care of them. So Abu Hurayra gave him his *kunya* since he took care of them. He was reliable with few *hadiths*. He died in Jarjaraya and his grave is there. He died before Muhammad ibn Sirin.

Hafsa bint Sirin said, "Anas said to me, 'How did Yahya ibn Sirin die?' I replied, 'Of the plague.' He said, 'The plague is martyrdom for every Muslim.'"

Anas ibn Sirin

His *kunya* was Abu Hamza. He was named after Anas ibn Malik and given his *kunya*. In some of the *hadiths* of Hammad ibn Zayd his *kunya* is given as Abu Musa. He was reliable with few *hadiths*.

Anas ibn Sirin said, "When I was born, my father took me to Anas ibn Malik and I was given his name and *kunya*."

Anas ibn Sirin said, "I was born in the last year of the khalifate of 'Uthman ibn 'Affan."

Qatada said, "Ibn az-Zubayr appointed Anas ibn Malik over Basra and he sent for Anas ibn Sirin to put him in charge of the taxes of Ubulla. Anas ibn Sirin said, 'Do you mean to appoint me as a customs collector?' He asked him, 'Are you content with what 'Umar ibn al-Khattab wrote in his letter?' He brought it out and in it he said to take one dirham for every forty from Muslim merchants, and one dirham from every twenty from the people of the *dhimma*, and one dirham from every ten from the merchants of the abode of war. Anas ibn Sirin died after Muhammad ibn Sirin.

Abu Nadra

His name was al-Mundhir ibn Malik ibn Quta'a. He was from 'Awaqa, a sub-tribe of Qays. He was reliable, Allah willing, with many *hadiths*. Not every one accepted him as an authority.

Shu'ba said, "Sulayman at-Taymi and Ibn 'Awn came to me to commiserate with me over the death of my mother. Sulayman said, 'Abu Nadra related to us.' Ibn 'Awn said, 'I saw Abu Nadra.' Sulayman said, 'I did not see him.'"

Abu Nadra's uncle said, "Al-Mu'aththira bint Arbak related to me that Abu Nadra went on an expedition to Khurasan with his wife Zaynab."

Salih ibn Rashid and others relate that they saw Abu Nadra dye his beard yellow. He said, "I saw Abu Nadra wearing a black turban."

Mahdi ibn Maymun said, "When Abu Nadra died, I saw al-Hasan lead us in the funeral prayer. Then *Dhuhr* came and he also led us in the prayer at al-Jabbana, and there was no *sutra* in front of him and the graves were on his right and left. Abu Nadra died while 'Umar ibn Hubayra was governor.

Sa'd ibn Hisham ibn 'Amr al-Ansari

Sa'd ibn Hisham said, "I visited 'A'isha and I told her my lineage and she asked, 'The son of the one killed in the Battle of Uhud?' I replied, 'Yes.'"

They say that Sa'd ibn Hisham was reliable, Allah willing.

'Alqama ibn 'Abdullah al-Muzani

He was reliable with few *hadiths*. He died while 'Umar ibn 'Abdu'l-'Aziz was khalif.

Bakr ibn 'Abdullah al-Muzani

He was not the brother of 'Alqama, He was firm, reliable and trustworthy with many *hadiths*. He was an authority and he was a *faqih*.

Mu'tamir said, "My father used to say, 'Al-Hasan is the shaykh of Basra and Bakr is its *mufti*.'"

'Abdullah ibn Bakr said, "My sister, Umm 'Abdullah bint Bakr said that she heard her father Bakr say, 'I resolved that I would not listen to any mention of *Qadar* without standing and praying two *rak'ats*.'"

Abu 'Abdullah said that Bakr was standing at 'Arafat and he was overwhelmed by a feeling of compassion and said, "If it were not that I was standing among you at 'Arafat, I would ask forgiveness for you."

Bakr al-Muzani said, "Beware of certain words. If you are correct in them, you will not be rewarded, and if you are wrong, you will incur a burden. That is a bad opinion of your brother."

Bakr ibn 'Abdullah al-Muzani said, "When a man keeps your company and his sandal strap breaks and you do not wait for him to mend his strap, then you are not his companion. If when he sits to urinate, you do not wait for him to finish, you are not his companion." Al-Hasan used to call Bakr 'the shrewd'.

When Bakr was made a qadi, he said, "I will inform you about myself with a report and you should investigate. Allah is the One other than Whom there is no god but Him. I have no knowledge of judgement. If I am telling the truth, it is not fitting for you to appoint me. If I am a liar, then it is not appropriate for you to appoint a liar."

Bakr said, "I hope to live the life of the rich and die the death of the poor." It was like that. So he donned his garment and then he went to the poor people and sat with them to speak to them. He said that they were delighted by that.

Mu'tamir said that he heard his father mention that Bakr ibn 'Abdullah's robe was worth 4000 dirhams and that his mother was wealthy. She had a husband with a lot of wealth. He used to dislike to refuse her anything.

Kulthum ibn Jawshan said, "Bakr ibn 'Abdullah purchased a shawl for 400 dirhams and the tailor wanted to cut it. He began to spread dust on it, and Bakr said to him, 'As you were,' and he commanded that camphor be ground and sprinkled on it."

Bakr ibn 'Abdullah al-Muzani was heard to say in his supplication, "I cannot hope for nor defend myself against what I dislike. My affair is in the hand of Someone else, and there is no poor man poorer than me." Then he said, "Son of Adam, have hope although you are not safe from the scheme of Allah. Be kind and you will not be alienated from the mercy of Allah."

Bakr ibn 'Abdullah said in his supplication, "O Allah, grant us from Your bounty a provision by which You will increase us in thankfulness to You, poverty and need of You, and independence and restraint from what is other than You."

Abu Hilal said, "On a Friday, the people visited Bakr when he was ill and sat with him. Bakr said, 'A sick person is visited and the healthy person is called upon.'"

Ziyad ibn Abi Muslim said, "I saw Bakr ibn 'Abdullah use black hair dye."

Mu'ammal ibn Isma'il said that Bakr ibn 'Abdullah died in 106 AH. Others said that he died in 108 AH, and I consider that to be more reliable.

Mubarak ibn Fadala said, "Al-Hasan attended the funeral of Bakr ibn 'Abdullah while he was on a donkey. He saw the people crowding and said, 'They are not burdened with more than what they are rewarded for.' The people were waiting. If they managed to carry the bier, their brothers followed them."

Abu 'Abdullah al-Jasri

He was from a sub-tribe of 'Anaza. He was famous with few *hadiths*. He related from Ma'qil ibn Yasar.

Sinan ibn Salama al-Hudhali

He was famous with few *hadiths*. He died at the end of the governorship of al-Hajjaj ibn Yusuf in Iraq.

His brother, Musa ibn Salama

He had few *hadiths*. He related from Ibn 'Abbas, and Qatada related from him.

'Abdullah ibn Rabah al-Ansari

He was reliable with *hadiths*.

Khalid ibn Sumayr as-Sadusi said, "'Abdullah ibn Rabah al-Ansari came to us in Basra. The Ansar had taught him *fiqh*."

'Abdullah ibn as-Samit

He was the son of the brother of Abu Dharr al-Ghifari. His *kunya* was Abu'n-Nadra. He was reliable with *hadiths*.

Abu Sa'id ar-Raqqashi

His name was Qays, the client of Husayn ibn al-Mundhir ar-Raqqashi. Abu Sa'id had few *hadiths* and he related from Ibn 'Abbas.

Unays Abu'l-'Uryan

He was with Muhammad ibn 'Ali ibn al-Hanafiyya among the people [i.e. with al-Mukhtar].

Abu Labid

His name was Lammaza ibn Zabbar al-Azdi then al-Jahdami. He listened to 'Ali. He is reliable with *hadiths*.

Muwarriq ibn al-Mushmarij al-'Ijli

His *kunya* was Abu'l-Mu'tamir. He was reliable and a man of worship.

Al-Mu'alla ibn Ziyad said, "Muwarriq al-'Ijli said, 'There is something I have been seeking for ten years and which I have not been capable of, but will not ever abandon seeking.' He was asked, 'What is it, Abu'l-Mu'tamir?' He replied, 'Silence about what does not concern me.'"

Muwarriq al-'Ijli said, "I studied silence for ten years."

Muwarriq said, "I rarely become angry and sometimes a year passes in which I do not become angry. When I am angry, rarely do I say anything that I might regret when I am pleased."

Muwarriq said, "I have never been filled with anger. I have asked Allah for something for about twenty years, and it has not been granted but I am not weary of supplication."

Hafsa bint Sirin said, "Muwarriq used to visit us. One day he visited us and greeted us and I returned the greeting to him. Then he asked after me and I asked after him. I said, 'How are your family and your children?' He replied, 'They are amply cared for.' I said, 'I praise Allah, your Lord.' He said, 'By Allah, I fear that their reckoning might entail destruction.'"

Sa'id al-Jurayri said, "Muwarriq al-'Ijli passed by a gathering in the district and he greeted them and they returned the greeting to him. A man from the area asked him. 'Is everything all right with you?' He replied, 'I only wish a tenth of it was in order.'" Muwarriq remarked, "Their conversation entailed insinuation."

Yazid al-'Araj ash-Shanni said that a man said to Muwarriq al-'Ijli, "Abu'l-Mu'tamir, I complain to you of my self. I cannot pray or fast." He replied, "Evil is what you praise of yourself! If you are too weak to do good, then you are too weak to do evil. I rejoice in a sleep that I sleep."

Muwarriq said, "I do not find any more apt metaphor for the believer in this world except that of a man clinging to a piece of wood in the sea saying, 'O Lord! O Lord!' Perhaps Allah will rescue him."

Muwarriq al-'Ijli said, "The one who holds to obedience to Allah when the people withdraw from it is like the one who returns to the fight after a retreat."

Muwarriq said, "There is no soul on the earth for whose death I will receive a reward but that I wish that he would die." Hammad said, "His mother was still alive."

Mu'tamir said that his father told him that Muwarriq used to delouse his mother.

Musa Abu Muhammad said, "Sometimes Muwarriq would visit some of his brothers and leave some dirhams with them. He would say, 'Keep them until I return to you.' When he left he said, 'You are in the lawful regarding them.'"

Jamil ibn Murra said, "Muwarriq used to come to take us to his family in Basra at Sura. He would say, 'Keep this for us. If you need it, then spend it.' It was the last trust he made."

Muwarriq al-'Ijli engaged in trade and received money. Whenever it was Friday and he had some of it, he would meet a brother of his and give him 400, or 500, or 300, and say, 'Keep it for us until we need it.' Then he would meet him later and say, 'Do what you wish with it.' The other would reply, 'We have no need of it.' He would say, 'By Allah, we will never take it back. Do what you want with it.'

A woman called Maymuna bint Madh'ur said, "Muwarriq al-'Ijli dropped in on us and a slave of ours cooked some eggs for him in a small pot. Muwarriq asked him, 'What is this pot?' He replied, 'Something left as a pledge with me.' Muwarriq said to him, 'Can you not use this for your eggs?' He disliked using a pledge."

Muwarriq al-'Ijli said, "He disliked selling the resale with fixed gain, 'eleven for ten' or 'twelve for ten'."

Ghaylan ibn Jarir said, "Al-Hajjaj put Muwarriq in prison. Mutarrif met me and said, 'What have you done with your companion?' I replied, 'He is in prison.' He said, 'Come and let us make supplication.' So Mutarrif made a supplication and we said 'Amen' to his supplication. In the evening al-Hajjaj went out and sat and gave permission to the people to come to him. Muwarriq's father came in among those who went and al-Hajjaj said, 'Take this shaykh to the prison and give him his son.'" They said that Muwarriq died while 'Umar ibn Hubayra was governor of Iraq.

Abu Mijlaz

His name was Lahiq ibn Humayd as-Sadusi. He was reliable and had *hadiths*. He died while 'Umar ibn 'Abdu'l-'Aziz was governor, before the death of al-Hasan al-Basri.

'Abdu'l-Malik ibn Ya'la al-Laythi

He was the Qadi in Basra before al-Hasan. He died while 'Umar ibn 'Abdu'l-'Aziz was khalif.

Ghazwan ibn Ghazwan ar-Raqqashi

He was excellent, a man of worship. Anas reported that Ghazwan did not laugh. Abu Musa said to him, "Ghazwan, I have heard that you do not laugh." He replied, "'Ha-ha'. What do I do with this?"

Yunus ibn 'Ubayd said that Ghazwan ar-Raqqashi used to recite from the Qur'an a lot. He had an old ignorant mother. One day she said to him, "Ghazwan, do you find in it a camel of ours that strayed in the *Jahiliyya*?" He did not condemn her or chide her, but said, "Mother, by Allah, I find a good promise in it."

It is mentioned that Ghazwan did not laugh for forty years. Ghazwan used to go on expeditions. When the companies returned, his mother would meet them and say to them, "Do you know Ghazwan?" They said, "Woe to you, old woman! He is the master of the people!"

Al-'Ala' ibn Ziyad al-'Adawi

He was from the Banu 'Adi. He was reliable with *hadiths*.

Al-'Ala' ibn Ziyad said that his father, Ziyad ibn Matar, left a will: "If anything happens to me, see what the *fuqaha'* of the people of Basra command and then do it." They agreed on the fifth, meaning in the will.

Abu Khulda said, "I saw al-'Ala' ibn Ziyad dye his beard yellow." Al-'Ala' died when al-Hajjaj was governor of Iraq.

Abu Hibara ad-Duba'i

His name was Shaykha ibn 'Abdullah. He related from 'Ali ibn Abi Talib. He had few *hadiths*.

Abu'l-Malih al-Hudhali

His name was 'Amir ibn Usama ibn 'Umayr. He was reliable with *hadiths*. Ayyub and others related from him. He died in 112 AH.

One of his children said, "Abu'l-Malih died about a year before al-Hasan." Al-Hasan attended his funeral.

Ibn 'Awn said that Abu'l-Malih was an administrator of Ubulla and attended the *Jumu'a* in Basra.

Abu'l-'Aliyya al-Qaysi said that Abu'l-Malih left a will requesting that when he died they take some of his moustache and nails.

Yazid ibn Hurmuz al-Farisi

The client of the Daws tribe. He was the commander of the clients in the Battle of al-Harra. He was reliable, Allah willing.

'Umayr ibn Ishaq

One of the people of Madina. He then moved to Basra and stayed there. The Basrans, Ibn 'Awn and others, related from him. None of the people of Madina related anything from him. 'Umayr ibn Ishaq related from Abu Hurayra and others.

Ibn 'Awn reported that 'Umayr ibn Ishaq said, "I met more of the Companions of the Prophet ﷺ than those before me. I did not see any people with more gentle behaviour or who were less harsh than they were."

Abu Yazid al-Madani

He was one of the people of Madina who moved to Basra, and the Basrans, 'Awf and others related from him. He related from Ibn 'Abbas and others.

Mu'awiya ibn Qurra ibn Iyas

His *kunya* was Abu Iyas. He was reliable with *hadiths*.

Khalid al-Hadhdha' said, "Mu'awiya ibn Qurra was asked, 'How does your son behave towards you?' He replied, 'He is an excellent son. He spared me worldly matters and freed me for the Next World.'"

'Abdullah ibn Burayda ibn al-Husayb al-Aslami

'Abdullah ibn Burayda said, "I was born in the last three years of 'Umar's khalifate." He and his brother Sulayman were twins. He said, "A slave of ours went to my father while he was sitting with 'Umar ibn al-Khattab and said, 'A boy has been born to you,' meaning 'Abdullah. He said, 'You are free.' Then another slave came and said, 'A boy has been born to you.' He said, 'So-and-so came before you.' He said, 'It is another.' 'Umar said, 'This,' meaning he should free him."

Ibn Burayda's *kunya* was Abu Sahl. They said that Abu Burayda related from his father and from 'Abdullah ibn 'Umar.

His brother, Sulayman ibn Burayda

He related from his father. Wukay' reported that they said that Sulayman ibn Burayda was the sounder and more reliable of the two in *hadith*.

Yusuf ibn Mihran

He related from Ibn 'Abbas. He was reliable. 'Ali ibn Zayd mentioned Yusuf ibn Mihran and said, "His memory resembles that of 'Amr ibn Dinar."

Abu'l-Jald al-Jawni

Jawn is a subtribe of Azd. His name was Jilan ibn Farwa. He was reliable.

Abu 'Imran said that Abu'l-Jald used to read books.

Maymuna bint Abi'l-Jald said, "My father used to recite the Qur'an every seven days and he read the Torah in six days. The day he finished it, he gathered together people for that. He said, 'It used to be said that mercy descends at the end of it.'"

Abu's-Salil al-Qaysi

His name was Durayb ibn Nuqayr. He was one of the Banu Qays. He was reliable, Allah willing.

Bashir ibn Nahik as-Sadusi

He was reliable. He related from Abu Hurayra and Bashir ibn al-Khassasiyya. Bashir ibn Nahik said, "I brought Abu Hurayra my book which I had written out and I read it to him and said, 'This is what I heard from you.' He said, 'Yes.'"

Abu'l-Jawza' ar-Rab'i'

'Amr ibn Malik an-Nukri said that the name of Abu'l-Jawza' was Aws ibn Khalid ar-Rab'i.

Al-Mustamirr ibn ar-Rayyan said, "I saw Abu'l-Jawza' ar-Rab'i dye his beard yellow."

'Amr ibn Malik an-Nukri said that Abu'l-Jawza' did not curse anything at all and did not ever eat anything that had been cursed. He said, "To such an extent that he used to bribe the servant with a dirham or two a month so that he would not curse the food which the oven had burned."

'Amr also said, "Abu'l-Jawza' was one of the most meticulous people in avoiding impurities. He had two separate garments: one for the prayer and another garment for the lavatory. Then later I saw him with two Marw garments and I asked, 'What is this, Abu'l-Jawza'?' He replied, 'I looked into the matter and it was easier than the position I had taken.'"

Abu'l-Jawza' said, mentioning the people of sects, "By the One Who has my soul in His name, I would prefer to fill my house with monkeys and to have pigs for my neighbours than to be a neighbour of one of them."

Abu'l-Jawza' said, "I have never cursed anything at all nor eaten anything cursed and I have never disputed with anyone at all."

'Amr ibn Malik said, "Abu'l-Jawza' did not ever curse anything, nor eat anything which had been cursed, and he never called a man a liar, and he never sat in shops."

Abu'l-Jawza' said, "I lived with Ibn 'Abbas in his house for twelve years during which there was no *ayat* of the Qur'an which I did not ask him about." They said that Abu'l-Jawza' went out with Ibn al-Ash'ath and was killed in the Battle of Dayr al-Jamajam in 83 AH.

'Abdullah ibn Ghalib

Al-Qasim ibn al-Fadl said, "I saw 'Abdullah ibn Ghalib come to Ibn al-Ash'ath when Ibn al-Ash'ath was on an iron minbar at az-Zawiya with 40 men in shrouds and funeral-perfume. Each man had a sword and shield. 'Abdullah ibn Ghalib went up to him and said, 'Extend your hand. On what basis do I offer you allegiance?' He said, 'On the Book of Allah and the *Sunna* of His Prophet.' So he wiped his palm against his and then threw away his shield, saying, 'No, by Allah, I will not put a shield between me and the people of Syria today!' He fought until he was killed."

'Uqba ibn 'Abdu'l-Ghafir

His *kunya* was Abu Nahar al-Azdi.

Thabit said, "There was no one in whose skin I would rather have been other than 'Uqba ibn 'Abdu'l-Ghafir. Then when the *fitna* occurred, we went to him and he said, 'I do not know you.'"

Murra ibn ad-Dabbab said, "I passed by 'Uqba ibn 'Abdu'l-Ghafir when he was lying wounded in the ditch when the people were routed. He called out to me, 'Abu'l-Mu'adhdhil! Abu'l-Mu'adhdhil!' I turned to him and he said, 'This world and the Next are lost!' That was in the time of Ibn al-Ash'ath."

Abu's-Siddiq an-Naji

His name was Bakr ibn 'Amr. They say things about his *hadiths* and object to them.

Abu Ayyub al-Azdi, then al-Muraghi

His name was Yahya ibn Malik. He was reliable and trustworthy. Qatada related from him.

Talq ibn Habib al-'Anazi

He was one of the people of Basra. He moved to Makka and was a Murji'ite. He was reliable, Allah willing. He related from Ibn 'Abbas and Jabir ibn 'Abdullah.

Yusuf ibn al-Harith said, "I saw Talq ibn Habib when Humayd ibn 'Abdu'r-Rahman al-Himyari said, 'Talq, I see that you are grey-haired.' He said, 'Yes, Allah has blessed me in it.'"

'Abdullah ibn Habib said that Talq used to delouse his mother.

Ayyub said, "Sa'id ibn Jubayr said to me, 'Do not sit with Talq.'"

Ayyub said, "Sa'id ibn Jubayr saw me sitting with Talq ibn Habib and he said, 'Did I see you sit with him? Do not sit with him!' He used to espouse the position of the Murji'ites."

'Abdu'r-Rahman ibn Jawshan al-Ghatafani

He is Abu 'Uyayna ibn 'Abdu'r-Rahman.

'Abdu'r-Rahman said, "In this mosque I met eighteen of the Companions of the Prophet ﷺ," meaning in the Basra mosque.

✻✻✻✻✻

Other men of knowledge of this generation include: **Jubayr ibn Abi Hayya**, who is Abu Ziyad ibn Jubay, and related from al-Mughira ibn Shu'ba; **Khalid ibn Ghallaq al-'Abasi** who had few *hadiths*; **Mudarib ibn Hazn**, one of the Banu Mazin with few *hadiths* who related from Abu Hurayra; **al-Hakam ibn al-'Araj**, who related from Ibn 'Abbas and has *hadiths*; **Hanzala ibn Sawada**, who saw 'Ali, and dyed his beard yellow; **Rufay' Abu Kabir**, who listened to 'Ali; **'Umar ibn Jawan,** who was one of the Banu Sa'd of Tamim and Abu 'Awana called him 'Amr ibn Jawan; **Abu Na'ama al-Hanafi**, who is Qays ibn 'Abaya who related from al-Jurayri and Kahmas; **Abu Na'ama as-Sa'di**, from whom 'Abdu Rabbih, Ayyub, Hammad ibn Salama and Shu'ba related; **Abu Na'ama as-Sa'di**, who is 'Awf ibn Qays, the uncle of 'Utiy ibn Damra; **Abu Mus'ab** al-Mazini, who is Hilal ibn Yazid, who related from Abu Hurayra; **Abu Hassan al-A'raj**, whose name was Muslim and was reliable, Allah willing; **Bushayr ibn Ka'b al-'Abdi**, who was reliable, Allah willing; **Abu'l-Mutawakkil an-Naji**, or 'Ali ibn Dawud; **Abu Hunayda al-'Adawi**, or al-Barra' ibn Nawfal, who was famous but had few *hadiths*; **Abu Harb ibn Abi'l-Aswad ad-Du'ali**, who was famous and had *hadiths*; **Abu'l-Ward ibn Thumama al-Qushayri**, who was famous and had *hadiths*; **Abu Salih**, whose name was Qayluwayh and from whom Yahya ibn Abi Kathir related; **Waqi' ibn Sahban**, from whom Qatada related and had few *hadiths*; **Abu'z-Zinba'**, whose name was Sadaqa ibn Salih; **Kinana ibn Nu'aym al-'Adawi**, who was famous and reliable, Allah willing; and **Talha ibn 'Ubaydullah al-Khuza'i**, who had few *hadiths*.

✲✲✲✲✲

The Third Generation

Qatada ibn Di'ama as-Sadusi

His *kunya* was Abu'l-Khattab. He was reliable and trustworthy, an authority in *hadith*. He used to say something about *Qadar*.

Qatada said, "Memorising in youth is like engraving in stone."

Abu Hilal said, "I asked Qatada about a problem and he said, 'I do not know.' I said, 'State what your opinion is.' He said, 'I have not stated my opinion for forty years.'" He was asked how old he was then and he said, "Fifty."

Shu'ba said, "I recognised in Qatada's *hadith* what he had not actually heard. When he gave us what he had actually heard, he would say, 'Anas ibn Malik related to us; al-Hasan related to us; Sa'id related to us; Mutarrif related to us.' When he quoted what he had not actually heard he would say, 'Sa'd ibn Jubayr said; Abu Qilaba said.'"

Qatada said, "I stayed with al-Hasan for twelve years and I prayed *Subh* with him for three years." He said, "The like of me took from the like of him."

Qatada said, "When you trace the *hadith* in an assembly, you remove its light. No one traced them for me," meaning those from whom he listened.

Third Generation

Qatada said to Sa'id ibn Abi 'Aruba, "Abu'n-Nadr, take the copy of the Qur'an." He read *Surat al-Baqara* to him, and did not err in a single letter of it. He said, "Abu'n-Nadr, you have mastered it well." He replied, "Yes." He said "No, by the page Jabir ibn 'Abdullah recalls *Surat al-Baqara* better than me." It used to be read to him.

Az-Zuhri was asked, "Who do you consider has more knowledge, Qatada or Makhul?" He replied, "Qatada. Makhul only had a little."

Ma'mar said, "We used to sit with Qatada when we were beginners and we asked about the *isnad*. His shaykhs around him said, 'Stop! Abu'l-Khattab is an *isnad*,' and they stopped us doing that."

Abu Hilal said, "Qatada was asked, 'Abu'l-Khattab, should we write what we hear?' He replied, 'No one will prevent you from writing when the All-Subtle, All-Aware has informed you that He wrote and read *'in a Book with My Lord who does not misplace nor does He forget.'* (20:52)"

'Imran ibn 'Abdullah said, "When Qatada came to Sa'id ibn al-Musayyab, he began to question him over the course of several days. Sa'id asked him, 'Do you remember all that you ask me?' He replied, 'Yes. I asked you about such-and-such and you said such-and-such about it. I asked you about such-and-such and you said such-and-such about it. Al-Hasan said such-and-such about it,' and he continued until he had repeated a great deal to him. Sa'id said, 'I did not think that Allah had created anyone like you.'"

Salam said, "There were questions he had studied before with al-Hasan and others and he asked him about them."

Ma'mar said that Qatada stayed with Sa'id ibn al-Musayyab for eight days. On the eighth day he said to him, "Travel on, blind man, you have drained me!"

'Affan ibn Muslim said, "Qatada used to use the words of Sa'id ibn al-Musayyab for analogy and then he related it from Sa'id ibn al-Musayyab." He said, "That is, a little."

Hammam said, "Vowel the *hadith*. Qatada did not use ungrammatical Arabic. When you see a grammatical error in his *hadith*, rectify it."

Hammad ibn Salama said, "We used to go to Qatada and he would say, 'We conveyed from the Prophet, peace be upon him; we conveyed from 'Umar, and we conveyed from 'Ali.' He almost did not use an *isnad*. When Hammad ibn Abi Sulayman came to Basra, he began to say, 'Ibrahim reported and so-and-so and so-and-so.' Qatada heard that and began to say, 'I asked Mutarrif; I asked Sa'id ibn al-Musayyab; Anas ibn Malik reported to me;' and he reported the *isnad*."

Qurra ibn Khalid said, "I saw Qatada's seal on his left hand."

Isma'il ibn 'Ulayya said that Qatada died in 118 AH. Sa'id ibn Bashir said that he died in 117 AH.

Humayd ibn Hilal al-'Adawi

His *kunya* was Abu Nasr. He was reliable.

Qatada was heard to say, "There was no man with more knowledge in Basra than Humayd ibn Hilal – and I do not exclude Muhammad or al-Hasan – although his residence there was imperfect," meaning that he actually lived at Dawlab in Ahwaz.

Sulayman ibn al-Mughira said, "I saw Humayd ibn Hilal wearing Yemeni garments, shawls and turbans." He died while Khalid ibn 'Abdullah was governor of Iraq.

Thabit ibn Aslam al-Bunani

Bunana is connected to Quraysh. His *kunya* was Abu Muhammad.

Anas said, "Everything has a key and Thabit is one of the keys of good."

Humayd said, "We used to go to Anas with Thabit. Whenever Thabit passed by a mosque, he would enter it and pray in it. We would go to Anas and he would ask, 'Where is Thabit? Thabit is a receptacle I love.'"

Thabit said, "I prefer to commit a wrong action, even if it is great, and ask Allah's forgiveness for it until I abandon it, than to commit a small wrong action for which I do not ask Allah's forgiveness until I abandon it."

Thabit said, "The worshipper is not a worshipper even if he possesses every good quality until he has these two qualities: prayer and fasting." Thabit said, "That is because, by Allah, they are part of his flesh and blood."

Sulayman ibn al-Mughira heard Thabit say, "By Allah, worship is harder than moving bales."

Hammad ibn Salama said, "Thabit and Humayd used to bathe and put on perfume and sprinkle perfume in the mosque on the night on which it was was hoped that it was the Night of Power [27 Ramadan]."

Hammad ibn Salama said that Thabit used to recite: *"Do you reject Him Who created you from dust, then from a drop of sperm?"* (18:37), while he was praying the night prayer, and he would weep and keep repeating it.

Thabit said, "It used to be said, 'There is no one who remembers death a lot but that it is seen in his actions.'"

Thabit said, "If it were not that you would do to me what you did to al-Hasan, I would recount pleasant stories to you." Then he said, "They denied him the midday nap. They denied him sleep."

Sulayman ibn al-Mughira said, "I saw Thabit al-Bunani wearing Yemeni garments, shawls and turbans."

Humayd said, "Thabit al-Bunani said to me, 'Wash me but do not scourge my skin.'" Thabit was trustworthy in *hadith* and he died while Khalid ibn 'Abdullah was governor of Iraq.

Bishr ibn Harb

His *kunya* was Abu 'Amr an-Nadabi. He was from Azd.

Bishr ibn Harb said, "I said to Ibn 'Umar, 'Engrave something from the Book of Allah on my ring.' He replied, 'No, by Allah, that is not a proper thing for you to do.'" So he engraved on it: "Bishr ibn Harb."

Bishr ibn Harb related from Rafi' ibn Khadij, Abu Sa'id al-Khudri and Samura. He was weak in *hadith*. He died while Yusuf ibn 'Umar was governor of Iraq.

Iyas ibn Mu'awiya ibn Qurra

His *kunya* was Abu Wa'ila. He was reliable. He was qadi of Basra and had *hadiths*. He was an intelligent and clever man.

Humayd reported, "When Iyas was appointed Qadi, al-Hasan went to him and Iyas wept."

Ibn 'Awn said, "Iyas was mentioned in Muhammad's presence, he said, 'He is a man of understanding.'"

Iyas ibn Mu'awiya said, "The person who does not recognise his fault is stupid." They said, "Abu Wa'la! What then is your fault?" He replied, "Superfluous words."

Sufyan ibn Husayn said, "When Iyas ibn Mu'awiya came to Wasit, they began to say, 'The Basran has come! The Basran has come!' Ibn Shubruma brought him some questions which he had prepared for him and he sat in front of him. He said, 'Will you give me permission to ask you about some things?' He replied, 'I had no misgivings about you until you asked my permission. If the question does not trouble the speaker nor harm those present, then ask.' So he asked about seventy topics and on that day they only disagreed about three or four which Iyas referred back to him and said, 'Ibn Shubruma, have you read the Qur'an?' He replied, 'Yes, from first to last.' He said, 'And have you read, *"Today I have perfected your deen for you and completed My blessing to you"* (5:3)?' He replied, 'Yes, and what is before it and after it.' He asked, 'Have you found that there remains anything which the family of Ibn Shubruma are seeking in it?' He said, 'No.' Iyas said to him, 'Practices have branches.' He mentioned fasting, the prayer, *hajj* and *jihad*. He said, 'I do not know that you are connected to any of the practices with anything better than the thing which is in your ability: to investigate opinion.'"

'Ali ibn Muhammad said, "Yusuf ibn 'Umar [the governor] caught Iyas ibn Mu'awiya and beat him."

'Asim al-Jahdari

One of the Banu Qays ibn Tha'laba.

Khalid al-Hadhdha' said that Iyas allowed the uncorroborated testimony of 'Asim al-Jahdari. The man said, "You allow the testimony of one man against me?" He said, 'He is "Asim! He is 'Asim!"

Abu Jamra ad-Duba'i

His name was Nasr ibn 'Imran. He was reliable. He died while Yusuf ibn 'Umar was governor of Iraq.

Abu Ghalib ar-Rasibi

The companion of Abu Umama al-Bahili. His name was Sa'id ibn al-Khazawwar. Some say that his name was Nafi'. He was weak and his *hadiths* objected to.

Abu Nawfal ibn Muslim al-Kinani

One of the Banu 'Urayj ibn Bakr. His name was Abu Nawfal Mu'awiya. He was reliable, Allah willing.

Abu Nawfal ibn Muslim said, "My father asked the Messenger of Allah ﷺ about fasting and it was the last of what he commanded him to do. He said, 'Fast three days of every month.'"

Abu'l-Muhazzim

His name was Yazid ibn Sufyan. Hammad ibn Salama related from him but Shu'ba considered him weak.

Shu'ba said, "I saw Abu'l-Muhazzim lying on the floor in the mosque of Thabit al-Bunani. If a man had offered him a penny, he would have related seventy *hadiths* to him."

Al-Muthanna ibn 'Abdullah

His mother was Kabsha ash-Shaybaniyya. Al-Muthanna was named after his great grandfather on his mother's side, al-Muthanna ibn Haritha ash-Shaybani.

'Abdullah ibn Muhammad ibn Sirin

Bakkar ibn Muhammad said that 'Abdullah ibn Muhammad ibn Sirin died in Makka in Rajab, 140 AH when he was 66.

'Amr ibn Sa'id

He was the client of Thaqif. He was reliable. Yunus ibn 'Ubayd related from him.

'Abdullah ibn al-Harith

He had few *hadiths*. Sulayman ibn Harb said that he was the son of Sirin's uncle.

Tawba al-'Anbari

His *kunya* was Abu'l-Muwarri'.

Tawba's son said that his name was Tawba ibn Kaysan and his family came from Sijistan. He was born in Yamana and grew up there. Then he moved to Basra. He was the client of Ayyub ibn Azhar al-'Adawi. Tawba's mother was Zabiyya bint Yazid ibn 'Uqayl. He went to the khalif, Sulayman ibn 'Abdu'l-Malik, and asked him to confirm two families for him in the stipend, give him permission to set up a bath-house in Basra and to dig a well in the desert, and he granted him that. It used to be the case that no one did that without the permission of the khalif. So he set up a bath-house beside his house in the Banu'l-'Anbar ar-Rabiyya, and he dug a well in the desert at al-Khirinq. There were three travel-stages between Basra and al-Khirinq. Then Tawba also went to 'Umar ibn 'Abdu'l-'Aziz when he was khalif.

Khabbab ibn 'Abdu'l-Akbar al-'Anbari said that when Tawba al-'Anbari came to 'Umar ibn 'Abdu'l-'Aziz, he saw his daughters playing around him wearing breeches.

Ishaq ibn Ibrahim said, "Tawba went to Hisham ibn 'Abdu'l-Malik and he sent him to Khurasan as an overseer over Asad ibn 'Abdullah, and then he sent him to Iraq and Yusuf ibn 'Umar appointed him over Sabur. Then he was appointed over Ahwaz. Then Yusuf was dismissed while Tawba was his governor over Ahwaz. Some people from the Banu'l-'Anbar tried to make Tawba claim to be among them but he refused. His uncles among the Banu Namir tried to make him claim to be among them and he refused. He had land in the desert and he died at Dabu' which is two days from Basra and was buried there. He was 74 when he died.

Muhammad ibn Wasi' ibn Jabir

One of the Banu Ziyad ibn Shams, a sub-tribe of Azd. The Banu Ziyad ibn Shams had four districts in Basra, including a district inside Bunana. People from the Banu'sh-Sha'ira' dominated it. They are the Sha'arun, the people who weave hair who have no lineage. The second is opposite the Banu Ghubar, the third opposite Hadad, and the fourth opposite al-Khurayba. Muhammad's *kunya* was Abu 'Abdullah. He died ten years after al-Hasan. He seems to have died in 120 AH.

Salam ibn Muti' said, "One day a man reported a *hadith* to Ayyub and Ayyub asked, 'Who reported this to you?' He replied, 'Muhammad ibn Wasi' reported it to me.' He exclaimed, 'Excellent!'

Then he asked, 'From whom?' He said, 'From so-and-so.' He said, 'Do not report it.'"

Sa'id ibn 'Amir said, "There was a quarrel between a son of Muhammad ibn Wasi' and a man who complained about him to his father. So Muhammad sent to his son, 'What are you then? By Allah, I only purchased your mother for 300 dirhams and as for your father, Allah has not had his like increased among the Muslims!'"

Various people said, "When Muhammad ibn Wasi' was very ill, his companions visited him. Harun ibn Ri'ab came after that and the people said, 'Harun, Abu'l-Hasan, make room for him.' So they made room for him and he sat in one side corner which they were in, neglecting Muhammad who was unconscious. Then he regained consciousness. He heard some of what they were saying and said, *The evil-doers will be recognised by their mark and seized hold of by their forelocks and their feet.* (55:41) My forelock and feet are taken together and I am thrown into the Fire – by Allah – nothing you say will help me. O my brothers, I will be taken – by Allah – from you to the Fire unless Allah forgives me.'"

Ishaq ibn Suwayd al-'Adawi

He was reliable, Allah willing. He died in the plague at the beginning of the khalifate of Abu'l-'Abbas as-Saffah in 131 AH.

Farqad ibn Ya'qub as-Sabakhi

His *kunya* was Abu Ya'qub. He was weak and his *hadiths* objected to. Hammad ibn Zayd said, "I asked Ayyub about Farqad and he said, 'He does not have *hadith*.'" They say that Farqad died during the plague in Basra in 131 AH.

Malik ibn Dinar

His *kunya* was Abu Yahya. He was the client of a woman of the Banu Sama ibn Lu'ayy. He was reliable with few *hadiths*. He used to write out copies of the Qur'an. He died shortly before the plague which occurred in 131 AH.

Harun ibn Ri'ab

One of the Banu Usayd ibn 'Amr. His *kunya* was Abu'l-Hasan. He was reliable with few *hadiths*. Sufyan ibn 'Uyayna related from Harun ibn Ri'ab, and he used to conceal his asceticism.

Kulthum ibn Jabr

He was famous and had *hadiths*. He related from Sa'id ibn Jubayr and Muslim ibn Yasar. His son said that his *kunya* was Abu Muhammad.

'Abdullah ibn Mutarrif

It is reported that his *kunya* was Abu Jaz'.

Thabit al-Bunani said, "''Abdullah ibn Mutarrif died and Mutarrif went out to his people wearing a fine garment. They became angry and said, 'Abu 'Abdullah! Allah has made 'Abdullah ibn Mutarrif die and you come out perfumed in this garment of yours!' Mutarrif said, 'Shall I abandon myself over it when Allah has promised me three qualities for my affliction, and each of them is dearer to me than all of this world? Allah says: *"The people who, when disaster hits them, say, 'We belong to Allah and we return to Him.' They are the people who have blessings and mercy from their Lord. It is they who are the guided."* (2:156-157) Shall I abandon myself over it after this?'"

Mutarrif said, "There is nothing which I will be given in the next World, even as little as a jug of water, but that I wish that I could have it in this world."

'Ata' ibn Abi Maymuna

He used to espouse the *Qadariyya* position. He died after the plague in Basra which was in 131 AH.

'Abdu'l-'Aziz ibn Suhayb

He was called 'Abdu'l-'Aziz ibn al-'Abd, the client of Anas ibn Malik. He was reliable.

Abu Harun al-'Abadi

His name was 'Umara ibn Juwayn. He was weak in *hadith*. He related from Abu Sa'id al-Khudri.

Musa ibn Salim

Abu Jahdam, the client of the Banu Hashim. He related from 'Abdullah ibn 'Ubaydullah ibn 'Abbas. 'Abdullah ibn 'Ubaydallah related *hadiths* from Ibn 'Abbas.

✻✻✻✻✻

Also among this generation were: **al-Azraq ibn Qays al-Harithi**, one of the Banu al-Harith ibn Ka'b who was reliable, Allah willing; **Abu'l-Minhal**, whose name was Sayyar ibn Salama and who was one of the Qays ibn Tha'laba and reliable; **Abu'l-Qamus**, whose name was Zayd ibn 'Ali and had few *hadiths*; **Abu'l-Hazmar al-'Ijli**, whose name was Nasr ibn Ziyad ibn 'Abbad and who had few *hadiths*; **Abu Hajib**, whose name was Sawada ibn 'Asim; **Abu Muraya al-'Ijli**, whose name was 'Abdullah ibn 'Amr and had few *hadiths*; **Abu'l-Wazi' ar-Rasibi**, whose name was Jabir ibn 'Amr and had few *hadiths*; **Abu Mawiya**, whose name was Hurayth ibn Malik, although some say Malik ibn Hurayth al-Usaydi; **Abu'l-'Aliyya al-Bara'**, whose name was Ziyad ibn Fayruz and had few *hadiths*; Abu'l-Bazri, whose name was Yazid ibn 'Utarid and had few *hadiths*; **Abu Bashshama**, whose name was Minqar; **Abu'l-Khalil**, whose name was Salih ibn Abi Maryam and was reliable; **Abu Hunayda al-Mazini**, whose name was Hurayth ibn Malik and had few *hadiths*; **Abu 'Imran al-Jawni**, whose name was 'Abdu'l-Malik ibn Habib and who was reliable and had *hadiths*; **Abu't-Tayyah ad-Duba'i**, whose name was Yazid ibn Humayd and was reliable and had *hadiths*; **Abu Rayhana**, whose name was 'Abdullah ibn Matar and related from Ibn 'Umar and had *hadiths*; **Thumama ibn 'Abdullah**, whose mother was Kabsha ash-Shaybaniyya, and he had had few *hadiths*; **'Abdullah ibn Muslim ibn Yasar**, the client of Talha ibn 'Ubaydullah at-Taymi; **Zayd ibn al-Hawari**, whose *kunya* was Abu'l-Hawari and who was weak in *hadith*; **Budayl ibn Maysara al-'Uqayli**, who was reliable and had *hadiths*; **Ghaylan ibn Jarir al-'Ataki**, who was reliable and had *hadiths*; **Kathir ibn Shinzir al-Mazini**, who was reliable, Allah willing, and related from 'Ata'; **Wasil**, who was the client of Abu 'Uyayna ibn al-Muhallab and had *hadiths*; **Yahya ibn Salam al-Bakka'**, who was reliable, Allah willing; **Yazid ar-Rashk ad-Duba'i**, who was reliable; and **Abu Raja'**, Salman, the client of Abu Qilaba.

*****

The Fourth Generation

Ayyub ibn Abi Tamima as-Sakhtiyani

His *kunya* was Abu Bakr. He was a client of 'Anaza. Abu Tamima's name was Kaysan. Ayyub was reliable and dependable in *hadith*, with extensive knowledge and good character. He was scrupulous and a very knowledgeable authority.

Ayyub was born a year before the Plague in 87 AH.

Maymun Abu 'Abdullah said, "We were with al-Hasan when Ayyub was with him and he asked him about something. Then he got up and al-Hasan followed him and when Ayyub could not hear, he said, 'This is the master of the young men.'"

Abu Khushayna said, "One day Muhammad related a *hadith* to us and they asked, 'From whom is this, Abu Bakr?' He replied, 'Ayyub as-Sakhtiyani related it to me. You must accept him.'"

Ayyub said, "When Muhammad read his bequest, I went to turn away and he said, 'Bring him near. There is no secret from him.'"

Hammad ibn Zayd said, "I have not seen anyone with more words which I do not know than Ayyub and Yunus. Ibn 'Awn is something extraordinary."

Hammad ibn Zayd said, "When a man asked Ayyub about something, he would ask him to repeat it. If he repeated to him the like of what he said the first time, he would answer him. If he erred in it, he would not answer him."

Ibn Shawdhab said, "When Ayyub was asked about something of which he knew nothing, he would say, 'Ask the people of knowledge.'"

Ayyub said, "Who is safe? A man relates a *hadith* and thinks that he has achieved a certain position with the people, so his heart becomes tainted with something of that."

Hammad ibn Zayd said, "Ayyub was asked about something and he said, 'Nothing about it has reached me.' He said, 'Say what your opinion on it is.' He said, 'No opinion has reached me.'"

Fourth Generation

Hammad ibn Zayd said, "I have no reservations about Ayyub and Ibn 'Awn except in *hadith*." 'Arim said, "I mentioned it to Yahya ibn Sa'id and he said 'I have no reservations about Sufyan except in *hadith*.'"

Hammad ibn Zayd said, "Our *fuqaha'* are Ayyub, Ibn 'Awn and Yunus." Arim said, "I mentioned it to Ibn Da'ud and he said that Sufyan ath-Thawri said, 'Our *fuqaha'* are Ibn Abi Layla and Ibn Shubruma.'"

Hammad ibn Salama said, "Ayyub used to let his hair grow from one year to the next."

Hammad ibn Zayd said that Ayyub said, "Some people want to rise and Allah refuses except to lower them, and others want to be humble and Allah refuses except to raise them."

He said, "Ayyub used to take me on a route which was longer and I would say, 'This one is shorter.' He would say, 'I am wary of these gatherings.' When he greeted, they would return a better greeting to him than they did to other people and he would say, 'O Allah, You know that I do not desire it. O Allah, You know that I do not desire it.' The devotees in those days used to roll up their garments, i.e. their shirts. So he would let his shirt drag."

Ma'bad said, "I saw Ayyub wearing a long shirt which he dragged. I spoke to him about it and he said, 'Abu 'Urwa, in the past reputation consisted in dragging it. Reputation today consists in rolling it up.'"

Hammad ibn Zayd said, "Ayyub met me while I was on my way to the market and he was in a funeral procession. I started to go with him and he said, 'Go to your market.'"

Ar-Rabi' ibn Muslim said, "We travelled with Ayyub as-Sakhtiyani and when we were at al-Abtah, a large rough man with coarse cotton garments began to go after the Basran men, saying, 'Where is Ayyub ibn Abi Tamima?' I said to Ayyub, 'This man wants you.' When Ayyub saw him, he rushed to him and they embraced. I asked about the man and they said, 'This is Salim ibn 'Abdullah ibn 'Umar.'"

Sulayman ibn al-Mughira said, "We were with Humayd ibn Hilal when Ayyub as-Sakhtiyani and Yunus ibn 'Ubayd were with him. Humayd got up to go to his family and Ayyub and Yunus followed him. I recognised from Humayd ibn Hilal that he disliked it and he turned to me and said, 'I used to think that when something happened to these two shaykhs (al-Hasan and Ibn Sirin), these two (Ayyub and Yunus) would take their place.' I said, 'We hope for that from them.' He said, 'Then why do I see them following me?' He intensely disliked that."

Hammad ibn Zayd said, "I did not see anyone more hopeful for the people of the *qibla* than Ayyub and Ibn 'Awn."

Hammad ibn Zayd said, "I did not see anyone smile at men when he met them more than Ayyub, and Harun ibn Ri'b was amazing."

Hammad ibn Zayd reported that Ayyub said, "I do not recognise the Qadarite position to be part of the *deen*."

Hammad ibn Zayd said that Ayyub said, "It is better for a man to conceal his asceticism than to display it."

Hammad ibn Zayd said, "I used to walk with Ayyub and he took me down various roads which I was amazed that he knew, keeping out of sight so that people would not say, 'There is Ayyub!'"

Ibn 'Awf said, "When Muhammad died, we said, 'Who will we have?' We said, 'We will have Ayyub.'"

Shu'ba said, "Ayyub said, 'I was mentioned and I do not like to be mentioned.' Sometimes I went with him on an errand and I wanted to walk with him and he would not let me. He went out and went this way and that so that he would not be recognised."

Hammad ibn Zayd said that Ayyub said, "There is no man on the face of the earth whom I love more than Bakr, my son. I would prefer to bury Bakr than for Hisham (or another of the khalifs) to come to visit me."

Hammad ibn Zayd said that one of Ayyub's neighbours told him that Ayyub's bowls of food went round to his neighbours on *'Id al-Fitr* before he went.

Hammad ibn Zayd said that when he wanted to go to Makka, Ayyub asked him to purchase for him a certain type of garment. He said, "When he came I saw him wearing it under his shirt and he was aware of it and said, 'If it were concealed for me, I would be happy to take it.'"

Hammad ibn Zayd said, "Ayyub had a red mantle which he used to wear when he went into *ihram*. He had prepared it to be a shroud. On the nights of the 23rd and 24th of Ramadan, he would wear it. One night his wife said, 'Ayyub went out in the night in a red garment.'

Fourth Generation

His baggage was stolen in Makka and that mantle was in it and so it was lost."

Hammad ibn Zayd said, "A man used to sit with Ayyub and the man did not think that Ayyub recognised him. But if he fell ill or one of his people died, he would go to him, so that the man would think that he was the most honoured of people with Ayyub."

Hammad ibn Zayd said, "Ya'la ibn Hakim died in Syria. He was a client of Thaqif. His house was near ours in the quarter and he left his mother on her own. Ayyub went to her for three days and sat at her door. We used to go and gather with him. We continued to go with Ayyub to his house. Sometimes he went at night, and this continued until his death."

Hammad ibn Zayd said, "We used to say to Ayyub, 'What did you hear Muhammad say about such and such?' He would say, 'This and this.' We would say, 'Mention it.' He would say, 'Did you not accept it?' We would say to him, 'Are you enough?' He said, 'Yes.'"

Shu'ba said, "I asked Ayyub about reading *hadiths*, and he said, 'It is good.'"

Ma'mar said, "Ayyub said, 'It is hard for me to listen to a *hadith* of Muhammad which I did not actually hear from him.' It is difficult for me to listen to a *hadith* from Ayyub which I did not actually hear from him."

Ayyub said, "I bequeath my books to Abu Qilaba." They were brought from Syria and their hire was about ten dirhams."

Hammad ibn Zayd said, "Ayyub used to dye his hair and beard red."

Hammad ibn Zayd said, "I once put Ayyub's wrapper on," meaning his shirt in which he was shrouded.

They agree that Ayyub died during the Plague in Basra in 131 AH when he was 63.

Humayd ibn Abi Humayd at-Tawil

The client of Talha at-Talahat al-Khuza'i. His *kunya* was Abu 'Ubayda. His name was Abu Humayd Tarkhan. Humayd was reliable with many *hadiths*, although he may have falsified from Anas ibn Malik.

It is reported from Humayd that he took the books of al-Hasan and copied them and then returned them to him. Humayd died in 142 AH.

'Ali ibn Zayd

One of the descendants of 'Abdullah ibn Jid'an al-Qurashi. He was born blind. He had many *hadiths* and there is some weakness in them and they are not used for evidence.

Sulayman ibn Tarkhan at-Taymi

His *kunya* was Abu'l-Mu'tamir.

Yazid ibn Harun said, "He was not from Taym, but Murra. However his house was in Taym and so he was ascribed to them. He was reliable with many *hadiths*. He was one of those who use *ijtihad*. He used to pray the entire night and would pray *Subh* with the *wudu'* from *'Isha'*. He and his son al-Mu'tamir used to go around to the mosques in the night and pray, sometimes in this mosque and sometimes in that mosque, until morning. Sulayman was a partisan for 'Ali ibn Abi Talib.

Sulayman said, "So-and-so and so-and-so took the paper of Jabir and said, 'Take it.' I said 'No.'" Sulayman died in Basra in 143 AH.

Shu'ayb ibn al-Habhab

His *kunya* was Abu Salih. He was the client of the Banu Zafir, a sub-tribe of al-Mu'awil which is part of Azd. I heard that from the descendants of Shu'ayb. He was reliable with *hadiths*.

Abu Bishr

His name was Ja'far ibn Abi Wahshiyya. Abu Wahshiyya's name was Iyas. Abu Bishr was reliable with many *hadiths*. Yahya ibn Sa'id al-Qattan said, "Shu'ba considered the *hadiths* of Abu Bishr weak." He said that Abu Bishr did not listen to Habib ibn Salim at all. Abu Bishr died in 125 AH.

Yahya ibn Abi Ishaq al-Hadrami

He was reliable and had *hadiths*. He had Qur'an, knowledge of Arabic and grammar.

Aban ibn Abi 'Ayyash ash-Shanni

He was from 'Abdu'l-Qays. His *hadiths* are abandoned.

Salim al-'Alawi said, "I saw Aban writing from Anas." 'Arim said, "From as-Sarraj." Yahya ibn 'Abbas said "in Sibburja."

Matar ibn Tahman al-Warraq

One of the people of Khurasan. He had some weakness in *hadiths*.

Matar al-Waraq said, "Those people are good in *hadith*. Abu'l-Qaddak said that it is an error and that they meant 'Abu'l-Waddak'.

Abu'l-'Ushara' ad-Darimi

One of the Banu Tamim. His name was Usama ibn Malik. Others said that his name was 'Utarid ibn Barz. He was a bedouin who settled at al-Hafr on the Basra road. His *hadith* are of unknown source. Hammad ibn Salama related from him.

Yazid ibn Hazim al-Azdi al-Jadhami

His *kunya* was Abu Bakr. He was reliable, Allah willing.

Jarir in Hazim said that Yazid ibn Hazim died at the end of 147 AH or the beginning of 148 AH.

Da'ud ibn Abi Hind

His *kunya* was Abu Bakr. Abu Hind's name was Dinar. 'Amr ibn 'Asim said that he was a client of the Quraysh.

Da'ud ibn Abi Hind said, "I fell ill (with the plague) and became unconscious. It seemed that two people came to me and one of them touched the skin of my tongue and the other touched the sole of my foot. He said, 'What do you find?' He replied, 'Glorification, *takbir* and some steps to the mosque and some recitation of the Qur'an.' I had not begun to learn the Qur'an then. I used to go on an errand and would say, 'If only I remember Allah until I finish my errand.' I became well and turned to learning the Qur'an."

Hammad ibn Salama said, "I visited Da'ud ibn Abi Hind and I saw a red rug, a red curtain and a red Yemeni garment." Yazid ibn Harun said, "Da'ud and Sa'id ibn Abi 'Aruba passed by us and I listened to them." Da'ud died in 139 AH. He was one of the people of Sarakhs and was born there. He was reliable with a lot of *hadiths*.

'Ali ibn al-Hakam al-Bunani

One of Bunana. His *kunya* was Abu'l-Hakam. He was reliable and had *hadiths*. He died in 131 AH.

'Asim ibn Sulayman al-Ahwal

His *kunya* was Abu 'Abdu'r-Rahman. He was the client of the Banu Tamim. He was a qadi in Mada'in when al-Mansur was khalif. In Kufa he was in charge of the market inspection of measures and weights. He was reliable and had numerous *hadiths*. He died in 141 or 142 AH.

Hafs ibn Sulayman

The client of the Banu Minqar. His *kunya* was Abu'l-Hasan. He was the most knowledgeable of them regarding what al-Hasan said.

Shu'ba said, "I took from a book of Hafs ibn Sulayman and he did not object to me." He used to take people's books and copy them. He died a little before the Plague which was in 131 AH.

'Uthman al-Batti

He is Ibn Sulayman ibn Jurmuz. He was reliable with *hadiths*. He had opinion *(ra'y)* and *fiqh*.

'Uthman al-Batti was one of the people of Kufa. He moved to Basra and settled there. He was a client of the Banu Zuhra. His *kunya* was Abu 'Amr. He used to sell a certain type of garment called *'batt'* and so he was called al-Batti.

Abu Raja' al-Azdi

His name was ibn Sayf. He was reliable. Hammad ibn Zayd, Yazid ibn Zuray', and Isma'il ibn 'Ulayya related from him. Abu Raja' related from al-Hasan.

'Awf ibn Abi Jamila al-A'rabi

His *kunya* was Abu Sahl, and he was a client of Tayy. He was reliable with many *hadiths*. Some say that he brought something from al-Hasan which no one else brought and that he was a Shi'ite.

Fourth Generation

Muhammad ibn 'Abdullah al-Ansari said, "I asked 'Awf ibn Abi Jamila, 'Abu Sahl, why do you say, "Al-Hasan reported to me"?' He replied, 'It has reached me that your companions say, "Al-Hasan said; the Messenger of Allah صلعم said;" and he said, 'Who says this? By Allah, al-Ash'ath did not object to it.' I said, "Amr ibn 'Ubayd says that.' He retorted, "Amr ibn 'Ubayd has lied. I listened to him before the rebellion of Ibn al-Ash'ath.'"

Al-Ansari said, "'Awf was the oldest of all of them. He died in 146 AH."[He was born in 59 AH.]

Khulayf ibn 'Uqba

His *kunya* was Abu Bakr. He received that *kunya* from Muhammad ibn Sirin and he was one of his companions. He used to dye his white hair a little. He died before Ibrahim ibn 'Abdullah ibn Hasan was killed in [the 'Alid revolt in] Basra, when he was 61 years old.

Abu Ayyub

His name was 'Abdullah ibn Abi Sulayman. He was a client of 'Uthman ibn 'Affan. Hammad ibn Salama and Ishaq ibn 'Uthman related from him.

Khalid ibn Mihran al-Hadhdha'

His *kunya* was Abu'l-Mubarak. He was a client of Quraysh through the family of 'Abdullah ibn 'Amir ibn Kurayz. He was not a shoemaker (*hadhdha'*), but he used to sit with them.

Fahd ibn Hayyan al-Qaysi said, "Khalid did not make shoes at all. He used to say, 'Follow (*hadh*) this example,' and so he got the nickname of al-Hadhdha'.

Khalid was reliable, and he was a fearsome man against whom no one was bold. He had many *hadiths*. He said, "I did not write down anything at all except a long *hadith*. When I had memorised it, I erased it." He was appointed over the working camels and the treasury of land taxes in Basra. Khalid died in 142 AH while al-Mansur was khalif.

Yunus ibn 'Ubayd

His *kunya* was Abu 'Abdullah. He was the client of 'Abdu'l-Qays. He was reliable with many *hadiths*. Yunus said, "I did not write anything at all."

Hammad ibn Zayd said, "Yunus used to relate *hadith* and then he would say, 'I ask forgiveness of Allah' three times." Fahd ibn Hayyan and others reported that he died in 139 AH.

Muhammad ibn 'Abdullah al-Ansari said, "I saw Sulayman and 'Abdullah, the sons of 'Ali ibn 'Abdullah ibn al-'Abbas ibn 'Abdu'l-Muttalib, and Ja'far and Muhammad, the sons of Sulayman ibn 'Ali, carrying the bed of Yunus ibn 'Ubayd on their shoulders. 'Abdullah ibn 'Ali said, 'There is honour in doing this.'"

Sawwar ibn 'Abdullah ibn Qudama

He had few *hadiths* and was in charge of judgement in Basra for al-Mansur.

Bakkar ibn Muhammad said, "I saw Sawwar ibn 'Abdullah when he was about to judge. He raised his head to heaven and his eyes were wet with tears. Then he gave judgement."

Sa'id ibn Iyas al-Jurayri

His *kunya* was Abu Mas'ud. He was reliable although he became somewhat muddled at the end of his life. Kahmas said, "We did not accept al-Jurayri in the time of the plague."

Yazid ibn Harun said, "I listened to al-Jurayri in 142 AH. It was the first year I came to Basra. We did not object to anything from him. We were told that he became muddled later." He said, "Ishaq al-Azraq listened to him after us." They said that al-Jurayri died in 144 AH.

'Abdullah ibn 'Awn ibn Artaban

His *kunya* was Abu 'Awn. He was the client of 'Abdullah ibn Durra al-Muzani. He was older than Sulayman at-Tamimi. He was a partisan of 'Uthman. He was reliable with many *hadiths* and was scrupulous.

Ibn 'Awn said, "I saw Anas ibn Malik when his mount was being led and he did not encounter what I encountered. They would not even let me go out for a need."

Hammad ibn Zayd said, "Ibn 'Awn was born three years before the Plague." [i.e. he was born in 66 AH]

'Abdullah al-Ansari said, "Ibn 'Awn did not greet the Qadaris when he passed by them."

161

Fourth Generation

Bakkar ibn Muhammad said, "Ibn 'Awn used to listen to much knowledge in Kufa. He read it to Muhammad and Muhammad did not say, 'How good is this! Relate it!' He kept the rest of it from him until he died. When he related a *hadith*, he became so humble that people asked for mercy for him because of his fear of adding or decreasing."

Isma'il ibn 'Ulayya said, "I heard Ibn 'Awn say, 'I seek refuge with Allah from the knowledge of the shaykhs!'"

Abu Qatan said, I heard Ibn 'Awn say, "I wished that I had emerged from it [knowledge] with what is just sufficient."

Bakkar ibn Muhammad said, "Ibn 'Awn said to me, 'Nephew, they have cut me off from the road so that I cannot even go out for a need,' meaning how frequently they pressed him for *hadith*."

Bakkar said, "Ibn 'Awn had brothers who came to him and he gave them special permission, but he did not give people in general permission."

Bakkar said, "When Ibn 'Awn's brothers came to him, they greeted him as if there were birds on their heads, out of humility and humbleness, which I have not seen for anyone. He used to reply to them, 'And peace be upon you and the mercy of Allah.' He would not allow any of the people of *hadith* or anyone else to follow him. Ibn 'Awn had followed Muhammad ibn Sirin one day and he said, 'Do you need something?' He replied, 'No,' and left."

Bakkar said, "I did not see Ibn 'Awn joke with anyone, and he did not argue with anyone and he did not recite any poetry. He was occupied with himself."

Bakkar ibn Muhammad said, "When Ibn 'Awn prayed in the morning, he would remain facing the *qibla* where he sat remembering Allah. When the sun rose, he would pray and then turn to his companions."

Bakkar said, "I did not see Ibn 'Awn curse anyone at all, slave or slavegirl, sheep or chicken, or anything. I did not see anyone control their tongue more than he did."

Bakkar ibn Muhammad said, "I did not hear Ibn 'Awn mention Bilal ibn Abi Burda at all. It has reached me that some people said, 'Ibn 'Awn! Bilal[1] has done something.' He said, 'If a man is wronged, he continues to speak until he wrongs. I do not think that

---
1. The grandson of Abu Musa al-Ash'ari. He was the governor and qadi of Basra.

anyone is harsher against Bilal than me.' Bilal had him whipped because he had married an Arab woman."

Bakkar ibn Muhammad said, "I kept the company of Ibn 'Awn for a long time until his death. He left a bequest to my father. I did not hear him swear a pious or impious oath until death parted us."

He said, "Ibn 'Awn used to fast every other day until his death. I did not ever see a dinar or dirham in Ibn 'Awn's hand. I did not ever see him weigh anything. When he did *wudu'* for the prayer, no one helped him in it [by pouring the water for him]. He used to wipe his face with a handkerchief or rag when he had finished his *wudu'*. He did not go very early to the *Jumu'a* nor did he go late. The things he loved the most were taking the middle way and keeping company with the community. He used to perform a *ghusl* on *Jumu'a* and the two *'Ids,* and he put on perfume for *Jumu'a* and the two *'Ids*. He thought that that was the *Sunna*. He was sweet-smelling on other days and wore soft garments. On *Jumu'a* and the two *'Ids* he wore his cleanest garments. He used to go to *Jumu'a* either walking or riding, and did not linger after the *Jumu'a* prayer. In the month of Ramadan he did not do more than the obligatory prayer in the group, and then he would withdraw to his house. When he withdrew to his house, he was silent and did not say more than, 'Praise be to Allah, our Lord.' I did not see Ibn 'Awn ever enter a bath-house.

"He had a Christian agent who arranged the revenue of his house. Those who lived in the house where he lived included both Christians and Muslims and the house was located in the market. He used to say, 'Let the Christians be under me and not the Muslims under me.' So he lived in the highest part of his house.

"Ibn 'Awn used to lead us in the *Maghrib* and *'Isha'* prayers. He had a mosque in his house in which he prayed all the prayers along with whichever of his brothers, inhabitants and children attended. A client of his called Zayd gave the *adhan*. He stood and prayed in pairs of *rak'ats* and did the *witr* with a single *rak'at*. Sometimes we went to Ibn 'Awn and we sometimes went to one of his sons. He did not ask for anything but that it was brought for him. When he knew that there was some garlic in his food, he would not taste it. His servant used to come to him before food was served and he would wash his hands and then he would bring a towel and he would wipe his hands with it."

Fourth Generation

Bakkar ibn Muhammad said, "A woman client of ours called 'Ayna reported to us that she served Ibn 'Awn while she was still the property of 'Abdullah ibn Muhammad. Then 'Abdullah ibn Muhammad's daughter was married to Ibn 'Awn and her mother was married to his son, 'Abdu'r-Rahman. She said, 'I used to serve him. I cooked a pot of food for Ibn 'Awn and he smelt the garlic in it. He asked me and I told him. He said, "May Allah bless you! May Allah bless you! Remove it from before me." I felt a kind of burning in my body and I ran to Sirin's house.'"

Bakkar ibn Muhammad said, "*Qadar* was mentioned in the presence of 'Abdullah ibn 'Awn and he said to me, 'Nephew, I am older than it. I have met people and only two men mentioned these words: Ma'bad al-Juhani and Sanhawayh, the husband of Umm Musa. It is evil.'"

Bakkar ibn Muhammad said, "The Mu'tazilites took steps against Ibn 'Awn with Ibrahim ibn 'Abdullah. They said, 'There is a man called 'Abdullah ibn 'Awn who is making the people turn from you.' So he sent to him, 'Where do you stand with me?' So Ibn 'Awn left Basra and settled at al-Qurayziyya and he remained there until what happened to Ibrahim happened."[1]

Bakkar said, "I saw Ibn 'Awn when Ibrahim ibn 'Abdullah ibn Hasan rebelled. He ordered that the doors which opened on the Mirbad Road be locked. He did not let anyone look out or see or even open a door."

Bakkar ibn Muhammad said, "When Ibn 'Awn brought something to a person, he brought it in secret. If he did anything, he did it in secret, disliking for anyone to look at him."

Muhammad ibn 'Abdullah al-Ansari mentioned that Ibn 'Awn said, "I dreamt that I was in a garden with Muhammad. He began to walk in it and passed by some stony ground and scattered the stones while I was doing that behind him. I went to him and I recounted that to him and I saw that he recognised it. He said, 'What Allah wills! What Allah wills! This is a man following a man learning good from him.' He saw that I was humbled."

---

1. At this time in Basra, the Mu'tazilites were pro-'Alid. In 145/762 there was a Shi'ite revolt against the Abbasids led by two grandsons of al-Hasan ibn 'Ali, Muhammad an-Nafs az-Zakiyya in Madina and Ibrahim in Basra. Both were killed and Ibrahim's head sent to the khalif.

When a man testified on behalf of his father, 'Uthman al-Batti was heard to say, "It is not permitted unless it is someone like Ibn 'Awn." Al-Ansari said, "I take that position. I testified before Sawwar ibn 'Abdullah on behalf of my father and he accepted it."

Muhammad ibn 'Abdullah al-Ansari said, "Ibn 'Awn reported to us that he brought Salm ibn Qutayba to me while he was a governor. He said, 'Peace be upon you.' He laughed and said, 'We endure it for ibn 'Awn.'"

Al-Ansari said, "Hisham ibn Hasan once related something and a man asked him, 'Who related it to you?' He replied, 'Someone, by Allah, whose like I have never seen – 'Abdullah ibn 'Awn, not even al-Hasan and Ibn Sirin.'"

Al-Ansari said, "Hisham once came from Makka and went to Ibn 'Awn while we were with him. He said, 'By Allah, I did not go to my family or anyone else before coming to you.'"

Ibn 'Awn said, "I dreamt that I was sitting in the mosque and some pebbles fell and landed into my ear and I tilted my head and they fell out. I asked Ibn Sirin about it and he said, 'This is a man who listens to unpleasant words which do not remain in his heart.'"

Bakkar ibn Muhammad said, "Ibn 'Awn used to dislike shaking hands. He did not shake hands with anyone. Sufyan ath-Thawri almost never shook hands. He said, 'Peace be upon you.'"

Bakkar said, "Ibn 'Awn's mosque inside his house did not have a *mihrab*."

Yahya ibn Khulayf said, "Ibn 'Awn and Muhammad ibn Sirin were walking along, and Ibn Sirin crossed over a puddle on a palm-trunk, but Ibn 'Awn walked through the puddle. Muhammad ibn Sirin asked him, 'What kept you from walking on the trunk?' He said 'I did not know if its owner would agree.'"

Yahya ibn Khulayf said, "When Ibn 'Awn made great effort in supplication, he would say, 'O One! O One!'"

Bakkar ibn Muhammad said, "Some of Ibn 'Awn's companions told me that he had a she-camel on which he went on expeditions and went on *hajj*. He was proud of it. He told a slave of his to water it. He brought it back and he had struck its face and its eye was watering down its face. We said, 'If Ibn 'Awn does anything, it will be today!' He soon came to us and when he looked at the she-camel, he said,

Fourth Generation

'Glory be to Allah! Shouldn't the face be avoided? May Allah bless you! Leave me. Bear witness that he is free.'"

Bakkar said, "Ibn 'Awn used to go on expeditions on his she-camel to Syria. When he went to Syria, he rode horses. Ibn 'Awn advanced against a Byzantine and slew him."

Bakkar ibn Muhammad said, "Ibn 'Awn recited the Qur'an in sevenths. He would recite every night. If he did not read it during the night, he would finish it in the day."

Hammad ibn Zayd said, "Ibn 'Awn said, 'There are three things I like for myself and my companions.' He mentioned them and they were: recitation of the Qur'an, the *Sunna*, and the third is that a man examines himself and it is only good in relation to people."

'Abdullah ibn Maslama said, "I heard them mention that Ibn 'Awn saw the mount of Abu Maslama ibn Qa'nab and mounted it without consulting him," meaning that he did that on trust.

Khalid ibn al-Harith said, "Ibn 'Awn used to call out, 'Sulaym! Sulaym! Azhar! Azhar!' They used to purchase his needs for him from the market."

Sufyan ibn 'Uyayna said, "I said to Ibn 'Awn, 'I see you love dirhams.' He said, 'They benefit us.'"

Bakkar ibn Muhammad said, "Ibn 'Awn's ring was silver. His bezel was silver and he engraved on it 'the ring of Sulayman'."

Bakkar ibn Muhammad said, "I saw Ibn 'Awn wearing a hat whose height was about a handspan and a shawl of this striped Yemeni cloth. I saw him wearing napless garments. I saw him wearing a waist-wrapper and a cloak and going out to the market. He wore two garments dyed with red ochre."

Bakkar ibn Muhammad said, "Ibn 'Awn did not clip his moustache. He took a medium amount from it. His hair reached the middle of his ears. If you had seen him, you would have said, 'He is not of this class,' because of the way in which he fraternised with the people."

Hammad ibn Zayd said, "Ibn 'Awn's navel used to show when he wore a waist-wrapper."

Mu'adh ibn Mu'adh al-'Anbari said, "I saw Ibn 'Awn wearing a burnous of fine excellent wool. One of his companions asked, 'What is this burnous, Ibn 'Awn?' He replied, 'This is a burnous which belonged to Ibn 'Umar. He gave it to Anas ibn Sirin and it was sold from the inheritance of Anas and I purchased it.'"

Basra

Bakkar ibn Muhammad said, "Ibn 'Awn's sandals had a single strap and were not tanned. The outer wrappers of Ibn 'Awn were spun, and his garments touched the back of his feet."

Abu Qatan said, "I saw that one of 'Abdullah ibn 'Awn's teeth was reinforced with gold."

Bakkar ibn Muhammad said, "Ibn 'Awn used to wish that he could see the Prophet صلعم [i.e. in a dream] and he saw him shortly before his death. He was absolutely delighted by that. He came down his stairs to the mosque in his house and slipped and injured his foot. It did not heal until he died. He was shrouded in a cloth which he had bought for 200 dirhams and over which we had haggled with his sons and said, 'We will not sell it for less than that.' My aunt, who was his wife said, 'Keep the rest against me.'"

He said, "I was present when Ibn 'Awn died. He was focused until he died, mentioning Allah until he gurgled with death. My aunt, Umm Muhammad bint 'Abdullah ibn Muhammad ibn Sirin, said, 'Recite *Sura Yasin* in Ibn 'Awn's presence.' So I recited it. I did not see anyone more conscious and composed at death than Ibn 'Awn. He did not do more than say that the garment should be moved from his belly. He died at dawn. We could not pray over him until we had placed him in the *mihrab* of the place of prayer. Sleep overcame us."

Bakkar ibn Muhammad said, "Ibn 'Awn died owing a debt of about 10,000 dirhams and he willed a fifth of his property after death to my father for his relatives, those who were needy and those who were not.

"During his illness, Ibn 'Awn was more steadfast than a lion. I did not see him complain about any of his illness until he died, and he did not leave a dirham or a dinar. He left a house among the perfumers and a house where he lived on the Mirbad Road."

He died, may Allah have mercy on him, in Rajab, 151 AH, while al-Mansur was khalif. Jamil ibn Mahfuz al-Azdi, the commander of the police of 'Uqba ibn Salm, prayed over him.

'Abdu'l-'Aziz ibn Qudayr

His house was in the 'Abdu'l-Qays. He was reliable, Allah willing. Sufyan and 'Abdullah ibn al-Mubarak related from him.

Fourth Generation

'Abbad ibn Mansur an-Naji

He was the Qadi in Basra. He was weak with contradicted *hadiths*.

Hawshab ibn Muslim

He used to sell shawls. He was reliable, Allah willing. Hisham ibn Hassan related from him.

Ghalib ibn Khuttaf ar-Rasibi

He was reliable. 'Abdu'l-A'la ibn Sulayman said, "Ghalib al-Qattan's *kunya* was Abu Salama. He was blind. He settled among the 'Abdu'l-Qays. I heard that he is Ghalib ibn Khuttaf."

Hisham ibn Hassan al-Qurdusi

One of Azd. There was seven years difference in age between him and Qatada.

Muhammad said, "Hisham is one of us, the People of the House."

Yahya ibn Sa'id al-Qattan said, "Hisham died in 147 AH. He was reliable, Allah willing, with many *hadiths*."

Makki ibn Ibrahim said, "Hisham died on the 1st Safar, 148 AH."

'Uyayna ibn 'Abdu'r-Rahman al-Ghatafani

He was reliable, Allah willing. Wukay' ibn al-Jarrah said, "I met 'Uyayna ibn 'Abdu'r-Rahman in Basra in 148 and he dictated to me."

Salih ibn Abi'l-Akhdar

Muhammad ibn 'Abdullah al-Ansari said, "I asked Salih ibn Abi'l-Akhdar, 'Have you heard this which you report from az-Zuhri?' He replied, 'From him is what he related to me, and from him is what I read to him. I cannot separate this from that.'"

Abu Hamza

Shu'ba related from him. He was his neighbour and his name was 'Abdu'r-Rahman ibn 'Abdullah.

Basra

'Amr ibn 'Ubayd

The client of Banu Tamim. His *kunya* was Abu 'Uthman. He was a Mu'tazili. He has opinion (*ra'y*) but nothing in *hadith*. He had many *hadiths* from al-Hasan and others. He died in 147 AH and was buried at Marran, some days journey from Makka on the Basra road.

✧✧✧✧✧

Also among this generation were: **Abu 'Abdullah ash-Shaqari**, whose name was Salama ibn Tammam and was reliable; **Rabi'a ibn Abi'l-Halal al-'Utaki**, who had few *hadiths*; **Yahya ibn 'Atiq**, who was reliable and had *hadiths*; **Abu Na'ama al-'Adawi,** whose name was 'Amr ibn 'Isa, and was weak; Rawh ibn 'Ubada related from him; **Sa'id ibn Yazid,** whose *kunya* was Abu Maslama and was reliable; Shu'ba, Hammad ibn Zayd and Isma'il ibn 'Ulayya related from him; **Sa'id ibn Abi Sadaqa**, whose *kunya* was Abu Qurra and who was reliable; **'Umara ibn Abi Hafsa**, whose *kunya* was Abu Rawh and was reliable; Shu'ba and Isma'il ibn 'Ulayya related from him; **Mansur ibn 'Abdu'r-Rahman al-'Adawi al-Ghuddani**, from whom Isma'il ibn 'Ulayya related; **'Isl ibn Sufyan at-Tamimi**, who was somewhat weak and Shu'ba related from him; **Ziyad al-A'lam**, the client of a woman of Bahila, who was reliable; **Abu Dhubyan**, whose name was Khalifa ibn Ka'b; **Abu Dilan**, whose name was Hayyan ibn Yazid and who had few *hadiths*; **Salama ibn 'Alqama**, whose *kunya* was Abu Bishr at-Tamimi and who was reliable; **Abu Marwan al-'Anawi**, whose name was Ibrahim ibn al-'Ala' and was reliable; **'Imran ibn Muslim al-Qasir**, who has *hadiths*; **'Abdu'l-Mu'min ibn Abi Shura'a**, who met Ibn 'Umar and related from him and has few *hadiths*; **Ghalib ibn Mihran at-Tammar**, who was reliable, and Shu'ba and Isma'il ibn 'Ulayya related from him; **'Abdu'l-Malik ibn Qudayr**, from whom people related; **Al-Hajjaj al-Aswad al-Qasamil**, one al-Azd, with *hadiths*; **Al-Hajjaj ibn Abi 'Uthman as-Sawwaf**, whose *kunya* was Abu's-Salt and was reliable; **Hatim ibn Abi Saghira**, whose *kunya* was Abu Yunus al-Qushayri, and was reliable, Allah willing; **Husayn ibn Dhakwan**, the teacher, who was reliable; **Kahmas ibn al-Hasan al-Qaysi**, who was reliable; **Husayn ash-Shahid**, a client of Muzayna who was reliable; **'Imran ibn Judayr as-Sadusi**, who was reliable with many *hadiths*; **Abu'l-**

Fifth Generation

Mu'alla al-'Attar whose name was Yahya ibn Maymun and who was reliable with many *hadiths*; and **Jarrad ibn Mujalid,** from whom Shu'ba related.

✯✯✯✯✯

The Fifth Generation

Sa'id ibn Abi 'Aruba

His *kunya* was Abu'n-Nadr. Abu 'Aruba's name was Mihran. He was reliable with many *hadiths*, and then he muddled things towards the end of his life.

'Abdu'l-Wahhab ibn 'Ata' said, "I sat with Sa'id ibn Abi 'Aruba in 136 AH and he died in 157 AH." Someone else said that it was 156 AH, while al-Mansur was khalif.

Quraysh ibn Anas said, "Sa'id ibn Abi 'Aruba swore to me that he had not written anything at all from Qatada except when Abu Mash'ar wrote to him to ask him to write out Qatada's *tafsir* for him. He said, 'You want to write it from me.' He said, 'I still have it.'"

Hammam said, "Sa'id ibn Abi 'Aruba came to me and asked me for the *'Awashir al-Qur'an* by Qatada. I said to him, 'I will copy it for you and present it to you.' He said, 'No, only your book.' I refused him and he kept at me but I did not lend it to him."

'Affan said, "Sa'id ibn Abi 'Aruba related from Qatada what he did not listen to a lot, and he did not say in it, 'He related to me.'"

Rawh ibn 'Ubada said, "Sa'id ibn Abi 'Aruba was one of the people with the best memory. When he related, he surprised himself. He would say, 'Pulverise the peppercorns with the pestle.'" Rawh mentioned from someone that he said, "I only remember it with its error."

Asma' ibn 'Ubayd

He used to live among the Banu Dubay'a. He was reliable, Allah willing. Sa'id ibn 'Amir, the grandson of Asma', said, "Asma' ibn 'Ubayd died in 141."

Isma'il ibn Muslim al-Makki

His *kunya* was Abu Ishaq. Muhammad ibn 'Abdullah al-Ansari said, "Isma'il ibn Muslim was Basran, but he lived in Makka for some years. He was known for that. When he returned to Basra, he was called 'Makkan'. He had opinion, *fatwa*, discernment and memory of *hadith* and other things. People relied on him and 'Uthman al-Batti. Isma'il and Yunus ibn 'Ubayd had the same gathering. I used to go and sit with them and I wrote from Isma'il and left Yunus for the pre-eminence of Isma'il with people since he was known for *fatwas*."

Abu'l-Ashhab

His name was Ja'far ibn Hayyan al-'Utaridi. He was reliable, Allah willing. He died in Basra in 165 AH while al-Mahdi was khalif.

'Ali ibn 'Ali ar-Rifa'i

Al-Fadl ibn Dukayn and 'Affan ibn Muslim said, "'Ali ibn 'Ali ar-Rifa'i resembled the Prophet صلعم."

Abu Hurra

His name was Wasil ibn 'Abdu'r-Rahman. He had some weakness and *hadiths* are related from him.

Sakhr ibn Juwayriyya

'Amr ibn 'Asim said, "Sakhr's *kunya* was Abu Nafi'. He was the client of Banu Tamim. He was firm and reliable."

'Affan ibn Muslim said, "Sakhr was firmer in *hadith* and more famous for it than Juwayriyya."

Ash'ath ibn 'Abdu'l-Malik al-Humrani

His *kunya* was Abu Hani'. Muhammad ibn 'Abdullah al-Ansari reported that Abu Hurra said, "When al-Hasan saw Ash'ath, he said, 'Come, Abu Hani'! Bring what you have!'"

Shu'ba said, "The *fiqh* of the questions of Yunus came from al-Hasan because it was said that he took them from Ash'ath. Ash'ath had immense knowledge. His sister was married to Hafs ibn Sulayman, the client of the Banu Minqar. He looked at his books, and Hafs was the most knowledgeable of them regarding the position of al-Hasan."

Muhammad ibn 'Abdullah al-Ansari reported that al-Ash'ath said, "We were in a gathering which we used to hold." Al-Batti, Sawwar, Dawud, 'Awf, al-Ash'ath and a number of others sat in it. There was an argument between Dawud and 'Awf regarding *Qadar*. 'Awf espoused *Qadar*. They got up and attacked each other. Al-Ash'ath said, "I went and held Dawud and Sawwar went to 'Awf and held him and so we separated them." Ash'ath died in 146, before 'Awf.

Al-Mubarak ibn Fadala ibn Abi Umayya

Abu Umayya was the client of 'Umar ibn al-Khattab by *kitaba*. He died in 165 AH while al-Mahdi was khalif. There was weakness in him. 'Affan ibn Muslim elevated him, trusted him, and related from him.

Ar-Rabi' ibn Sabih

His *kunya* was Abu Hafs, the client of the Banu Sa'd. He went out on an expedition to India by sea and died and was buried on an island in 166 AH, at the beginning of the khalifate of al-Mahdi. A shaykh from the people of Basra who was with him told me that. He was weak in *hadith*. Ath-Thawri related from him. 'Affan abandoned him and did not relate from him.

As-Sari ibn Yahya ash-Shaybani

His *kunya* was Abu'l-Haytham and his grandfather was Harmala ibn Iyas who related from Abu Qatada.

Harmala reported from Abu Qatada that the Prophet صلعم said, "Fasting 'Arafa is equivalent to fasting two years, and fasting 'Ashura' is equivalent to one year."

Yazid ibn Ibrahim at-Tustari

He was firm and reliable. 'Affan elevates him. He settled in Bahila at the cemetery of the Banu Sahm.

Jarir ibn Hazim al-Jahdami

One of Azd. His *kunya* was Abu'n-Nadr, He was reliable although he muddled things towards the end of his life.

His son, Wahb, said, "My father was born in 85 AH while 'Abdu'l-Malik ibn Marwan was khalif." He said that he died in 170 AH.

Abu Hilal ar-Rasibi

His name was Muhammad ibn Sulaym. There was some weakness in him. Musa ibn Isma'il said, "Abu Hilal was blind. He used to not relate until he had heard the lineage of those with him." He died in 165 AH while al-Mahdi was khalif.

Hisham ibn Abi Hisham

His *kunya* was Abu'l-Miqdam. Abu Hisham's name was Ziyad, the client of 'Uthman ibn 'Affan. Hisham was weak in *hadith*.

Al-Hasan ibn Dinar

He was weak in *hadith* and is inconsequential. Muhammad ibn Ishaq, al-Mu'afi ibn 'Imran and others related from him.

Musa ibn Isma'il said, "I listened to al-Hasan ibn Dinar. He asked to borrow a book from me and I did not give it to him. He said, '*Hadith* is more than that. Whoever is niggardly with what he has will receive blame and wrong action. We got it from someone else.'"

Hisham ibn Abi 'Abdullah ad-Dastawa'i

Abu 'Abdullah's name was Sanbar. He was a client of the Banu Sadus. He was reliable and firm and an authority in *hadith* although he is accused of being a Qadari.

Muhammad ibn Hafs at-Taymi said, "When Hisham ad-Dastawa'i did not have a lamp in his room, he tossed and turned on his bed. His wife would bring him a lamp. She asked him about that and he said, 'When I have no lamp I remember the darkness of the grave.'"

'Abdu's-Samad ibn al-Warith said that Hisham died in 152 AH, but Zayd ibn al-Hubab said, "I visited him in 153 AH and he died after that."

Fifth Generation

Sulayman ibn al-Mughira al-Qaysi

His *kunya* was Abu Sa'id. He was reliable and firm.

Wuhayb said, "Ayyub used to tell us, 'Take from Sulayman ibn al-Mughira.' We used to go to him in one corner, while his father was in another corner."

Musa ibn Isma'il said, "Sulayman ibn al-Mughira related to me that Ayyub said, 'There is no one with better memory of the *hadiths* of Humayd ibn Hilal than Sulayman ibn al-Mughira.'"

Mahdi ibn Maymun al-Azdi

He is the client of al-Mu'awil. His *kunya* was Abu Yahya.

'Ubaydullah ibn Muhammad al-Qurashi said, "Maymun was a Kurd and he was the client of Yazid ibn al-Muhallab. Mahdi was reliable. He died while al-Mahdi was khalif."

Shu'ba ibn al-Hajjaj ibn Ward

He was one of Azd, and a client of Ashaqir through emancipation. His *kunya* was Abu Bistam.

He was reliable, trustworthy and firm, an authority in *hadith*.

Shu'ba was ten years older than ath-Thawri.

Shu'ba said, "By Allah, I am safer in poetry than in *hadith*." Abu Qatan said that Shu'ba said, "I am not worried about anything I fear will make me enter the Fire except it," meaning *hadith*.

Shu'ba said, "My mother said to me, 'There is a woman who relates from 'A'isha. Go and listen to her.' I went to her and listened to her and then told her, 'I listened to her.' She said, 'Allah will not question you.'" He died in Basra at the beginning of 160 AH when he was 75.

Juwayriyya ibn Asma' ibn 'Ubayd

'Affan ibn Muslim said, "Juwayriyya ibn Asma' possessed immense knowledge. He used to refuse to dictate to us. A man came to him and asked him about reciting the Qur'an without purity and he said, 'I do not have anything about it.' So I reported to him about it from Ibn 'Abbas, Abu Hurayra and others. He said, 'I did not see you here. Relate to me and dictate to me.' When he dictated to me, I left him and did not go to him."

Salih al-Murri

'Abdu'r-Rahman ibn Mahdi said, "I used to mention Salih al-Murri to Sufyan ath-Thawri and he said, 'Stories! Stories!'[1] as if he disliked him. When he had a need, he went early to do it. He went early one day and I went with him and our path passed the mosque of Salih al-Murri. I said, 'Abu 'Abdullah, let us go in and pray in this mosque.' So we went in and prayed. It was the day of Salih's gathering. When we had prayed, the people crowded in and we were unable to get up. Salih spoke and I saw Sufyan weeping profusely. When he finished and got up, I said to him, 'Abu 'Abdullah, what do you think of this man?' He replied, 'This is not a rebel. This is a warner of people.'"

Humam ibn Yahya

His *kunya* was Abu 'Abdullah. The client of the Banu 'Awdh of Azd. He was reliable. Sometimes he erred in *hadith*.

Hammad ibn Salama

His *kunya* was Abu Salama. His father Salama's *kunya* was Abu Sakhr. He was the client of Banu Tamim. He was the nephew of Humayd at-Tawil.

Hammad ibn Zayd said, "We did not go to anyone with the intention of learning anything at all in that time except for Hammad ibn Salama. We used to say, 'Today we will not go to anyone except with the intention of learning.'" They said that Hammad ibn Salama was reliable with many *hadiths*. Sometimes he related contradicted *hadiths*.

Hammad ibn Salama said, "Iyas ibn Mu'awiya took my hand while I was a boy and said, 'Do not die or tell stories. I said this to your uncle (Humayd at-Tawil), and he did not die until he told stories." Abu Khalid said, "I said to Hammad ibn Salama, 'Did you tell stories?' He said, 'Yes.'"

Qasim ibn al-Fadl al-Huddani

His *kunya* was Abu'l-Mughira. Musa ibn Isma'il said, "He was not a Huddani, but he lived in Huddan. He was a man of the Banu Luhayy of Azd. He was reliable."

---

1. Many of the 'storytellers' (*qussâs*, sing. *qâss*) incorporated doubtful legends in their preaching. Sometimes they became very partisan to one party or another.

Sallam ibn Miskin

His *kunya* was Abu Rawh. He was a man from the Yemen. He was reliable. He died before Hammad ibn Salama.

Sulayman al-Aswad an-Naji

We do not know whether he was one of them or their client. He has *hadiths*.

Bahr ibn Kunayz as-Saqqa' al-Bahili

His *kunya* was Abu'l-Fadl. He was weak. He died in 160 AH while al-Mahdi was khalif.

Abu 'Ubayda an-Naji

He was the client of Kabis ibn Rabi'a an-Naji. He lived in the Banu Najiyya and then moved to the Banu 'Uqayl.

'Ubaydullah ibn al-Hasan

He was made qadi of Basra after Sawwar ibn 'Abdullah. He was praised, reliable, and intelligent among men.

*****

Other men of this generation include: **Abu Khulda Khalid ibn Dinar**; **Sa'id ibn 'Abdu'r-Rahman**, from whom *hadiths* are also related; **Qurra ibn Khalid as-Sadusi**, whose *kunya* was Abu Khalid and was reliable; **Rabi'a ibn Kulthum**, a shaykh with *hadiths*; **'Abdu'r-Rahman ibn Fadala**, whose *kunya* was Abu Umayya; *hadith* were related from him; **Abu 'Aqil ad-Dawraqi**, who is Bashir ibn 'Uqba; **As-Salt ibn Dinar,** who was weak and is inconsequential; **Sallam ibn Sulayman**, who is Abu'l-Mundhir, the client of Muzayna; **'Umara ibn Zadhan as-Saydalani**, whose *kunya* was Abu Ṣalama; **'Abdu'l-'Aziz ibn Muslim**, who died in 167 AH while al-Mahdi was khalif; **Aban ibn Yazid al-'Attar**, whose *kunya* was Abu Yazid; **Hazm ibn Abi Hazm al-Quta'i,** who died in 175 AH; **Husam ibn Misakk**, one of Azd who was weak; **Abu'l-'Awwam al-Qattan**, who is 'Imran ibn Dawar; **Al-Husayn ibn Abi Ja'far al-Jufri,** one of the Banu 'Awdh from Azd; he died in 160 AH; **Salama**

ibn 'Alqama, the Imam of the mosque of Dawud ibn Abi Hind; **Mu'awiya ibn 'Abdu'l-Karim ad-Dall**, so-called because he lost his way (*dalla*) on the Makka road; **'Uthman ibn Miqsam al-Barsami**, who is of no consequence; his *hadiths* are abandoned, and he died in al-Mahdi's khalifate; and **Abu Jurayy Nasr ibn Tarif**, who is of no consequence and his *hadiths* are abandoned.

*****

The Sixth Generation

Hammad ibn Zayd

His *kunya* was Abu Isma'il. He was a partisan for 'Uthman. He was dependable, reliable, and an authority with many *hadiths*.

Sulayman ibn Harb said, "Hazim ibn Hazim died while Zayd, the father of Hammad ibn Zayd, was his slave, and Yazid and Jarir, Hazim's sons, set him free."

It is said that Hammad ibn Zayd was born in 96 AH.

Hammad ibn Zayd said, "My mother stated that I was born while 'Umar ibn 'Abdu'l-Aziz was khalif. My aunt said that it was at the end of the reign of Sulayman ibn 'Abdu'l-Malik."

Hammad ibn Zayd said, "Hammad ibn Abi Sulayman came to us in Basra but Ayyub did not go to him. If Ayyub did not go to someone, we would not go to him. Layth ibn Abi Sulaym came to us and Ayyub went to him, so we went to him." Someone else said, "Ayyub died when Hammad ibn Zayd was 34."

Hammad ibn Zayd said, "We were with 'Amr ibn Dinar when Ayyub and Abu 'Amr ibn al-'Ala' came and asked him about a book. When they came to a *hadith* which they had heard, they left it. He said, 'I say, "I related thus and thus," so ask about what you left.'"

'Affan ibn Muslim said, "Hammad ibn Zayd wore a tall fine white hat."

'Arim ibn al-Fadl said, "Hammad ibn Zayd died on Friday, 10th Ramadan, 179 AH when he was 81. Ishaq ibn Sulayman al-Hashimi prayed over him. He was governor of Basra at that time for Harun ar-Rashid, the Amir al-Mu'minin."

Sixth Generation

His brother, Sa'id ibn Zayd

He was reliable. He is related from. He died before his brother, Hammad ibn Zayd.

Wuhayb ibn Khalid

He was the client of Bahila. His *kunya* was Abu Bakr. Khalid's *kunya* was Abu Ghibta. Wuhayb was imprisoned and went blind. He was reliable with many *hadiths* and was an authority. He had a better memory than Abu 'Awana. He would dictate from memory. He died when he was 58.

Abu 'Awana

His name was al-Waddah. He was the client of Yazid ibn 'Ata'. He was reliable and truthful.

Mahdi ibn Maymun said, "I saw Abu 'Awana when he was a boy, in the time of Khalid ibn 'Abdullah's governorship, reciting with modulated tones."

Abu 'Awana said, "On the Day of 'Arafa I saw al-Hasan ibn Abi'l-Hasan leave the *maqsura* and sit in the courtyard of the mosque and people sat around him."

Al-Jurayri used to say, "Who will be good to al-Wasiti for me? Who will be good to al-Wasiti for me?" meaning Abu 'Awana. Yazid said, "He used to give him excellent dates."

Abu 'Awana said, "I gave the wife of al-A'mash a donkey. When I concealed myself she took his hand and brought him to me."

Abu 'Awana said, "I asked al-A'mash, 'I need something from you.' He said, 'What do you need?' I said, 'I need that if you do not fulfil it you will not be angry with me.' He replied, 'My heart is not in my control about whether or not I get angry with you. Either my anger will harm you secretly or openly.' I said, 'Dictate to me.' He replied, 'I will not do it.'"

'Affan ibn Muslim said, "Abu 'Awana used to memorise and dictate to us and he would produce long *hadiths* which he would either read or dictate."

Abu 'Ubayda al-Haddad said, "Abu 'Awana said to me, 'What do people say about me?' I said, 'They say that everything that you relate is from a book and so it is memorised. What you have not brought from a book is not memorised.' He said, 'They will not leave me alone.'"

'Affan ibn Muslim said that 'Abu 'Awana wore a hat.

Yahya ibn Hammad said that Abu 'Awana died in 176 AH, while Harun ar-Rashid was khalif and Ja'far ibn Sulayman was our governor. He was originally from the people of Wasit and then he moved to Basra and lived there until his death.

Ja'far ibn Sulayman ad-Duba'i

He was the client of the Banu'l-Harish. His *kunya* was Abu Sulayman. He was reliable although there was some weakness in him. He was a Shi'ite. He died in Rajab, 178 AH, according to various people.

'Abdu'l-Wahid ibn Ziyad

His *kunya* was Abu Bishr. He was known as ath-Thaqafi. He was the client of 'Abdu'l-Qays. He was reliable with many *hadiths*. He died in 177 AH while Harun ar-Rashid was khalif.

'Abdu'l-Warith ibn Sa'id

His *kunya* was Abu 'Ubayda. He was the client of the Banu'l-'Anbar. He was reliable and an authority. He died at the beginning of Muharram 180 AH while Harun ar-Rashid was khalif.

Yazid ibn Zuray'

His *kunya* was Abu Mu'awiya. He was reliable, an authority with many *hadiths*. He died in Basra in Shawwal, 182 AH. He was a partisan of 'Uthman.

'Abdu'l-Wahhab ibn 'Abdu'l-Majid ath-Thaqafi

His *kunya* was Abu Muhammad. He was reliable although there was some weakness in him. 'Abdu'l-Wahhab was born in 108.

Wuhayb said, "Ayyub said to us when 'Abdu'l-Majid died, 'Cling to this young man,' meaning 'Abdu'l-Wahhab. 'Abdu'l-Wahhab died in Basra in 194 AH while al-Amin was khalif.

Sixth Generation

Bishr ibn al-Mufaddal

His *kunya* was Abu Isma'il. He was the client of the Banu Raqqash. He was reliable with many *hadiths*. He was a partisan of 'Uthman. He died in 186 AH.

'Abdu'l-A'la ibn 'Abdu'l-A'la al-Qurashi

One of the Banu Sama ibn Lu'ayy. His *kunya* was Abu Humam. He was not strong in *hadith*. He died in 189 AH.

'Ubbad ibn 'Ubbad ibn Habib al-'Ataki

One of Azd. His *kunya* was Abu Mu'awiya. He was famous for excellent medicine. He was not strong in *hadith*. He died in 181AH while Harun ar-Rashid was khalif.

Al-Mu'tamir ibn Sulayman at-Taymi

His *kunya* was Abu Muhammad. He was reliable. Al-Mu'tamir ibn Sulayman said, "My father said to me, 'Count from the year 106 AH," meaning he was born in it. He died in 187 AH in Basra while Harun ar-Rashid was khalif.

Sulaym ibn Ahdar

He was the strongest of them in keeping close to 'Abdullah ibn 'Awn. He was reliable.

Ibn 'Awn used to say, "Sulaym! Sulaym! Azhar! Azhar!" They used to purchase his needs for him from the market.

'Umar ibn 'Ali al-Muqaddami

His *kunya* was Abu Hafs. He was a reliable person, although he often used to falsify. He used to say, "I heard," and "He related to us," and then was silent. Then he would say, "Hisham ibn 'Urwa al-A'mash." 'Affan ibn Muslim, Sulayman ibn Harb and others related from him.

'Affan ibn Muslim said, "'Umar ibn 'Ali was a righteous man. They did not hold anything against him other than the fact that he was a forger. I did not accept from him unless he said, 'He related to us.'"

Khalid ibn al-Harith al-Hujaymi

His *kunya* was Abu 'Uthman. He was reliable. He died in Basra in 186 AH while Harun ar-Rashid was khalif.

'Ar'ara ibn al-Birnid

His *kunya* was Abu Muhammad. He died in Jumada al-Akhira or Rajab, 192 AH, while Harun ar-Rashid was khalif, at the age of 82.

Muhammad ibn Abi 'Adi

His *kunya* was Abu 'Amr. Abu 'Adi's name was Ibrahim. He was the client of the Banu Sulaym. He was reliable. He died in Basra in 194 AH, while al-Amin was khalif.

Yusuf ibn Khalid ibn 'Umayr as-Samti

His *kunya* was Abu Khalid. He was the client of Sahl ibn Sakhr al-Laythi who was a Companion who set 'Umayr free. Yusuf ibn Khalid was born in 120 AH, while Yusuf ibn 'Umar ath-Thaqafi was governor and was named after him. He devoted himself to knowledge and met Khalid al-Hadhdha', Yunus, Ibn 'Awn, Hisham, and their generation. He met al-A'mash, Isma'il ibn Abi Khalid, 'Abdu'l-Malik ibn Abi Sulayman and other Kufans. He met Musa ibn 'Uqba, Muhammad ibn 'Ajlan and their companions. He had insight into opinion, *fatwa*, books and preconditions. People used to be wary of his *hadith* by his opinion. He was weak in *hadith*. It is said that he was called 'as-Samti' (from *samt*, road) because of his beard, appearance and manner. The house where Yusuf was in Basra was the house of Sahl ibn Sakhr. Yusuf died in Basra in Rajab, 189 AH when he was 69.

Mu'adh ibn Mu'adh

His *kunya* was Abu'l-Muthanna. He was reliable. He was born in 119 AH while Hisham was khalif. He was made qadi in Basra for Harun, the Amir al-Mu'minin. Then he was dismissed. He died in Basra in the month of Rabi' al-Akhir, 196 AH, while Al-Amin was khalif, at the age of 77. Muhammad ibn 'Abbad ibn 'Abbad al-Muhallabi prayed over him. On that day he was in charge of the prayer and amirate in Basra.

Safwan ibn 'Isa az-Zuhri

His *kunya* was Abu Muhammad. He was reliable and righteous. He died in Basra in Jumada, 200 AH, while al-Ma'mun was khalif.

Hammad ibn Mas'ada

His *kunya* was Abu Sa'id. He was reliable, Allah willing. He died in Basra in Jumada, 202 AH, while al-Ma'mun was khalif.

Azhar ibn Sa'd as-Samman

His *kunya* was Abu Bakr, the client of Bahila. He was reliable. 'Abdullah ibn 'Awn made him his executor. Azhar died when he was 94.

Muhammad ibn 'Abdullah al-Ansari

His *kunya* was Abu 'Abdullah. He was descended from Anas ibn Malik. He was truthful.

Muhammad ibn 'Abdullah al-Ansari said, "My father told me, 'You were born, my son, in Shawwal, 118 AH, while Hisham ibn 'Abdu'l-Malik was khalif.'"

Muhammad ibn 'Abdullah al-Ansari was appointed qadi of Basra after Mu'adh ibn Mu'adh. Then he moved to Baghdad and was appointed over the army of al-Mahdi, after al-'Awfi, at the end of Harun's khalifate. When al-Amin became khalif, he dismissed him and replaced him with 'Awn ibn 'Abdullah al-Mas'udi as qadi. Muhammad ibn 'Abdullah al-Ansari was put in charge of grievances, after Isma'il ibn 'Ulayya, and then he was appointed qadi of Basra for a second time. Then al-Ma'mun dismissed him and appointed Yahya ibn Aktham in his place. Al-Ansari continued to transmit *hadith* in Basra until he died there in Rajab, 215 AH.

'Abdullah ibn Da'ud al-Hamdani

From Hamadan. He moved from Kufa and settled in al-Khutayba, a district of Basra. He was reliable and a man of devotion and worship. He died in Shawwal, 213 AH, while al-Ma'mun was khalif.

Abu 'Asim an-Nabil

His name was ad-Dahhak ibn Makhlad ash-Shaybani. He was a reliable *faqih*. He died in Basra on Thursday night, the 14th of Dhu'l-Hijja, 212 AH, while al-Ma'mun was khalif.

'Abdullah ibn Bakr as-Sahmi

He was from Bahila. His *kunya* was Abu Wahb. He was reliable and truthful. He died in Baghdad in Muharram, 208 AH.

Muhammad ibn Bakr al-Bursani

He was from Azd. His *kunya* was Abu 'Abdullah. He was reliable. He died in Basra in Dhu'l-Hijja, 203 AH, while al-Ma'mun was khalif.

Ghundar

His name was Muhammad ibn Ja'far. His *kunya* was Abu 'Abdullah, the client of Hudhayl. He was reliable, Allah willing. He died in Basra in 194 AH, while al-Amin was khalif.

Sa'id ibn 'Amir al-'Ujayfi

He settled among the Banu Dubay'a. His *kunya* was Abu Muhammad. He was reliable and righteous. 'Affan said, "I wrote *zuhd* from him." He died in Basra in Shawwal, 208 AH.

Bakkar ibn Muhammad

Bakkar ibn Muhammad said, "I was born in Rajab, 201 AH." He said that his father said that he was given the name and *kunya* of Muhammad ibn Sirin (his grandfather). They said that he lived to be 66.

'Abbad ibn Suhayb al-Kalbi

His *kunya* was Abu Bakr. He sought knowledge and listened to people. He was old, but he was a Qadarite and a missionary and so his *hadith* are abandoned. He died in Basra in Shawwal, 214 AH, while al-Ma'mun was khalif and Tahir ibn 'Ali al-Hashimi, governor of Basra at that time, prayed over him.

✲✲✲✲✲

Other men of this generation include: **Nuh ibn Qays at-Tahi** who settled in Suwayqat Tahiyya; **Al-Hakam ibn Sinan**, who was weak in *hadith* and died in 186 AH, while Harun was khalif; **Yahya ibn Sa'id al-Qattan**, whose *kunya* was Abu Sa'id and who was a reliable, trustworthy authority; **Muhammad ibn Sawa'**, who related from Sa'id ibn Abi 'Aruba; **Rawh ibn 'Ubada al-Qaysi**, one of the Banu Qays, whose *kunya* was Abu Muhammad and who was reliable; and **'Uthman ibn 'Umar**, who was reliable.

✻✻✻✻✻

The Seventh Generation

'Abdu'r-Rahman ibn Mahdi

His *kunya* was Abu Sa'id. He was reliable with many *hadiths*. He was born in 135 AH and died in Basra in Jumada al-Akhira, 198 AH, when he was 63.

Wahb ibn Jarir al-Jahdami

He was from Azd. His *kunya* was Abu'l-'Abbas. He was reliable. 'Affan mentioned him. He died at Manjashaniyya about six miles from Basra while returning from *hajj*. He was carried to Basra and buried.

Abu Da'ud at-Tayyalasi

His name was Sulayman ibn Da'ud. He had many *hadiths* and was reliable. Sometimes he erred. He died in Basra in 203 AH when he was 92. Yahya ibn 'Abdullah, the governor of Basra at that time, prayed over him.

Bahz ibn Asad

His *kunya* was Abu'l-Aswad. He was from Bal'am. He was reliable and an authority with many *hadiths*.

'Affan ibn Muslim as-Saffar

His *kunya* was Abu 'Uthman. He was the client of 'Azra ibn Thabit al-Ansari. He was reliable and dependable, an authority with many *hadiths*. Someone heard 'Affan say on Thursday, 18th Jumada al-Akhira, 210 AH, "I am 76," which would mean he was born in 134 AH. He died in Baghdad in 220 AH and 'Asim ibn 'Ali prayed over him.

Habban ibn Hilal al-Bahili

His *kunya* was Abu Habib. He was reliable, firm, an authority. He refrained from *hadith* before he died. He died in Basra in Ramadan, 216 AH.

Rayhan ibn Sa'id

His *kunya* was Abu 'Isma. He died in Basra in 203 or 204 AH while al-Ma'mun was khalif.

Abu Bakr al-Hanafi

His name was 'Abdu'l-Kabir ibn 'Abdu'l-Majid. He was reliable. He died in Basra in 204 AH while al-Ma'mun was khalif.

Abu 'Amir al-'Aqadi

His *kunya* was Abu 'Amr. He was the client of Banu Qays ibn Tha'laba. He was reliable and died in Basra in 224 AH.

'Abdu's-Samad ibn 'Abdu'l-Warith

His *kunya* was Abu Sahl. He was reliable. He died in 224 AH.

Sulayman ibn Harb al-Washihi

He was from Azd. His *kunya* was Abu Ayyub. He was reliable with many *hadiths*. He was made qadi of Makka and then dismissed. He returned to Basra where he remained until he died at the end of Rabi'a al-Akhira, 224 AH, when he was 84.

Bishr ibn 'Umar az-Zahrani

His *kunya* was Abu Muhammad. He was reliable in the transmission of Malik ibn Anas. He died in Basra in Sha'ban, 209 AH. Yahya ibn Aktham, who was Qadi of Basra at that time, prayed over him.

185

Seventh Generation

Abu'l-Walid at-Tayyalasi

His name was Hisham ibn 'Abdu'l-Malik. He was reliable and a dependable authority. He died in Basra in the beginning of Rabi' al-Awwal, 227 AH, when he was 94.

Al-Hajjaj ibn al-Minhal al-Anmati

His *kunya* was Abu Muhammad. He was reliable with many *hadiths*. He died in Basra on Saturday, 25 Shawwal, 217 AH.

'Ubaydullah ibn Muhammad at-Taymi

He is of Quraysh. He is Ibn 'A'isha. His *kunya* was Abu 'Abdu'r-Rahman. He listened to the books of Hammad ibn Salama. He died in Basra in Ramadan, 228 AH.

'Abdullah ibn Salama al-Harithi

His *kunya* was Abu 'Abdu'r-Rahman. He was a man of worship and virtue. He related the books of Malik ibn Anas. He related from 'Abdu'l-'Aziz ad-Darawardi and other shaykhs of Madina.

Rawh ibn Aslam

He was a client of Bahila. His *kunya* was Abu Hatim. He related from Hammad ibn Salama and Shu'ba.

Harami ibn Hafs

He settled in al-Qasamil. He related from Shu'ba and Hammad ibn Salama.

'Ali ibn 'Uthman

He was the cousin of Bishr ibn al-Mufaddal. He died in Basra in his house among the Banu'l-'Anbar in 227 AH.

Muslim ibn Ibrahim

His *kunya* was Abu 'Amr, the client of Azd. He was known as ash-Shahham. He was reliable with many *hadiths*. He died in Basra in Safar, 222 AH.

Abu Hudhayfa Musa ibn Mas'ud an-Nahdi

He had many *hadiths* and is reliable, Allah willing. He has excellent transmission from 'Ikrima ibn 'Ammar, Zuhayr ibn Muhammad and Sufyan ath-Thawri. They mention that Sufyan married his mother when he came to Basra. Abu Hudhayfa died in Basra in Jumada al-Akhira, 220 AH.

Ya'qub ibn Ishaq al-Hadrami al-Muqri

His *kunya* was Abu Muhammad. He is not considered dependable by them. They mention that he related from men whom he met when he was still a child.

His brother, Ahmad ibn Ishaq al-Hadrami

His *kunya* was Abu Ishaq. He was reliable. He was older than his brother. He died in Basra in Ramadan, 211 AH.

'Amr ibn Marzuq al-Bahili

He was reliable with many *hadiths* from Shu'ba. He died in Basra in Safar, 224 AH.

Muhammad ibn 'Ar'a'ra

His *kunya* was Abu 'Umar. He had *hadiths* from Shu'ba and others. He died in Shawwal, 213 AH, when he was 76.

'Arim ibn al-Fadl as-Sadusi

His *kunya* was Abu'n-Nu'man. 'Arim was a nickname. His actual name was Muhammad ibn al-Fadl. He died in Basra in Rabi' al-Awwal, 224 AH.

Abu 'Umar al-Hawdi

His name was Hafs ibn 'Umar. He died in Basra on Wednesday, 28th Jumada al-Akhira, 225 AH.

Musa ibn Isma'il at-Tabudhki

His *kunya* was Abu Salama. He was reliable with many *hadiths*. He died in Basra, Tuesday, 13th Rajab, 223 AH.

Al-Muʻalla ibn Asad the blind

He was the brother of Bahz ibn Asad. His *kunya* was Abu'l-Haytham. He was a teacher. He died in Basra in Ramadan, 218 AH.

Yahya ibn Hammad

His *kunya* was Abu Muhammad. He was reliable with many *hadiths*. He related from Abu ʻAwana. He related from his father Hammad ibn Abi Ziyad. His father related from al-Hasan, Ibn Sirin, and ʻAta' al-Khurasani that he asked ʻAbdu'l-Aʻla ibn Hammad an-Nursi about buying bottles on credit.

✶✶✶✶✶

Other men of this generation also include: **ʻUbaydullah ibn ʻAbdu'l-Majid,** who is related from and is reliable; **Ibrahim ibn Abi Suwayd,** who had the works of Hammad ibn Salama and died in Basra in 224 AH; **Umayya ibn Khalid al-Qaysi,** who is Umayya al-Aswad; **Hudba ibn Khalid al-Qaysi,** whose *kunya* was Abu Khalid; he was the brother of Umayya ibn Khalid al-Aswad; **Ishaq ibn ʻUmar,** who related from Hammad ibn Salama; **Muslim ibn Qutayba,** Abu Qutayba, who related from Shuʻba and others; **Muhammad ibn Sinan al-ʻAwfi,** who related from Hammam ibn Yahya; **ʻAbdullah ibn Yunus ibn ʻUbayd,** who has a few *hadiths*; **Da'ud ibn Shabib,** who related from Hammad ibn Salama; **ʻAbdu'r-Rahman ibn al-Mubarak,** who is Abu Bakr at-Tufawi; he settled among the Banu ʻAbs; **Al-Hajjaj ibn Basir al-Fusatiti,** who was weak; **ʻAmr ibn ʻAsim al-Kilabi,** whose *kunya* was Abu ʻUthman and who was reliable; **Muhammad ibn Kathir al-ʻAbdi,** the brother of Sulayman ibn Kathir; and **ʻAbdullah ibn Sawwar ibn ʻAbdullah the Qadi,** who died in Basra in 228 AH.

✶✶✶✶✶

The Eighth Generation

Musaddad ibn Musrahad ibn Musarbal al-Asadi

His *kunya* was Abu'l-Hasan. He died in Basra in Ramadan, 228 AH.

'Abdullah ibn 'Abdu'l-Wahhab al-Hujani

He related from Hammad ibn Zayd and others.

Sulayman ibn Da'ud Abu'r-Rabi' az-Zahrani

He died in Basra at the end of 234 AH.

'Abdullah ibn Muhammad ibn Asma'

He related from his uncle, Juwayriyya ibn Asma'.

Muhammad ibn Abi Bakr ibn 'Ali

He was the client of Thaqif. He died in Basra in 234 AH.

Ibn Ma'mar al-Minqari

His name was 'Abdullah ibn 'Amr. He had much transmission from Abdu'l-Warith at-Tannawri.

Abu Zafar

His name was 'Abdu's-Salam ibn Mutahhar ibn Husam.

'Ali ibn 'Abdullah ibn Ja'far al-Madini

His *kunya* was Abu'l-Hasan. He died in the army of the Amir al-Mu'minin at Surramanra'a on Monday, 28th Dhu'l-Qa'da, 234 AH.

Ibrahim ibn Bashshar ar-Ramadi

His *kunya* was Abu Ishaq, the companion of Ibn 'Uyayna. He died in Basra.

Ibrahim ibn Muhammad ibn 'Ar'ara

He died in Baghdad in Ramadan, 231 AH. He fell ill in the army of the Khalif at Samarra and was brought to Baghdad where he died.

'Ali ibn Barri

Hadith were recorded from him. He died in Basra, 234 AH.

Sulayman ibn ash-Shadhkuni

He memorised *hadith*. He died in Basra in 234 AH.

{End of the Basrans}

✽✻✽✻✽

The *Fuqaha'* and *Hadith* Scholars in Wasit

Ya'la ibn 'Ata'

He was the client of 'Abdullah ibn 'Amr ibn al-'As. He was reliable. He was from the people of Ta'if. He came to Wasit and settled there at the end of the Umayyad reign. Shu'ba ibn al-Hajjaj, Abu 'Awana, Hushaym and their companions listened to him.

Abu 'Aqil

Shu'ba related from him. His name was Hashim ibn Sallal or Sallam. He was reliable, Allah willing. He was one of the people of Syria. He went to Wasit and became Qadi there.

Abu Balj

His name was Yahya ibn Abi Sulaym al-Fazari. He was reliable, Allah willing. Shu'ba, Hushaym and Abu 'Awana related from him. Yazid ibn Harun said, "I saw Abu Balj. He was a neighbour of ours and he had no need for women. A bathhouse was set up in his house and he was friendly with them. He used to remember Allah often. If the Resurrection had come, he would have entered the Garden. He used to say, 'Allah is owed our remembrance.'"

Mansur ibn Zadhan

The companion of Al-Hasan. He is the one from whom Hushaym and his companions related. He was reliable and firm, a fast reciter. He used to try to slow down, but could not. He could do the entire Qur'an in a morning. That was known from him by the prostrations of the Qur'an. He moved and settled in al-Mubarak, nine parsangs (approx. 54 km) from Wasit. Yazid ibn Harun said that he died in the year of the plague in 131 AH.

Al-'Awwam ibn Hawshab

He was reliable. Yazid ibn Harun said that his *kunya* was Abu 'Isa. He was in charge of commanding the correct and forbidding the reprehensible. He died in 148 AH.

Sufyan ibn Husayn as-Sulami

He was their client. Yazid ibn Harun said that Sufyan's *kunya* was Abu'l-Hasan. Another said that it was Abu Muhammad. He was basically reliable although made several mistakes in *hadith*. He was a Qur'an teacher for al-Mahdi, the Amir al-Mu'minin. He died in Rayy while al-Mahdi was khalif.

Abu'l-'Ala' al-Qassab

His name was Ayyub ibn Abi Miskin. He was reliable. Yazid ibn Harun said that he died in 140 AH.

Asbagh ibn Zayd al-Warraq

He was the client of Juhayna. He used to write out copies of the Qur'an. He was weak in *hadith*. His *kunya* was Abu 'Abdullah. He died in 159 AH while al-Mahdi was khalif.

Khalaf ibn Khalifa

His *kunya* was Ahmad. He was the client of Ashja'. He was one of the people of Wasit and moved to Baghdad. He was reliable and then had semiparalysis before he died so that he became weak, his complexion altered and he muddled things. He died before Hushaym in Baghdad in 181 AH when he was about 90.

Hushaym ibn Bashir

His *kunya* was Abu Mu'awiya, the client of Banu Sulaym. He was basically reliable with many *hadiths* and dependable, although forged several times. When he says in his *hadith*, "He informed us," he is an authority, but when he does not say, "he reported to us," it is worthless.

His son Sa'id said, "My father was born at the beginning of 105 AH and died in Baghdad in Sha'ban, 183 AH, while Harun ar-Rashid was khalif, when he was 79, and was buried in the graves of al-Khayzuran."

'Ali ibn 'Asim

The client of Banu Tamim. His *kunya* was Abu'l-Hasan. He was born in 109 AH and died in Wasit in Jumada al-Ula, 201 AH, when he was 92.

Muhammad ibn Yazid al-Kala'i

His *kunya* was Abu Sa'id. He was reliable. He died in Wasit in 188 AH while Harun ar-Rashid was khalif.

Abu Sufyan al-Himyari al-Hadhdha'

He was a weak shaykh who had few *hadiths*. He died in Wasit on Wednesday, 23rd Sha'ban, 202 AH.

Yazid ibn Harun

His *kunya* was Abu Khalid, the client of the Banu Sulaym. He was reliable with many *hadiths*. He was born in 118 AH. He said, "I devoted myself to *hadith* when Husayn was alive. He was at al-Mubarak and people used to read to him. He forgot. Sometimes al-Jurayri gave me a *hadith* first and it would be contradicted." Yazid said in Shawwal, 199 AH, "I am 81 or 82." He died when he was 87 or 88, while al-Ma'mun was khalif.

Ishaq ibn Yusuf al-Azraq

His *kunya* was Abu Muhammad. He was reliable. Sometimes he muddled. He died in Wasit 195 AH while al-Amin was khalif.

Muhammad ibn al-Hasan

He was one of the people of Syria and was made qadi in Wasit. He was reliable.

Al-Fadl ibn 'Abasa al-Khazzar

His *kunya* was Abu'l-Hasan. He was reliable and known. He related from Yazid ibn Ibrahim at-Tustari, Hammad ibn Salama and others.

Surur ibn al-Mughira

He related *tafsir* from 'Abbad ibn Mansur from al-Hasan. He was commonly accepted.

'Asim ibn 'Ali

He used to relate from Shu'ba, Sulayman ibn al-Mughira, Layth ibn Sa'd, al-Mas'udi and others. He was reliable but was not known for *hadith*. There are a lot of errors in what he related. He died in Wasit on Monday, 15th Rajab, 221 AH while Abu Ishaq al-Mu'tasim was khalif. Al-Muttalib ibn Fahm al-Khurasani, the governor of Wasit at that time, prayed over him.

'Amr ibn 'Awn

His *kunya* was Abu 'Uthman. He died in Wasit in 225 AH while Abu Ishaq ibn Harun al-Mu'tasim was khalif.

✾✾✾✾✾

Other men of this generation also include: **Abu Hashim ar-Rumani,** or Yahya ibn Dinar, a reliable man; **Abu Khalid ad-Dalani,** or Yazid ibn 'Abdu'r-Rahman, whose *hadith* are ignored; **Al-Qasim ibn Abi Ayyub,** reliable with few *hadiths*; **Yazid ibn 'Ata' al-Bazzaz,** the client of Abu 'Awana, weak in *hadith*; **Khalid ibn 'Abdullah at-Tahhan,** the client of Muzayna, reliable, and he died in Wasit in 182 AH; **'Abdu'l-Hakim ibn Mansur,** the client of Khuza'a, weak in hadith; **Qurra ibn 'Isa,** who related from al-A'sha; and **Sila ibn Sulayman,** who was well-known.

✾✾✾✾✾

The Companions of the Messenger of Allah in Mada'in

Hudhayfa ibn al-Yaman

His mother was ar-Rabab bint Ka'b. His *kunya* was Abu 'Abdullah.

Hudhayfa was not present at Badr, but he, his father and brother Safwan ibn al-Yaman, were at Uhud. His father was killed that day. Hudhayfa was with the Messenger of Allah ﷺ at the Ditch and at the other battles after it. 'Umar ibn al-Khattab put him in charge of Mada'in.

Talha said, "Hudhayfa came to Mada'in and died some months after that in 36 AH and he has descendants in Mada'in."

Salman al-Farisi

Sufyan reported from his shaykhs that Salman's *kunya* was Abu 'Abdullah.

Abu 'Uthman an-Nahdi said, "Salman al-Farisi asked me, 'Do you know the site of Ramhurmuz?' I said, 'Yes. I am one of its people.' Salman said, 'I am one of the people of Jiy.'"

Ibn 'Abbas said, "Salman al-Farisi related to me, 'I was one of the people of Isfahan from a village called Jiy. My father was a landowner. I left him to collect a debt and some people from Kalb seized me and sold me to a Jewish man. Then that man sold me to a Jewish man of the Banu Qurayza who brought me to Madina. The Messenger of Allah ﷺ emigrated and I was kept from him by slavedom and so I missed Badr and Uhud. Then the Messenger of Allah ﷺ said to me, "Write a *kitaba*," and I wrote it and the Messenger of Allah ﷺ helped me in my *kitaba* with something like an egg of gold. I paid the money which I owed and was free and was present at the Ditch and the rest of the battles of the Messenger of Allah as a free Muslim.'"

Al-Hasan said that the Messenger of Allah ﷺ said, "Salman is the forerunner of Persia."

Kathir ibn 'Abdullah al-Muzani related that his grandfather said, "The Muhajirun and Ansar quarrelled about Salman on the Day of the Ditch and the Messenger of Allah ﷺ said, 'Salman is one of us, the People of the House.'"

Mada'in

Thabit ibn Qutba said, "Salman was governor of Mada'in." Salman al-Farisi died in Mada'in while 'Uthman was khalif.

✶✶✶✶✶

The *Fuqaha'* and *Hadith* Scholars in Mada'in

Abu Ja'far al-Mada'ini

His name was 'Abdullah ibn al-Miswar. He was the grandson of Ja'far ibn Abi Talib. He was commonly accepted, with few *hadith*s.

'Asim al-Ahwal ibn Sulayman

His *kunya* was Abu 'Abdu'r-Rahman, the client of Banu Tamim. He was reliable and was one of the people of Basra. He was given various appointments in the government. He was in charge of market inspection of weights and measures in Kufa. He was qadi in Mada'in while al-Mansur was khalif. He died in 141 or 142 AH.

Hilal ibn Khabbab

He was originally one of the people of Basra. Then he settled in Mada'in and died there at the end of 144 AH.

Al-Hudhayl ibn Bilal al-Fazari

He was weak in *hadith*.

Nu'aym ibn Hakim

He does not have a position in transmitting *hadith*.

Nasr ibn Hajib al-Qurashi

He was one of the Banu'l-Harith ibn Lu'ayy. His *kunya* was Abu Yahya. He was originally from Khurasan and he settled in Mada'in and died there in 145 AH when he was about 50 years old.

Shabbaba ibn Sawwar al-Fazari

He was their client. His *kunya* was Abu 'Amr. He was reliable, and correct in *hadith*. He was a Murji'ite.

Shu'ayb ibn Harb

His *kunya* was Abu Salih. He was one of the people of Khurasan among the people of Baghdad and then he moved to Mada'in and settled there and retired there. He was reliable and excellent. Then he went to Makka and remained there until he died.

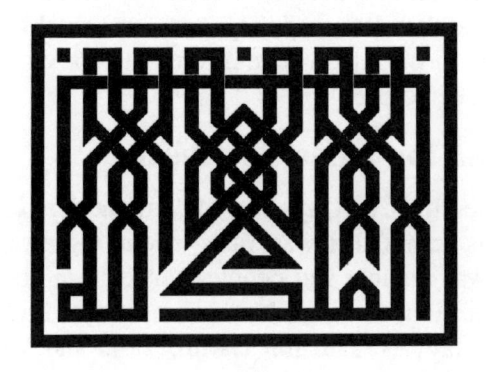

The *Fuqaha'* and *Hadith* Scholars in Baghdad

Isma'il ibn Salim al-Asadi

Hushaym and his people related from him. He was reliable and dependable. He was originally one of the people of Kufa and then he moved to Baghdad[1] before it was built and inhabited. Hisham ibn 'Abdu'l-Malik and other Umayyad khalifs had five hundred thousand Persians stationed in Baghdad as a defensive force against the Kharijites when they emerged in the region before their authority became weak.

Hisham ibn 'Urwa ibn az-Zubayr ibn al-'Awwam

His *kunya* was Abu'l-Mundhir. His mother was an *umm walad*. He was reliable and dependable, an authority with a lot of *hadith*. He listened to 'Abdullah ibn az-Zubayr and went to al-Mansur in Kufa and joined him in Baghdad where he died in 146 AH. He is buried in the Khayzuran cemetery.

Muhammad ibn Ishaq ibn Yasar

He was the client of Qays ibn Makhrama. His *kunya* was Abu 'Abdullah. His grandfather was Yasar, one of those captured at 'Ayn at-Tamr. He was reliable and people related from him. Ath-Thawri, Shu'ba, Sufyan ibn 'Uyayna, Yazid ibn Zuray', Ibrahim ibn Sa'd, Isma'il ibn 'Ulayya, Yazid ibn Harun, Ya'la and Muhammad, the sons of 'Ubayd, 'Abdullah ibn Numayr and others related from him. Some people spoke about him. He left Madina early on and went to Kufa, Mesopotamia, Rayy and Baghdad. He settled there and died there in 151 AH and is buried in the Khayzuran cemetery.

Abu Hanifa

His name was an-Nu'man ibn Thabit, the client of the Banu Taymullah. He was weak in *hadith*. He had judicial opinion (*ra'y*). He came to Baghdad and died there in Rajab or Sha'ban, 150 AH when he was 70. He is buried in the Khayzuran cemetery.

---
1. Al-Mansur started the construction of Baghdad in 146/763.

Abu Mu'awiya an-Nahawi

His name was Shayban ibn 'Abdu'r-Rahman, the client of the Banu Tamim. He was a teacher of the children of Da'ud ibn 'Ali and others. He was reliable in *hadith*. He died in Baghdad in 164 AH while al-Mahdi was khalif. He was buried in the cemetery of Quraysh at Bab at-Tibn.

Ibrahim ibn Sa'd az-Zuhri

His *kunya* was Abu Ishaq. He was reliable with many *hadiths*. Sometimes he erred in *hadith*. He came to Baghdad and he and his dependants and children settled there. He was put in charge of the Treasury by Harun, Amir al-Mu'minin. He died in Baghdad in 183 AH and was buried in the cemetery of the Bab at-Tibn.

'Abdu'l-'Aziz b.'Abdullah b. Abi Salama al-Majishun

His *kunya* was Abu 'Abdullah, the client of the Taymi family of al-Hudayr. He was reliable with many *hadiths*. The people of Iraq related from him more than the people of Madina. He came to Baghdad and lived there until he died in the khalifate of al-Mahdi. Al-Mahdi attended and prayed over him and buried him in the cemetery of Quraysh. He died in 164 AH.

'Abdu'l-Malik ibn Muhammad ibn Abi Bakr

One of the Najjar. His mother was Amatu'l-Wahhab bint 'Abdullah, the great granddaughter of Hanzala the Washed.[1] He came to Baghdad and took up residence there and Harun, the Amir al-Mu'minin, asked him to be Qadi of the army-camp of al-Mahdi. He died and Harun prayed over him and he was buried in the cemetery of al-'Abbasiyya bint al-Mahdi. He had few *hadiths*. His *kunya* was Abu Tahir.

Muhammad ibn 'Abdullah al-Kilabi

His *kunya* was Abu'l-Yasir. He was reliable, Allah willing. He was one of the people of Harran. He came to Baghdad and al-Mahdi

---

1. Hanzala was killed at the Battle of Uhud. As martyrs are buried without being washed, Hanzala's family were worried because he had been in a state of major impurity. The Prophet ﷺ informed them that the angels had washed him. Hence he is called 'the Washed' or 'Washed by the angels'.

made him qadi of the army-camp of al-Mahdi. Then 'Afiyya ibn Yazid al-Awdi was also appointed qadi along with him.

'Ali ibn al-Ja'd said, "I saw them both giving judgement in the Communal Mosque at Rusafa, one in the nearer part and one in the further part." 'Afiyya visited al-Mahdi more than he did.

Ziyad ibn 'Abdullah al-Kilabi

He was the deputy of his brother, Muhammad ibn 'Abdullah, in charge of judgement for al-Mahdi.

Isma'il ibn 'Umar

His *kunya* was Abu'l-Mundhir. He related from Sufyan ath-Thawri and Malik ibn Anas.

Muhammad ibn Sabiq

His *kunya* was Abu Ja'far, the client of Banu Tamim. He was one of the people of Kufa who settled in Baghdad in the region of ar-Rabi' and traded there. He died in Baghdad.

Sa'id ibn 'Abdu'r-Rahman al-Jumahi

He was appointed qadi in Baghdad in the army-camp of al-Mahdi and died there.

'Abdu'r-Rahman ibn Abi'z-Zinad

His *kunya* was Abu Muhammad. He came to Baghdad for something he needed and the Baghdadis listened to him. He had many *hadiths*. His transmission from his father was weak. He died in Baghdad in 174 AH while Harun ar-Rashid was khalif. He was buried in the cemetery of Bab at-Tibn.

His son, Muhammad ibn 'Abdu'r-Rahman

His *kunya* was Abu 'Abdullah. He met most of the men of his father's generation and he was reliable with a lot of knowledge. He died before people listened to him. He died in Baghdad 21 days after his father in 174 AH when he was 54. He was buried in the cemetery of al-Khayzuran.

Hushaym ibn Bashir al-Wasiti

His *kunya* was Abu Mu'awiya. He settled in Baghdad and died there on a Tuesday in Sha'ban, 183 AH while Harun ar-Rashid was khalif. He was reliable but forged.

Isma'il ibn Ibrahim ibn Miqsam

He was the client of 'Abdu'r-Rahman ibn Qutba al-Asdi. He was one of the people of Kufa. Miqsam was one of the captives from Qiqaniyya, which is between Khurasan and Zabulistan. Ibrahim ibn Miqsam was a merchant from the people of Kufa. He used to bring his goods to Basra, sell them, and then return. He stayed behind and married 'Ulayya bint Hassan, a client of the Banu Shayban. She was a noble intelligent woman of great dignity who did not conceal herself. She had a house in al-'Awaqa in Basra for which she was famous. Salih al-Murri and other notable scholars and *fuqaha'* of the people of Basra used to visit her and she would come out to them and converse with them and question them.

She bore Ibrahim ibn Isma'il in 110 AH and he is called by her name, "Ibn 'Ulayya", and he lived in Basra. After Isma'il, she bore Ibrahim Rib'i ibn Ibrahim. Isma'il's *kunya* was Abu Bishr. He was reliable and a dependable authority. He was put in charge of the *zakat* of Basra and was put in charge of injustices in Baghdad at the end of Harun's khalifate. He and his children settled in Baghdad and he bought a house there. He died in Baghdad on Tuesday, 13th Dhu'l-Qa'da, 193 AH, and was buried on Wednesday morning in the cemetery of 'Abdullah ibn Malik. His son, Ibrahim ibn Isma'il, prayed over him. Wukay' ibn al-Jarrah was in Baghdad on the day that Isma'il died.

Isma'il ibn Zakariyya

He was the client of the Banu Suwa'a. His *kunya* was Abu Ziyad. He was a merchant in foodstuffs and other things. He was one of the people of Kufa and settled in Baghdad in the Humayd ibn Qahtaba suburb. He died there at the beginning of 171 AH when he was 75.

Abu Sa'id al-Mu'addib the tutor

His name was Muhammad ibn Muslim. He was from a subtribe of Quda'a. He came from Mesopotamia. When al-Mansur took control of Mesopotamia, he made Abu Sa'id the tutor of his son, al-Mahdi. At that time al-Mahdi was about ten years old. He went to Baghdad with them. Then al-Mansur appointed Sufyan ibn Husayn as al-Mahdi's tutor. Al-Mahdi appointed Abu Sa'id tutor of his son, 'Ali. He remained with him until Abu Sa'id died in Baghdad while al-Hadi was the khalif. He was buried in the cemetery of al-Khayzuran. His house was in Rusafa.

Abu Sa'id used to relate from Salim al-Aftas, Khusayf, 'Abdu'l-Karim al-Jazari, 'Ali ibn Badima, Ibrahim ibn Abi Hurra, Hisham ibn 'Urwa, Yahya ibn Sa'id, Muhammad ibn 'Amr ibn 'Alqama, al-A'mash, Isma'il ibn Abi Khalid, Mis'ar, al-Ajlah al-Kindi, Sulayman at-Taymi and others. He was reliable.

'Ubbad ibn 'Ubbad ibn Habib al-'Ataki

His *kunya* was Abu Mu'awiya. He was reliable and sometimes erred. He related from Abu Hamza and from Wasil, the client of Abu 'Uyayna. He was one of the people of Basra who went to Baghdad and settled there and died there.

Al-Faraj ibn Fadala

His *kunya* was Abu Fadala. He was one of the people of Syria from the people of Hims. He came to Baghdad and was put in charge of the Treasury at the beginning of Harun's khalifate. He lived in the city of al-Mansur and died there in 176 AH. He was weak in *hadith* and was related from.

Isma'il ibn Ja'far al-Madani

He was reliable and he had 500 *hadiths* which people heard from him. He was one of the people of Kufa. He came to Baghdad and remained there until his death.

'Ubaydullah ibn 'Ubaydu'r-Rahman al-Ashja'i

His *kunya* was Abu 'Abdu'r-Rahman. He related the books of ath-Thawri properly and related *al-Jami'* from him. He was one of the people of Kufa and he came to Baghdad and remained there until his death.

'Ammar ibn Muhammad

His *kunya* was Abu'l-Yaqzan. He was the nephew of Sufyan ath-Thawri. He was reliable. He related from 'Ata' ibn as-Sa'ib and other Kufans. He was one of the people of Kufa and he came to Baghdad and remained there until his death.

Talha ibn Yahya al-Ansari

He settled in the suburb of the Ansar. He related from Yunus ibn Yazid al-Ayli, and 'Abbad ibn Musa listened to him a lot.

Marwan ibn Shuja'

He was called al-Khusayfi. He was from Harran in Mesopotamia. He related from Khusayf and came to Baghdad and was the teacher of the children of al-Hadi, the Amir al-Mu'minin. He remained in Baghdad until his death.

'Abida ibn Humayd at-Taymi

His *kunya* was Abu 'Abdu'r-Rahman. He was reliable and sound in *hadith*. He was one of the people of Kufa and a master of grammar, Arabic and Qur'an recitation. He came to Baghdad in the days of Harun, the Amir al-Mu'minin, and he went with his son, al-Amin, and remained with him until his death in Baghdad.

Abu Hafs al-Abbar

His name was 'Umar ibn 'Abdu'r-Rahman al-Asadi. He was reliable. He related from Mansur ibn al-Mu'tamir and others. He was one of the people of Kufa and came to Baghdad and stayed there until his death.

Marwan ibn Mu'awiya ibn al-Harith al-Fazari

His *kunya* was Abu 'Abdullah. He was one of the people of Kufa. Then he went to the frontier area with Byzantium and stayed there. Then he went to Baghdad and stayed there and settled there. The Baghdadis listened to him. He was reliable. Then he went to Makka and stayed there and died there on the 10th Dhu'l-Hijja a day before the *Tarwiya* in 193 AH. He was 81 when he died.

'Abbad ibn al-'Awwam

His *kunya* was Abu Sahl. He was one of the people of Wasit. He was a Shi'ite. Harun ar-Rashid had him imprisoned for a time and then let him go. He stayed in Baghdad and the Baghdadis listened to him. He was reliable. He settled in Karkh on the river of the Bazzaris. He died in 185 AH while Harun was Amir al-Mu'minin.

'Ali ibn Thabit

His *kunya* was Abu'l-Hasan, the client of al-'Abbad ibn Muhammad al-Hashimi. He was from Mesopotamia and came to Baghdad where he lived until his death. He was reliable and truthful.

Abu Yusuf the Qadi

His name was Ya'qub ibn Ibrahim ibn Habib ibn Sa'd. Sa'd's mother was from the Banu 'Amr of the Ansar, and Sa'd was known by his mother's name, Ibn Habta. They were allies of the Banu 'Amr. Abu Yusuf had many *hadiths* from Abu Khusayf, al-Mughira, Husayn, Mutarrif, Hisham ibn 'Urwa, al-A'mash and other Kufans. He was famous for his memory of *hadith*. He would attend a *hadith* scholar and memorise fifty or sixty *hadiths* and stand up and recite them to people. Then he attached himself to Abu Hanifa an-Nu'man ibn Thabit and studied his *fiqh* and so opinion (*ra'y*) dominated him and he avoided *hadith*. Al-Mahdi attached him to his son Musa and he was responsible for his judicial decisions. He remained with him at Jurjan until he became khalif. Then he went to Baghdad with him and became its qadi. He and his children remained there and he died on 5th Rabi' al-Akhir 185 AH while Harun ar-Rashid was khalif.

Al-Husayn ibn Hasan ibn 'Atiyya al-'Awfi

His *kunya* was Abu 'Abdullah, and he was one of the people of Kufa. He listened a lot, and was weak in *hadith*. Then he came to Baghdad and was made qadi of its eastern side after Hafs ibn Ghiyath. Then he was transferred from the eastern side and made qadi of the army-camp of al-Mahdi while Harun ar-Rashid was khalif. Then he was dismissed and remained at Baghdad until he died there in 201 or 202 AH.

Asad ibn 'Amr al-Bajali

His *kunya* was Abu'l-Mundhir. He had many *hadiths* and was reliable, Allah willing. He accompanied Abu Hanifa and studied *fiqh* with him. He was one of the people of Kufa and was brought to Baghdad and appointed qadi of the eastern part of the city after al-'Awfi.

'Afiyya ibn Yazid al-Awdi

He was one of the people of Abu Hanifa and was appointed qadi for al-Mahdi in Baghdad over the army-camp of al-Mahdi.

'Isma ibn Muhammad al-Ansari

He was the Imam of the Great mosque of the Ansar in Baghdad. He related from Sahl ibn Abi Aflah, Yahya ibn Sa'id and 'Ubaydullah ibn 'Umar. He was considered weak in *hadith* in their eyes.

Al-Musayyab ibn Sharik

His *kunya* was Abu Sa'id. He was one of the Banu Shuqra Tamim. He was born in Khurasan and grew up in Kufa. He listened to *hadith* from al-A'mash, Isma'il ibn Abi Khalid, 'Abdu'l-Malik ibn Abi Sulayman and others. He was weak in *hadith* and was not an authority in it. Then he came to Baghdad and settled there and was put in charge of the Treasury for Harun, the Amir al-Mu'minin. His home was in the city of al-Mansur. He had descendants and died in Baghdad 186 AH.

Abu'l-Bakhtari the qadi

His name was Wahb ibn Wahb. He was one of the people of Madina and then left it and settled in Syria. Then he came to Baghdad and Harun, Amir al-Mu'minin, appointed him qadi in the army-camp of al-Mahdi. Then he dismissed him and put him in charge of Madina after Bakkar ibn Muhammad az-Zubayri. He put him in charge of its prayer, war and judgement. He was a chivalrous shaykh among the men of Quraysh. He did not have that position in *hadith*. He related contradicted *hadiths* and so his *hadith* are abandoned. Then he was dismissed from Madina and he went to Baghdad where he remained until his death in 200 AH.

Al-Hajjaj ibn Muhammad al-A'war

His *kunya* was Abu Muhammad, the client of Salman ibn Mujalid, the client of al-Mansur. His family is still in Baghdad. He moved to Massisa with his children and dependants and stayed there for two years. Then he returned to Baghdad because of something he needed and remained there until his death in Rabi' al-Awwal, 206 AH. He was reliable and truthful, Allah willing. He made alterations at the end of his life when he returned to Baghdad.

'Abdu'l-Wahhab ibn 'Ata' al-'Ijli-Khaffaf

His *kunya* was Abu Nasr. He was one of the people of Basra. He attached himself to Sa'id ibn Abi Aruba and was known as his companion and wrote out his books. He related from Yunus ibn 'Ubayd, Khalid al-Hadhdha', Humayd at-Tawil, 'Awf al-A'rabi, Ibn 'Awn, Da'ud ibn Abi Hind, 'Imran ibn Judayr and others. He has many *hadiths* and was known and truthful, Allah willing. Then he came to Baghdad and settled there and lived there and kept to the market in Karkh where he remained until his death.

Abu Badr

His name was Shuja' ibn al-Walid as-Sakuni. He related from al-A'mash, Hisham ibn 'Urwa, Khusayf and others. He lived to more than 90. He prayed a lot and was scrupulous. He died in Baghdad in 204 AH. That was in Ramadan while al-Ma'mun was khalif.

His son, Abu Humam

His name was al-Walid ibn Shuja'. He related from Baqiyya, Isma'il ibn 'Ayyash, al-Walid ibn Muslim and others.

'Abdullah ibn Bakr as-Sahmi

Sahm was a subtribe of Bahila. He was one of the people of Basra. He was reliable and truthful. He settled in Baghdad and stayed with Sa'id ibn Muslim and the Baghdadis listened to him. He remained there until his death on Tuesday, 17th Muharram, 208 AH while al-Ma'mun was khalif.

Kathir ibn Hisham

His *kunya* was Abu Sahl. He was the companion of Ja'far ibn Burqan. He settled in Baghdad at Bab al-Karkh in the market. He used to equip the traders going to ar-Raqqa and elsewhere in Mesopotamia and Syria. He was reliable and truthful. Then he went to al-Hasan ibn Sahl who was at Fam as-Silh. He died there in Sha'ban, 207 AH.

Muhammad ibn 'Umar al-Aslami

He was the client of 'Abdullah ibn Burayda al-Aslami. His *kunya* was Abu 'Abdullah. He was one of the people of Madina. He came to Baghdad in 180 AH to seek a debt connected to him and remained there. He went to Syria and ar-Raqqa and then returned to Baghdad and remained there until al-Ma'mun came from Khurasan [after defeating his brother, al-Amin]. He was appointed qadi in the army-camp of al-Mahdi and he remained qadi until he died in Baghdad on Tuesday night, 11th Dhu'l-Hijja, 207 AH. He was buried on Tuesday in the al-Khayzuran cemetery. He was 78.

He mentioned that he was born in 130 AH at the end of the khalifate of Marwan II. He related from Muhammad ibn 'Ajlan, Rabi'a, ad-Dahhak ibn 'Uthman, Ma'mar, Ibn Jurayj, Thawr ibn Yazid, Mu'awiya ibn Salih, al-Walid ibn Kathir, 'Abdu'l-Hamid ibn Ja'far, Usama ibn Zayd, Makhrama ibn Bukayr, Aflah ibn Sa'id, Aflah ibn Humayd, Yahya ibn 'Abdullah ibn Abi Qatada, and Ibn Abi Dhib. He had knowledge of expeditions, the disagreements of people and their words.

Hashim ibn al-Qasim al-Kinani

His *kunya* was Abu'n-Nadr. He was one of the Banu Layth. He was one of the *abna'*[1] of Khurasan who settled in Baghdad. He was reliable. He related from Sulayman ibn al-Mughira, Shu'ba, al-Mas'udi, Ibn Abi Dhib, Hariz ibn 'Uthman, Zuhayr ibn Mu'awiya, Muhammad ibn Talha, Abu Ja'far ar-Razi, Sharik and others. He died in Baghdad at the beginning of Dhu'l-Qa'da, 207 AH, while al-Ma'mun was khalif and was buried in the cemetery of 'Abdullah ibn Malik.

---

1. *Abna'*, short for *abna' ad-dawla*, 'sons of the state', a term used to describe the new generation of Khurasanis whose fathers had settled in Baghdad after the 'Abbasid revolution.

Qurrad Abu Nuh

He was the client of 'Abdullah ibn Malik. He was reliable. He related a lot from Shu'ba and al-Hajjaj.

Shadhan

His name was al-Aswad ibn 'Amir. He was from Syria and he was correct in *hadith*. He settled in Baghdad and remained there until his death in 208 AH.

'Affan ibn Muslim

He was the client of 'Azra ibn Thabit al-Ansari. His *kunya* was Abu 'Uthman. He was reliable with many *hadiths* and sound books. He was one of the people of Basra and he came to Basra and remained there until he died in 220 AH. 'Asim ibn 'Ali prayed over him. He was put through the Inquisition [*Mihna*][1] and was questioned about the Qur'an but refused to say that the Qur'an is created.

Muhammad ibn al-Hasan

His *kunya* was Abu 'Abdullah, the client of Banu Shayban. He originated from the people of Mesopotamia. His father was in the army of the people of Syria and came to Wasit.[2] Muhammad was born there in 132 AH and he grew up in Kufa and devoted himself to *hadith* and listened a lot to Mis'ar, Malik ibn Mighwal, 'Umar ibn Dharr, Sufyan ath-Thawri, al-Awza'i, Ibn Jurayj, Muhill ad-Dabbi, Bakr ibn Ma'iz, Abu Hurra, 'Isa al-Khayyat and others. He sat with Abu Hanifa and listened to him. He studied judicial opinion (*ra'y*) and it dominated him and he was known for it and acted on it. He came to Baghdad and settled there and people came to him and listened to *hadith* and opinion from him. He went to ar-Raqqa when Harun, the Amir al-Mu'minin, was there and he appointed him qadi of ar-Raqqa. Then he dismissed him and he went back to Baghdad. When Harun went out to Rayy the first time, he went with him and he died in Rayy in 189 AH when he was 58.

---

1. The Inquisition instituted by the Abbasid khalif, al-Ma'mun, which required all important people to publicly state the belief that the Qur'an was created.

2. Wasit was a major Umayyad base in Iraq.

Yusuf ibn Ya'qub ibn Ibrahim the Qadi

He listened to *hadith* and related *ra'y* from his father, Abu Yusuf. He was appointed qadi in Baghdad on the western side while his father was still alive. He led the people in the *Jumu'a* prayer in the city of al-Mansur at the command of Harun, the Amir al-Mu'minin. He remained qadi for him there until he died in Rajab, 192 AH.

Abu Kamil Muzaffar ibn Mudrik

He was one of the *abna'* of Khurasan. He was reliable. He related from Hammad ibn Salama and others.

Yunus ibn Muhammad the tutor

His *kunya* was Abu Muhammad. He was reliable and truthful. He died in Baghdad on Saturday, 7th Safar, 208 AH.

Al-Hasan ibn Musa al-Ashyab

He was one of the *abna'* of Khurasan. His *kunya* was Abu 'Ali. He was appointed qadi of Hims and Mosul for Harun, the Amir al-Mu'minin. Then he came to Baghdad while al-Ma'mun was khalif. He remained in Baghdad until al-Ma'mun appointed him Qadi of Tabaristan. He set out for it but died on the way at Rayy in the month of Rabi', 209 AH. He was reliable and truthful in *hadith*. He related from Shu'ba, Hammad ibn Salama, Warqa' ibn 'Umar, Zuhayr ibn Mu'awiya, Ibn Lahi'a, Abu Hilal, Jarir ibn Hazim and others.

Husayn ibn Muhammad al-Marwazi

His *kunya* was Abu Ahmad. He was reliable. He related from Shu'ba and Harir ibn Hazim. He mentioned that he listened to him in Jurjan in the time of Sulayman ibn Rashid. He related *tafsir* from Ibn Abi Dhib, Shayban ibn 'Abdu'r-Rahman and others. He related *Expeditions* from Abu Ma'shar. He died at the end of al-Ma'mun's khalifate.

Hujayr ibn al-Muthanna

His *kunya* was Abu 'Amr. He was one of the people of Yamama. He came to Baghdad and settled there. He dealt in pearls and gems.

He stayed in the market in Baghdad. He was reliable. He related a lot from Layth ibn Sa'd and 'Abdullah al-Majishun. He died in Baghdad.

'Ali ibn al-Ja'd

The client of Umm Salama al-Makhzumiyya, the wife of Abu'l-'Abbas, the Amir al-Mu'minin.

'Abdu'r-Rahman ibn Ishaq the Qadi said, "'Ali ibn al-Ja'd brought me a scroll belonging to his father which contained his freedom from Umm Salama which was witnessed by the grandfathers of Ibrahim ibn Salama and another man who used to visit her."

'Ali ibn al-Ja'd said, "I was born in 136 AH at the end of the khalifate of Abu'l-'Abbas (as-Saffah)." He related from Shu'ba, Zuhayr ibn Mu'awiya, Sakhr ibn Juwayriyya, Layth ibn Sa'd, Hammad ibn Salama, Sufyan ath-Thawri, Abu Ja'far ar-Razi and others. He died in Baghdad on the 25th Rajab 230 AH, and was buried in the cemetery of Bab Harb. He was 96 when he died.

Hawdha ibn Khalifa ibn 'Abdullah

His *kunya* was Abu'l-Ashhab. His mother was az-Zuhra bint 'Abdu'r-Rahman and her mother was Hawla bint 'Abdu'r-Rahman. Hawdha was born in 125 AH and devoted himself to *hadith*. He wrote from Yunus, Hisham, 'Awf, Ibn 'Awn, Ibn Jurayj, Sulayman at-Taymi and others. His books have disappeared and there only remains the book of 'Awf and a little of Ibn 'Awn, Ibn Jurayh, Ash'ath and at-Taymi. Hawdha died in Baghdad on Tuesday, 11th Shawwal 216 AH, while al-Ma'mun was khalif and was buried outside the Khorasan Gate. His son prayed over him. He was a brown-skinned man who used henna.

Yahya ibn Sa'id ibn Aban

His *kunya* was Abu Ayyub. He was one of the people of Kufa and went to Baghdad where he settled. He was reliable with many *hadiths*. He related from Hisham ibn 'Urwa, Yahya ibn Sa'id al-Ansari, al-A'mash, Isma'il ibn Abi Khalid, 'Abdu'l-Malik ibn Abi Sulayman and others. He related *Expeditions* from Muhammad ibn Ishaq. He settled in Baghdad in the army of al-Mahdi at as-Sib at the

Mill of 'Abdu'l-Malik. He died there in 194 AH while Muhammad al-Amin was khalif when he was eighty.

Abu Zakariyya as-Saylihini

His name was Yahya ibn Ishaq al-Bajali. He was reliable. He related from Yahya ibn Ayyub, Ibn Lahi'a and others. People wrote from him. He memorised his *hadith*. He settled in Baghdad in Dar ar-Raqiq and died there in 210 AH while al-Ma'mun was khalif.

Sa'id ibn Sulayman al-Wasiti

His *kunya* was Abu 'Uthman. His name was Sa'dawayh. He was reliable with many *hadiths*. He related from Sulayman ibn al-Mughira, al-Mubarak ibn Fadala, Layth ibn Sa'd, Abu Ma'shar and others. He settled in Baghdad and traded there. His home was at al-Karkh near the road of the paper people. He died there on Tuesday in the evening. He was buried the following day, at the beginning of the day, on the 4th Dhu'l-Hijja 225 AH. His nephew, 'Ali ibn Hunayn the merchant, prayed over him.

Abu Nasr at-Tammar

His name was 'Abdu'l-Malik ibn 'Abdu'l-'Aziz, one of the *abna'* of Khurasan from the people of Nasa. He mentioned that he was born six months after Abu Muslim, the Abbasid recruiting officer, was killed. He settled in Baghdad in the suburb of Abu'l-'Abbas at-Tusi, and then in the Darb an-Nassabiyya where he traded in dates and other commodities. He was reliable and excellent, scrupulous and worthy. He related from Hammad ibn Salama, Sa'id ibn 'Abdu'l-'Aziz at-Tanukhi, Kawthar ibn Hakim and others.

He died in Baghdad on Tuesday at the beginning of the day in Muharram 228 AH. He was buried at Bab Harb. He was 91 and had gone blind.

Shurayh ibn an-Nu'man

His *kunya* was Abu'l-Husayn. He dealt in pearls. He was reliable and related from Hammad ibn Salama, Fulayh ibn Sulayman, and Abu 'Awana. His home was in the army camp of al-Mahdi at Sib al-

Qadi. He died on the *'Id al-Adha* in the seventh year of al-Ma'mun's khalifate.

Yahya ibn Ghaylan

One of Khuza'a. He was reliable. He settled in Baghdad and then went to Basra for something he needed and died there in 210 AH. He related from the Basrans.

Mu'awiya ibn 'Amr al-Azdi

His *kunya* was Abu 'Amr. He related the books and works of Za'ida ibn Qudama. He related the *Book of Travel in Dar al-Harb* from Abu Ishaq al-Fazari. He settled in Baghdad and the people of Baghdad listened to him. He died in Baghdad in 214 or 215 AH while al-Ma'mun was khalif.

Al-Mu'alla ibn Mansur ar-Razi

His *kunya* was Abu Ya'la. He settled in Baghdad and devoted himself to hadith. He was truthful with *hadith*, judicial opinion (*ra'y*) and *fiqh*. Some of the people of *hadith* relate from him and some do not relate opinion from him. He settled in Karkh in the Qati'a ar-Rabi'. He died in 211 AH.

Muhammad ibn as-Sabah al-Bazzaz ad-Dulabi

His *kunya* was Abu Ja'far. He settled at the gate of Karkh and died at the end of Muharram, 227 AH.

Bishr ibn al-Harith

May Allah be pleased with him. His *kunya* was Abu Nasr. He was one of the *abna'* of Khurasan from the people of Marw. He settled in Baghdad and devoted himself to *hadith* and listened a lot to Hammad ibn Zayd, Sharik, 'Abdullah ibn al-Mubarak, Hushaym and others. Then he devoted himself to worship and withdrew from people and did not relate.

He died in Baghdad on Wednesday, 11th Rabi' al-Awwal 227 AH. Many people of Baghdad and elsewhere were present and he was buried at the Harb Gate. He was 76.

Al-Haytham ibn Kharija

His *kunya* was Abu Ahmad. He was one of the *abna'* of Khurasan from the people of Marwurrudh. He settled at Baghdad. He remained there until he died on Monday, 22th Dhu'l-Hijja, 227 AH.

Sa'd ibn Ibrahim az-Zuhri

His *kunya* was Abu Ishaq. He was appointed qadi in Wasit while Harun ar-Rashid was khalif. Then he was appointed qadi of the army-camp of al-Mahdi at the beginning of al-Ma'mun's khalifate while he was still in Khurasan. He used to relate the books of his father and some of the Baghdadis listened to him. Then he was dismissed as qadi in Baghdad and joined al-Hasan ibn Sahl while he was at Fam as-Silh and was appointed qadi of its army. He died at al-Mubarak when he was 63 in 201 AH.

His brother, Ya'qub ibn Ibrahim az-Zuhri

His *kunya* was Abu Yusuf. He was reliable and trustworthy. He used to relate *The Expeditions* from his father and other people. The Baghdadis listened to him. He used to be given precedence over his brother in virtue, scrupulousness and *hadith*. He remained in Baghdad and then he went to al-Hasan ibn Sahl when he was at Fam as-Sulh and remained there with him until he died there in Shawwal, 208 AH. He was four years younger than his brother Sa'd.

Sulayman ibn Da'ud

He was a Hashimi whose *kunya* was Abu Ayyub. He was reliable and listened to Ibrahim ibn Sa'd, 'Abdu'r-Rahman ibn Abi'z-Zinad and others. The Baghdadis wrote from him and related from him. He died in Baghdad in 229 AH.

Qurran ibn Tammam al-Asadi

His *kunya* was Abu Tammam. He was one of the people of Kufa. He came and settled in Baghdad. He was a broker in animals. He was listened to although he was weak.

'Umar ibn Hafs

His *kunya* was Abu Hafs al-'Abdi. He related from Thabit al-Bunani, Yazid ar-Raqqashi, Aban ibn Abi 'Ayyash, Umm Shabib al-'Abdiyya, Malik ibn Anas and others. He was considered by them to be weak in *hadith*. They wrote from him and then abandoned him. He died in Baghdad in 198 AH at the beginning of al-Ma'mun's khalifate.

Mus'ab ibn 'Abdullah

His *kunya* was Abu 'Abdullah. He settled in Baghdad and related the *Muwatta'* from Malik ibn Anas, and he related from ad-Darawardi, Ibrahim ibn Sa'd, 'Abdu'l-'Aziz ibn Abi Hazim, his father ('Abdullah ibn Thabit) and others. When he was asked about whether the Qur'an was created, he would take a stand and reprove the one who did not take a stand. He died in Baghdad in Shawwal, 236 AH.

Nasr ibn Zayd

His *kunya* was Abu'l-Hasan. He was reliable and had *hadiths*. He listened to Jarir ibn Hazim, Abu Hilal, Wuhayb and others. He died early on before he could transmit *hadith*. His family came from Sijistan. He was the client of Ja'far, the son of al-Mansur (the khalif).

'Anbasa ibn Sa'id ibn Aban

His *kunya* was Abu Khalid. He was reliable and had *hadith*. He came to Baghdad and stayed there and the Baghdadis listened to him.

Mansur ibn Salama

His *kunya* was Abu Salama. He was reliable and listened to several people. He refrained from *hadith* and then he reported historical events. Then he went to the frontier and died there at Massisa in 214 AH while al-Ma'mun was khalif.

Nasr ibn Bab al-Khurasani

His *kunya* was Abu Sahl. He listened to Da'ud ibn Abi Hind, 'Awf al-A'rabi, al-Hajjaj ibn Arta' and others. He settled in Baghdad and they listened to him and related from him. Then he reported from

Ibrahim as-Sa'igh,[1] so they suspected him and abandoned his *hadith*. He died in Baghdad in the army-camp of al-Mahdi.

Musa ibn Da'ud ad-Dabbi

His *kunya* was Abu 'Abdullah. He was reliable and had *hadith*. He listened to Sufyan ath-Thawri, Zuhayr and others. He settled in Baghdad. Then he was made qadi of Tarsus and went there and remained qadi there until his death.

Ibrahim ibn al-'Abbas

His *kunya* was Abu Ishaq. He was known as as-Samiri. He related from Abu Uways, Sharik and others. He became muddled at the end of his life and his family secluded him in his house until his death.

Al-Hakam ibn Musa al-Bazzaz

His *kunya* was Abu Salih. He was reliable with many *hadiths*. He was one of the *abna'* of Khurasan from the people of Nasa. He related from the Syrians, from Yahya ibn Hamza, Fadl ibn Ziyad and others of the people of Syria. He was a righteous man who was reliable in *hadith*. He died in Baghdad in Shawwal, 232 AH.

Hisham ibn Sa'id al-Bazzaz

His *kunya* was Abu Ahmad. He transmitted from Ibn Lahi'a and Hammad ibn Zayd. He was reliable but died before people listened to him.

Muhammad ibn al-Hajjaj al-Musaffir

His *kunya* was Abu Ja'far. He listened to Shu'ba, Ibn Abi Dhib and others. He was considered by them to be weak in *hadith*.

Sa'd ibn 'Abdu'l-Hamid

An ally of the Ansar. His *kunya* was Abu Mu'adh. He mentioned that he listened to Malik ibn Anas and others.

---

1. An opponent of Abu Muslim and the Abbasids. See p. 229-30.

Baghdad

Khalid ibn Khidash

His *kunya* was Abu'l-Haytham, the client of the family of al-Muhallab ibn Abi Sufra. He was reliable. He related from Hammad ibn Zayd, Abu 'Awana and others. He died in 223 or 224 AH.

Mansur ibn Bashir

He is the son of Abu Muzahim. His *kunya* was Abu Nasr, and he was a client of Azd. He was one of the Turkish captives. He had a *diwan* which he left and people wrote from him. He was reliable and was a proponent of the *sunna*. He died in Baghdad in Dhu'l-Qa'da, 235 AH, when he was 80 or more.

Muhammad ibn Bakkar

His *kunya* was Abu 'Abdullah. He related from Ma'shir, Muhammad ibn Talha, Qays ibn ar-Rabi', 'Anbasa ibn 'Abdu'l-Wahid and others. He died in Baghdad in Rabi' al-Akhir, 238 AH.

Muhammad ibn Ja'far al-Warakani

His *kunya* was Abu 'Imran. He related from Ibrahim ibn Sa'd, Abu Ma'shar, Sharik, al-Mu'afi ibn 'Imran, Ibn Abi'z-Zinad, Abu 'Aqil, the companion of Buhayya, and others. He died in Baghdad in Ramadan, 228 AH.

Yahya ibn Yusuf ar-Raqqi

His *kunya* was Abu Zakariyya. He used to related from 'Ubaydullah ibn 'Amr ar-Raqqi and others. He died in Baghdad while al-Wathiq was khalif.

Khalaf ibn Hisham al-Bazzaz

His *kunya* was Abu Muhammad. He listened to Sharik, Abu 'Awana, Hammad ibn Zayd and others. He had Qur'an and its readings. He read to Salim, the companion of Hamza. He died in Baghdad on Saturday, 7th Jumada al-Akhira, 229 AH and was buried in the Kunasa cemetery.

Al-Husayn ibn Ibrahim ibn al-Hurr

His *kunya* was Abu 'Ali. His nickname was Ishkab. He was one of the *abna'* of Khurasan from Nasa. His father was one of those who rallied to the call of the 'Abbasids with Usayd ibn 'Abdu'r-Rahman who took power in Nasa. Usayd was put in charge of Isfahan and Ibrahim ibn al-Hurr was among his companions. Al-Husayn was born to him in Isfahan in 145 AH. Al-Husayn grew up in Baghdad and devoted himself to *hadith* and met Muhammad ibn Rashid, Sharik ibn 'Abdullah, Fulayh, Hammad ibn Zayd and others. He kept close to Abu Yusuf al-Qadi and had insight into *ra'y*. Then he stayed with them and did not become involved in any judgeship or any other position. He remained in Baghdad giving *hadith* and *fiqh* until he died in 218 AH at the age of 71, while al-Ma'mun was khalif.

Da'ud ibn 'Amr

His *kunya* was Abu Sulayman. He died in Baghdad in Rabi' al-Awwal, 228 AH.

Da'ud ibn Rushayd

He settled in the city of Abu Ja'far and was one of the *abna'* of Khurasan from Khwarizm. He related from al-Walid ibn Muslim, Baqiyya ibn al-Walid, Isma'il ibn 'Abbas and other Syrians. The people of Baghdad wrote from him. He was reliable with a lot of *hadiths*.

Fudayl ibn 'Abdu'l-Wahhab al-Qannad

He was the brother of Muhammad ibn 'Abdu'l-Wahhab from whom Harun ibn Ishaq al-Hamdani related.

'Abdu'l-Jabbar ibn 'Asim

His *kunya* was Abu Talib. He was one of the *abna'* of Khurasan who were in Mesopotamia. He wrote from 'Ubaydullah ibn 'Amr, Isma'il ibn 'Ayyash, Abu'l-Malih, Baqiyya and others. He died in Baghdad in the army of al-Mahdi in Rabi' al-Akhir, in 233 AH.

'Ubaydullah ibn 'Umar al-Qawariri

His *kunya* was Abu Sa'id. He was one of the people of Basra. He came to Baghdad and settled there. He related from Hammad ibn

Zayd, Yazid ibn Zuray', 'Abdu'r-Rahman ibn Mahdi and others. He had many *hadiths* and was reliable. He died in Baghdad on the 13th Dhu'l-Hijja 235 AH in the Days of *Tashriq*. Many people attended and he was buried in the army-camp of al-Mahdi outside the three gates. He was 84 when he died.

Muhammad ibn Abi Hafs al-Mu'ayti

He was their client. His *kunya* was Abu 'Abdullah. Abu Hafs's name was 'Umar. He was reliable with *hadith*. He related from Baqiyya, 'Abdullah ibn al-Mubarak, Abu'l-Ahwas, Sharik, Hushaym and others. He was one of the people of Baghdad. He prayed *Jumu'a* one day and went to his home and went to bed on Saturday night. He was afflicted by semiparalysis in the night and lived for the rest of the night and Saturday until *'Asr*. Then he died and was buried in the al-Khayzuran cemetery on Monday, the 6th Sha'ban 222 AH while al-Mu'tasim was khalif. The funeral prayer was performed outside the three arches and many people attended.

Salm ibn Qadim

His *kunya* was Abu'l-Layth. He related from Baqiyya, Muhammad ibn Harb and others. He died in Baghdad in Dhu'l-Qa'da 228 AH.

Nu'aym ibn Haysam

His *kunya* was Abu Muhammad. He was one of the people of Khorasan. He related from Hammad ibn Zayd and others. He died in Baghdad in Shawwal 228 AH.

Yahya ibn 'Uthman

His *kunya* was Abu Zakariyya. He was one of the *abna'* of Khurasan. He lived at Darb Abi'l-Jahm. He related from the Syrians, Rushayd ibn Sa'd, Hiql ibn Ziyad, Baqiyya, Isma'il ibn 'Ayyash and others. He died in Rabi' al-Awwal, 238 AH.

Ibrahim ibn Ziyad Sablan

His *kunya* was Abu Ishaq. He died in Baghdad and was buried on Wednesday, the 6th Dhu'l-Hijja 228 AH.

Bashshar ibn Musa al-Khaffaf

His *kunya* was Abu 'Uthman. He died in Baghdad in Ramadan 228 AH and was buried on Friday after *'Asr*.

Abu'l-Ahwas

His name was Muhammad ibn Hayyan al-Baghi. He listened a lot and was reliable. He died in Dhu'l-Hijja, 229 AH.

Shuja' ibn Mukhallad

His *kunya* was Abu'l-Fadl. One of the *abna'* of Khurasan from Bagha. He related all of Hushaym's books and he also related from Isma'il ibn 'Ulayya and others. He was reliable and dependable. He died in Baghdad on the 10th Safar 235 AH. Many people attended and he was buried in the cemetery of Bab at-Tibn.

'Abbad ibn Musa al-Khuttali

His *kunya* was Abu Muhammad. He related from Ibrahim ibn Sa'd, Talha ibn Yahya az-Zuraqi and Isma'il ibn Ja'far. He went to Tarsus and died there at the beginning of 230 AH.

Ahmad ibn Muhammad ibn Ayyub

His *kunya* was Abu Ja'far. He was a copyist who wrote for al-Fadl ibn Yahya ibn Ja'far ibn Barmak. He mentioned that he heard the *Expeditions* from Ibrahim ibn Sa'd with al-Fadl ibn Yahya. He mentioned that he heard from Abu Bakr ibn 'Ayyash what happened to al-Fadl ibn Yahya.[1] He died in Baghdad on Tuesday night, the 26th of Dhu'l-Hijja 228 AH.

Ishaq ibn Ibrahim ibn Kamhar

His *kunya* was Abu Ya'qub. He was the son of Abu Isra'il from Khorasan from the people of Marw. He confused and transposed things. He would stop while reciting Qur'an and repeat it several times. He related from Ibrahim ibn Sa'd, Hammad ibn Zayd, 'Abdu'r-Rahman ibn Abi'z-Zinad, Ja'far ibn Sulayman, and Sulayman ibn

---

1. Al-Fadl ibn Yahya al-Barmaki, who was governor of Khurasan before the Barmakids fell from their position of power in the Abbasid administration. He died in prison after the execution of his brother Ja'far and the disgrace of the entire family.

Akhdar. He listened a great deal. He travelled to Muhammad ibn Jabir in Yamama and wrote out his books. He went from Yamama to Basra two or three days after Abu 'Awana died and did not meet him.

Yahya ibn Ma'in

His *kunya* was Abu Zakariyya. He was one of the most extensive recorders of *hadith* and was known for that, but he almost never related them. He died in Madina on his way to *hajj*.

Zuhayr ibn Harb ibn Ashtal

One of the people of Nasa. Then he Arabicised Ashtal and it became Shaddad. His *kunya* was Abu Khaythama. He was the client of the Banu Harish. He related from Jarir ibn 'Abdu'l-Hamid, Hushaym, Sufyan ibn 'Uyayna, Ibn 'Ulayya, 'Abdullah ibn Wahb, al-Walid ibn Muslim and other Kufans, Basrans and Hijazis. He compiled a *Musnad* and books of that sort. He died in Baghdad in Sha'ban, 234 AH. Many people attended. He was reliable and dependable.

Khalaf ibn Salim al-Mukharrami

His *kunya* was Abu Muhammad. He was a client of the Muhallab family. He wrote a *Musnad* from the Messenger of Allah ﷺ and he had many *hadiths*. People wrote from him. He died in Baghdad in Ramadan, 231 AH.

Ahmad ibn Muhammad ibn Hanbal

His *kunya* was Abu 'Abdullah. He was reliable, dependable, truthful with many *hadiths*. He was subjected to the Inquisition (*Mihna*) and beaten with whips. Al-Mu'tasim, the Amir al-Mu'minin, commanded that he be beaten to make him state that the Qur'an was created and he refused to say it. He was imprisoned on that account but remained firm in his position and did not acquiesce at all. Then he was summoned to go to the khalif al-Mutawakkil. Then he was offered money but he refused to accept it. He died on a Friday at midday and was buried after *'Asr*. Many of the people of Baghdad and others attended.

Al-Qasim ibn Sallam

His *kunya* was Abu 'Ubayd. He was one of the *abna'* of Khurasan. He was a tutor and had knowledge of grammar and Arabic. He devoted himself to *hadith* and *fiqh*. He was appointed qadi of Tarsus in the time of Thabit ibn Nasr ibn Malik and remained with him and his children. He came to Baghdad where he explained unusual *hadith* and wrote books and people listened to him. He went on *hajj* and died in Makka in 224 AH.

Bishr ibn al-Walid al-Kindi

He related from Abu Yusuf the Qadi, both from his books and by his dictation. He related from Sharik, Hammad ibn Zayd, Malik ibn Anas, Salih al-Murri and others. He related from Muhammad ibn Talha. He was appointed Qadi of Baghdad on both sides of the river. He related and gave *fatwa* to the people in Baghdad. A man took action against him and said, "He does not say that the Qur'an is created." The Amir al-Mu'minin al-Mu'tasim commanded that he be put under house arrest. He was put under house arrest and police were assigned to his door. He was forbidden to give *fatwa* to anyone in any matter. When al-Mutawakkil became khalif, he commanded that he be released and give *fatwa* to people and transmit to them. So he continued until he was old and spoke of the *waqf*.[1] The people of *hadith* then withdrew from and abandoned him.

Muhammad ibn Sulaym

His *kunya* was Abu 'Abdullah al-'Abdi. He listened a lot and was appointed qadi in Badraya and Bakisba in the time of al-Ma'mun. I saw that the people of *hadith* were wary about his *hadith* and transmission from him.

Bishr ibn Adam

He listened a lot and I saw that the people of *hadith* were wary of his *hadith* and writing from him.

---

1. There was a disagreement about the nature of the *waqf* between *fuqaha'* of different schools.

'Abdu'r-Rahman ibn Yunus

His *kunya* was Abu Muslim, one of the clients of al-Mansur. We were informed that he was born in 164 AH and that he devoted himself to *hadith* and travelled in search of it and listened to it a lot and took dictation from Sufyan ibn 'Uyayna, Yazid ibn Harun and others. He died on Wednesday at sunrise suddenly, in the mosque of Asad ibn al-Marzban on the 10th Rajab 224 AH.

Abu'l-Qasim

The husband of Abu Muslim's daughter. He was the grandfather of Husayn ibn al-Fahm on his father's side. He lived in the army of al-Mahdi. He was reliable, scrupulous and a scholar. He spoke of the *Sunna* and censured those who took the position of Jahm[1] and opposed the *Sunna*. He died on Sunday the 12th Rabi' al-Awwal 224 AH.

'Abdullah ibn 'Awn al-Khazzaz

His *kunya* was Abu Muhammad. He died in Baghdad while al-Wathiq was khalif.

Shurayh ibn Yunus al-Marwrudhi

His *kunya* was Abu'l-Harith. He was the husband of the daughter of Quraysh al-Mustamli. He wrote books and produced them and related them. He was reliable. He died on Tuesday the 23rd Rabi' al-Awwal 235 AH.

Ahmad ibn Da'ud

His *kunya* was Abu Sa'id al-Haddad al-Wasiti. He lived in Baghdad. He was reliable and died before he could be related from and written from.

Isma'il ibn Ibrahim at-Tarjumani

His *kunya* was Abu Ibrahim, one of the *abna'* of Khurasan. His home was near the desert of Abu's-Sarri. He related from Hushaym, al-'Attaf ibn Khalid, 'Abdu'l-'Aziz al-Majishun, Khalaf ibn Khalifa,

---

1. The Jahmite Qadarites believed that Allah created good but not evil, and that the Qur'an is created.

Salih al-Murri and others. He related also from Sharik. He died in Baghdad on the 25th Muharram 236 AH. He had *sunna*, virtue and good.

'Amr an-Naqid

His *kunya* was Abu 'Uthman. He was reliable with dependable *hadith*. The people of Baghdad wrote many books from him. He was one of the few memorisers. He was a *faqih*. He died in Baghdad on Thursday the 4th Dhu'l-Hijja 202 AH.

Muhammad ibn 'Abbad al-Makki

The companion of Sufyan ibn 'Uyayna. He died in the army of the khalif in Samarra in 234 AH.

Hajib ibn al-Walid al-A'war the teacher

His *kunya* was Abu Ahmad. He died in Baghdad in the month of Ramadan 228 AH.

Abu Ma'mar

His name was Isma'il ibn Ibrahim al-Harawi from Hudhayl. He had *sunna*, virtue and good. He died in Baghdad in Jumada al-Ula 236 AH and many people attended his funeral.

Muhammad ibn Hatim al-Marwazi

His *kunya* was Abu 'Abdullah. He produced a book on the *tafsir* of the Qur'an which people wrote down in Baghdad. He lived at Qati'a ar-Rabi' at Karkh. He died in Baghdad on Thursday the 26th Dhu'l-Hijja 235 AH.

Ibrahim ibn Muhammad

One of the Banu Sama. His *kunya* was Abu Ishaq. He died in Baghdad in Ramadan 231 AH after coming from the khalif's army in Samarra.

'Abdu'r-Rahman ibn Salih al-Azdi

His *kunya* was Abu Muhammad. He was one of the people of Kufa and settled in Baghdad. He related from Sharik, Ibn Abi Za'ida,

Abu Bakr ibn 'Ayyash and others, and from Mulazim ibn 'Amr. He died in Baghdad on a Monday at the end of Dhu'l-Hijja in 235 AH.

Ahmad ibn Ibrahim

His *kunya* was Abu 'Ali. He was known as al-Mawsuli. He related from Hammad ibn Zayd, Sharik, Abu 'Awana and others. He died in Baghdad in Rabi' al-Awwal 236 AH.

Ibrahim ibn Abi'l-Layth

His *kunya* was Abu Ishaq. He was the companion of al-Ashja'i. He settled in Baghdad in the army of al-Mahdi. He had *sunna* and was weak in *hadith*.

'Abdu'l-Mun'im ibn Idris

His *kunya* was Abu 'Abdullah. He was the son of the daughter of Wahb ibn Munabbih [the *Tabi'i* who died in 114 AH]. He related the books of Wahb about the stories of the Prophets and men of worship, and the stories of the tribe of Israel, from his father from Wahb ibn Munabbih. He mentioned that he met Ma'mar ibn Rashid in Yemen and listened to him. He read the books of Wahb ibn Munabbih and his wisdom. He died in Baghdad in Ramadan 228 AH when he was nearly 100.

Muhammad ibn Mus'ab

His *kunya* was Abu Ja'far. He was a Qur'an reciter. He listened to *hadith* and sat with people. He was reliable, Allah willing. He died in Baghdad in Dhu'l-Qa'da 228 AH.

Muhriz ibn 'Awn

His *kunya* was Abu'l-Fadl. He said that his father told him that he was born in 144 AH. He said, "In that year al-Mansur went on *hajj* with the people." He died in Baghdad in 231 AH when he was 88. He related *hadith* and people wrote from him a lot. He was reliable and dependable.

Al-Walid ibn Salih an-Nahhas

His *kunya* was Abu Muhammad. He related from 'Ubaydullah ibn 'Amr, Abu Ma'shar, Baqiyya ibn al-Walid, Hammad ibn Salama and 'Isa ibn Yunus. He related the *Musnad* of Wukay' and others. He died in Baghdad in Safar 233 AH.

Rabah ibn al-Jarrah

His *kunya* was Abu'l-Walid, one of the people of Mosul. He came to Baghdad and related from al-Mu'afi ibn 'Imran and 'Afif ibn Salim.

Al-Walid ibn Shuja'

His *kunya* was Abu Humam as-Sakuni. He related from Baqiyya ibn al-Walid and other Syrians and Iraqis.

Nuh ibn Yazid the tutor

His *kunya* was Abu Muhammad. He was the companion of Ibrahim ibn Sa'd. He was reliable.

Kamil ibn Talha al-Jahdari

One of the people of Basra. His *kunya* was Abu Yahya. He died in Basra in 232 AH.

Yusuf ibn Musa al-Qattan

He was one of the people of Kufa and settled in Rayy and traded there and listened to Jarir ibn 'Abdu'l-Hamid and others. He came to Baghdad and settled in Dar al-Qutn.

Mardawayh as-Sa'igh

His name was 'Abdu's-Samad ibn Yazid. His nickname was Mardawayh. His *kunya* was Abu 'Abdullah. He related from al-Fadl ibn 'Iyad, Ibn 'Uyayna and others. He was reliable among the people of the *Sunna* and scrupulousness. People wrote from him. He died on the last day of Dhu'l-Hijja 235 AH.

Abu 'Amr al-Muqri'

He is Hafs ibn 'Umar al-Azdi. People recited the Qur'an to him. He had knowledge of the Qur'an and *tafsir*. He wrote from Sharik and other people of Iraq, Madina and Syria.

Muhammad ibn Sa'd, the companion of al-Waqidi

He was the client of al-Husayn ibn 'Abdullah of the 'Abbasid family. He died at the age of 62 in Baghdad on Sunday the 4th Jumada al-Akhira, 236 AH, and was buried in the cemetery of the Syrian gate. He is the one who wrote the *Kitab at-Tabaqat*, worked it out and composed it. He is related from. He had an abundance of knowledge and many *hadiths* and transmission, many books of *hadith* and other books on strange terms and *fiqh*.

✳✳✳✳✳

Other Baghdadis also include: **Abu Isma'il al-Mu'addib the tutor**, who is Ibrahim ibn Sulayman; **Abu 'Ubayda al-Haddad**, who was 'Abdu'l-Wahid; **Abu Qatan**, whose name was 'Amr ibn al-Haytham al-Quta'i; **Ghassan ibn al-Mufaddal al-Ghalabi**, whose *kunya* was Abu Mu'awiya; **'Isa ibn Hisham an-Nakhkhas**, who listened a lot and had *hadith*, but died before he could relate; **Mahdi ibn Hafs,** whose *kunya* was Abu Ahmad and who lived at the Kufa gate; **Sahl ibn Nasr**, who lived at al-Matbakhiyya; **Harun ibn Ma'ruf**, whose *kunya* was Abu 'Ali, and who died in Baghdad in Ramadan 231 AH; **Sahl ibn Muhammad**, whose *kunya* was Abu's-Sarri, the client of al-'Abbad ibn 'Abdullah, and who was reliable; **Yahya ibn Ayyub**, who was Abu Zakariyya, the client of Abu'l-Qasim Muharrar; **Ibrahim ibn Hatim al-Harawi**, who is Abu Ishaq; **Ahmad ibn Muhammad as-Saffar**, whose *kunya* was Abu Hafs; **Ya'qub ibn Ibrahim al-'Abdi**, who is Abu Yusuf, Ibn ad-Dawraqi; his brother, **Ahmad ibn Ibrahim**, who is Abu 'Abdullah; **'Abdu'l-'Aziz ibn Bahr the tutor,** who related from Isma'il ibn Ja'far and others; and **Yahya ibn Isma'il al-Wasiti**, whose *kunya* was Abu Zakariyya.

✳✳✳✳✳

The Companions of the Prophet who went to Khurasan and died there

Burayda ibn al-Husayb

His *kunya* was Abu 'Abdullah. He became Muslim when the Messenger of Allah صلعم passed him on the *Hijra* and recited the beginning of *Surat Maryam* (19) to him. Then Burayda emigrated to him in Madina after Uhud and he learned the rest of *Surat Maryam* and went on the later expeditions of the Messenger of Allah صلعم after that. He lived in Madina until the death of the Messenger of Allah صلعم. When Basra was set out and became a city, Burayda moved there and built a house there. Then he left it to go on an expedition to Khurasan and died in Marw while Yazid ibn Mu'awiya was khalif. He left children there and some of them came to Baghdad and died there.

Abu Ya'qub ad-Dabbi said that he was told that Burayda al-Aslami was heard to say beyond the river of Balkh, "There is no life except in the transport of horses!"

Abu Barza al-Aslami

Abu Barza became Muslim early on and was present with the Messenger of Allah at the conquest of Makka. He killed 'Abdu'l-'Uzza ibn Khattal when he was clinging to the curtains of the Ka'ba. Abu Barza continued to go on expeditions with the Messenger of Allah صلعم until the Messenger of Allah died. Then he moved to Basra and settled there when the Muslims settled there and he built a house there. He had descendants there. Then he went on an expedition to Khurasan and died there.

Al-Hakam ibn 'Amr ibn Mujadda'

He was called al-Hakam ibn 'Amr al-Ghifari as he was descended from Nu'ayla, the brother of Ghifar. Al-Hakam was a companion of the Prophet صلعم until the Prophet died. Then he moved to Basra and settled there. Ziyad ibn Abi Sufyan appointed him governor of Khurasan and he went there and remained its governor until he died during the khalifate of Mu'awiya.

'Abdu'r-Rahman ibn Samura

His mother was Arwa bint Abi'l-Fari'a. 'Abdu'r-Rahman moved to Basra and settled there and related *hadiths* from the Messenger of Allah ﷺ. His name had been 'Abdu'l-Ka'ba and the Messenger of Allah ﷺ renamed him 'Abdu'r-Rahman when he became a Muslim. He said to him, "'Abdu'r-Rahman, do not ask for command." 'Abdullah ibn 'Amir appointed him over Sijistan and he attacked Khurasan and achieved victories there. Then he returned to Basra and died there in 50 AH. Ziyad ibn Abi Sufyan prayed over him.

Qutham ibn al-'Abbas ibn 'Abdu'l-Muttalib

His mother was Umm al-Fadl or Lubaba the elder al-Hilaliyya. Qutham resembled the Messenger of Allah ﷺ. Qutham raided Khurasan when Sa'id ibn 'Uthman was in charge of it. He said to him, "Take a thousand shares for yourself." He said, "No, take a fifth and then give the people their rights and then give me what you wish." Qutham was scrupulous and virtuous and died in Samarqand.

'Abdu'r-Rahman ibn Ya'mur ad-Di'li

Bukayr ibn 'Ata' reported from him that the Prophet ﷺ said, "*Hajj* is 'Arafa. Whoever catches 'Arafa [on the night of Muzdalifa] before *Subh* has caught the *hajj*."

✻✻✻✻✻

The *Fuqaha'* and *Hadith* Scholars in Khurasan after them

Yahya ibn Ya'mar al-Laythi

One of the Banu Kinana. He was one of the people of Basra. He was a grammarian with great knowledge of Arabic and the Qur'an. Then he went to Khurasan and settled in Marw and was made its qadi. He judged by the oath with the witness. He was reliable.

Abu't-Tayyib Musa ibn Yasar said, "I saw Yahya ibn Ya'mar when he was qadi in Marw. Sometimes I saw him giving judgement in the market and on the road. Sometimes two litigants would come to him while he was on a donkey and he stopped on the donkey until he had judged between them."

Abu Mijlaz Lahiq as-Sadusi

He was reliable with *hadiths*. He went to Marw and settled there and built a house there. He was put in charge of the Treasury there. He only had one eye. He died while 'Umar ibn 'Abdu'l-'Aziz was khalif.

Muhammad an-Nakh'i

His *kunya* was Abu Yusuf. He was reliable, Allah willing. He related from Sa'id ibn Jubayr. He was appointed qadi of Marw.

'Ata' al-Khurasani

He was reliable. He went to Syria and related from the Syrians. Malik ibn Anas and others related from him.

Abu'l-Munib

His name was 'Isa ibn 'Ubayd. He had *hadiths* and he related from 'Ikrima.

Ar-Rabi' ibn Anas

'Ammar ibn Basr al-Khurasani said that ar-Rabi' ibn Anas was one of Bakr ibn Wa'il. He was one of the people of Basra. He met Ibn 'Umar, Jabir ibn 'Abdullah and Anas ibn Malik. He fled from al-Hajjaj to Marw and settled in one of its villages called Burz and then moved to another village called Sadhawwar, where he remained until his death. He was also pursued in Khurasan when the Abbasid movement began. He hid and sought to escape with 'Abdullah ibn al-Mubarak who was also in hiding. He listened to forty *hadiths* from him. 'Abdullah used to say, "How this delights me!" about something he named. Ar-Rabi' ibn Anas died while al-Mansur was khalif.

Ibrahim ibn Maymun as-Sa'igh

He and Muhammad ibn Thabit al-'Abdi were companions of Abu Muslim, the Abbasid recruiting officer in Khurasan. They sat with him and listened to what he had to say. When the Abbasid movement emerged in Khurasan and this business [of revolution] began, he sent agents to them to ask them about himself and whether he should be assassinated. Muhammad ibn Thabit said, "I do not think that he should be assassinated because belief is a bar to assassination." Ibrahim as-Sa'igh said, "I think that he should be assassinated and killed." Abu Muslim appointed Muhammad ibn Thabit al-'Abdi as qadi of Marw and sent for Ibrahim ibn as-Sa'igh and killed him. It is reported that Ibrahim as-Sa'igh used to come to Abu Muslim and admonish him. He told him, "Go to your home. We know your views." So he went back and then later put on funeral perfume and shrouded himself and went to him while he was in a gathering of people and admonished him and spoke some strong words. He commanded that he be killed and thrown into a well.

Muhammad ibn Thabit al-'Abdi

He came from Basra. He related from Abu'l-Mutawakkil and was made qadi of Marw. 'Abdullah ibn al-Mubarak and others related from him.

Ya'qub ibn al-Qa'qa'

He was one of the people of Marw who was qadi there. He related from 'Arta' ibn Abi Rabah, and ath-Thawri and 'Abdullah ibn al-Mubarak related from him.

Al-Fadl ibn Musa as-Sinani

Sinan is one of the villages of Marw from the region of as-Saqadham. He was reliable and Waki' ibn al-Jarrah and others related from him.

'Abdullah ibn al-Mubarak

His *kunya* was Abu 'Abdu'r-Rahman. He was born in 118 AH and devoted himself to knowledge and related a lot of transmission, and wrote many books on the categories and types of knowledge which people took from him, and people wrote from him. He had poetry and encouragement for *jihad*. He went to Iraq, the Hijaz, Syria, Egypt and Yemen and listened to a great deal of knowledge. He was reliable and a trustworthy Imam, an authority with many *hadiths*. He died at Hit while returning from an expedition in 181 AH when he was 63.

An-Nadr ibn Muhammad al-Marwazi

He was given pre-eminence by them in knowledge, *fiqh*, intellect and virtue. He was a companion of 'Abdullah ibn al-Mubarak. He was one of the people of Abu Hanifa.

Makki ibn Ibrahim al-Balkhi

His *kunya* was Abu's-Sakan. He died in Balkh in 215 AH. He was reliable and came to Baghdad intending to go on the *hajj* and he went on the *hajj* and returned and related to the people on his journey there and back and they wrote from him. He was reliable in *hadith*.

An-Nadr ibn Shumayl al-Marwazi

He was one of the people of Basra of the Banu Mazin. He was reliable, Allah willing, and had *hadith* and transmission of poetry and knowledge of grammar and the historical events of people. He died in Khurasan in 203 AH while al-Ma'mun was khalif. That was before al-Ma'mun left Khurasan.

Muqatal ibn Sulayman al-Balkhi

The one who had a *tafsir*. He related from ad-Dahhak ibn Muzahim and 'Ata'. The people of *hadith* were wary of his *hadith* and objected to them.

Abu Muti' al-Balkhi

His name was al-Hakam ibn 'Abdullah, He was in charge of judging in Balkh. He was a Murji'ite.[1] He met 'Abdu'r-Rahman ibn Harmala and others. They considered him weak in *hadith*. He was blind.

'Amr ibn Harun al-Balkhi

He related from Ibn Jurayj and others. People wrote a large book from him but abandoned his *hadiths*.

---

1. The Murji'ites were opponents of the Kharijites. They held that it is faith and not actions which is important.

Salm ibn Salim al-Balkhi

His *kunya* was Abu Muhammad. He was a Murji'ite who was weak in hadith, but he was strict in commanding the correct and forbidding the objectionable. He had leadership in Khurasan, and Harun, the Amir al-Mu'minin, sent for him and he was brought to him and he imprisoned him. He remained in prison until Harun died. Then al-Amin released him from the prison of ar-Raqqa when he became khalif. He came to Baghdad and remained there a short time and then went to Khurasan where he died.

Abu Tumayla al-Marwazi

His name was Yahya ibn Wadih. He was the client of the Ansar. He met Muhammad ibn Ishaq and related from him. He was reliable and related from.

Al-Hasan ibn Sawwar

His *kunya* was Abu'l-'Ala' al-Marwrudhi. He was reliable. He came to Baghdad intending to go on *hajj* and people related from him and wrote from him. Then he returned to Khurasan and died there at the end of al-Ma'mun's khalifate.

'Abdu's-Samad ibn Hassan al-Marwrudhi

He was a qadi there and in Nishapur and Herat. He was reliable. He died during al-Ma'mun's khalifate.

'Ali ibn al-Hassan

He was one of the companions of 'Abdullah ibn al-Mubarak. He met al-Husayn ibn Waqid and related from him. He was one of the people of Marw and died there.

Nasr ibn Bab

His *kunya* was Abu Sahl, one of the people of Marw. He listened to Da'ud ibn Abi Hind, 'Awf al-A'rabi, al-Hajjaj and others. He came to Baghdad and they listened to him. Then he related from Ibrahim as-Sa'igh[1] so they suspected him and left his *hadiths*.

---

1. See p.230.

'Ali ibn Ishaq ad-Darakani

Darakan is a village of Marw. He was one of the people of 'Abdullah ibn al-Mubarak and was famous for being his companion. He was reliable and came to Baghdad and they listened to him.

Sahl ibn Muzahim

He was one of the people of Marw. He was a *faqih* and *mufti*, a man of worship. His *kunya* was Abu Bishr.

His brother, Muhammad ibn Muzahim

His *kunya* was Abu Wahb. He was informed and virtuous. He died in 221 AH. He used to relate from 'Abdullah ibn al-Mubarak.

Sufyan ibn 'Abdu'l-Malik

One of the people of Marw. 'Abdullah ibn al-Mubarak trusted him and presented his books to him.

Salama ibn Sulayman

One of the people of Marw. He was the companion of Abdullah ibn al-Mubarak and known for that.

'Iyadh ibn 'Uthman

His name was 'Abdullah and he was the son of the daughter of 'Abdu'l-'Aziz ibn Abi Rawwad. He met Shu'ba and he had books from Abdullah ibn al-Mubarak.

Abu Ishaq az-Zayyat

He was one of the people of Balkh. His name was Ibrahim ibn Sulayman. He was a Murji'ite.

Qutayba ibn Sa'id

His *kunya* was Abu Raja' al-Balkhi. He related from Layth ibn Sa'd and Ibn Lahi'a.

*****

Khurasan

Other Khurasanis also include: **Yazid ibn Abi Sa'id an-Nahawi**, one of the people of Marw who had *hadiths*; **ad-Dahhak ibn Muzahim**, Abu'l-Qasim, one of the people of Balkh; **Abu Jarir**, the Qadi of Sijistan, whose name was 'Abdullah ibn Husayn; **Mansur ibn Abi Surayra**, from whom 'Abdullah ibn al-Mubarak related; **Husayn ibn Waqid**, who related from 'Abdullah ibn Burayda and had excellent *hadiths*; **Kharija ibn Mus'ab as-Sarkhasi,** people were wary of his *hadith* and abandoned them; **Nuh ibn Abi Maryam**, whose *kunya* was Abu 'Isma; **Abu Hamza as-Sukari**, one of the people of Marw; **Hafs ibn 'Abdu'r-Rahman al-Balkhi**, Abu 'Amr, who lived in Nishapur; **'Ubaydullah as-Sajari**, one of the people of Sijistan who related from Sufyan ath-Thawri and others; **Nahshal ibn Sa'id**, who related from ad-Dahhak ibn Muzahim; **Muqatal ibn Hayyan**, Abu Mu'an al-Balkhi, who is was related from; **Khalaf ibn Ayyub**, Abu Sa'id, one of the people of Balkh, who is related from; **Shaddad ibn Hakim**, Abu 'Uthman al-Balkhi, who is related from; **'Abdu'l-'Aziz ibn Abi Rizma al-Marwazi**, who related from Hammad ibn Salama, Hammad ibn Zayd and others, and was reliable; **Al-Husayn ibn al-Walid**, Abu 'Abdullah, a client of Quraysh; **'Attab ibn Ziyad al-Marwazi**, a reliable companion of Abdullah ibn al-Mubarak; **Ibrahim ibn Rusaym**, one of the people of Marw; **Muhammad ibn al-Fadl**, one of the people of Marw whose *hadiths* are abandoned; **'Umara ibn al-Mughira**, one of the people of Sarakhas; his brother, **al-Qasim ibn al-Mughira**, one of the people of Sarakhas; **Abu Sa'id as-Saghani**, Muhammad ibn Muyassar, he was reliable and blind; **'Isam ibn Yusuf**, one of the people of Balkh; **Abu Mu'adh an-Nahawi**, one of the people of Marw who related from Abdullah ibn al-Mubarak; and **Ya'mar ibn Bishr**, Abu 'Amr, a companion of Abdullah ibn al-Mubarak.

✻✻✻✻✻

The *Fuqaha'* and *Hadith* Scholars in Rayy

Abu Ja'far ar-Razi

His name was 'Isa ibn Mahan. He was one of the people of Marw from a village called Burz. It is the village where ar-Rabi' ibn Anas first settled and it was there that Abu Ja'far listened to him. Then Abu Ja'far moved to Rayy where he died and so he is called ar-Razi. He was reliable and he came to Baghdad and Kufa for *hajj* and they listened to him.

Yahya ibn Durays

He was a qadi in Rayy and died there.

Sa'id ibn Sinan ash-Shaybani

He originated from Kufa, but he lived in Rayy later. He went on *hajj* every year and had bad character.

Jarir ibn 'Abdu'l-Hamid

His *kunya* was Abu 'Abdullah. He was born in 107 AH in Kufa and grew up there. He sought *hadith* and listened and had a lot. Then he settled in Rayy and died there. He was reliable with a lot of knowledge and people travelled to him.

Hakkam ibn Salm ar-Razi

He was reliable, Allah willing.

Salama al-Abrash ibn al-Fadl

His *kunya* was Abu 'Abdullah. He was reliable and truthful. He was the companion of Muhammad ibn Ishaq. He related the *Expeditions* and *Al-Mubtada'* from him. He died in Rayy having reached the age of 110. He was a tutor. It is said that he was the humblest of people in his prayer.

Ishaq ibn Sulayman

His *kunya* was Abu Yahya. He was the client of 'Abdu'l-Qays. He was reliable with virtue and scrupulousness. He moved to Kufa and spent two years there and then returned to Rayy where he died in 199 AH.

Ishaq ibn Isma'il ar-Razi

His nickname was Hayyawayh. He died in Rayy. He transmitted and is related from.

The *Fuqaha'* in Hamadan

Asram ibn Hawshab al-Hamadani

He came to Baghdad and the people of Baghdad wrote from him. Then he returned to Hamadan and died there.

The *Hadith* Scholars in Anbar

Muhammad ibn 'Abdullah al-Hadhdha'

His *kunya* was Abu Ja'far. He had *hadiths* and was reliable.

Suwayd ibn Sa'id

His *kunya* was Abu Muhammad al-Anbari. He settled in al-Haditha, Haditha an-Nura, some parasangs from Anbar.

Ishaq ibn al-Bahlul

His *kunya* was Abu Ya'qub.

Chapter Two:
The Companions of the Messenger of Allah who settled in Syria

Abu 'Ubayda ibn al-Jarrah

His name was 'Amir ibn 'Abdullah ibn al-Jarrah. His mother was Umayma bint Ghanm. Abu 'Ubayda became Muslim before the Messenger of Allah ﷺ entered the house of al-Arqam [in 614 AH] and he emigrated to Abyssinia in the second Abyssinian emigration. Then he returned and was present at Badr, Uhud, the Ditch and all the battles alongside the Messenger of Allah ﷺ. The Messenger of Allah sent him on an expedition with 300 Muhajirun and Ansar along the coast to a branch of Juhayna. That was the al-Khabt expedition.

Anas ibn Malik reported that the Prophet ﷺ said, "Every community has a trusty one and the trusty one of this community is Abu 'Ubayda ibn al-Jarrah." Muhammad ibn 'Umar said, "When 'Umar ibn al-Khattab became khalif, he appointed Abu 'Ubayda over Syria and he was commander-in-chief at the Battle of Yarmuk."

Malik ibn Yukhamir described Abu 'Ubayda ibn al-Jarrah and said, "He was a thin man with a gaunt face, thin beard, tall with a slight hunching of shoulders, and with a gap between his front teeth."

Abu Bakr ibn 'Abdullah reported from some men of the people of Abu 'Ubayda that Abu 'Ubayda ibn al-Jarrah was present at Badr when he was 41. He died in the 'Amwas plague in 18 AH while 'Umar ibn al-Khattab was khalif. Abu 'Ubayda was 58 when he died. His grave is at 'Amwas, which is four miles from Ramla in the direction of Jerusalem. Abu 'Ubayda dyed his head and hair with henna and privet. Abu 'Ubayda also related from 'Umar.

Bilal ibn Rabah

He was a client of Abu Bakr as-Siddiq. His *kunya* was Abu 'Abdullah. He was one of the half-castes of the nobles. His mother's name was Hamama. His mother belonged to one of the Banu Jumah.

Al-Hasan said that the Messenger of Allah ﷺ said, "Bilal is the forerunner of the Abyssinans."

Qays ibn Abi Hazim said, "Abu Bakr purchased Bilal for five *uqiyyas*."

'Umar used to say, "Abu Bakr is our master and he freed our master," meaning Bilal.

Al-Qasim ibn 'Abdu'r-Rahman said, "Bilal was the first to give the *adhan*."

Muhammad ibn 'Amr said, "Bilal used to carry the staff before the Messenger of Allah ﷺ on the day of the *'Id* and for the rain prayer." Muhammad ibn 'Umar said, "Bilal was present at Badr and Uhud and all the battles with the Messenger of Allah ﷺ. When the Messenger of Allah died, he went to Abu Bakr and asked his permission to go to Syria to join the defences in the way of Allah. Abu Bakr said, 'I ask you by Allah, Bilal, and by my respect and my due, I am old and weak and my end is near.' So Bilal remained with Abu Bakr until his death. Then he went to 'Umar and said the like of what he had said to Abu Bakr and he gave him permission. So he went to Syria where he remained until he died."

Qays said, "Bilal said to Abu Bakr when the Messenger of Allah ﷺ died, 'If you bought me for yourself, keep me. If you bought me for Allah, then leave me to Allah's work.'"

Muhammad ibn Ibrahim at-Taymi said, "Bilal died in Damascus in 20 AH and was buried at the Bab as-Saghir in the Damascus cemetery when he was about 60, while 'Umar ibn al-Khattab was khalif."

Shu'ayb ibn Talha reported that one of Abu Bakr's children said that Bilal was the same age as Abu Bakr. Muhammad ibn 'Umar said, "If this is the case and Abu Bakr died in 13 AH when he was 63, then there are seven years between this and what is related to us about Bilal. Shu'ayb ibn Talha has the best knowledge of when Bilal was born when he said that he was the same age as Abu Bakr. Allah knows best."

Makhul said, "Someone who saw Bilal said that he was man of very dark skin, thin, humped shoulders, with a lot of hair, a sparse beard, and much grey hair which he did not dye."

'Ubada ibn as-Samit

One of Khazraj. His *kunya* was Abu'l-Walid. His mother was Qurratu'l-'Ayn bint 'Ubada of Khazraj. 'Ubada was present at 'Aqaba with seventy of the Ansar. He was one of the twelve chiefs present there. He was present at Badr, Uhud, the Ditch and all the battles alongside the Messenger of Allah صلم. Then he went to Syria when the Muslims attacked it and remained in Syria until his death.

Al-Walid ibn 'Ubada said, "'Ubada ibn as-Samit was a tall handsome stout man. He died in Ramla in Syria in 34 AH while 'Uthman ibn 'Affan was khalif. He was 72 and had descendants."

Muhammad ibn Sa'd said that he heard people say that he lived on in Syria until Mu'awiya ibn Abi Sufyan was the khalif.

Mu'adh ibn Jabal

One of Khazraj. His *kunya* was Abu 'Abdu'r-Rahman. His mother was Hind bint Sahl from Juhayna. His half-brother on his mother's side was 'Abdullah ibn al-Jadd, one of the people of Badr. Mu'adh was at 'Aqaba with seventy of the Ansar and he was at Badr when he was 20 or 21. He was present at Uhud, the Ditch and all the battles of the Messenger of Allah صلم. The Messenger of Allah صلم sent him to Yemen as a tax collector and teacher. The Prophet died while he was in Yemen and Abu Bakr became khalif when he was in charge of it over the army. Then he came to Makka and went to 'Umar who was on hajj that year.

Anas ibn Malik said that the Messenger of Allah صلم said, "Mu'adh ibn Jabal is the knowledgeable one of my community regarding the lawful and unlawful."

Muhammad ibn 'Umar said, "Then Mu'adh went to Syria for *jihad* in the way of Allah."

'Abdullah ibn Rafi' said, "When Abu 'Ubayda ibn al-Jarrah was struck down by the plague of 'Amwas, Mu'adh ibn Jabal was appointed in his place and the pestilence was severe. People said to Mu'adh ibn Jabal, 'Pray to Allah to remove this filth from us.' He

Companions

said, 'It is not filth, but the supplication of your Prophet ﷺ, the death of the righteous before you and martyrdom which Allah will single out for whomever He wills among you. O Allah! Give the family of Mu'adh their fullest portion of this mercy!' His two sons fell ill with the plague and he said, 'How are you?' They said, 'Father, The truth is from your Lord, so on no account will we be among the doubters.' [cf 2:147; 10:94] He said, 'You will find me, Allah willing, one of the steadfast.' [cf 37:102] Then both his wives fell ill with the plague and died. He himself was afflicted in his thumb and began to suck it and say, 'O Allah, it is little, so bless it. You bless the small,' until he died."

Al-Harith ibn 'Amira az-Zubaydi said, "I was sitting with Mu'adh ibn Jabal when he was dying. He would lapse in and out of consciousness. I heard him say when he came round, 'Throttle Your throttled! I promise You that I love You.'"

Abu Muslim al-Khawlani said, "I entered the mosque of Hims and there were about thirty Companions of the Prophet ﷺ. There was a young man with dark eyes and shining teeth there who was silent and did not speak. When the people were uncertain about something, they turned to him and asked him. I asked someone who was sitting beside me, 'Who is this?' He replied, 'Mu'adh ibn Jabal.'"

'Abdullah ibn Ka'b said, "Mu'adh ibn Jabal was a tall fair man with handsome teeth and large eyes, eyebrows which joined together, and short and curly hair. He was at Badr when he was 20 or 21. He went to Yemen after he had gone with the Prophet ﷺ on the Tabuk expedition when he was 28. He died in the 'Amwas plague in Syria in the region of Jordan in 18 AH when 'Umar ibn al-Khattab was khalif, at the age of 38. He left no descendants.

Sa'id ibn al-Musayyab said, "'Isa ﷺ was taken up when he was 33, and Mu'adh died when he was 33."

'Ata' said that Mu'adh's grave is at Qusayr Khalif in the district of Damascus.

Sa'd ibn 'Ubada

One of the Khazraj of the Ansar. His *kunya* was Abu Thabit. His mother was 'Amra bint Mas'ud of Banu'n-Najjar. He was the cousin of Mas'ud ibn Zayd al-Ashhali, one of the people of Badr. Sa'd ibn 'Ubada used to write Arabic in the *Jahiliyya* and was a good swimmer and shooter. He was one of the best in that and was called 'the perfect'. Sa'd was at 'Aqaba with the seventy Ansar. He was one of the twelve Helpers. He was a generous master. He was not present at Badr. He got ready to set out for Badr and went to some houses of the Ansar to encourage them to set out and he missed it. The Messenger of Allah صلعم said, "Even if Sa'd was not there, he was eager for it."

After that he was present with the Messenger of Allah صلعم at Uhud, the Ditch and all of the battles. When the Messenger of Allah صلعم died, the Ansar met in the Hall of Sa'ida and Sa'd ibn 'Ubada was with them. They discussed offering him their allegiance. The news reached Abu Bakr and 'Umar and they came along with some of the Muhajirun. There was some debate and argument between them. 'Umar then said to Abu Bakr, "Stretch out your hand," and he gave him his allegiance and the Muhajirun and Ansar also gave him their allegiance. Sa'd ibn 'Ubada did not give him allegiance. He left him and did not go to him until Abu Bakr died and 'Umar was appointed. He did not give him allegiance either. One day 'Umar met him on one of the roads of Madina and said to him, "Speak, Sa'd! Speak, Sa'd!" Sa'd said, "Speak, 'Umar!" 'Umar said, "You are a Companion. What is your position?" Sa'd said, "Yes, I am that. Allah has given you this command, and your companion who was in charge of it was dearer to me than you. By Allah, I have begun to dislike being near you." 'Umar said, "Whoever dislikes a neighbour close to him should move from him." Sa'd said, "I do not conceal that. I will move to a neighbourhood better than yours!" He soon left and emigrated to Syria at the beginning of 'Umar's khalifate.

Sa'd's descendants report that he died at Harran in Syria two and a half years into 'Umar's rule.

Muhammad ibn 'Umar said, "It seems that he died in 15 AH." 'Abdu'l-'Aziz said, "His death was not known in Madina until some boys heard a voice in the well of Munabbih, or Sakan, while they were drawing water at midday in the intense heat saying:

We killed the master of Khazraj, Sa'd ibn 'Ubada.
We shot him with two arrows and we did not miss his heart.

The boys were frightened, so that day was remembered, and they discovered that that was the very day on which Sa'd had died. He sat to urinate in a hole and had a bath and then died immediately. They found that his skin had gone green.

Muhammad ibn Sirin related that Sa'd ibn 'Ubada urinated standing up and when he returned, he said to his friends, "I feel something crawling," and then he died. They heard a jinn saying:

> We killed the master of Khazraj, Sa'd ibn 'Ubada.
> We shot him with two arrows and we did not miss his heart.

Abu'd-Darda'

His name was 'Uwaymir ibn Zayd of Khazraj. His mother was Muhibba bint Waqid. Abu'd-Darda' was the last of the people of his house to become Muslim. 'Abdullah ibn Rawaha, who was a brother to him in the *Jahiliyya* and in Islam, came and took an axe and began to smash the idol of Abu'd-Darda', saying:

> You are free from all the names of the Shaytans.
> All that is prayed to with Allah is false.

Abu'd-Darda' came and told his wife what 'Abdullah ibn Rawaha had done and he thought about it and said, "If there had been any good in this, it would have defended itself." So he went to the Messenger of Allah ﷺ with 'Abdullah ibn Rawaha and became a Muslim.

Abu'd-Darda' said, "I was a merchant before the Prophet ﷺ was sent. When Muhammad was sent I pursued both trade and worship but they did not go together and so I chose worship and left trade."

Muhammad ibn 'Umar said, "Some of them relate that Abu'd-Darda' was present at Uhud and that the Prophet ﷺ looked at him on that day when people were running in every direction. He said, "Uwaymir is an excellent horseman who does not hold back.' Abu'd-Darda' was one of the high-ranking Companions of the Messenger of Allah ﷺ and the people of resolve among them. He related many *hadiths* from the Messenger of Allah ﷺ and was present with him in many battles."

Rabi'a ibn Yazid reported that when Abu'd-Darda' reported a *hadith* from the Prophet ﷺ, he would say, "O Allah! If it is not like this, then make it similar to it!"

Muhammad ibn 'Umar said, "Abu'd-Darda' went to Syria and remained there until he died."

Yahya ibn Sa'id said, "Abu'd-Darda' was appointed qadi and they began to congratulate him. He said, 'Do you congratulate me for the qadiship when I have been placed on the top of an abyss into which a slip takes one further than Aden. If people had known what was involved in being qadi, they would take it in turns out of aversion to it and dislike for it. If people had known what was in the *adhan*, they would have taken it in turns out of desire for it and eagerness for it.'"

Umm ad-Darda' reported that Abu'd-Darda' said, "An hour of reflection is better than a night of standing in prayer."

Abu'd-Darda' said, "I love poverty out of humility to my Lord and I love death out of yearning for my Lord, and I love illness for expiation of my wrong actions."

Ya'la ibn al-Walid reported that Abu'd-Darda' was asked, "What do you like for the one you love?" He replied, "Death." They asked, "And if he does not die?" He replied, "That he has little wealth and few children."

Mu'awiya ibn Qurra reported that Abu'd-Darda' fell ill and his friends visited him. They said, "Abu'd-Darda', what is your complaint?" He said, "I complain of my sins." They asked, "What do you desire?" He replied, "I desire the Garden." They said, "Have you called a doctor?" He replied, "He is the One who has put me to bed."

Muhammad ibn Ka'b al-Qurazi said, "When Abu'd-Darda' was dying. Habib ibn Maslama came to him and asked, 'How do you feel, Abu'd-Darda'?' He replied, 'I feel heavy.' He said, 'I think it must be death.' He replied, 'Yes.' He said, 'May Allah repay you well.'"

Muhammad ibn 'Umar said that Abu'd-Darda' died in Damascus in 32 while 'Uthman was khalif. He has descendants in Syria.

Khalid ibn Ma'dan said that he died in Syria in 31 AH.

Shurahbil ibn Hasana

Hasana was his mother, an 'Adawi woman. He was the son of 'Abdullah ibn al-Muta', from Kinda, the ally of the Banu Zuhra. His *kunya* was Abu 'Abdullah. He became Muslim early on in Makka. He was one of those who emigrated to Abyssinia the second time. He was one of the high-ranking Companions of the Messenger of Allah صلعم and went on expeditions with him. He was one of the generals whom Abu Bakr as-Siddiq sent to Syria. Shurahbil ibn Hasana died in the 'Amwas plague in Syria in 18 AH while 'Umar ibn al-Khattab was khalif. He was 67.

Khalid ibn al-Walid

One of Makhzum. His *kunya* was Abu Sulayman. His mother was 'Isma', Lubaba the younger, daughter of al-Harith ibn Harb. She was the sister of Umm al-Fadl bint al-Harith, the mother of the sons of 'Abbas ibn 'Abdu'l-Muttalib. Khalid was one of the warriors of Quraysh and their strong men. He was with the idolaters at Badr, Uhud and the Ditch.

Then Allah cast love of Islam into his heart when Allah desired good for him. The Messenger of Allah ﷺ entered Makka in the year of the Fulfilled *'Umra* and Khalid stayed away. The Messenger of Allah ﷺ asked his brother about him, "Where is Khalid?" He said, "Allah will bring him." The Messenger of Allah ﷺ said, "Someone like Khalid will not remain ignorant of Islam. It would be better for him to devote his power to inflict defeat and good fortune on the side of the Muslims against the idolaters and we would promote him over others." Khalid ibn al-Walid heard about that and it increased his desire for Islam and encouraged him to leave Makka. He decided to go to the Messenger of Allah ﷺ.

Khalid said, "I looked for someone to accompany me and I met 'Uthman ibn Talha and I mentioned to him what I wanted to do and he readily agreed. We left together. When we reached al-Hadda, we met 'Amr ibn al-'As who said, 'Greetings to the people!' We replied, 'And to you.' He asked, 'Where are you going?' We told him and he informed us that he also was going to the Prophet ﷺ. So we all went together to Madina to the Messenger of Allah, arriving on the first day of Safar 8 AH. When I looked at the Prophet ﷺ, I greeted him as the Prophet and he returned the greeting to me with a cheerful face. So I became Muslim and gave the testimony of the Truth. The Messenger of Allah ﷺ said, 'I thought you were intelligent and I hoped that it would only lead you to good.' I gave my allegiance to the Messenger of Allah ﷺ and said, 'Ask forgiveness for me for all I have done to impede the way of Allah.' He said, 'Islam cuts through what was before it.' I said 'Messenger of Allah, pray for that for me.' He said, 'O Allah, forgive Khalid ibn al-Walid all that he did

Syria

to impede Your way.' I came forward, and then 'Amr ibn al-'As and 'Uthman ibn Talha came forward and became Muslim and gave allegiance to the Messenger of Allah ﷺ. By Allah, on the day I became Muslim the Messenger of Allah ﷺ did not make me equal to any of his Companions in what he repaid."

Abu Qatada al-Ansari, the warrior of the Messenger of Allah ﷺ, said that he heard the Prophet ﷺ mentioning the army of the Amirs[1] one by one, announcing their death and asking forgiveness for them. The Prophet ﷺ said, "Then Khalid ibn al-Walid, the Sword of Allah, took the banner." He was not one of the amirs. The Messenger of Allah ﷺ raised his fingers and said, 'O Allah, he is one of Your swords, so give him victory!' On that day Khalid received the name of 'Sword of Allah'."

Qays ibn Abi Hazim said that the Messenger of Allah ﷺ said, "Khalid is one of the swords of Allah which Allah has unsheathed against the unbelievers."

Qays ibn Abi Hazim said, "I heard Khalid ibn al-Walid say at Hira, 'On the day of Mu'ta nine swords broke in my hand and I had to make do with a Yamani broadsword."

Muhammad ibn 'Umar said, "On the Day of the Conquest of Makka, the Messenger of Allah ﷺ ordered him to enter Makka by al-Layt. He entered and encountered a group of Quraysh and their Confederates, including Safwan ibn Umayya, 'Ikrima ibn Abi Jahl and Suhayl ibn 'Amr, who tried to prevent him from entering. They drew their weapons and shot arrows at him. Khalid shouted to his companions and fought them, killing 24 of them. When the Messenger of Allah ﷺ conquered Makka, he sent Khalid ibn al-Walid to the idol, al-'Uzza, which he destroyed. Then he returned to the Messenger of Allah while he was still in Makka and he sent him to the Banu Jadhima, who are part of Banu Kinana. They were one day away from Makka in a place called al-Ghumaysa'. He went and attacked them. When the Arabs apostatised after the death of the Messenger of Allah ﷺ, Abu Bakr sent Khalid ibn al-Walid to deal with them, and call to them to Islam. He went and attacked the people of the Ridda."

---

1. This was the Raid on Mu'ta in 8 AH, where a force of 3000 Muslims met 200,000 Byzantines and their allies. The Muslim force had three successive Amirs who fell: Zayd ibn Haritha, Ja'far ibn Abi Talib and 'Abdullah ibn Rawaha.

'Urwa said, "There was a Ridda among the Banu Sulaym and Abu Bakr sent Khalid ibn al-Walid and he collected some of their men in groups and then burned them. 'Umar went to Abu Bakr and said, 'Remove a man who has punished with the punishment of Allah.' Abu Bakr said, 'No, by Allah, I will not sheathe a sword which Allah has unsheathed against the unbelievers, until He is the One Who sheathes it.' Then he commanded him to deal with those whom he encountered on the way to Musaylima."

Al-Bara' ibn 'Azib and Sa'id ibn al-Musayyab said, "After Khalid ibn al-Walid finished with the people of Yamama, Abu Bakr as-Siddiq wrote to him, ordering him to go to Iraq. So Khalid left Yamama and went to Hira and stopped at Khaffan. The *marzban* at Hira was a king who was subject to Khusraw and had become king when an-Nu'man ibn Mundhir died. The Banu Qabisa, Banu Tha'laba and 'Abdu'l-Masih ibn Hayyan met him and made peace with him on behalf of Hira and paid a *jizya* of 100,000 dirhams provided that he would withdraw to the Sawad.[1] He agreed to that and made peace with them and wrote out a document for them. This was the first *jizya* paid in Islam.

"Then Khalid went to 'Ayn at-Tamr and called them to Islam. They refused, so he fought a terrible battle against them and Allah gave him victory over them. He killed and took captives and sent the captives to Abu Bakr as-Siddiq. Then he stopped at the people of Ullays, a town on the lower part of the Euphrates and made peace with them for 2,000,000 dirhams. The one in charge of the truce was Hani ibn Habir at-Ta'i. Then he stopped at Baniqya on the bank of the Euphrates and they fought him for a night until morning. Then they asked for peace and he made peace with them and wrote a document for them. He made peace with Busbuhra ibn Saluba, whose residence was on the bank of the Euphrates, for a *jizya* of 100,000 dirhams.

"Then Abu Bakr as-Siddiq wrote to him instructing him to go to Syria. He wrote to him, 'I have appointed you over your army and have given you instructions to read. You should act by what is in them. Go to Syria until my letter reaches you.'

"Khalid said, "Umar ibn al-Khattab envied me because Iraq was conquered by me. He appointed al-Muthanna ibn Haritha ash-Shaybani

---

1. The name of the huge area of agricultural land bordering the Tigris in Iraq which was called Sawad (meaning 'black') because of the intensity of cultivation and trees there.

Syria

in my place.' Khalid set out with guides and proceeded to Dumat al-Jandal. He received Abu Bakr's letter and his instructions from Sharik ibn 'Abda al-'Ajlani. Khalid was one of the generals in Syria while Abu Bakr was khalif. He had many victories there. He concluded a treaty with the people of Damascus and wrote a document for them with which they complied. When Abu Bakr died and 'Umar ibn al-Khattab was appointed, he dismissed Khalid and appointed Abu 'Ubayda ibn al-Jarrah. Khalid continued to fight in Abu 'Ubayda's army. He experienced affliction, wealth and advancement in the way of Allah until he died in Hims in 21 AH and left instructions for 'Umar ibn al-Khattab. He was buried in a village about a mile from Hims."

Muhammad ibn 'Umar said, "I asked about the village and they said that it no longer existed."

Nafi' said, "When Khalid ibn al-Walid died, he only left his horse, his weapons and a slave." That reached 'Umar ibn al-Khattab and he said, 'May Allah have mercy on Abu Sulayman. He was not how we thought he was.'"

'Iyad ibn Ghanm

One of Fihr. He became Muslim early on, before al-Hudaybiyya, and was present at al-Hudaybiyya with the Messenger of Allah صلعم. He was a righteous and generous man. He was with Abu 'Ubayda ibn al-Jarrah in Syria. When Abu 'Ubayda was dying, he appointed 'Iyad ibn Ghanm who had been his subordinate. 'Umar ibn al-Khattab asked, "Who did Abu 'Ubayda appoint to his post?" They replied, "'Iyad ibn Ghanm." He confirmed him and wrote to him, "I have appointed you to what Abu 'Ubayda had, so do what Allah has imposed on you."

It is reported that when 'Umar appointed 'Iyad ibn Ghanm over the army of Hims, he provided him with a dinar, a sheep and a *mudd of grain* a day."

Muhammad ibn 'Umar said, "'Iyad remained governor for 'Umar ibn al-Khattab over Hims until he died in Syria in 20 AH at the age of 60 while 'Umar was still khalif. He died without any property and without owing any debts to anyone.

Sa'id ibn 'Amir

He became Muslim before Khaybar and emigrated to Madina and was at Khaybar with the Prophet ﷺ and on his subsequent expeditions. We do not know whether he had a house in Madina. 'Umar ibn al-Khattab appointed him to 'Iyad ibn Ghanm's post when 'Iyad died. He was in charge of Hims and the surrounding part of Syria. He had fainting spells when he was among his companions. That was mentioned to 'Umar and he said, "Ask him." He said, "I was among those present when Khubayb was killed. I heard his supplication. By Allah, it does not come to my heart when I am in an assembly but that I faint." 'Umar's good opinion of him increased.

Muhammad ibn 'Umar said that Sa'id ibn 'Amir died in 20 AH when 'Umar was khalif.

Al-Fadl ibn al-'Abbas ibn 'Abdu'l-Muttalib

His *kunya* was Abu Muhammad. He was the oldest son of al-'Abbas. He was with the Messenger of Allah ﷺ in the Conquest of Makka and at Hunayn. He stood on that day with the Messenger of Allah ﷺ when the people retreated, and he was present at the Farewell *Hajj* with him and rode behind the Messenger of Allah ﷺ on the same animal. He was among those who washed the Messenger of Allah ﷺ and was in charge of his burial. Then he later went to Syria, and he died in a part of Jordan in the 'Amwas plague, in 18 AH, while 'Umar ibn al-Khattab was khalif.

Abu Malik al-Ash'ari

He became a Muslim and was a Companion of the Messenger of Allah ﷺ and went on expeditions with him and related from him.

Abu Musa al-Ash'ari said that the Messenger of Allah ﷺ set Abu Malik al-Ash'ari on the horse of at-Talb and commanded him to go after Hawazin when they retreated.

'Awf ibn Malik al-Ashja'i

He became Muslim before Hunayn and was at Hunayn. He held the banner of Ashja' on the day that Makka was conquered. He moved to Syria while Abu Bakr was khalif. He settled in Hims and lived on until the beginning of the khalifate of 'Abdu'l-Malik ibn Marwan and died in 73 AH. His *kunya* was Abu 'Amr.

Thawban, the client of the Messenger of Allah

His *kunya* was Abu 'Abdullah. He was one of the noble people. They mentioned that he was from Himyar and was caught by Siba, and the Messenger of Allah ﷺ purchased him and freed him. He remained with the Messenger of Allah ﷺ until his death, and then moved to Syria and settled in Hims. He had the Dar as-Sadaqa there. He died there in 54 AH while Mu'awiya was khalif.

Sahl ibn al-Hanzaliyya

He is Sahl ibn 'Amr. His mother was from Tamim and then Banu Hanzala. He is known by his mother's lineage and is thus called Ibn al-Hanzaliyya. He was present at Uhud, the Ditch and the battles with the Messenger of Allah ﷺ and then moved to Syria and lived in Damascus until he died there.

Shaddad ibn Aws

One of Banu'n-Najjar. He was the nephew of Hassan ibn Thabit the poet. He moved to Palestine and settled there and died there in 58 AH at the end of Mu'awiya's khalifate. He was 95 when he died and has descendants in Jerusalem. He had worship and striving in action. He related from Ka'b al-Ahbar.

Fadala ibn 'Ubayd

One of the Ansar. He was present at Uhud, the Ditch and all the battles alongside the Messenger of Allah ﷺ. Then he went to Syria and settled in Damascus and built a house there. He was qadi there in the time of Mu'awiya ibn Abi Sufyan. He died in Damascus while Mu'awiya was khalif and has descendants.

Abu Ubayy

This Abu Ubayy was the son of the wife of 'Ubada ibn as-Samit. His name was 'Abdullah ibn 'Amr of Banu'n-Najjar of the Ansar from Khazraj. His father and brother Qays ibn 'Amr were at Badr but Abu Ubayy was not. His mother was Umm Hiram bint Milhan, the aunt of Anas ibn Malik. Abu Ubayy moved to Syria and settled in Jerusalem. He has descendants there. He related from the Messenger of Allah ﷺ.

Abu'l-Muthanna al-Himsi reported that Ubayy, the son of the wife of 'Ubada ibn as-Samit said, "We were sitting with the Messenger of Allah ﷺ and he said, 'Amirs will come who are distracted by things so that they delay the prayer until they do not pray the prayer in its time. Pray the prayer at its time.' A man asked, 'Messenger of Allah, should we pray with them then?' He said, 'Yes.'"

'Abdu'r-Rahman ibn Shibl

One of the Ansar. He settled in Syria and related from the Messenger of Allah ﷺ that he forbade moving like a pecking crow and prostrating like sitting animals [in the prayer].

'Umayr ibn Sa'd

One of Banu 'Amr ibn 'Awf. His father was one of those who was present at Badr. He was Sa'd al-Qari'. 'Umayr ibn Sa'd was a Companion of the Prophet ﷺ and related from him. 'Umar ibn al-Khattab made him governor of Hims after Sa'id ibn 'Amir.

'Amr ibn 'Abasa as-Sulami

His *kunya* was Abu Nujayh. 'Amr ibn 'Abasa said, "I went to the Messenger of Allah ﷺ when he was camped at 'Ukaz. I said, 'Messenger of Allah, who is with you in this business?' He replied, 'Two men are with me: Abu Bakr and Bilal.' I became Muslim then. I saw myself as a quarter of Islam. I said, 'Messenger of Allah, shall I remain with you or rejoin my people?' He replied, 'Rejoin your people. It is almost the point that you will attract those you see and give life to Islam.' Then I went to him after the conquest of Makka and greeted him, saying, 'Messenger of Allah, I am 'Amr ibn 'Abasa as-Sulami. I want to ask you about what you know of which I am ignorant and will benefit me and not harm me.'"

Muhammad ibn 'Umar said, "After 'Amr ibn 'Abasa became Muslim in Makka, he returned to his people's land, the Banu Sulaym. He lived at Safna Wahhadha, which is part of the land of the Banu Sulaym. He remained there until after Badr, Uhud, the Ditch, al-

Hudaybiyya and Hunayn were over. Then he went to the Messenger of Allah ﷺ after that in Madina and accompanied him and listened to him and related from him. Then after the death of the Messenger of Allah he went to Syria and settled there, living there until his death.

Al-Harith ibn Hisham

He became Muslim on the day that Makka was conquered and was present with the Messenger of Allah ﷺ at Hunayn, and the Messenger of Allah gave him a hundred camels from the booty of Hunayn. He remained in Makka after he became Muslim until the Messenger of Allah ﷺ died. Then he received the letter from Abu Bakr as-Siddiq encouraging people to volunteer to go and fight against the Byzantines. Al-Harith ibn Hisham, 'Ikrima ibn Abi Jahl, and Suhayl ibn 'Amr went together to Abu Bakr in Madina. Abu Bakr went to them in their camps and greeted them and welcomed them and was delighted with their attitude. Then they went out to Syria on the expedition with the Muslims. They were present at Fihl [13/635] and Ajnadayn [13/634]. He died in Syria in the 'Amwas plague in 18 AH while 'Umar ibn al-Khattab was khalif.

'Ikrima ibn Abi Jahl

Abu Jahl's name was 'Amr ibn Hisham of Makhzum. 'Ikrima became Muslim when Makka was conquered and the Messenger of Allah ﷺ put him in charge of the *zakat* of Hawazin in the year when he made *hajj*. The Messenger of Allah ﷺ died while 'Ikrima was at Tabala as governor of Hawazin. 'Ikrima went on *jihad* to Syria while Abu Bakr as-Siddiq was khalif. He was killed as a martyr in the battle of Ajnadayn and left no descendants.

Suhayl ibn 'Amr

His *kunya* was Abu Yazid. He went to Hunayn with the Messenger of Allah ﷺ. He remained an idolater until he became Muslim at al-Ji'rrana when the Messenger of Allah ﷺ was leaving Hunayn. On that day the Messenger of Allah gave him a hundred camels from the booty of Hunayn.

Abu Sa'id ibn Abi Fadala al-Ansari, who was a Companion, said, "Suhayl ibn 'Amr and I went to Syria in the days when Abu Bakr as-

Siddiq sent us on expeditions. I heard Suhayl say, 'I heard the Messenger of Allah ﷺ say, "The standing of one of you in the way of Allah for an hour is better than all his actions in his life among his people."' Suhayl ibn 'Amr said, 'I will remain in the front lines until I die and I will never return to Makka.'" He remained in Syria until he died there in the 'Amwas plague in 18 AH while 'Umar was khalif.

Abu Jandal ibn Suhayl

He became Muslim early on in Makka and his father locked him up and chained him up to keep him from making *hijra*. Then he escaped after al-Hudaybiyya and went to Abu Basir[1] at al-'Is. He remained with him until Abu Basir died. Then Abu Jandal and some Muslims came to Madina to the Messenger of Allah ﷺ. He continued to go on expeditions with him until the Messenger of Allah ﷺ died. Then he went to Syria among the first Muslims to go there. He continued to fight and strive in the way of Allah until he died in Syria in the 'Amwas plague in 18 AH while 'Umar was khalif. Abu Jandal left no descendants.

Yazid ibn Abi Sufyan

He became Muslim on the day that Makka was conquered and was present with the Prophet ﷺ at Hunayn. The Messenger of Allah gave him a hundred camels and 40 *uqiyyas* from the booty of Hunayn. He always spoke well of him. Abu Bakr as-Siddiq commissioned him with the generals of the armies sent to Syria. He said, "When you agree on a stratagem, then Yazid is in charge of the people. When you are separate, then whoever in the battle is near his army is in charge of his companions." Abu Bakr as-Siddiq went out on foot to bid him farewell and said, "I reckon that these steps of mine are in the way of Allah." Abu Bakr began to instruct him. Abu Bakr died while he was governor and 'Umar ibn al-Khattab appointed him over Damascus. He remained governor there until he died in the 'Amwas plague in 18 AH. He left no descendants.

---

1. He collected various Muslims who could not go to Madina because of the terms of the treaty of al-Hudaybiyya. They raided caravans belonging to the unbelievers until they were given permission to go to Madina.

Syria

Mu'awiya ibn Abi Sufyan

His mother was Hind bint 'Utba. His *kunya* was Abu 'Abdu'r-Rahman. He has descendants. He mentioned that he became Muslim in the year of al-Hudaybiyya and that he concealed his Islam from Abu Sufyan. He said, "The Messenger of Allah ﷺ entered Makka in the conquest and I declared my Islam and met him and he welcomed me." He acted as his scribe. Mu'awiya was present with the Messenger of Allah ﷺ at Hunayn and Ta'if. The Messenger of Allah gave him 100 camels and 40 *uqiyyas* of the booty of Hunayn which Bilal weighed out for him. He related *hadiths* from the Messenger of Allah ﷺ and when his brother Yazid died, 'Umar ibn al-Khattab appointed him to Yazid's position. He remained governor for 'Umar until 'Umar was killed. Then 'Uthman ibn 'Affan appointed him to that office and the rest of Syria until 'Uthman was murdered. So he was governor of Syria for twenty years. Then he was given allegiance as the khalif and people agreed on him after 'Ali ibn Abi Talib. He was khalif for twenty years until he died on Thursday night in the middle of Rajab in 60 AH, when he was 78.

Abu Hashim ibn 'Utba

He became Muslim the day that Makka was conquered. He went to Syria and lived there until his death. He lived in Damascus.

'Abdullah ibn as-Sa'di

As-Sa'di's name was 'Amr ibn Waqdan. He became Muslim the day that Makka was conquered and became a Companion of the Prophet ﷺ and related from him. He went to Syria and settled in Damascus where he died.

Dirar ibn al-Khattab

He was a poet. He became Muslim the day that Makka was conquered. He was a mounted warrior. He became a Companion of the Prophet and a good Muslim. He went to Syria on *jihad* and died there.

Wathila ibn al-Asqa'

One of Banu Kinana. His *kunya* was Abu Qirsafa. He lived in a part of Madina. Islam fell into his heart and he came to the

Messenger of Allah ﷺ while he was preparing to go to Tabuk. He became Muslim and went out with the Messenger of Allah ﷺ to Tabuk. He was one of the *Ahl as-Suffa*. He said, "I was among twenty of the Companions of the Messenger of Allah ﷺ among the *Ahl as-Suffa* and I was the youngest of them." He listened to the Messenger of Allah. When the Messenger of Allah ﷺ died, he went to Syria.

Abu'z-Zahriyya said, "Wathila ibn al-Asqa' died in Syria in 85 AH at the age of 98." Ibn Khalid said, "Wathila ibn al-Asqa' died in 83 AH when he was 105. He settled in Jerusalem and died there. He went on expeditions and passed through Damascus and Hims."

Makhul said, "Abu'l-Azhar and I visited Wathila ibn al-Asqa' and we said to him, 'Abu'l-Asqa', relate to us a *hadith* which you heard from the Messenger of Allah ﷺ.'"

Abu'l-Mus'ab said, "I saw Wathila ibn al-Asqa' having lunch or supper in the courtyard of his house and inviting people to share his food."

Tamim ad-Dari

He is Tamim ibn Aws. He came to the Messenger of Allah ﷺ with his brother Nu'aym ibn Aws and they became Muslim and the Messenger of Allah ﷺ gave them a land grant of Hibra and Bayt 'Aynun in Syria. The Messenger of Allah did not give any land grant other than that in Syria. Tamim kept the company of the Messenger of Allah ﷺ and went on expeditions with him and related from him. He remained in Madina until he moved to Syria after the death of 'Uthman ibn 'Affan. Tamim ad-Dari's *kunya* was Abu Ruqayya.

Busr ibn Abi Arta'

Abu Arta's name was 'Umayr ibn 'Uwaymir.

Muhammad ibn 'Umar said, "The Messenger of Allah ﷺ died while Busr ibn Abi Arta' was young and none of the Madinans related that he listened to the Prophet ﷺ. Then he moved and settled in Syria." In other transmissions from the Syrians and others it is said that he met the Prophet ﷺ and related *hadith* from him. He kept the company of Mu'awiya and was a partisan of 'Uthman. He lived until the khalifate of 'Abdu'l-Malik ibn Marwan.

Habib ibn Maslama al-Fihri

Habib ibn Maslama al-Fihri reported that he went to the Prophet while he was in Madina and his father met him. He said, "Messenger of Allah, my hand and my foot." The Prophet ﷺ said to him, "Return with him. He is about to die." He died that same year.

Muhammad ibn 'Umar said, "Our people in our transmission state that the Messenger of Allah ﷺ died while Habib ibn Maslama was twelve. He did not go on any expeditions with him. In other transmissions it states that he went on expeditions with the Messenger of Allah ﷺ and memorised *hadiths* from him which he reported. Habib ibn Maslama moved to Syria and remained with Mu'awiya ibn Abi Sufyan, participating in his battles at Siffin and elsewhere. Mu'awiya sent him to attack the Byzantines, and he inflicted damage on them. Then he sent him to Armenia as its governor and he died there in 42 AH before reaching the age of 50.

Ad-Dahhak ibn Qays

Muhammad ibn 'Umar said, "In our transmission it states that the Messenger of Allah ﷺ died while ad-Dahhak ibn Qays was a boy who had yet not reached puberty. In another variant it states that he met the Prophet ﷺ and listened to him.

Al-Hasan said that ad-Dahhak ibn Qays wrote to Qays ibn al-Haytham when Yazid ibn Mu'awiya died, "Peace be upon you. I heard the Messenger of Allah ﷺ say, 'Before the Last Hour there will be seditions like concentrations of smoke in which the heart of a man will die as his body dies. A man will be a believer in the morning and an unbeliever in the evening. People will sell their character and their *deen* for the goods of this world.' Yazid ibn Mu'awiya has died when you were our brothers and our full brothers. Do not go ahead of us until we choose for ourselves."

Muhammad ibn 'Umar said, "When Mu'awiya ibn Yazid died and people in Syria disagreed, ad-Dahhak ibn Qays called for 'Abdullah ibn az-Zubayr and Ibn az-Zubayr wrote to him to appoint him governor of Syria. Allegiance was given to Marwan ibn al-Hakam and he went to him and they met at the Battle of Marj Rahit and fought. Ad-Dahhak ibn Qays was killed at Marj Rahit in the middle of Dhu'l-Hijja 64 AH.

Qubath ibn Ashyam

One of Kinana. He was present with the idolaters at Badr. He had some renown in it. Then he became Muslim later and was present with the Prophet ﷺ in some of his battles. He was in charge of the flank of Abu 'Ubayda ibn al-Jarrah at the Battle of Yarmuk. He settled in Syria after that and is related from.

Qubath ibn Ashyam reported that the Messenger of Allah ﷺ said, "The prayer of two men in which one of them leads his companion is purer with Allah than the prayer of eight separate men. The prayer of four men in which one leads them is purer with Allah than the prayer of 100 separate men."

Abu Umama al-Bahili

His name was as-Sudayy ibn 'Ajlan. He related from Sulayman.

Abu Umama said, "I was at Siffin, and they did not finish off anyone who was wounded, nor go after a retreater, nor loot the dead."

Abu Ghalib said, "I saw Abu Umama dye his beard yellow."

Habib ibn 'Ubayd said that Abu Umama used to relate *hadith* like a man who is obliged to convey what he has heard. Al-Hasan ibn Jabir said that he asked Abu Umama al-Bahili about the *Book of Knowledge* and he said, "There is nothing wrong with that," or, "I do not know anything wrong about it."

Sulayman ibn Habib said that Abu Umama al-Bahili said to them, "These gatherings are part of Allah conveying to you. The Messenger of Allah ﷺ conveyed what he was sent with to you, so convey from us the best of what you hear." They say that Abu Umama died in Syria in 86 AH while 'Abdu'l-Malik ibn Marwan was khalif at the age of 61.

Al-'Irbad ibn Sariyya as-Sulami

His *kunya* was Abu Nujayh.

Muhammad ibn 'Umar said that he died in Syria in 75 AH at the beginning of the khalifate of 'Abdu'l-Malik ibn Marwan.

'Utba ibn 'Abd as-Sulami

He settled in Syria. He died in 91 or 92 AH. Muhammad ibn 'Umar said that he died in 87 AH when he was 94.

'Abdullah ibn Busr al-Mazini

His *kunya* was Abu Safwan.

Jarir ibn 'Uthman and Safwan ibn 'Amr said that they saw 'Abdullah ibn Busr, the Companion of the Prophet صلعم, dyeing his beard and hair as well as removing the hair from his head.

Jarir ibn 'Uthman said, "I saw the garment of 'Abdullah ibn Busr wrapped up and his cloak was above his shirt. When he passed a stone on the road, he would remove it."

Safwan ibn 'Amr said, "I saw on 'Abdullah ibn Busr's forehead the mark of prostration." Muhammad ibn 'Umar said that 'Abdullah ibn Busr died in 88 AH, and he was the last of the Companions of the Messenger of Allah صلعم to die in Syria. He was 94 when he died.

Ka'b ibn Murra al-Bahzi

Bahz is part of the Banu Sulaym. He lived in Jordan and he related from the Prophet صلعم. He died in 57 AH.

Ka'b ibn 'Iyad

He was a Companion of the Prophet صلعم. He related from him. He said, "I heard the Prophet صلعم say, 'Every community has a trial, and the trial of my community is wealth.'"

Al-Miqdam ibn Ma'dikarib al-Kindi

His *kunya* was Abu Yahya. He died in Syria in 87 AH while 'Abdu'l-Malik ibn Marwan was khalif, when he was 91.

Al-Hakam ibn 'Umayr ath-Thumali

One of Azd. He lived in Hims.

Musa ibn Abi Habib said, "I heard al-Hakam ibn 'Umayr ath-Thumali, one of the Companions of the Prophet صلعم say that the Messenger of Allah صلعم said, 'Two or more is a group.'"

'Abdullah ibn 'A'idh ath-Thumali

He was a Companion of the Prophet صلعم and settled in Syria. Khusayf ibn al-Harith said to 'Abdullah ibn A'idh ath-Thumali when he was dying, "If you can meet us, tell us what you met in death." Then later he saw him in a dream and he asked him, "Will you not inform us?" He said, "We were saved but we were almost not saved. We were saved after white hairs, and we found our Lord to be good, a Lord who forgives wrong actions and overlooks evil except what the contemptible do." He asked, "Who are the contemptible?" He said, "Those who are pointed out by people."

Abu Tha'laba al-Khushani

Khushayn is part of Quda'a. The name of Abu Tha'laba, according to what our companions say, was Jurhum ibn Nash. Abu Mushir ad-Dimishqi said that his name was Jarthuma ibn 'Abdu'l-Karim. Abu Tha'laba said that the Messenger of Allah صلعم saw a gold ring on his hand and began to knock his hand with a stick he had. He understood the Prophet صلعم, and took the ring and threw it away. The Prophet looked and did not see it on his hand and said, "We only think we hurt you and are indebted to you."

Mihjan ibn Wuhayb said, "Abu Tha'laba al-Khushani came to the Messenger of Allah صلعم when he was preparing to go to Khaybar. He was at Khaybar with the Messenger of Allah صلعم. Then the delegation of Khushayn, who were seven, came to the Messenger of Allah صلعم and stayed with Abu Tha'laba al-Khushani.

Muhammad ibn 'Umar said, "Abu Tha'laba al-Khushani died in Syria in 75 AH at the beginning of the khalifate of 'Abdu'l-Malik."

'Abdu'r-Rahman ibn Qatada as-Sulami

He was a Companion of the Messenger of Allah صلعم and related from him and settled in Syria.

'Abdu'r-Rahman ibn Qatada as-Sulami, one of the Companions of the Messenger of Allah, said, "I heard the Messenger of Allah صلعم say, 'Allah Almighty created Adam and took creation from his back and said, "These are in the Garden and I do not care and these are in the Fire and I do not care."' A man asked, 'Messenger of Allah, on what basis should we act?' He replied, 'As Fate decrees.'"

Nu'aym ibn Habbar al-Ghatafani

Kathir ibn Murra reported that Nu'aym ibn Habbar said, "Al-Walid ibn Muslim used to say in what he related from Nu'aym ibn

Habbar 'Nu'aym ibn Hammar'." He was a Companion of the Prophet and related from him and settled later in Damascus.

'Abdu'r-Rahman ibn Abi 'Amira al-Muzani

He was one of the Companions of the Messenger of Allah صلعم who settled in Syria. He said, "I heard the Messenger of Allah صلعم say, 'The allegiance to guidance will take place in Jerusalem.'"

'Abdu'r-Rahman ibn Abi 'Amira said that the Prophet صلعم said about Mu'awiya, "O Allah, make him a guided guide and guide him and guide by him."

Abu Sayyara al-Mut'i

He was an ally of Banu Bajala. It is related that Abu Sayyara al-Mut'i said, "I said, 'Messenger of Allah, I have palm trees.' He said, 'Pay their *zakat*.' I said, 'Make their mountain a reserve for me.' He said, 'Its reserve is yours.'"

Wahshi ibn Harb al-Habashi

He was the killer of Hamza ibn al-Muttalib. He became Muslim after that and was a Companion of the Prophet صلعم and listened to *hadiths* from him and participated in killing Musaylima the Liar. He used to say, "I killed the best of people and I killed the worst of people." He settled in Hims where he lived until he died there and his descendants are still there today.

Al-Walid ibn Muslim reported that one of his descendants, who was also called Wahshi ibn Harb, had *hadiths* going back to Wahshi himself from the Prophet صلعم. He said, "When Abu Bakr as-Siddiq commissioned Khalid ibn al-Walid to set out against the people who had rebelled in the Ridda, he said to me, 'Wahshi, go with Khalid and fight in the way of Allah as you fought to block the way of Allah.' So I set out with him and we fought the Banu Hanifa, and the Muslims were defeated two or three times. Then Allah turned to them and they stood fast with the swords slashing at their heads until I could see sparks of fire coming from the swords and I heard from them something like the sound of bells. I struck with my sword until its pommel was sticky with blood. Then Allah Almighty sent down His victory and Allah defeated the Banu Hanifa and Allah killed Musaylima." He

Companions

also said, "Abu Bakr said, 'I heard the Prophet صلعم say, "Khalid is one of the swords of Allah which Allah Almighty has unleashed against the idolaters."'"

Rashid ibn Sa'd said, "The first to wear pressed clothes and be beaten for drinking wine in Hims was Wahshi."

'Uthman ibn 'Uthman ath-Thaqafi

The Companion of the Messenger of Allah صلعم.

'Uthman ibn 'Uthman ath-Thaqafi, reported that the Messenger of Allah said, "Allah Almighty accepts repentance from His slave a week before his death. Allah Almighty accepts repentance from His slave a month before his death. Allah Almighty accepts repentance from His slave the time between two camel milkings before his death."

Muslim ibn Harith at-Tamimi

He was a Companion of the Messenger of Allah صلعم.

Muslim ibn Harith at-Tamimi said, "The Messenger of Allah صلعم sent us on an expedition. When we approached a fortress, we heard the tumult of its people and I spurred my horse forward and went up to them and said, 'Say: "There is no god but Allah," and you will be protected.' They said, 'There is no god but Allah.' My companions said, 'You have denied us booty after it was firmly in our hands.' When we came to the Messenger of Allah صلعم, he was informed of that and he approved of what I had done and said to me, 'You will have such-and-such a reward in number as great as every man of them!' Then he said, 'I will write you a letter in which I recommend you to the Imams of the Muslims after me.' So he wrote a letter for me and sealed it. When the Prophet صلعم died, I took the letter to Abu Bakr and he opened it and gave me something and then sealed it. When Abu Bakr died, I took the letter to 'Umar ibn al-Khattab and he opened it and gave me something and then sealed it. When 'Uthman became khalif, I took the letter to him and he read it and gave me something and then sealed it."

When 'Umar ibn 'Abdu'l-'Aziz became khalif, he sent for al-Harith, Muslim's son. He brought him the letter and he gave him something. He said, "I wanted to come to you, but I want you to

Syria

report to me your *hadith* from your father from the Prophet صلعم." So he reported it.

Malik ibn Hubayra as-Sulami

Malik ibn Hubayra as-Sulami, a Companion, reported that the Messenger of Allah صلعم said, "Three rows do not form for a dead person [in the funeral prayer] but that it [the Garden] is mandatory."

'Abdullah ibn Mu'awiya al-Ghadiri

'Abdullah ibn Mu'awiya al-Ghadiri reported that the Messenger of Allah صلعم said, "Whoever does three things has been fed with the food of belief: Whoever worships Allah alone, says that there is no god but Him, and pays the *zakat* on his property cheerfully."

'Amr al-Bakali

Abu Tamima al-Hujaymi said, "I came to Syria and there was a man with his fingers cut off, around whom they gathered to hear him relate. I asked, 'Who is this?' They said, 'This is the one with the most *fiqh* of the Companions of the Messenger of Allah صلعم remaining on the face of the earth. This is 'Amr al-Bakali.' I asked, 'What happened to his fingers?' They replied, 'He was wounded in the Battle of Yarmuk.'"

Sinan ibn Gharafa

One of the Companions of the Messenger of Allah صلعم who lived in Syria and who related from the Prophet صلعم concerning the woman who dies among men, or a man who dies among women. *Tayammum* is done for them and they are not washed.

Abu Hind ad-Dari

Makhul heard that he heard Abu Hind ad-Dari say, "I heard the Messenger of Allah صلعم say, 'Whoever stands in a position of showing-off and reputation, Allah will put in a place of reputation and show on the Day of Resurrection.'" Abu Hind ad-Dari was Tamim ad-Dari's brother.

Mu'awiya al-Hudhali

Mu'awiya al-Hudhali, the Companion of the Messenger of Allah, said, "The hypocrite prays and Allah denies him. He gives *sadaqa* and Allah denies him. He fights and Allah denies him. He is killed and Allah makes him one of the people of the Fire."

Nahik ibn Sarim as-Sakuni

Nahik ibn Sarim said that the Messenger of Allah ﷺ said, "Those who are left of you will fight the Dajjal at the Jordan River. You will be on the eastern side of the river and they will be on the western. I do not know where 'the Jordan' is."

Sufyan ibn Usayd al-Hadrami

Sufyan ibn Usayd al-Hadrami reported that he heard the Messenger of Allah ﷺ say, "It is terrible treachery to tell your brother something which he believes when you are lying to him."

Abu'l-Bujayr

He was a Companion of the Prophet ﷺ. He said, "One day the Messenger of Allah ﷺ was hungry and placed a stone on his belly. Then he said, 'O Lord, many a soul may be fed and comfortable in this world and hungry and naked on the Day of Rising! O Lord, someone may be deferential to his self while he despises it! O Lord, someone may despise his self while he is deferential to it! O Lord, someone absorbed and blessed in the booty which Allah has given His Messenger might have no portion with Allah. Action for the sake of the Garden is a sorrow for which there is elevation. Action for the sake of the Next World is ease in exchange for a hardship. O Lord, an hour's worth of appetite bequeaths long sorrow.'"

The grandfather of Abu'l-Asad as-Sulami

He said, "I was one of seven with the Prophet ﷺ. The Messenger of Allah commanded us and each of us brought a dirham and we shared in a sacrifice for seven dirhams. We said 'Messenger of Allah, by Allah, he has raised the price for us.' The Prophet ﷺ said, 'The best of sacrifices is the most expensive and plumpest.' The Prophet commanded one man who took its foreleg, another man who took another leg, another man took another leg, and another man took another leg, and one man a horn and another man another horn, and the seventh man sacrificed, and they all said, 'Allah is great!'"

Thawban ibn Yamrad

The Companion of the Messenger of Allah ﷺ who was called 'Dhu'l-Asabi'' (he with fingers), a man of the people of Yemen from the reinforcements who settled in Syria at Jerusalem.

Dhu'l-Asabi' said, "O Messenger of Allah, if we are tested by continuing on after you, where do you command us to settle?" He replied, "Settle at Jerusalem. Perhaps Allah will provide you with offspring who will frequent that mosque, going to it morning and evening."

Mazin ibn Khaythama

Mu'adh ibn Jabal sent for Mazin ibn Khaythama and Hanbal, the-granfather of Zamil, on the day that he camped between Sakun and Sakasik and fought until the people submitted. Then he sent them to the Messenger of Allah ﷺ and the Messenger of Allah made brotherhood between Sakun and Sakasik.

Abu Hanash al-Ansari

The Prophet ﷺ told him, "Do not ask for command."

Abu Rayhana al-Ansari

He was the Companion of the Messenger of Allah. Abu Rayhana said, "I heard the Messenger of Allah ﷺ say, 'Nothing of pride will enter the Garden.' Someone said, 'Messenger of Allah, I like the handle of my whip and the straps of my sandals to look beautiful.' The Messenger of Allah ﷺ said, 'That is not part of pride. Allah is Beautiful and loves beauty. Pride means to renounce the truth and hold people in contempt.'"

Dhu Mikhmar

He was the nephew of the Negus. Some say Mikhbar, but Mikhmar is more correct and frequent. He was one of the people of Yemen and later settled in Syria. People related from him and he was a Companion of the Messenger of Allah ﷺ.

Dhu Mikhmar said, "I heard the Messenger of Allah ﷺ say, 'The Greeks will make a secure truce with you.'"

'Abdullah as-Sunabihi

Ata' ibn Yasar said that he heard 'Abdullah as-Sunabihi say that he heard the Messenger of Allah ﷺ say, "The sun rises and with it is the horn of Shaytan, and when the sun gets higher the horn leaves it. Then when the sun reaches the meridian, the horn joins it, and when the sun declines the horn leaves it, and when the sun has nearly set it joins it again. Do not pray at these three times."

Qays al-Judhami

Qays al-Judhami, a Companion, reported that the Messenger of Allah ﷺ said, "The martyr is given six qualities at the first drop of his blood which expiates every error for him, and he sees his seat in the Garden, and he marries the dark-eyed houris, and he will be safe from the Greatest Terror and from the punishment of the grave, and he will be robed in the robe of belief."

Busr ibn Jahhash al-Qurashi

It is related from Busr ibn Jahhash al-Qurashi that one day the Messenger of Allah ﷺ spat on his palm and placed it on his finger and said, "Allah says, 'O son of Adam, you think that you can thwart Me when I created you from the like of this and I shaped you and proportioned you. You walk between two similar states and will be buried in the earth. Yet you gather and deny until you reach this,'" and he pointed to his throat. "'You say, "I give *sadaqa*," and you are slack in *sadaqa*.'"

Salama ibn Nufayl al-Hadrami

Salama ibn Nufayl al-Hadrami said, "Allah gave victory to the Messenger of Allah ﷺ and I went to the Messenger of Allah and drew near him until my garment was almost touching his garment and I said, 'Messenger of Allah, the horses are released and the weapons idle and they say that war has put down its burdens.' The

Messenger of Allah ﷺ said, 'They have lied. Now fighting comes. Now fighting comes. Allah will continue to make the hearts of the people whom you fight swerve and Allah Almighty will provide for you from them until the command of Allah comes and they follow that and the centre of the Abode of Islam is in Syria.'"

Salama ibn Nufayl said, "I asked the Messenger of Allah ﷺ and said, 'Are you given food from heaven?' He said, 'Yes.' I said, 'Was there anything left of it?' He said, 'Yes.' I said, 'What happened to it?' He said, 'It was taken back to heaven.'"

Yazid ibn Asad

He came in a delegation to the Prophet ﷺ and related a *hadith* from the Prophet. He said, "The Messenger of Allah ﷺ said to me, 'Yazid ibn Asad, love for other people what you love for yourself.'"

Muhammad ibn 'Umar and others said, "Yazid ibn Asad was not one of those who laid out Kufa in the khalifate of 'Umar ibn al-Khattab. He did not settle there. He settled in Syria and one of his descendants was Khalid ibn 'Abdullah al-Qasri. He was made governor of Makka for al-Walid I, and was governor of Iraq for Hisham ibn 'Abdu'l-Malik. He built a house in Kufa and has many descendants there.

Ghutayf ibn al-Harith al-Kindi

Ghutayf ibn al-Harith said, "In those things I forgot, I did not forget that I saw the Messenger of Allah ﷺ pray with his right hand on his left hand in the prayer."

Ghutayf said, "The Messenger of Allah ﷺ said, 'If anyone innovates something in Islam, cut his tongue.'"

Bashir ibn 'Aqraba al-Juhani

His *kunya* was Abu'l-Yaman. 'Abdullah ibn 'Awf al-Kindi, the governor of Ramla for 'Umar ibn 'Abdu'l-'Aziz, reported that he was present when 'Abdu'l-Malik ibn Marwan said to Bashir ibn 'Aqraba al-Juhani on the day when 'Amr ibn Sa'id ibn al-'As was killed, "Abu Yaman! Today I rely on your words. Stand up and speak!" He said, "I heard the Messenger of Allah ﷺ say, 'Whoever stands to speak out of the desire for showing off or reputation, Allah will make him stand on the Day of Rising in a position of showing off and reputation.'"

Al-Jullah

I think he is Ibn al-Ashadd. Al-Jullah said, "We used to work in the market and the Messenger of Allah ﷺ brought a man who had been stoned to death. A man came and asked us where he was. We did not direct him to where he was until the Messenger of Allah came to us with him. We said, 'Messenger of Allah, this man came to ask us about that foul individual whom you had stoned today.' The Messenger of Allah ﷺ said, 'Do not say, "Foul." He is better with Allah than musk.'"

'Atiyya ibn 'Amr as-Sa'di

One of the Banu Sa'd. 'Atiyya said, "I came to the Messenger of Allah ﷺ with a group of the Banu Sa'd ibn Layth. He said to me, 'Accept what Allah has given you and do not ask people for anything. The upper hand is the giver and the lower hand is the receiver. The property of Allah will be asked about.' The Messenger of Allah ﷺ spoke to us in our dialect."

'Utba ibn 'Amr as-Sulami

'Utba ibn 'Amr said, "The Messenger of Allah ﷺ said, 'The Garden has eight gates and the Fire has seven gates.'"

'Isma

He was the Companion of the Messenger of Allah ﷺ. 'Isma said that he used to seek refuge in his prayer from the trial of the west.

Gharafa ibn al-Harith al-Kindi

Gharafa was heard to say, "I saw the Messenger of Allah ﷺ in the Farewell *Hajj* when the sacrificial animals were brought. He said, 'Call Abu Hasan ('Ali) for me.' He was called and he said, 'Take the bottom of the spear,' and the Messenger of Allah ﷺ took the upper part and then we pierced the sacrificial animals with it. When he had finished, he mounted his camel and 'Ali mounted behind him."

Sharahbil ibn Aws

Sharahbil ibn Aws, one of the Companions of Prophet, reported that the Messenger of Allah ﷺ said, "Whoever drinks wine, flog him. Whoever drinks wine, flog him.' three times. If he does it again, kill him."

Habis ibn Sa'd at-Ta'i

'Abdullah ibn 'Abir said, "Habis ibn Sa'd, who had met the Messenger of Allah ﷺ entered the mosque at dawn. He saw the people praying in the front of the mosque and said, 'Those who make a show of themselves. By the Ka'ba of Allah, warn them! Whoever warns them has obeyed Allah and His Messenger.' So one man took a man from behind him to bring him back from the front of the mosque. It was said that the angels are in the front of the mosque at dawn."

Jabala ibn al-Azraq

He was a Companion of the Messenger of Allah. He said that the Messenger of Allah ﷺ prayed next to the side of the wall with a lot of stone. He prayed *Dhuhr* or *'Asr*. When he had prayed two *rak'ats*, a scorpion came and stung him and the people made a talisman. When he came round he said, 'Allah healed me, and not by your talisman.'"

Ibn Mis'ada

He is 'the one with armies'. Ibn Mis'ada said that he heard the Prophet ﷺ say [towards the end of his life], "I have become heavy, so do not rush to precede me in bowing nor precede me in prostration. Whoever misses my bowing, catches it when I am slow in my standing."

'Umara ibn Za'kara

He said that he heard the Messenger of Allah ﷺ say, "Allah says, 'My slave is every slave of Mine who remembers Me, even when he meets his opponent.'"

Abu Salma

The herdsman of the Messenger of Allah ﷺ. Abu Salam al-Aswad said that he heard Abu Salma say, "I heard the Messenger of Allah ﷺ say, 'Excellent! Excellent and how heavy they are in the balance: "Glory be to Allah," "Praise be to Allah," "There is no god

Companions

but Allah," "Allah is greater," and a righteous child of a Muslim man who dies and for whom he is rewarded.'"

'Urayb

'Urayb reported that the Messenger of Allah ﷺ was asked about the words of Allah, *"And others besides them whom you do not know. Allah knows them,"* (8:60), and replied, "It is the jinn."

He said that the Messenger of Allah ﷺ said, "The jinn do not disorder anyone who has swift noble horses in his house."

He said that the Prophet ﷺ was asked about His words, *"Those who give away their wealth secretly and openly will have their wage with their Lord. They will feel no fear; they will know no sorrow."* (2:274) He said, "They are people who have horses."

He said that the Messenger of Allah ﷺ said, "Good will remain tied to the forelocks of horses until the Day of Rising, and for their people who spend on them."

He also said that the Messenger of Allah ﷺ said, "The one who spends on horses is like the one who stretches out his hand with *sadaqa* which is not diminished. On the Day of Rising their urine and dung will be like the fragrance of musk in the sight of Allah."

Abu Ruhm ibn Qays al-Ash'ari

He was one of the Ash'arites who came with Abu Musa al-Ash'ari to the Messenger of Allah ﷺ when he was at Khaybar. They were 54 men including six of their brothers from 'Akk. They became Muslim and accompanied the Messenger of Allah ﷺ. Abu Ruhm went to Syria after the death of the Messenger of Allah ﷺ and settled there.

Sahm ibn 'Amr al-Ash'ari

He was one of those who came with Abu Musa al-Ash'ari to the Messenger of Allah ﷺ when he was at Khaybar. He became a Muslim and accompanied the Prophet ﷺ. Then he went to Syria after the death of the Messenger of Allah and settled there.

'Amr ibn Malik al-'Akki

His maternal uncles were the Ash'arites. He was among those who came with Abu Musa al-Ash'ari to the Messenger of Allah صلعم. He became Muslim and accompanied the Prophet صلعم. He is Abu Malik ibn 'Amr. Mutahhar ibn Hayy al-'Akki claimed that he was his mother's maternal uncle.

Rifa'a ibn Zayd al-Judhami

He came in a delegation to the Messenger of Allah صلعم and became Muslim. The Prophet gave him permission and he stayed for some days in Madina, learning the Qur'an, and then he asked the Prophet صلعم to write for him a letter to his people calling them to Islam. They responded quickly. The Messenger of Allah صلعم had sent Zayd ibn Haritha to that area and he attacked them and killed people and took captives. Rifa'a returned to the Prophet and with him from among his people were Abu Yazid ibn 'Amr, Abu Asma' ibn 'Amr, Suwayd ibn Zayd and his brother Bardha' ibn Zayd, and Tha'laba ibn 'Adi. Rifa'a gave the letter to the Prophet and he read it, and he informed him what Zayd ibn Haritha had done. He said, "What shall I do about the slain?" Abu Yazid said, "Release for us those who are still alive, and those who have been killed are under these two feet." The Messenger of Allah صلعم said, "Abu Yazid has spoken the truth." So the Prophet صلعم sent 'Ali to Zayd and he released those of them whom he had captured and returned what he had taken from them.

Farwa ibn 'Amr al-Judhami

Zamil ibn 'Amr said, "Farwa ibn 'Amr al-Judhami was a governor for the Byzantine Emperor over 'Amman in the region of Balqa'. The Messenger of Allah صلعم had written to Heraclius and to al-Harith ibn Abi Shammar, but he did not write to him. Farwa became Muslim and wrote to the Messenger of Allah صلعم about his Islam and sent him a messenger called Mas'ud ibn Sa'd from his people. He gave the Messenger of Allah صلعم a mule called Fidda, a donkey called Ya'fur, a horse called az-Zarb, and some cotton garments and a man's gown of silk brocade mixed with gold. The Messenger of Allah صلعم accepted his letter and his gifts, and wrote him a reply, and authorised 200 *uqiyyas* and a *nashsh* (20 dirhams) for his messenger Mas'ud. The

Companions

Emperor heard about the Islam of Farwa ibn 'Amr and sent for him and imprisoned him until he died in prison. When he died, he crucified him.

Abu 'Inaba al-Khawlani

Abu 'Inaba al-Khawlani said, "I had pledged to shave my hair for an idol of ours in the *Jahiliyya* and Allah delayed that for me until I shaved it in Islam."

Abu Sufyan Madluk

Abu Sufyan was heard to say, "I went with my clients to the Messenger of Allah ﷺ and I became Muslim with them. The Messenger of Allah ﷺ called me and wiped my head with his hand and prayed for blessing for me." They say that the front of Abu Sufyan's head was marked where the hand of the Messenger of Allah had touched it while the rest of it was pale.

Hani' al-Hamdani

Hani' reported that he came to the Messenger of Allah ﷺ from the Yemen and became Muslim. The Messenger of Allah ﷺ stroked his head and prayed for blessing for him. He lodged him with Yazid ibn Abi Sufyan until he went with him to Syria when Abu Bakr sent him there.

Abu Maryam al-Ghassani

He was the grandfather of Abu Bakr ibn 'Abdullah ibn Abi Maryam, from whom al-Walid ibn Muslim and others related.

Abu Maryam reported that he put some stones in front of the Messenger of Allah ﷺ and he liked that and prayed for him.

Abu Maryam

One of the men of Asad who was a Companion of the Messenger of Allah ﷺ. It is reported from al-Qasim ibn Mukhaymara that a man of Palestine from Asad called Abu Maryam came to Mu'awiya ibn Abi Sufyan and said, "What shall we bestow on you?" He said, "There is a *hadith* which I heard from the Messenger of Allah. I heard him say, 'If Allah puts someone in charge of any of the Muslims and he is veiled from their needs, their illness and their want, then Allah will be veiled from his need, want and loss on the Day of Rising.'"

'Abdu'r-Rahman ibn 'A'ish al-Hadrami

He related that he heard the Messenger of Allah ﷺ say, "I saw my Lord in the best form."

Rabi'a ibn 'Amr al-Jurshi

It says in some *hadiths* that he was a Companion of the Messenger of Allah ﷺ. He is related from and he is reliable. He was killed at the Battle of Marj Rahit in Dhu'l-Hijja 64 AH.

'Abdullah ibn Saydan as-Sulami

They mentioned that he saw the Prophet ﷺ and related from Abu Bakr that he prayed *Jumu'a* behind him, and his *khutba* and prayer were before the middle of the day.

He said, "I prayed behind 'Umar and his *khutba* and prayer were before the middle of the day. I prayed with 'Uthman, and his *khutba* and prayer were before noon."

Khalid ibn al-Hawatiri

A man of the Abyssinians, He was one of the Companions of the Prophet ﷺ.

'Umayr ibn Jabir al-Kindi

He was a Companion and used henna.

Hashraj

The Prophet ﷺ placed him in his lap and stroked his head and prayed for him.

✽✽✽✽✽

Other Companions in Syria also include: **'Amr ibn Murra al-Juhani**, who was an old man in the time of the Prophet; **'Utba ibn**

Companions

an-Nudhar as-Sulami, who settled in Damascus and died in 84 AH; **Abu Kabsha al-Anmari,** who was at Tabuk with the Messenger of Allah; and '**Abdullah ibn Sufyan al-Azdi**.

The First Generation of the People of Syria after the Companions

Junada ibn Abi Umayya

He met Abu Bakr, Umar and Mu'adh and memorised from them. He was reliable, and went on an expedition. Muhammad ibn 'Umar said that he died in 80 AH while 'Abdu'l-Malik ibn Marwan was khalif.

Abu'l-'Ufayf

He said, "I was present when Abu Bakr as-Siddiq was receiving the allegiance of the people."

Jubayr ibn Nufayr al-Hadrami

His *kunya* was Abu 'Abdu'r-Rahman. He was a pagan who became Muslim while Abu Bakr was khalif. He was reliable in the *hadith* which he related. He died in 80 AH while 'Abdu'l-Malik was khalif. He related from 'Umar, Mu'adh, Abu'd-Darda' and Abu Tha'laba.

Jubayr said, "I welcomed Islam from its beginning and I continued to see that people are both righteous and wicked."

Abu'z-Zahriyya and Ibn Jubayr said, "We never saw Jubayr sit in the gathering of his people at all."

Yazid ibn 'Amira az-Zubaydi

Some say that he was from Kalb. He was the companion of Mu'adh. He met Abu Bakr and 'Umar. He was reliable, Allah willing.

'Abdu'r-Rahman ibn Ghanm al-Ash'ari

He was reliable, Allah willing. 'Umar ibn al-Khattab sent him to Syria to teach the people *fiqh*. He met Mu'adh ibn Jabal and related from him and his father.

Ghanm ibn Sa'd

He was one of the Ash'arites who came with Abu Musa al-Ash'ari to the Messenger of Allah ﷺ, and he accompanied the Messenger of Allah and died on one of the expeditions after the Messenger of Allah.

Malik ibn Yakhmir al-Alhani or as-Saksaki

One of the companions of Mu'adh. He was reliable, Allah willing. He died while 'Abdu'l-Malik ibn Marwan was khalif.

Awsat ibn 'Amr al-Bajali

He is Abu Isma'il ibn Awsat. He met Abu Bakr and related from him. He had few *hadiths*.

Abu 'Adhaba al-Hadrami

He said, "I came to 'Umar ibn al-Khattab with three other Syrians. We were on *hajj*." Then he recounted a story from him about the people of Iraq when they came to him and were present and what he said to them.

Abu 'Adhaba al-Hadrami said, "I was one of four who came to 'Umar ibn al-Khattab from the people of Syria making *hajj*. While we were with him, news came that the people of Iraq had thrown pebbles at their Imam. He replaced him with another Imam and they threw pebbles at him. [Probably 'Ammar, and then Abu Musa in Kufa.] He went out to the prayer angry and was forgetful in his prayer. Then he came over to the people and said, 'Who is there here from among the people of Syria?' My companions and I stood up. He said, 'People of Syria, prepare yourselves for the people of Iraq. Shaytan has taken up residence among them and is at work.' Then he said, 'O Allah, they have made me befuddled, so befuddle them! O Allah, hasten the Thaqafi youth to them who will judge among them with the judgement of the *Jahiliyya*, and who will not accept from their good-doer nor overlook their evildoer.'"

'Umayr ibn al-Aswad

He asked Abu'd-Darda' about the food of the people of the Book. He related from Mu'adh ibn Jabal. He had few *hadiths* and is reliable.

Syria

Abu Bahriyya al-Kindi

His name was 'Abdullah ibn Qays. He said, "I came to Mu'adh in Syria."

'Asim ibn Humayd as-Sakuni

The companion of Mu'adh ibn Jabal. He related from Mu'adh from the Prophet ﷺ, about delaying the *'Isha'* prayer.

Ghudayf ibn al-Harith al-Kindi

He was reliable. Safwan ibn 'Amr said, "Some shaykhs from the army were present with Ghudayf when he was critically ill. He asked, 'Is there anyone among you who can recite *Surat Yasin*?' So Salih ibn Shurayh al-Kindi recited it. He had only recited forty *ayats* of it when he died. The shaykhs said, 'When it is read in the presence of a dying person, Allah alleviates it for him.'"

It is related that when Khalid ibn Yazid was absent or ill, Ghudayf ibn al-Harith commanded Abu Asma' ath-Thumali to lead the people in prayer. When the army heard about it, they attended. It was a *Jumu'a* in which the furthest people of the mosque heard his admonishment. He said, "O people! Do you know which pledge is your pledge? It is not a pledge of gold or silver. If it had been gold or silver, you would have answered that its pleasure is not connected to you. Allah Almighty says, *'Every self is held in pledge against whatever it has earned.'* (74:38) You are people on a journey. Whoever has his mount brought to him mounts it without returning in that to Allah." Ghudayf died while Marwan ibn al-Hakam was khalif.

Abu 'Abdullah as-Sunabihi

The companion of 'Ubada ibn as-Samit. Yazid ibn Bahram reported that as-Sunabihi said to him, "Yazid ibn Bahram, if you remain in my house for three days, do not bury me until you find a safe grave for me." He was not disinterred.

'Amr ibn al-Harith al-'Anbasi

He asked 'Umar, "From where should one of us go into *ihram* for *hajj*?" He replied, "Dhu'l-Hulayfa."

Al-Harith ibn Mu'awiya al-Kindi

He travelled to 'Umar ibn al-Khattab and listened to him and 'Umar asked him about Syria and its people, and he began to inform him. He listened to 'Umar and related from him.

Yazid ibn al-Aswad al-Jurashi

'Amir al-Khaba'iri said, "There was a drought, and Mu'awiya ibn Abi Sufyan and the people of Damascus went out to pray for rain. When Mu'awiya sat on the minbar, he asked, 'Where is Yazid ibn al-Aswad al-Jurashi?' The people called for him and he came up. Mu'awiya commanded him to ascend the minbar and he sat on it at his feet. Mu'awiya said, 'O Allah, we intercede for the people with you by the best and most excellent of us! O Allah, we seek intercession with you by Yazid ibn al-Aswad al-Jurashi! O Yazid, lift your hands to Allah!' Yazid raised his hands and the people raised their hands. There was soon a cloud in the west which the wind brought and we had rain until the people could almost not reach their homes."

Sharahbil ibn as-Samt

Yahya al-Hawazini said, "I was present at the funeral of Sharahbil ibn as-Samt with Habib ibn Maslama, and he is the one who was allotted Hims in the last district, or the second, in the time of 'Uthman. Habib ibn Maslama al-Fihri came, and Habib turned his face to us like some one looking down from his mount on us because of his great height. He said, 'Pray over your brother and strive for him in supplication and let part of your supplication for him be: "O Allah, forgive this natural Muslim soul, and make him among those who repented and followed Your path, and protect him from the punishment of Jahim." And ask for help against your enemies.'"

Abu Sallam al-Aswad

He moved from Hims to Damascus. He said, "Blessing has become weak in it. Blessing has become weak in it."

Ka'b al-Ahbar ibn Mati'

His *kunya* was Abu Ishaq. He was from Himyar, from the family of Dhu Ru'ayn. He was a Jew and then became Muslim and came to

Madina. Then he went to Syria and settled in Hims until his death there in 32 AH while 'Uthman ibn 'Affan was khalif.

Sa'id ibn al-Musayyab said, "Al-'Abbas asked Ka'b, 'What kept you from becoming a Muslim in the time of the Messenger of Allah صلعم and Abu Bakr, so that you waited to become Muslim until now?' He replied, 'My father wrote out a book for me from the Torah and gave it to me. He said, "Act according to this." He sealed the rest of his books and took from me the right of a father from his son that I would not break the seal. When the time came and I saw that Islam had emerged and I did not see any harm in it, I said to myself, "Perhaps my father has concealed some knowledge from me. I should read it." I opened the seal and read it and in it I found the description of Muhammad and his community. So now I have come as a Muslim.' He was the client of al-'Abbas."

Qatada said that Ka'b became Muslim while 'Umar was the ruler.

Abu'd-Darda' mentioned Ka'b and said, "The son of the Himyarite has a lot of knowledge."

Yazid ibn Shajara ar-Ruhawi

He and his companions perished at sea in 58 AH while Mu'awiya ibn Abi Sufyan was khalif.

✻✻✻✻✻

Other people of this generation include: **Sufyan ibn Wahb al-Khawlani**, who met 'Umar ibn al-Khattab; **Dhu'l-Kala'**, whose name was Sumayfa' ibn Hawshab; **'Amr ibn al-Aswad as-Sakuni**, who related *hadiths* from 'Umar and Mu'adh; **Ma'dan ibn Abi Talha al-Yamuri**, who related from 'Umar ibn al-Khattab and was reliable; and **al-Harith ibn 'Abd'l-Azdi as-Saluki**, the companion of Mu'adh who had *hadiths*.

✻✻✻✻✻

The Second Generation

'Abdullah ibn Muhayriz

'Abdullah ibn Ja'far said, "Ibn Muhayriz met Qabisa ibn Dhu'ayb and said, 'Abu Ishaq! you neglect the Greek frontiers while you send armies against the Hijaz and against Mus'ab ibn az-Zubayr.'[1] Qabisa said to him, 'Watch your tongue! By Allah, this is not done!' 'Abdu'l-Malik sent for him and he was brought blind-folded. He was made to stand before him. He said, 'What is this you have said which unsettles the land from the Euphrates to 'Arish?' i.e. Egypt. Then he softened to him and said, 'Keep quiet. Whoever sees the outstanding men of Quryash show forbearance to them.' Ibn Muhayriz saw that he had saved himself that day."

Qabisa ibn Dhu'ayb al-Khuza'i

One of the Banu Qumayr. His *kunya* was Abu Ishaq. He was reliable. Az-Zuhri related from him. He was in charge of the seal of 'Abdu'l-Malik ibn Marwan and he brought az-Zuhri to 'Abdu'l-Malik, and he gave him something, rewarded him, and he became one of his people. Qabisa died in Syria in 86 or 97 AH at the end of 'Abdu'l-Malik's khalifate.

Kathir ibn Murra al-Hadrami

His *kunya* was Abu Shajara. He was reliable. Yazid ibn Abi Habib said that 'Abdu'l-'Aziz ibn Marwan wrote to Kathir ibn Murra al-Hadrami. In Hims he had met 70 veterans of Badr from among the Companions of the Messenger of Allah صلعم. (Layth said, "Hims was called the frontier district.") He wrote to him to write out for him what he had heard of *hadiths* from the Companions of the Messenger of Allah صلعم, except for the *hadiths* of Abu Hurayra, who was already with him."

---

1. During the rebellion of 'Abdullah ibn az-Zubayr, his brother, Mus'ab ibn az-Zubayr was his governor in Basra.

Abu Muslim al-Khawlani

His name was 'Abdullah ibn Thawb. He was reliable. He died while Yazid ibn Mu'awiya was khalif.

Qatada reported that Ka'b met Abu Muslim al-Khawlani and said to him, "Where are you from, Abu Muslim?" He replied, "From the people of Iraq." He asked, "Where in Iraq?" He said, "The people of Basra."

Abu Idris al-Khawlani

His name was 'A'idh ibn 'Abdullah. Yahya ibn Ma'in said, "Abu Idris al-Khawlani was born in the year of Hunayn." He was asked, "Who told you?" and replied, "It is clear in the account of the Syrians." He was reliable and related from az-Zuhri.

Ya'la ibn Shaddad al-Ansari

He was the son of the brother of Hassan ibn Thabit the poet. Ya'la was reliable, Allah willing, and is related from.

Shahr ibn Hawshab al-Ash'ari

Muhammad ibn 'Umar said that Shahr ibn Hawshab died in 112 AH. He was weak in *hadith*.

Abu 'Abdullah ash-Shami said, "I asked 'Abdu'l-Hamid ibn Bahram, 'When did Shahr ibn Hawshab die?' He replied, 'In 98 AH.'"

Al-Qasim ibn 'Abdu'r-Rahman

His *kunya* was Abu 'Abdu'r-Rahman. He was the client of Juwariyya bint Abi Sufyan ibn Harb. It is said that he was the client of Mu'awiya. He had many *hadiths*. In some of the accounts of the Syrians it says that he met forty of the veterans of Badr. He died in 112 AH, while Hisham ibn 'Abdu'l-Malik was khalif.

Ibn Jabir said, "I saw that al-Qasim Abu 'Abdu'r-Rahman did not dye his white hair."

Muslim ibn Mishkam

He was the scribe of Abu'd-Darda'. He related from Abu'd-Darda' and Mu'awiya. 'Abdullah ibn al-'Ala' ibn Zayd related from him.

Sa'id ibn Hani al-Khawlani

His *kunya* was Abu 'Uthman. He was reliable, Allah willing. He died in 127 AH.

Abu'z-Zahariyya al-Hadrami

Some say he is al-Himyari. His name was Hudayr ibn Kurayb. He was reliable, Allah willing, with many *hadiths*. He died in 129 AH while Marwan ibn Muhammad was khalif.

'Abdullah ibn Mikhmar

Ibn Abi 'Awf reported that once 'Abdullah ibn Mikhmar was on the minbar and saw that the people were in a muddle. He said, "O Handsomeness! O Beauty! After the lack of and desire for fine food, turbans and mantles, you have flowered into splendour, although people have become dust! People began to give and so you took. People began to breed animals and so you rode. People began to weave and so you wore. People began to cultivate and so you ate."

Kulthum ibn Hani' al-Kindi

It is related from Abu Zur'a ash-Shaybani that Kulthum ibn Hani' was asked, "Abu Sahl, relate to us!" He said, "He feared conceit when they appointed him and said, 'My heart has no good in it! How often it has not been listened to and forgotten!' If he had wished to relate to them, he would have done so."

Kulthum ibn Hani' said, "When one of your brothers is given a position, say to him, 'And peace be upon you.'"

Hakim ibn 'Umayr

He was accepted and has few *hadiths*. He is Abu'l-Ahwas ibn Hakim ash-Sha'mi. Safwan ibn 'Amr said, "I saw the mark of prostration on the forehead of Hakim ibn 'Umayr."

Tubay'

He was the son of the wife of Ka'b al-Ahbar. He was a man of knowledge who read books and listened to Ka'b a lot. His *kunya* was Abu 'Ubayda. In some sources he is called Abu 'Amir.

Syria

Muslim ibn Kabis or Kubays

His *kunya* was Abu Hasana. Safwan ibn 'Amr related from him, and he used to write out copies of the Qur'an for people for free. He did not stipulate a wage for that. When he had finished and was given something, he accepted it. Otherwise he did not ask anyone for anything.

*****

Other people of this generation include: **'Abdu'r-Rahman ibn 'Amr as-Sulami**, who died in 110 AH while Hisham ibn 'Abdu'l-Malik was khalif; **'Abdullah ibn 'Amir al-Yahsubi**, who had few *hadiths* and died in 118 AH; **Muslim ibn Qaraza al-Ashja'i**, who related from his uncle 'Awf ibn Malik al-Ashja'i; **Al-Hajjaj ibn 'Abdu'th-Thumali**, who died in the khalifate of 'Abdu'l-Malik ibn Marwan; and **Nawf al-Bikali**, the son of the wife of Ka'b.

*****

The Third Generation

Makhul ad-Dimishqi

'Abdullah ibn al-'Ala' said, "I heard Makhul say, 'I belonged to 'Amr ibn Sa'id ibn al-'As and he gave me to a man of Hudhayl in Egypt. He was generous to me there, and when I left it I thought that there was no knowledge there but that I had heard it. Then I went to Madina and I did not leave but that I thought that there was no knowledge there but that I had heard it. Then I met ash-Sha'bi and I have not seen his equal.'"

Numayr ibn 'Uqba al-'Abasi said, "I heard Makhul say, 'I kept company with Shurayh for six months, during which I did not ask him about anything I wanted to hear but that he granted it.'"

Makhul said, "I saw Anas ibn Malik in the Damascus mosque. I said, 'One of the Companions of the Messenger of Allah ﷺ whom I have not greeted or questioned!' So I greeted him and asked him about *wudu'* on account of carrying a bier and attending a funeral. He said, 'We were in a prayer and then returned to prayer. What is the sense of *wudu'* in what is between that?'"

Sa'id ibn 'Abdu'l-'Aziz said that he saw Makhul wearing an iron ring overlaid with silver so that the iron could not be seen at all, engraved with: "Lord, put Makhul far from the Fire. "

'Abdullah ibn Rashid ash-Sahmi said, "I saw Makhul wearing a ring on his left hand."

Muhammad ibn Rashid said, "When Makhul prayed, he let the shawl hang on him a lot."

Sa'id ibn 'Abdu'l-'Aziz said that Makhul was among those allotted a stipend. He would take it and use it to strengthen the *jihad* against the enemies of Allah.

Sa'id ibn 'Abdu'l-'Aziz said, "Makhul visited Hisham [the khalif]. When he came, he had him transported by the postal service. "

Another of the people of knowledge said that Makhul was one of the people of Kabul and he used some incorrect grammar. He used to espouse *Qadar*. He was weak in *hadith* and transmission.

'Umar ibn Sa'id said, "Makhul died in 118." Someone else said it was 113 AH. Abu Malik said, "My father let me ride behind him when Makhul died in 112 AH."

Raja' ibn Haywa

He lived in Jordan. He was reliable, knowledgeable, excellent with a lot of knowledge. Ibn 'Awn said that Raja' ibn Haywa related *hadiths* in their dialects. It is reported that his *kunya* was Abu Nasr.

Jarir ibn Hazim said, "I saw Raja' ibn Haywa, and his hair was red and his beard white."

Khalid ibn Ma'dan al-Kila'i

He was reliable. Khalid ibn Ma'dan said, "There is no animal in the land or sea who can ransom me from death. If death is a post to which one races, then I am the first to race to it unless a man gets ahead of me by virtue of more strength."

Safwan ibn 'Amr said, "I saw the mark of prostration on the forehead of Khalid ibn Ma'dan." He said that Khalid ibn Ma'dan used to dye his beard yellow.

They agree that Khalid ibn Ma'dan died in 103 AH while Yazid I was khalif. Yazid ibn Harun said, "Khalid ibn Ma'dan died while he was fasting."

'Abdu'r-Rahman ibn Jubayr al-Hadrami

He was reliable. Some people object to his *hadith*. He died in 118 AH while Hisham ibn 'Abdu'l-Malik was khalif.

Rashid ibn Sa'd al-Himyari

One of the people of Hims. He was reliable and died in 108 AH while Hisham ibn 'Abdu'l-Malik was khalif.

Sa'id ibn Marthad

Jarir ibn 'Uthman related from him. He was one of those who was at the Battle of Siffin.

Numayr ibn Aws al-Ash'ari

He was a qadi in Damascus. He had few *hadiths*. He died in 122 AH while Hisham ibn 'Abdu'l-Malik was khalif.

'Abdullah ibn Abi Zakariyya al-Khuza'i

He was reliable with few *hadiths* and went on an expedition. He was one of the people of Damascus and died in 117 AH while Hisham was khalif.

Ibn Jabir said, "I noticed that Ibn Abi Zakariyya did not dye his white hair."

'Abdu'r-Rahman ibn Maysara al-Hadrami

'Abdu'r-Rahman ibn Maysara said, "I saw the Prophet صلعم in a dream and I said, 'O Prophet of Allah, pray to Allah for me that I understand *hadith* and retain them!' He made a supplication for me, and afterwards I did not hear anything but that I understood it."

Abu Makhrama as-Sa'di

Jabir said, "I saw that Abu Makhrama did not dye his white hair."

Sulayman ibn Musa al-Asdhaq

His *kunya* was Abu Ayyub. He was reliable and Ibn Jurayj raised him. Burd said, "They used to meet with 'Ata' during the festivals and Sulayman ibn Musa was the one who asked on their behalf." Sulayman died in 129 AH while Hisham was khalif.

Abu Rashid al-Hubrani

One of Himyar. It is reported that he used to dye his beard.

'Ali ibn Abi Talha

He related *tafsir* from Ibn 'Abbas. Mu'awiya ibn Salih related from him.

Yahya ibn Jabir at-Ta'i

He had *hadiths*. He died in 126 AH while al-Walid ibn Yazid was khalif.

Damdam Abu'l-Muthanna al-Umluki

Safwan ibn 'Amr reported that Damdam Abu'l-Muthanna used to dye his beard.

Yunus ibn Sayf

He was accepted. He had *hadiths*. He died in 120 AH while Hisham was khalif.

'Abdu'r-Rahman ibn 'Urayb al-Himyari

Safwan reported that he used to dye his beard.

'Amr ibn Qays al-Kindi

He had correct *hadiths*. Muhammad ibn 'Umar said that he died in 125 AH, while al-Walid ibn Yazid was khalif.

Abu Talha

He had *hadiths*. Muhammad ibn 'Umar said that he died in 124 AH.

Abu 'Anbasa

He had *hadiths*. Muhammad ibn 'Umar said that he died in 124 AH.

Abu 'Utba al-Kindi

He had few *hadiths*. Muhammad ibn 'Umar said that he died in 118 AH while Hisham was khalif.

Yazid ibn Sumayy

He was reliable. Muhammad ibn 'Umar said that he died in 125 AH while Hisham was khalif.

Muhasir ibn Habib

He was accepted. He died in 128 AH while Marwan ibn Muhammad was khalif.

*****

Other people of this generation include: **'Ubada ibn Nusayy al-Kindi**, who was reliable and died in 118 AH while Hisham was khalif; **Sulayman ibn Habib al-Muharibi**, who had few *hadiths* and died in 120 AH; **'Abdullah ibn Qays al-Lakhmi**, who died in 124 AH; **Yahya ibn 'Amr ash-Shaybani**, whose *kunya* was Abu Zur'a.

*****

The Fourth Generation

'Urwa ibn Qu'aym al-Lakhmi

He had many *hadiths*. He died in 132 AH.

'Atiyya ibn Qays

He was accepted. He had *hadiths*. Ibn Jabir said, "I saw that 'Atiyya ibn Qays did not dye his white hair."

Azhar ibn Sa'id al-Harrazi

One of Himyar. He had few *hadiths*. He died in 129 AH while Marwan II was khalif.

Sa'id ibn Hani'

He died in 129 AH while Marwan II was khalif.

Asad ibn Wada'a at-Ta'i

One of the people of Hims. He was old. He related from Abu'd-

Fourth Generation

Darda' and lived until 137 AH, dying at the beginning of the khalifate of al-Mansur.

Bilal ibn Sa'd

He was reliable. Ibn Jabir said, "I saw that Bilal ibn Sa'd did not dye his white hair."

Al-Walid ibn Abi Malik al-Hamdani

His *kunya* was Abu'l-'Abbas. He has *hadiths*. His office was in Kufa and he died there in 125 or 126 AH while al-Walid II was khalif. He was 72 when he died.

His brother, Yazid ibn Abi Malik al-Hamdani

He had *hadiths*. He died in Damascus in 136 AH while Marwan II was khalif, at the end of the power of the Umayyads, at the age of 72.

Khalid ibn 'Abdullah

Ibn Jabir said that they say that he did not dye his white hair.

An-Nu'man ibn al-Mundhir al-Ghassani

One of the people of Damascus. He had many *hadiths*. He died in 132 AH at the beginning of the Abbasid khalifate.

'Amr ibn al-Muhajir

He was the client of Asma' bint Yazid al-Ansariyya by emancipation. He was the master of the guard of 'Umar ibn 'Abdu'l-'Aziz.

Al-Muhajir Abu 'Amr said, "I heard my client, Asma' bint Yazid say, 'I heard the Messenger of Allah ﷺ say, "Do not kill your children secretly," meaning by *ghila*. "By the One Who has my soul in His hand, it will overtake the horseman and throw him from his horse!"'" Muhammad ibn 'Umar said, "By that he meant intercourse while breast-feeding."

'Amr ibn al-Muhajir was reliable and had many *hadiths*. He died in 139 AH while al-Mansur was khalif, at the age of 74.

Abu Luqman al-Hadrami

He was accepted. Muhammad ibn 'Umar said, "He died in 130 AH while Marwan II was khalif."

Al-'Ala' ibn al-Harith

He had few *hadiths*. But he had the most knowledge of the companions of Makhul and was the oldest of them, He used to give *fatwa* until he became muddled. He died in 136 AH at the end of the khalifate of Abu'l-'Abbas as-Saffah.

Yahya ibn al-Harith adh-Dhimari

He had few *hadiths*. He had knowledge of recitation in his time and the Qur'an was recited to him. He died in 145 AH while Abu Ja'far al-Mansur was khalif, at the age of 70.

Al-Husayn ibn Jabir

He was early. He listened to Abu Umama and 'Abdullah ibn Busr al-Mazini, and lived until Mu'awiya ibn Salih related from him.

Sulaym ibn 'Amir

He was reliable. He was early and recognised. Sulaym ibn 'Amir said, "I went to Jerusalem and visited Umm ad-Darda' in Damascus and she commanded a dinar for me and let me drink thickened juice." Sulaym ibn 'Amir died in 130 AH while Marwan II was khalif.

Abu 'Ubayda

Ibn Jabir said that Abu 'Ubayda did not dye his white hair.

Hatim ibn Hurayth al-Himsi

He was accepted. He died in 132 AH at the beginning of the khalifate of Abu Ja'far al-Mansur.

Abu 'Abdu Rabb

Ibn Jabir said, "I noticed that Abu 'Abdu Rabb did not dye his white hair."

Abu Bishr

He was the *mu'adhdhin* of the mosque of Damascus. He died in 130 AH while Marwan II was khalif.

✻✻✻✻✻

Fifth Generation

Other people of this generation include: **Hujayr ibn Sa'd**, who was reliable; **'Arim ibn Abu'l-Jashib**, who had few hadiths; **as-Saqar ibn Nusayr**, who died in 133 AH; **Damra ibn Habib**, who was reliable; and **Rabi'a ibn Yazid**, who was reliable.

✽✽✽✽✽

Fifth Generation

Muhammad ibn al-Walid az-Zubaydi

He was reliable, Allah willing. He had the greatest knowledge of *fatwa* and *hadith* among the people of Syria. He met az-Zuhri and wrote from him. He died at the age of 70 in 148 AH, when al-Mansur was khalif.

Yahya ibn Yahya al-Ghassani

He was the scholar of *fatwa* and judgement in Damascus. He had hadiths. He died in 135 AH at the end of the khalifate of as-Saffah.

Al-Wasin ibn 'Ata'

One of Kinana. His *kunya* was Abu Kinana. He was weak in *hadith*. He died in Damascus, on the 10th Dhu'l-Hijja 149 AH while al-Mansur was khalif.

'Abdu'r-Rahman ibn Yazid al-Azdi

He was older than his brother Yazid ibn Yazid. 'Abdu'r-Rahman died in 154 AH while al-Mansur was khalif, when he was about 80. He was reliable.

His brother, Yazid ibn Yazid al-Azdi

He was reliable, Allah willing. He was younger than 'Abdu'r-Rahman, but died before him. Yazid died in 134 AH before the age of 60.

Yunus ibn Maysara

He was reliable. When the black turbans [Abbasid supporters] entered Damascus at the beginning of the reign of the Banu Hashim [the Abbasids], they entered its mosque and killed everyone they found in it. Yunus ibn Maysara was killed that day as was the grandfather of Abu Mushir 'Abdu'l-A'la ibn Mushir al-Ghassani. That was in 132 AH, at the beginning of the khalifate of Abu'l-'Abbas as-Saffah.

Thawr ibn Yazid al-Kila'i

One of the people of Hims. His *kunya* was Abu Khalid. He was reliable in *hadith*. It is said that he was a Qadarite. He died in Jerusalem in 153 AH, while al-Mansur was khalif at the age of 60.

Thawr's grandfather was present at the Battle of Siffin on Mu'awiya's side, and was killed on that day. When 'Ali was mentioned, Thawr said, "I do not like a man who killed my grandfather."

Abu Bakr ibn 'Abdullah al-Ghassani

He had many *hadiths*, but was weak. He is related from a great deal. Yazid ibn Harun said, "Abu Bakr ibn 'Abdullah was one of the striving worshipping servants of Allah. Death came while he was fasting. He continued to strive with his fast until they peeled him an apple and he broke his fast with it."

His wife was asked, "Don't you delouse his clothes?" She said, "When could I delouse them? He does not remove them at night or during the day because he is so busy praying."

Safwan ibn 'Amr as-Saksaki

He was reliable and dependable.

Sa'id ibn 'Abdu'l-'Aziz at-Tanukhi

He was reliable, Allah willing. 'Umar ibn Sa'id said, "The *kunya* of Sa'id ibn 'Abdu'l-'Aziz was Abu Muhammad." He died in Damascus in 167 AH at the age of about 70, while al-Mahdi was khalif.

Sa'id ibn Bashir al-Azdi

His *kunya* was Abu 'Abdu'r-Rahman. He was one of the people of Basra. He moved to Syria and settled in Damascus. He was a Qadarite. He died in Damascus in 170 AH, at the beginning of the khalifate of Harun ar-Rashid.

Fifth and Sixth Generations

Hisham ibn al-Ghazi al-Jurashi

His *kunya* was Abu'l-'Abbas. They related from him. He was reliable.

'Abdullah ibn al-'Ala'

He was reliable, Allah willing.

Shu'ayb ibn Abi Hamza

Abu Hamza's name was Dinar. He was one of the people of Hims.

Yahya ibn Hamza

His *kunya* was Abu 'Abdu'r-Rahman. He had many *hadiths* which were correct. He was a Qadi in Damascus. He died in 183 AH while Harun ar-Rashid was khalif.

Sadaqa ibn Khalid as-Samin

He was reliable.

Al-Faraj ibn Fadala al-Himsi

His *kunya* was Abu Fadala. He was weak. He was in charge of the Treasury of Baghdad. He died there in 176 AH while Harun was khalif.

✽✽✽✽✽

The Sixth Generation

Baqiyya ibn al-Walid al-Himsi

His *kunya* was Abu Yuhmid. He was reliable in his transmission from reliable sources. His transmission is weak when it is from other than reliable sources. He died in 197 AH at the end of the khalifate of al-Amin.

Suwayd ibn 'Abdu'l-'Aziz

He was a client of the Banu Sulaym. His *kunya* was Abu Muhammad. He used to relate contradicted *hadiths*. He was born in 90 AH at the end of the khalifate of al-Walid I. He died in 167 AH while al-Mahdi was khalif.

Syria

Abu 'Abdullah ash-Shami said, "Suwayd ibn 'Abdu'l-'Aziz was appointed qadi of Baalbaak. He was needy. Da'ud ibn Abi Shayban ad-Dimishqi met him and said to him, 'Abu Muhammad, you have been appointed qadi after knowledge and *hadith*?' He said, 'Yes. I ask you by Allah, is there barley under your cloak?' Da'ud said, 'Yes.' Suwayd lifted his cloak and said, 'But my cloak has no barley under it.' Then he said, 'I ask you by Allah, does this shawl belong to you?' Da'ud said, 'Yes.' Suwayd said, 'By Allah, this shawl which you see me wearing is not mine. It is rented. Is there qadiship after this? By Allah, if I was were to be appointed to the treasury, it would be worse than being appointed qadi!'"

'Abdu'l-Malik ibn Muhammad al-Barsami

From Himyar. He is Abu'z-Zurqa'.

Muhammad ibn Harb al-Abrash al-Khawlani

His *kunya* was Abu 'Abdullah. He was appointed qadi of Damascus.

Al-Walid ibn Muslim

His *kunya* was Abu'l-'Abbas. Abu 'Abdullah ash-Sham'i said, "Al-Walid ibn Muslim was one of the slaves who worked the land for the government. He belonged to the family of Maslama ibn 'Abdu'l-Malik. When the Banu Hashim [the Abbasids] came to power, they went to Syria and took their slaves who worked the land and others with them. Al-Walid ibn Muslim and the people of his house went to Salih ibn 'Ali. He gave them to his son, al-Fadl ibn Salih and al-Fadl freed them. Al-Walid rode to the family of Maslama and purchased himself from them.

Sa'id ibn Maslama said, "Al-Walid ibn Muslim came to me and acknowledged his slavedom to me and I freed him." Al-Walid ibn Muslim had a brother called Jabala. He had importance and distinction in Syria. Al-Walid was reliable with a lot of *hadith* and knowledge. He went on hajj in 194 AH while al-Amin was khalif. Then he left and died on the journey before he reached Damascus.

'Umar ibn 'Abdu'l-Wahid

He was reliable and is related from.

Damra ibn Rabi'a

His *kunya* was Abu 'Abdullah. He was a client. He was reliable, trustworthy, and well-informed. There was no one better than him – not al-Walid nor anyone else. He died at the beginning of Ramadan in 202 AH, while al-Ma'mun was khalif.

Mubashshir ibn Isma'il al-Halabi

His *kunya* was Abu Isma'il. He was a client of Kalb. He lived in Aleppo. He was reliable and trustworthy. He died in Aleppo in 200 AH, while al-Ma'mun was khalif.

Shu'ayb ibn Ishaq

He was the client of Ramla bint 'Uthman ibn 'Affan. He was trustworthy. He died in Damascus in 189 AH while Harun was khalif.

✻✻✻✻✻

The Seventh Generation

Abu'l-Mughira al-Himsi

His name was 'Abdu'l-Quddus ibn al-Hajjaj.

Abu'l-Yaman al-Himsi

His name was al-Hakam ibn Nafi'. He died in Hims in Dhu'l-Hijja 222 AH while al-Mu'tasim was khalif. Someone asked him, "From whom are you?" He replied, "From Rabi'a."

Abu Mushir

His name was 'Abdu'l-A'la ibn Mushir al-Ghassan, one of the people of Damascus. He related from Sa'id ibn 'Abdu'l-'Aziz at-Tanukhi and other Syrians. He was taken from Damascus to al-Ma'mun when he was in Raqqa. He questioned him about the Qur'an and he replied, "It is the Word of Allah." He refused to say that it was created. Al-Ma'mun called for a sword and the leather mat to behead him. When he saw that, he said that it was created. So he did not kill him. He said, "If you had said that before I called for the sword, I would have accepted it from you and returned you to your land and family, but now you will leave and say, 'I said that out of fear of death.' Dispatch him to Baghdad and imprison him there until he dies." So he was taken from Raqqa to Baghdad in Rabi' al-Akhir 218 AH and imprisoned before Ishaq ibn Ibrahim. He remained in prison except for a short time until he died at the beginning of Rajab 218 AH. He was taken out and buried and many of the people of Baghdad attended.

Hisham ibn 'Ammar

One of the people of Damascus who related from al-Walid ibn Muslim.

'Ali ibn 'Ayyash al-Himsi

His *kunya* was Abu'l-Hasan. He related from Jarir ibn 'Uthman and Shu'ayb ibn Abi Hamza.

Yahya ibn Salih al-Wuhazi al-Himsi

His *kunya* was Abu Zakariyya. He related from Sa'id ibn 'Abdu'l-'Aziz and Yahya ibn Hamza.

Al-Hajjaj ibn Abi Mani'

The name of Abu Mani' was Yusuf ibn 'Ubaydullah ibn Abi Ziyad, the client of 'Abda bint 'Abdullah ibn Yazid ibn Mu'awiya. 'Ubaydullah ibn Abi Ziyad was the foster brother of the wife of Hisham ibn 'Abdu'l-Malik. She was 'Abda bint 'Abdullah ibn Yazid. When az-Zuhri came to Hisham in Rusafa and accepted that, he stayed with them for twenty years except for a few months. 'Ubaydullah ibn Abi Ziyad stayed with him and listened to his knowledge and his books. His son, Yusuf ibn 'Ubaydullah, listened to them from him, and his son, al-Hajjaj ibn Yusuf, listened to them from him, and then his son, al-Hajjaj ibn Abi Mani' listened to them at the end of the khalifate of al-Mansur. He said, "I used to carry the books to him and he would read them to people."

Al-Hajjaj said, "'Ubaydullah ibn Abi Ziyad died in 158 or 159 AH, when he was more than 80. He had black hair and a white beard. He had a lot of hair. The *kunya* of al-Hajjaj was Abu Muhammad. Al-Hajjaj said in Jumada al-Ula 210 AH, "Today I am 76."

Eighth Generation

Abu 'Amr

His name was al-Khattab ibn 'Uthman al-Fawzi al-Himsi, the Imam of the mosque of the Muharrarites [a tribe]. His grandfather, Sulaym, was the client of Layy'. He related from Isma'il ibn 'Ayyash and Muhammad ibn Humayd.

Yazid ibn 'Abdu Rabbih al-Jurjushi al-Himsi

His *kunya* was Abu'l-Fadl. He related from Baqiyya and others.

Abu 'Abdu'l-Malik al-'Attar al-Khuza'i

He related from Muhammad ibn Shu'ayb ibn Shabur and others.

Bishr ibn Shu'ayb

One of the people of Hims. They wrote from him. He died with Ibn Ma'ruf, before Abu'l-Yaman al-Himsi.

[End of the generations of the people of Syria]

The Companions of the Messenger of Allah in Mesopotamia

'Adi ibn 'Amira

He is the one from whom Qays ibn Abi Hazim reported that he heard that the Prophet ﷺ said, "If someone is put in an administrative position on our behalf and conceals even a needle from us, that will be considered faithlessness on the Day of Rising."

'Adi fled from 'Ali ibn Abi Talib in Kufa and settled in Mesopotamia (al-Jazira) where he died. He was the father of 'Adi ibn 'Adi al-Jazari, the companion of 'Umar ibn 'Abdu'l-'Aziz.

Wabisa ibn Ma'bad al-Asadi

He related that he prayed behind the rows on his own and the Prophet ﷺ commanded him to repeat the prayer.

One of his descendants was 'Abdu'r-Rahman ibn Sakhr who was qadi of ar-Raqqa in the time of Harun ar-Rashid.

Al-Walid ibn 'Uqba

His *kunya* was Abu Wahb. His mother was Arwa bint Kurayz, the mother of 'Uthman ibn 'Affan. Al-Walid ibn 'Uqba left Kufa to withdraw from 'Ali and Mu'awiya, and settled in Northeast Syria at ar-Raqqa where he died, and his descendants are still there today.

Abu 'Udhra

'Abdullah ibn Shaddad reported that Abu 'Udhra al-Jazari met the Prophet ﷺ.

The grandfather of Muhammad ibn Khalid as-Sulami

He said, "I heard the Prophet ﷺ say, 'When a position is preordained for a servant by Allah which he has not obtained by action, then He tests him in his body, family and property, and then makes him steadfast in that until he obtains the station intended for him with Allah.'"

The *Fuqaha'* and *Hadith* Scholars in Mesopotamia

Maymun ibn Mihran

His *kunya* was Abu Ayyub. He was reliable with many *hadiths*.

'Amr ibn Maymun said, "I asked my father, 'Whom are you from?' He said, 'My father was a *mukatib* of the Banu Nasr ibn Mu'awiya who was freed. I belonged to a woman of Azd from Thumala called Umm Nimar. She freed me and I remained in Kufa until the agitation of Jamajim and then I moved to Mesopotamia.'" Al-Haytham said,"The beginning of the Jamajim business was in 80 AH, the Battle of Dujayl was at the end of 81 AH, and the end of the business was the Battle of Dayr al-Jamajim at the beginning of 82 AH.

Maymun ibn Mihran said, "I was born in the Year of the Community, 40 AH."[1]

They say that Maymun was a cloth merchant. He was in charge of the *kharaj*. He sat in his shop and wrote to 'Umar ibn 'Abdu'l-'Aziz, asking to be relieved of collecting the *kharaj*, and 'Umar wrote to him: "It is a dirham which you take as its right, and place it in its right. Why would you ask to be freed of this?" He remained in charge of the *kharaj* during the reign of 'Umar ibn 'Abdu'l-'Aziz, until 'Umar's death and Yazid II became khalif. Maymun was his agent in charge of *kharaj* for some months. Before that, Maymun had been in charge of the Treasury in Harran for Muhammad ibn Marwan, before 'Umar ibn 'Abdu'l-'Aziz. Ghaylan the Qadarite wrote a letter to him to admonish him about that. Maymun said, "I wish that I had been unknown, and I had not held an office before either for him or for 'Umar ibn 'Abdu'l-'Aziz." He said, "Nor for 'Umar ibn 'Abdu'l-'Aziz!"

Abu'l-Malih said that Maymun ibn Mihran did not dye his hair.

'Isa ibn Kathir said, "Maymun ibn Mihran died in 117 AH while Hisham was khalif. He dominated the people of Mesopotamia in *fatwa* and *fiqh*."

---

1. The year in which it was accepted by all parties that Mu'awiya was the khalif.

Mesopotamia

Abu'l-Malih said that Maymun ibn Mihran died in 117 AH.

Yazid ibn al-Asamm

His name was 'Abdu 'Amr ibn 'Udas. His mother was Barza bint al-Harith. Barza was the sister of Maymuna bint al-Harith, the wife of the Prophet ﷺ, and the sister of Lubaba bint al-Harith, the mother of the Banu'l-'Abbas, and the sister of Lubaba the younger, who is 'Isma' bint al-Harith, the mother of Khalid ibn al-Walid. He was reliable with many *hadiths*. He related from Abu Hurayra, Ibn 'Abbas, and his aunt Maymuna the wife of the Prophet, and others. He settled in ar-Raqqa.

Yazid ibn al-Asamm said, "I spent the night with my aunt Maymuna and I brought the *sahur* and saw the dawn and was anxious about it and drew it to her attention. She said, 'What will teach you? Take it and drink.'"

Yazid ibn al-Asamm died in 103 AH when Yazid II was khalif.

'Adi ibn 'Adi al-Kindi

He was reliable, Allah willing. Maymun ibn Mihran said that 'Adi ibn 'Adi was qadi of Mesopotamia while 'Umar ibn 'Abdu'l-'Aziz was khalif.

'Abdu'r-Rahman ibn as-Sa'ib al-Hilali

He was the son of the brother of Maymuna bint al-Harith al-Hilaliyya, the wife of the Messenger of Allah ﷺ, and related from her. He had few *hadiths*.

Zayd ibn Rufay'

One of the people of Nasibin. He had *hadiths*. He died in 130 AH, at the end of the khalifate of Marwan ibn Muhammad.

Salim al-Aftash ibn 'Ajlan

He was the client of Muhammad ibn Marwan ibn al-Hakam. 'Abdullah ibn 'Ali killed him at the beginning of the entry of the black-turbans (Abbasid partisans) into Syria in 132 AH. He lived in Harran. He was reliable, with many *hadiths*.

'Abdullah ibn Malik al-Jazari

His *kunya* was Abu Sa'id, the client of Muhammad ibn Marwan ibn al-Hakam. One of the people of Harran. He had been one of the people of Istakhr, and then moved to Harran. He was the close cousin of Khasif. He was reliable, with many *hadiths*.

Zayd ibn Abi Unaysa

He lived in Ruha and died there. He was the client of a rich man. He was reliable with many *hadiths*, a *faqih* and a transmitter of knowledge. A man of Harran said that Zayd died in 129 AH.

'Ali ibn Nadima

He was reliable. Al-Hakam ibn Junada as-Suwa'i said, "On the day when Mada'in fell, Sa'd ibn Abi Waqqas gave Jabir ibn Samura as-Suwa'i two slaves from among the dependants of the Sasanid emperor, one of whom was Nadima, the father of 'Ali ibn Nadima, and the other Abu Zuhayr, the grandfather of al-Muttalib ibn Ziyad. Jabir ibn Samura freed both of them." 'Ali ibn Nadima died in Harran in 136 AH, at the beginning of the khalifate of al-Mansur. His *kunya* was Abu 'Abdullah.

Khasif ibn 'Abdu'r-Rahman

His *kunya* was Abu 'Awn. He was one of the people of Harran, the client of either 'Uthman ibn 'Affan, or Mu'awiya ibn Abi Sufyan. He was reliable. He died in 137 AH at the beginning of the khalifate of al-Mansur.

'Amr ibn Maymun

He was reliable, Allah willing. He settled in ar-Raqqa. Muhammad ibn 'Umar said that he died in 145 while al-Mansur was khalif.

Ja'far ibn Burqan al-Kilabi

He was reliable and truthful. He had transmission, *fiqh*, and *fatwa* in his time. There are a lot of errors in his *hadiths*. He settled in ar-Raqqa. He died in 154 AH while al-Mansur was khalif.

Musa ibn A'yan

His *kunya* was Abu Sa'id, the client of the Banu Umayya. He was truthful. He died in Harran in 197 AH while Harun ar-Rashid was khalif.

Sulayman ibn 'Abdullah al-Kilabi

He had few *hadiths*. He settled in Harran and was in charge of the judiciary.

Muhammad ibn 'Abdullah al-Kilabi

His *kunya* was Abu'l-Yusr. He was reliable, Allah willing. He was in charge of the judiciary for al-Mahdi.

Ziyad ibn 'Abdullah al-Kilabi

He was the deputy of his brother over the judiciary for al-Mahdi.

Bujayr ibn Abi Unaysa

He lived in Ruha and died there. He was younger than his brother Zayd. He was weak, and the people of *hadith* did not write down his *hadiths*.

Abu'l-Malih

His name was al-Hasan ibn 'Umar. Abu'l-Malih was born in ar-Raqqa and he was a client of 'Umar ibn Hubayra al-Fazari. He transmitted from Maymun ibn Mihran, and he continued to pray between *Maghrib* and *'Isha* beside the minbar, adding a *rak'at* to that. He died in 181 AH at the age of 95, while Harun ar-Rashid was khalif.

'Ubaydullah al-Ansari ar-Raqqi said, "I saw Abu'l-Malih using henna."

'Ubaydullah ibn 'Amr al-Asadi

The client of Asad. His *kunya* was Abu Wahb. He was reliable and truthful with many *hadiths*. Sometimes he erred. He had the greatest memory of those who related from 'Abdu'l-Karim al-Jazari. No one contended with him in *fatwa* in his time. He died in ar-Raqqa in 180 AH, while Harun ar-Rashid was khalif.

Marwan ibn Shuja'

His *kunya* was Abu 'Amr, the client of Marwan ibn Muhammad. He was one of the people of Harran. He was reliable and truthful and transmitted from Khasif. He was the one who is called al-Khusayfi. He came to Baghdad as a tutor with Musa al-Hadi, Amir al-Mu'minin, and his children. He died in Baghdad in 184 AH while Harun was khalif.

'Attab ibn Bashir

His *kunya* was Abu'l-Hasan. He was the client of the Banu Umayya. He resided in Harran. He was truthful and reliable, Allah willing, transmitting from Khasif. He did not have that in *hadith*. He died in Harran in 190 AH, while Harun was khalif.

Muhammad ibn Salama

His *kunya* was Abu 'Abdullah, a client of Bahila. He lived in Harran. He was truthful and reliable, Allah willing. He had excellence, transmission and *fatwa*. He died at the end of 191 AH, while Harun was khalif.

Abu Qatada al-Harrani

His name was 'Abdullah ibn Waqid, the client of Banu Himman. He had excellence and worship, but did not have that in *hadith*.

Al-Fayd ibn Ishaq

His *kunya* was Abu Yazid. He was one of the people of Raqqa. He had *hadith*, goodness and raids. He died in Raqqa in 210 AH, while al-Ma'mun was khalif.

Ma'mar ibn Sulayman ar-Raqqi an-Nakh'i

He died in Sha'ban 191 AH while Harun ar-Rashid was khalif.

Khalid ibn Hayyan

His *kunya* was Abu Yazid al-Khazzaz. He was reliable and dependable. He died in ar-Raqqa in Dhu'l-Qa'da 191 AH, while Harun ar-Rashid was khalif. He was just 70 the year he died.

'Abdullah ibn Ja'far ibn Ghaylan

His *kunya* was Abu 'Abdu'r-Rahman, the client of the family of Abu Mu'ayt. He transmitted from Abu'l-Malih and 'Ubaydullah ibn 'Amr. He had poor eye-sight and used henna. He died in ar-Raqqa on the 21st Sha'ban 210 AH, while al-Mu'tasim was khalif.

Yahya ibn 'Abdullah al-Harrani

His *kunya* was Abu Sa'id. His great-grandfather was one of the great kings of the people of Tukharistan. He related from Abu Bakr ibn Abi Maryam and Safwan ibn 'Amr.

'Abdullah ibn Muhammad ibn 'Ali al-Harrani

He was the companion of Zuhayr ibn Mu'awiya. His *kunya* was Abu Ja'far. He was at Mosul.

Al-Mu'afi ibn 'Imran

He was one of Azd. Ahmad ibn 'Abdullah said, "Sufyan ath-Thawri used to call al-Mu'afi ibn 'Imran 'the ruby'. He was the pride of the people of Mosul.

✽✽✽✽✽

Other people of this generation include: **Thabit ibn al-Hajjaj al-Kilabi**, who was reliable, and Ja'far ibn Burqan and others related from him; **Abu Fazara**, one of the people of ar-Raqqa; **Ibrahim ibn Abi Hurra**, who had few *hadith;* **Khassaf ibn 'Abdu'r-Rahman**; **an-Nadr ibn 'Arabi al-'Amiri**, who was weak in *hadith* and died while al-Mahdi was khalif; **Ghalib ibn 'Ubaydullah al-Jazari al-'Uqayli**, who was weak in *hadith* and died while al-Mansur was khalif; **'Abdullah ibn Muharrar al-'Amiri**, who was weak in *hadith* and died while al-Mansur was khalif; **Abu'l-'Atuf**, who was al-Jarrah ibn al-Minhal, and who was weak in *hadith.*

✽✽✽✽✽

Those at the Inner and Outer Frontiers[1]

Abu 'Amr al-Awza'i

His name was 'Abdu'r-Rahman ibn 'Amr. Al-Awza' is a sub-tribe of Hamdan. He was one of them. He was born in 88 AH. He was reliable and trustworthy, truthful, virtuous, good, with many *hadiths* and abundant knowledge and he was an authority in *fiqh*. His office was in Yamama. That is why he listened to Yahya ibn Abi Kathir and other shaykhs of the people of Yamama. He lived in Beirut and died there in 157 AH, at the end of the khalifate of al-Mansur, at the age of 70.

Abu Ishaq al-Fazari

His name was Ibrahim ibn Muhammad al-Harith. He was trustworthy and virtuous, one who followed the *Sunna* and went on expeditions. He had many mistakes in his *hadiths*. He died in Massisa in 188 AH, while Harun ar-Rashid was khalif.

'Isa ibn Yunus as-Sabi'i

One of Hamdan. His *kunya* was Abu 'Amr. He was one of the people of Kufa who moved to the frontier and settled in al-Hadath. He was reliable and dependable. He died in al-Hadath at the beginning of 191 AH, while Harun ar-Rashid was khalif.

Makhlad ibn al-Husayn

His *kunya* was Abu Muhammad. He was one of the people of Basra. He was the son of the wife of Hisham ibn Hassan. He related from him. He was trustworthy and virtuous. He moved and settled in Massisa and died there in 191 AH, while Harun ar-Rashid was khalif.

Muhammad ibn Kathir

His *kunya* was Abu Yusuf. He was one of the people of San'a and grew up in Syria and settled in Massisa. He was trustworthy. He

---

1. This is with reference to the border areas with the Byzantines.

related from Ma'mar, al-Awza'i and others. They mention that he muddled things at the end of his life. He died at the end of 216 AH while al-Ma'mun was khalif,

Al-Hajjaj ibn Muhammad al-A'war

His *kunya* was Abu Muhammad. He was the client of Sulayman ibn Mujalid, the client of al-Mansur, the Amir al-Mu'minin. He was one of the people of Baghdad who moved to Massisa with his family and settled there, remaining for many years. Then he returned to Baghdad and died there in 206 AH while al-Ma'mun was khalif. He was trustworthy, with many *hadiths* from Ibn Jurayj and others. He changed when he reached Baghdad and died like that.

Muhammad ibn Yusuf al-Firyabi

His *kunya* was Abu 'Abdullah. He was the companion of Sufyan ath-Thawri.

Adam ibn Abi Iyas

His *kunya* was Abu'l-Hasan. He was one of the *abna'* of Khurasan from Marwurrudh. He devoted himself to *hadith* in Baghdad and listened to Shu'ba a lot in a sound manner. Then he moved and settled in 'Asqallan where he remained until his death in Jumada al-Akhira 220 AH while al-Mu'tasim was khalif, at the age of 88. He was a paper-maker.

Al-Haytham ibn Jamil

Musa ibn Da'ud said, 'Al-Haytham went bankrupt twice in his devotion to *hadith*. He was one of the people of Baghdad who moved to Antioch where he died. He was reliable.

'Ali ibn Bakkar al-Basri

His *kunya* was Abu'l-Hasan. He had knowledge and *fiqh*. He died in Massisa in 208 AH, while al-Ma'mun was khalif.

Harith ibn 'Atiyya al-Basri

His *kunya* was Abu 'Abdullah. He died in Massisa in 199 AH, while al-Ma'mun was khalif. He was a scholar.

Khalaf ibn Tamim al-Kufi

He was a scholar. He died in Massisa in 213 AH, while al-Ma'mun was khalif.

Muhammad ibn 'Uyayna al-Fazari

His *kunya* was Abu 'Abdullah. He was a man of knowledge. He died in Massisa in 217 AH, while al-Ma'mun was khalif.

Abu 'Uthman Sa'id al-Qari' as-Sayyad

He was one of the people of Khurasan. He lived at the frontier. He was a *faqih*, scholar and ascetic. He died in Massisa in 221 AH, while al-Mu'tasim was khalif.

Abu'l-Muwaffaq

He was a *faqih*. He settled in Kafarbaya and died in Massisa in 220 AH, while al-Mu'tasim was khalif.

Abu'l-Mundhir

He was a qadi in Massisa. He was a scholar and *faqih*. He died in Massisa in 222 AH, while al-Mu'tasim was khalif.

Mansur ibn Harun

His *kunya* was Abu'l-Hasan. He was a scholar and *faqih*. He died in Massisa in 222 AH, while al-Mu'tasim was khalif.

Abu Zakariyya at-Tahhan

He was a scholar. He died in Massisa in 225 AH while Abu Ishaq al-Mu'tasim was khalif.

Chapter Three:
The Companions of the Messenger of Allah who settled in Egypt

'Amr ibn al-'As

His *kunya* was Abu 'Abdullah. He became Muslim in Abyssinia with the Negus. Then he came to Madina to the Messenger of Allah صلعم as an emigrant at the beginning of Safar 8 AH. He was a Companion of the Messenger of Allah, and he made him commander of the expedition to Dhat as-Salasil. The day Makka was conquered, he sent him to Suwa', the idol of Hudhayl, which he demolished. He also sent him to Jayfar and 'Abd, the sons of al-Julanda, who were part of Azd in 'Uman, to call them to Islam. The Messenger of Allah صلعم died while 'Amr was still in 'Uman. He left and returned to Madina.

Abu Bakr as-Siddiq sent him as one of the generals on the expedition to Syria and appointed him over what he conquered. He was at the Battle of Yarmuk. 'Umar ibn al-Khattab appointed him over Palestine and its adjoining area. Then he wrote to him to proceed to Egypt, and he went there with 3500 Muslims and conquered Egypt. 'Umar appointed him over Egypt until he died. 'Uthman ibn 'Affan then appointed him over Egypt for two years and then dismissed him and appointed 'Abdullah ibn Sa'd ibn Abi Sarh in his place. 'Amr returned to Madina and remained there.

When the people were agitated about 'Uthman, he went to Syria and settled near there on some land which belonged to him at as-Sab', in the land of Palestine, where he remained until 'Uthman was murdered, may Allah have mercy on him. Then he went to Mu'awiya and remained with him, promoting the case for revenge for the blood of 'Uthman. He was with him at the Battle of Siffin. Then Mu'awiya appointed him over Egypt and he went there and remained there as governor and built a house there and lived in it until he died on the *'Id al-Fitr* in 43 AH while Mu'awiya was khalif. He was buried in al-

Companions

Muqattam, the cemetery of the people of Egypt which is on the plateau of a hill

When he was dying he said, "Sit me up." So they sat him up. He ordered, "When you see that I have died, then prepare me and shroud me in three garments and tie my wrapper. I have a quarrel. Dig my grave for me and spread the earth over me and take me quickly to my grave." Then he said, "O Allah, you commanded 'Amr ibn al-'As certain things and he left them, and You forbade him certain things and he committed them. There is no god but You. There is no god but You!' three times, holding his hands tightly together until he died.

Abu Nuwas, the client of 'Abdullah ibn 'Amr, reported that 'Amr ibn al-'As died on the night of the *'Id al-Fitr,* and in the morning 'Abdullah ibn 'Amr took him and brought him out and placed him in Jabbana until all the people had passed through the alley of people and then he prayed over him and buried him. Then he prayed the *'Id* prayer with the people. He said, "I reckon that there was no one present at the *'Id* who had not prayed over him and attended his burial."

'Abdullah ibn 'Amr ibn al-'As

Muhammad ibn 'Umar said, "'Abdullah ibn 'Amr became Muslim before his father and was a Companion of the Prophet صلم. He was good and virtuous."

'Abdullah ibn 'Amr said, "I asked the Prophet صلم for permission for a letter which I heard from him and he gave me permission and I wrote it down." 'Abdullah used to call that paper of his 'the truthful'.

Mujahid said, "I saw a paper in the possession of 'Abdullah ibn 'Amr and asked him about it. He said, "This is 'the truthful' which contains what I heard from the Messenger of Allah صلم. There was no one between me and him."

Someone who saw 'Abdullah ibn 'Amr said that he had a white head and beard.

Al-'Uryan ibn al-Haytham said, "I came with my father to Yazid ibn Mu'awiya and a tall swarthy man with a large belly came and gave the greeting and then sat down. My father asked, 'Who is this?' It was said, "Abdullah ibn 'Amr.'"

Sharik ibn Khalifa said, "I saw 'Abdullah ibn 'Amr read in Syriac."

Muslim, the client of the Banu Makhzum said, "'Abdullah ibn 'Amr went around the house after he was blind."

'Abdullah ibn 'Amr withdrew with his father during the business about 'Uthman. When his father went to Mu'awiya, he went with him and was present at Siffin. Then he later regretted that and said, "What do I have to do with Siffin? What do I have to do with the Muslims fighting one another?" He went with his father to Egypt. When 'Amr ibn al-'As was dying, he appointed him over Egypt and Mu'awiya confirmed him. Then he dismissed him. He went on *hajj* and *'umra* and went to Syria. Then he returned to Egypt where he had built a house. He remained there until his death and was buried in his house in 77 AH while 'Abdu'l-Malik ibn Marwan was khalif.

Various people state this about his death. Muhammad ibn 'Umar said that he died in Syria in 65 AH when he was 92. He related from Abu Bakr and 'Umar.

Kharija ibn Hudhaqa

He became Muslim early on and was a Companion of the Prophet صلعم, and then he went and settled in Egypt. He was a qadi there for 'Amr ibn al-'As. On the morning of the day when the Kharijites had arranged to murder 'Amr ibn al-'As, 'Amr did not go out that day and commanded Kharija to lead the people in prayer in his stead. So the Kharijite went and struck Kharjia with his sword, thinking that he was 'Amr ibn al-'As, and killed him. He was seized and brought to 'Amr. They said, "By Allah, you have not killed 'Amr! You have killed Kharija." He said, "I intended 'Amr and Allah intended Kharija," which became a proverb.

Yazid ibn Abi Habiba said that 'Umar ibn al-Khattab wrote to 'Amr ibn al-'As, "Allot to everyone from those who gave allegiance under the Tree[1] a stipend of 200 dirhams, and give yourself that because you are the Amir, and also give Kharija ibn Hudhaqa this top stipend because of his courage. Allot 'Uthman ibn Qays as-Sahmi this top stipend because of his hospitality."

'Abdullah ibn Sa'd ibn Abi Sarh

He became Muslim early on and wrote down the revelation for the Messenger of Allah. Then he was tempted and left Madina for Makka as an apostate. Then the Messenger of Allah صلعم declared that he

---
1. i.e. shortly before the Treaty of al-Hudaybiyya was made.

Companions

could be killed on the Day of the Conquest, and 'Uthman ibn 'Affan went to the Prophet and asked for an amnesty for him, which he granted to him. He was his milk brother. He asked him, "Messenger of Allah, will you accept his allegiance?" The Messenger of Allah صلعم accepted his allegiance in Islam on that day. He said, "Islam removes what went before." 'Uthman ibn 'Affan appointed him over Egypt after 'Amr ibn al-'As. He settled there and built a house there. He remained governor there until 'Uthman was murdered.

Mahmiyya ibn Jaz'

He was an ally of Banu Sahm. Mahmiyya became Muslim early on in Makka and emigrated to Abyssinia in the second emigration. The first of his battles was al-Muraysi', which was the expedition against Mustaliq. The Messenger of Allah صلعم put him in charge of the *khums* and the shares of the Muslims on that day. He appointed him over the fifths after that. Then he moved to Egypt and settled there.

'Abdullah ibn al-Harith az-Zubaydi

He was a Companion of the Prophet صلعم and settled in Egypt. The Egyptians related from him. 'Ubaydullah ibn Abi Ja'far said, "I saw a *harqani* turban on 'Abdullah ibn al-Harith and I asked Ibn Lahi'a about *'harqani'* and he said that it is black."

'Uqba ibn 'Amir al-Juhami

His *kunya* was Abu 'Amr. He was a Companion of the Prophet صلعم. When the Messenger of Allah صلعم died and Abu Bakr sent the people to Syria, 'Uqba ibn 'Amir went and took part in the conquest of Syria and Egypt. He was with Mu'awiya at Siffin and then he moved to Egypt where he settled and built a house. He died there at the end of the khalifate of Mu'awiya ibn Abi Sufyan and was buried at Muqattam, the cemetery of the people of Egypt.

Abu 'Ushshana said, "I saw that 'Uqba ibn 'Amir dyed his hair black. He said, "We change the top of it, but its roots refuse."

Nubayh ibn Sawab al-Mahri

Nubayh ibn Sawab al-Mahri, one of the Companion of the Prophet صلعم said, "A man from Himyar came to the Messenger of

Allah ﷺ and became Muslim and then died. The Prophet said, 'Look for a Muslim heir of his.' They looked but could not find one. He said, 'Give it to the one with the closest lineage of Quda'a to him.' That was 'Abdullah ibn Unays, the closest of Quda'a in lineage. He was from the Banu'l-Bark ibn Wabara, the brother of Kalb ibn Wabara. He was the ally of the Banu Salama of the Ansar.

'Alqama ibn Rimtha al-Balawi

One of Quda'a. 'Alqama said, "The Prophet ﷺ sent 'Amr ibn al-'As to Bahrayn and then the Messenger of Allah ﷺ went out on an expedition and we went with him. The Messenger of Allah dozed off and then woke up and said, 'May Allah have mercy on 'Amr.' We discussed every man we knew whose name was 'Amr. Then the Messenger of Allah ﷺ dozed off again and woke up and said, 'May Allah have mercy on 'Amr.' Then he fell asleep a third time and woke up and said, 'May Allah have mercy on 'Amr.' We asked, 'Which 'Amr, Messenger of Allah?' He said, "'Amr ibn al-'As.' They said, 'What has he done?' He said, 'I remember him when I recommended that people give *sadaqa*. He brought *sadaqa* and was generous. I said, "From where do you have this, 'Amr?" He replied, "From Allah." 'Amr spoke the truth and 'Amr has much good with Allah.'"

Zuhayr said, "When there was a *fitna*, I said, 'I will follow this man about whom the Messenger of Allah ﷺ said what he said,' and I did not part from him."

Abu Zam'a al-Balawi

He was one of the Companions of the Messenger of Allah ﷺ. It is reported that when he was dying in North Africa, he said to them, "When you bury me, level my grave."

Abu Khirash as-Sulami

It is reported that Abu Khirash as-Sulami heard the Messenger of Allah ﷺ say, "If someone ostracises his brother for a year it is as if he has shed his blood."

Abu Basra al-Ghifari

He was a Companion of the Prophet ﷺ. He settled in Egypt and died there and was buried in Muqattam, the cemetery of the people of Egypt.

His son, Basra ibn Abi Basra

He was a Companion of the Prophet ﷺ, and related from him.

His son, Jamil ibn Basra al-Ghifari

He was also a Companion of the Prophet ﷺ, along with his father and grandfather. He is related from.

Abu Burda

He was a Companion of the Prophet ﷺ who settled in Egypt.

Abu Burda said, "I heard the Messenger of Allah ﷺ say, 'A man will emerge from among the rabbis who will study the Qur'an in a way in which no one after him will study it.'"

Rabi'a said, "We used to say that it was Muhammad ibn Ka'b al-Qurazi. The rabbis are Qurayza and an-Nadir."

'Abdullah ibn Sa'd

A man of the Companions of the Prophet who settled in Egypt.

'Abdullah ibn Sa'd said, "I asked the Messenger of Allah ﷺ about eating with a menstruating woman. He said, 'Eat with her.'"

He said, "I asked the Messenger of Allah ﷺ about praying in my house and the prayer in the mosque. He said, 'You do not see anyone with a house nearer to the mosque than me. I prefer to pray in my house than to pray in the mosque, except for the obligatory prayer."

Kharasha ibn al-Harith

Kharasha ibn al-Harith, the Companion of the Prophet ﷺ, said that the Messenger of Allah ﷺ said, "When you see a man killed with steadfastness do not be present. Perhaps he was killed unjustly and anger will descend and alight on you."

Junada al-Azdi

Junada al-Azdi said, "I visited the Messenger of Allah ﷺ with seven people from Azd, some of whom were women, on *Jumu'a*. We were fasting. The Messenger of Allah ﷺ invited us to eat with him and we said, 'We are fasting.' He asked, 'Did you fast yesterday?' We replied, 'No.' He asked 'Will you fast tomorrow?' We replied, 'No.' He said, 'Break your fast.' So we broke our fast and then the Messenger of Allah ﷺ went out to *Jumu'a*. When he sat on the minbar, he called for a vessel of water and drank, to teach the people that he did not fast on *Jumu'a*."

Abu Sa'd al-Khayr al-Anmari

It is reported that Abu Sa'd al-Khayr related to them at Qartasa that the Messenger of Allah ﷺ said, "70,000 of my community will enter the Garden and there will be 70,000 with every thousand. That includes our Muhjarun and that is made up by a group of our desert Arabs."

Mu'adh ibn Anas al-Juhani

He was a Companion of the Prophet ﷺ and *hadiths* are related from him. He settled in Egypt. He is Abu Sahl ibn Mu'adh, from whom Zabban ibn Fa'id and other Syrians and Egyptians related.

Abu'l-Yaqzan

He was a Companion of the Messenger of Allah. It is reported that Abu 'Ushshana said that he heard Abu'l-Yaqzan say, "Receive good news! By Allah, you have the greatest love for the Messenger of Allah ﷺ although you were not one of the group who saw him."

Mu'awiya ibn Hudayj

The Companion of the Prophet ﷺ. He is related from. He met 'Umar ibn al-Khattab and related a *hadith* from him about wiping. He was a partisan of 'Uthman.

Mu'awiya ibn Hudayj, who was a Companion, said, "Whoever washes a dead person, shrouds him, follows him and turns him on his side will return forgiven."

Ziyad ibn al-Harith as-Suda'i

He was with the Messenger of Allah ﷺ on some of his journeys. He went with the Messenger of Allah and clung to his stirrup. When it was before dawn, the Prophet ﷺ said, "Give the *adhan*, brother of

Suda'.' He gave the *adhan* and then Bilal came and gave the *iqama*. The Messenger of Allah ﷺ said, "The brother of Suda' gave the *adhan*. Whoever gives the *adhan* gives the *iqama*." So he gave the *iqama*, and the Messenger of Allah ﷺ went forward and led the people in prayer.

Ziyad ibn al-Harith settled in Egypt, and the Egyptians related from him.

Maslama ibn Makhlad ibn as-Samit

One of Khazraj of the Ansar. His *kunya* was Abu Ma'mar.

Maslama ibn Makhlad said, "I became Muslim when I was four. The Messenger of Allah ﷺ died when I was fourteen."

Muhammad ibn 'Umar said, "Maslama ibn Makhlad reported from the Messenger of Allah ﷺ and moved to Egypt where he settled. He was with the people of Khurbata, and they were the strongest people of North Africa and the most aggressive. He had renown and eminence there. Then he went to Madina where he died, while Mu'awiya was khalif.

Surraq

'Abdu'r-Rahman ibn al-Baylamani said, "I was in Egypt and a man said to me, 'Shall I direct you to one of the Companions of the Prophet?' I said, 'Yes, indeed!' So he directed me to a man and I went up to him and asked, 'Who are you, may Allah have mercy on you?' He replied, 'I am Surraq [meaning 'thief'].' I said, 'Glory be to Allah! You have such a name when you are one of the Companions of the Messenger of Allah?' He said, 'The Messenger of Allah ﷺ named me Surraq and I will never abandon it!' I asked, 'Why did he name you Surraq?'

"He said, 'One of the men of the desert Arabs came with two camels he had to sell. I bought them from him and said to him, "Wait until I pay you." I went into my house and then I went out by a back entrance and spent the money for the price of the camels on something I needed. Then I stayed away until I thought that the bedouin had left. I went out and found the bedouin standing there. He grabbed me and brought me to the Messenger of Allah ﷺ and told him the story. The Prophet asked, "What led you to do what you did?" I replied, "I bought something I needed with their price, Messenger of

Egypt

Allah." He said, "Pay him." I said, "I do not have it." He said, "You are a thief (*surraq*). Take him, Bedouin, and sell him so that you receive your due." The people began to haggle with him for me, and he turned to them and asked, "What do you want?" They said, "What do you want? We want to ransom him from you." He said, "By Allah, one of you is more in need of Allah than me. Go, I have freed you.'"'

Surraq reported that the Messenger of Allah ﷺ judged by the testimony of a witness and by the oath of a claimant.

Sandar

He was the client of the Messenger of Allah. Some say his name was Ibn Sandar.

Shu'ayb reported that his father said, "Zinba' al-Judhami had a slave called Sandar. He saw him kiss a slavegirl of his. So he cut off his testicles and sliced the end of his nose and ears. Sandar went to the Prophet ﷺ who sent for his master and admonished him. 'Do not make them bear what they are incapable of and feed them from what you eat and clothe them from what you wear. If you are pleased with them, keep them. If you dislike them, sell them. Do not torture Allah's creatures. Whoever is mutilated or burned with fire is free and is the client of Allah and the client of his Messenger.' So he set Sandar free, and he said, 'Messenger of Allah, command guardians for me.' He said, 'I entrust you to every Muslim.'

"When the Prophet ﷺ died, he went to Abu Bakr and said, 'Maintain the instruction of the Messenger of Allah ﷺ about me.' So Abu Bakr provided his food for him until he died.

"Then 'Umar came to power and Sandar said, 'Maintain the instruction of the Messenger of Allah ﷺ about me.' He said, 'Choose: If you want to remain with me, I will pay you the same as Abu Bakr did. Or if you wish, seek which of the garrisons you prefer and I will write a document for you.' Sandar said, 'Write to Egypt on my behalf. It is a fertile land.' So 'Umar wrote for him to 'Amr ibn al-'As: 'Sandar has been sent to you, so maintain the instruction of the Messenger of Allah ﷺ about him.' When he came to 'Amr ibn al-'As, he allotted him land and a house, and he lived in it. When he died, it was taken back into the property of Allah. Then it was made a grant to al-Asbagh ibn 'Abdu'l-'Aziz. They did not have any better land than it."

Muhammad ibn 'Umar said, "The Muna al-Asbagh is famous today in Egypt. Muna is like two gardens there."

One of the transmitters said that Sandar was an unbeliever.

It is reported that 'Amr ibn 'As was going to travel one day and Ibn Sandar, the client of the Prophet صلعم, went with him, along with some people. They were travelling in front of 'Amr ibn al-'As. They stirred up the dust and 'Amr began to pull his turban over his nose. He said, "Be careful of the dust. It is the quickest thing to enter and the last to leave. When it settles in the lung, it becomes part of it." Some people said to those people, "Move aside." They did so, except for Ibn Sandar. He was asked, "Why don't you move aside, Ibn Sandar?" 'Amr said, "Leave him. The dust of a eunuch is not harmful." Ibn Sandar heard him and got angry. He said, "'Amr! By Allah, if you were one of the believers, I would not harm you!" 'Amr said, "May Allah forgive you! By the praise of Allah, I am one of the believers." Ibn Sandar said, "You know that I asked the Messenger of Allah صلعم to give me guardians and he said, 'I entrust you to every believer.'"

Abu Fatima al-Azdi

Abu Fatima al-Azdi said, "I was sitting with the Messenger of Allah صلعم when he said, "Who would like to be healthy and not ill?' We said, 'We would, Messenger of Allah!' The Messenger of Allah صلعم said, 'Why!' We saw his displeasure in his face. He said, 'Do you want to be like the biting donkey?' They said, 'No, Messenger of Allah.' He said, 'Do you not want to be people of testing and people of expiation?' They said, 'Yes indeed, Messenger of Allah.' The Messenger of Allah صلعم said, 'By Allah, Allah tests the believer and He only tests him because of his honour with Him. If he has a position with Him that he has not attained by any of his actions, He puts him in it by affliction which will make him reach that position.'"

Abu Fatima said, "The Messenger of Allah صلعم said to me, 'Do a lot of prostration after me. There is no one who prostrates one prostration to Allah but that Allah will elevate him by it one degree in the Garden and remove one error from him.'"

Abu Jum'a

The Companion of the Messenger of Allah ﷺ. He was in Syria and then moved to Egypt and settled there. He related *hadiths* from the Messenger of Allah ﷺ.

'Abdullah ibn Muhayriz said, "I said to one of the Companions of the Messenger of Allah whom I think was called Abu Jum'a, 'Relate to us a *hadith* which you heard from the Messenger of Allah ﷺ.' He said, 'I will report an excellent *hadith* to you. We had lunch with the Messenger of Allah ﷺ one day when Abu 'Ubayda ibn al-Jarrah was with us. We said, "Messenger of Allah, is there anyone better than us? We became Muslim with you and we emigrated with you." He replied, "Yes, some people of my community who will come after me and who will believe in me."'"

Abu Su'ad

He was a Companion of the Messenger of Allah ﷺ, who lived in Egypt.

'Abdu'r-Rahman ibn 'Udays al-Balawi

He was a Companion of the Messenger of Allah ﷺ and listened to him. He was a leader of those men who went to attack 'Uthman when he was besieged and murdered.

Abu'sh-Shamus al-Balawi

He was a Companion of the Messenger of Allah ﷺ, who settled in Egypt.

The First Generation of the people of Egypt after the Companions

'Abdu'r-Rahman ibn 'Usayla as-Sunabihi

One of Himyar. His *kunya* was Abu 'Abdullah. He was reliable, with few *hadiths*. He related from Abu Bakr, 'Umar and Bilal.

'Abdu'r-Rahman ibn 'Usayla said, "I only missed the Messenger of Allah ﷺ by five days. The Messenger of Allah died when I was in al-Juhfa. I went to many Companions. I asked Bilal about the Night of Power and he said, 'The night of the 23rd is not dark.'"

Abu Tamim al-Jayshani

He was reliable. He related from 'Umar and 'Ali. He died early on in 77 or 78 AH, while 'Abdu'l-Malik was khalif.

'Abdullah ibn Zurayr al-Ghafiqi

He was reliable with *hadiths*. He related from 'Umar and 'Ali. He was present with 'Ali at the Battle of Siffin. He died in 81 AH while 'Abdu'l-Malik ibn Marwan was khalif.

Abu Wahb al-Jayshani

Jayshan is part of Quda'a. Abu Wahb's name was Daylam ibn al-Hawsha'. He was reliable, with few *hadiths*.

'Abdu'r-Rahman ibn Shammasa

He had correct *hadiths*.

✶✶✶✶✶

The Second Generation

Abu'l-Khayr

His name was Marthad ibn 'Abdullah al-Bazani, from Himyar. He was reliable, with virtue and worship. He died in 90 AH while al-Walid ibn 'Abdu'l-Malik was khalif.

Egypt

Abu 'Abdu'r-Rahman al-Jubuli

One of Himyar. His name was 'Abdullah ibn Yazid. He was reliable. He related from 'Abdullah ibn 'Amr ibn al-'As.

Abu Qays

He was the client of 'Amr ibn al-'As. He was reliable, Allah willing. He related from 'Amr ibn al-'As.

Wardan

He was the client of 'Amr ibn al-'As. His *kunya* was Abu 'Ubaydullah. He is also related from. The market in Egypt is named after him: the Wardan Market.

Qanbar

The client of 'Amr ibn al-'As. He is also related from.

'Ali ibn Rabah al-Lakhmi

The people of Egypt call him 'Ali ibn Rabbah, and the people of Iraq call him 'Ali ibn Rabah. He was reliable. He related from 'Amr ibn al-'As and others.

Abu 'Ushshana al-Mu'afiri

His name was Hayy ibn Yu'min. He had *hadiths*. He is related from. He died in 118 AH while Hisham was khalif.

Abu Qabil al-Mu'afiri

His name was Hayy ibn Hani'. He said, "I remember the murder of 'Uthman ibn 'Affan." He has *hadiths*. He is related from and lived on until he died in 127 AH while Marwan ibn Muhammad was khalif.

'Abdullah ibn Hubayra as-Sabba'i

He had *hadiths* and he died while Yazid ibn 'Abdu'l-Malik was khalif.

Shufayy ibn Mati' al-Asma'i

One of Himyar. He had *hadiths*. He died while Hisham ibn 'Abdu'l-Malik was khalif.

Tabi'un

Shaym ibn Baytan
He had *hadiths*.

Mishrah ibn Ha'an
His *kunya* was Abu Mus'ab. He had *hadiths*.

Abu'l-Haytham
The companion of Abu Sa'id al-Khudri. His name was Sulayman ibn 'Amr al-'Utwari.

✵✵✵✵✵

The Third Generation

Yazid ibn Abi Habib
His *kunya* was Abu Raja', the client of the Banu 'Amir ibn Lu'ayy of Quraysh. He was reliable, with many *hadiths*. He died in 128 AH while Marwan II was khalif.

Ja'far ibn Rabi'a al-Azdi
He was an ally of the Banu Zuhra ibn Kilab and Shurahbil ibn Hasana, one of the generals of the armies sent by Abu Bakr to Syria. Ja'far died in Egypt in 132 AH. He was reliable.

'Ubaydullah ibn Abi Ja'far
He was a client of Banu Umayya. He was reliable, outstanding in his time. He died in 135 or 136 AH.

Bakr ibn Sawada al-Judhami
He was reliable, Allah willing. He died while Hisham ibn 'Abdu'l-Malik was khalif.

'Abdullah ibn Rafi' al-Ghafiqi
One of Himyar. He had *hadiths*. He died while Hisham ibn 'Abdu'l-Malik was khalif.

Al-Walid ibn Abi Hilal
He was reliable, Allah willing.

Sa'id ibn Abi Hilal

He was reliable, Allah willing.

Zuhra ibn Ma'bad

His *kunya* was Abu 'Aqil.

*****

The Fourth Generation

'Amr ibn al-Harith

The client of the Ansar. He was reliable, Allah willing. He died in 147 or 148 AH, while Abu Ja'far al-Mansur was khalif.

Haywa ibn Shurayh

His *kunya* was Abu Yazid at-Tujibi, from Kinda. He was reliable. He died while Abu Ja'far al-Mansur was khalif.

Musa ibn 'Ali ibn Rabah al-Lakhmi

He was reliable, Allah willing. Makki ibn Ibrahim said, "I came to Egypt in 164 AH and was told that Musa ibn 'Ali had died in Alexandria."

Muhammad ibn 'Umar said that Musa ibn 'Ali died in 163 AH, while al-Mahdi was khalif.

Sa'id ibn Abi Ayyub

He was reliable and dependable. Abu Ayyub's name was Miqlas.

'Abdu'r-Rahman ibn Shurayh

His *hadith* are contradicted. He died in 167 AH while al-Mahdi was khalif.

Yahya ibn Ayyub al-Ghafiqi

His *hadith* are contradicted.

*****

Fifth Generation

'Abdullah ibn 'Uqba ibn Lahi'a al-Hadrami

One of them. His *kunya* was Abu 'Abdu'r-Rahman. He was weak, and had many *hadiths*. Those who listened to him at the beginning of his affair have a better state in his transmission than those who listened to him at the end of it. The people of Egypt mention that he did not become muddled, and the beginning and end of his life were the same. However things which were not part of his *hadith* were read to him and he was silent about it. He was asked about that and he said, "Where is my wrong action? They brought a book which they read. If they had asked me, I would have told them that it was not part of my *hadiths*."

He died in Egypt on Sunday, the 15th Rabi' al-Awwal 174 AH, while Harun ar-Rashid was khalif.

Al-Layth ibn Sa'd

His *kunya* was Abu'l-Harith, the client of Qays. He was born in 93 or 94 AH, while al-Walid I was khalif. He was reliable, with many *hadiths* which are sound. He was the only one to give *fatwa* in his time in Egypt. He was noble, eminent, and a generous man with hospitality. He died on Friday the 16th Sha'ban 165 AH while al-Mahdi was khalif.

Al-Fadl ibn Fadala al-Qayni

He was qadi in Egypt. His *hadiths* are contradicted.

Rishdin ibn Sa'd al-Qayni

He is Rishdin ibn Abi Rishdin. He was weak. He died in 188 AH while Harun ar-Rashid was khalif.

Ghawth ibn Sulayman al-Hadrami

He died while al-Mahdi was khalif.

✺✺✺✺✺

The Sixth Generation

'Abdullah ibn Wahb

He was a client of Quraysh. He had much knowledge and was reliable in what he transmitted when he said, "He related to me." He used to forge.

'Abdullah ibn Salih al-Juhani

His *kunya* was Abu Salih. He was a scribe for al-Layth ibn Sa'd and was his transmitter. He died in Egypt on the Day of 'Ashura' in Muharram 223 AH, while al-Mu'tasim was khalif.

'Amr ibn Khalid

The companion of Zuhayr ibn Mu'awiya.

Nu'aym ibn Hammad

He was one of the people of Khurasan from Marw. He devoted himself extensively to *hadith* in Iraq and the Hijaz. Then he settled in Egypt where he remained until he was investigated [about the Qur'an] while al-Mu'tasim was khalif. He was arrested and questioned about the Qur'an. He refused to give any answer at all to what he was asked. So he was imprisoned in Samarra and remained a prisoner there until he died in 228 AH.

[End of the generations of the people of Egypt]

Other Locations

Those who were in Ayla

Talha ibn 'Abdu'l-Malik al-Ayli
He was reliable. He related from Malik ibn Anas and others.

'Aqil ibn Khalid
The companion of az-Zuhri. He was reliable.

Abu Sakhr al-Ayli
His name was Yazid ibn Abi Sumayya. He had correct *hadiths*.

Muhammad ibn 'Umar said that Abu Sakhr was one of the people of worship. He used to pray for the entire night, weeping. He had a Jewish woman who lived in the house with him, and she used to weep out of compassion for him. One night he said in his supplication, "O Allah! This Jewish woman weeps out of compassion for me and yet her *deen* is different from mine. You are more entitled to be merciful to me."

Abu Sakhr al-Ayli came to the *hajj* '*ids* (*mawsims*) every year with Muhammad ibn al-Munkadir, Safwan ibn Sulaym, Yazid ibn Khusayfa, Sulayman ibn Suhaym, and Abu Hazim. They met 'Umar ibn Dharr and he recounted to them and reminded them about the Next World. They remained like that until the '*id* ended. Then they did not meet again until the next festival.

Zurayq ibn Hakam
He was reliable.

Yunus ibn Yazid al-Ayli
He had sweet *hadith*, and a lot of them. He is not an authority. Sometimes he brought something contradicted.

'Abdu'l-Jabbar ibn 'Umar al-Ayli
His *kunya* was Abu's-Sabbah. He was reliable. He related from Yazid ibn Abi Sumayya from Ibn 'Umar from the Prophet صلعم, regarding dragging the shirt and what he said about dragging the wrapper. 'Abdu'l-Jabbar was related from.

Those who were in North Africa

Khalid ibn Abi 'Imran

One of the people of Tunis from North Africa. He was reliable, Allah willing. He did not forge.

*****

Those who were in Andalusia

Mu'awiya ibn Salih al-Hadrami

He was their qadi. He was reliable with a lot of *hadith*. He went on one *hajj* in his lifetime and visited Madina. There he met those of the people of Iraq that he met. In that *hajj* he met 'Abdu'r-Rahman ibn Mahdi, Zayd ibn al-Hubab al-'Ukali, Muhammad ibn 'Umar al-Waqidi, Hammad ibn Khalid al-Khayyat and Ma'n ibn 'Isa.

*****

Praise belongs to Allah, the Lord of the worlds.
May Allah bless our master Muhammad, the Messenger of Allah,
and his pure family and grant them peace abundantly.

*****

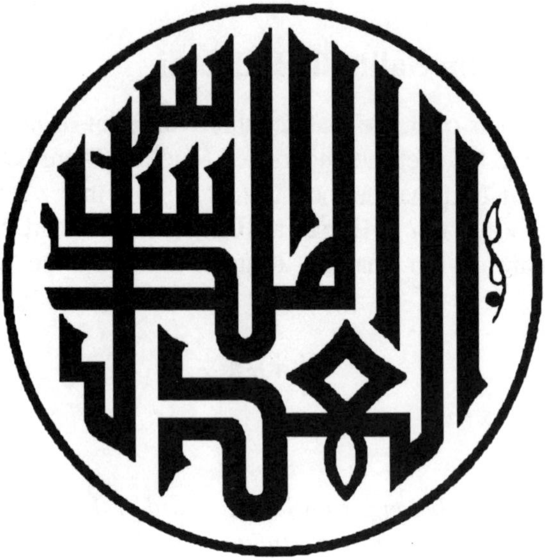

Glossary

abna': short for *abna' ad-dawla*, 'sons of the state', used to describe the new generation of Khurasanis whose fathers had settled in Baghdad after the 'Abbasid revolution and who were loyal supporters of the 'Abbasids.

Abu Muslim: 'Abdu'r-Rahman ibn Muslim al-Khurasani, the mysterious individual who was the chief recruiting officer for the Abbasid revolution in Khurasan in 128/747. He was murdered by the Abbasids in 132/750.

adhan: the call to prayer.

Ahl as-Suffa: the people of the Bench, the poor and needy amongst the Companions of the Prophet, may Allah's blessings be upon him, who lived on a verandah (*suffa*) in a courtyard next to the house of the Prophet and the mosque in Madina.

Amir al-Mu'minin: the Commander of the Believers, a title of respect given to the Khalif.

Ansar: the "Helpers", the people of Madina who welcomed and aided the Prophet, and the *Muhajirun.*

'Arafa: a plain 15 miles to the east of Makka. One of the essential rites of the *hajj* is to stand on 'Arafa on the 9th of Dhu'l-Hijjah.

'arif: a prefect or sergeant, lit. 'one who knows', an official in charge of a military division in Basra, or Kufa in the time of Ziyad.

'Ashura': the 10th day of the month of Muharram. It is considered a highly desirable day to fast.

'Asr: the mid-afternoon prayer.

awaq: see *uqiyya.*

awsaq: see *wasq.*

ayat: a verse of the Qur'an.

Badr: a place near the coast, about 95 miles to the south of Madina, where, in 2 AH in the first battle fought by the newly established Muslim community, the 314 outnumbered Muslims led by the Messenger of Allah overwhelmingly defeated 1000 Makkan idolaters.

Banu: lit. sons, a tribe or clan.

basmala: the words "In the Name of Allah, the All Merciful, the All Compassionate."

Dajjal: the false Messiah whose appearance marks the imminent end of the world.

Dar al-Harb: the abode of conflict, the domain and territory of unbelievers.
Dar al-Islam: the abode of Islam where the *Shari'a* is in force.
deen: the life-transaction, lit. the debt between two parties, in this usage between the Creator and created.
dhimma: obligation or contract, in particular a treaty of protection for non-Muslims living in Muslim territory.
dhimmi: a non-Muslim living under the protection of Muslim rule.
Dhuhr: the noon prayer.
Dhu'l-Hijja: the twelfth month of the Muslim calendar, the month of the *Hajj*.
Dhu'l-Qa'da: the eleventh month of the Muslim calendar.
diwan: a collection of poems written by one person; also the account books of the treasury, or a register.
Duha: the voluntary mid-morning prayer.
Fajr: the dawn, or pre-dawn, prayer.
faludhaj: a Persian sweet dish similar to fudge prepared with almonds, sugar, rose-water and other ingredients. Someone who offered it to guests was considered to have refined taste and culture.
faqih, pl. *fuqaha':* a man learned in knowledge of *fiqh* (see below) who by virtue of his knowledge can give a legal judgement.
fatwa: an authoritative legal opinion or judgement given by a *mufti*.
fiqh: the science of the application of the *Shari'a*. A practitioner or expert in *fiqh* is called a *faqih*.
fitna: a word which means 'testing' or 'temptation', which refers to social and civil unrest, civil war, sedition or schism.
fitra: the first nature, the natural, primal condition of mankind in harmony with nature.
fuqaha': plural of *faqih.*
furqan: discrimination.
ghila: a term used to designate having intercourse with a woman while she is still breast-feeding an infant.
ghusl: the full ritual washing of the body.
hadd: Allah's boundary limits which define the lawful and unlawful. The *hadd* punishments are specific fixed penalties laid down by Allah for specified crimes.
hadith: reported speech of the Prophet.
hajj: the yearly pilgrimage to Makka.
Harra: A stony tract of black volcanic rock east of Madina, where a terrible battle took place in 63 AH (26 August 683 CE) between the

Glossary

forces of Yazid I and 'Abdullah ibn az-Zubayr which culiminated in Madina being sacked and plundered.

Hijra: emigration in the way of Allah, especially designating the emigration of the Prophet ﷺ from Makka to Madina.

Ibadiyya: the remnants of the Kharijite rebellion in the second civil war between the Umayyads and Ibn az-Zubayr.

'Id: a festival, either the festival at the end of Ramadan or at the time of the *hajj*.

'Id al-Adha: the *'Id* at the time of the *hajj*.

'Id al-Fitr: the *'Id* at the end of Ramadan.

ihram: the ritual condition adopted by a person performing *hajj* or *'umra* which involves certain garments and rules of behaviour.

ijtihad: to struggle, to exercise personal judgement in legal matters based on the Qur'an and *Sunna*.

iqama: the call which announces that the obligatory prayer is about to begin.

'Isha': the evening prayer.

isnad: the record of the names of the people who form the chain of human transmission by means of which a *hadith* is preserved.

Jahannam: One of the names for the Fire, Hell.

Jahiliyya: the Time of Ignorance before the coming of Islam.

janaba: the state of impurity in which a person requires a *ghusl*.

jarib: a grain measure of capacity of either 16, 26, or 29.5 litres; also a measure of land sixty cubits square.

jihad: struggle, particularly fighting in the way of Allah to establish Islam.

jinn: unseen beings created from smokeless fire who co-habit the earth together with mankind.

jizya: a protection tax imposed on non-Muslims under the protection of Muslim rule.

jubbah: a long outer garment with an open front and wide sleeves.

Jumada: Jumada al-Ula and Jumada al-Akhira are the fifth and sixth months of the Muslim lunar calendar:

Jumu'a: the day of gathering, Friday, and particularly the *Jumu'a* prayer which is performed instead of *Dhuhr* by those who attend it.

kharaj: land tax.

Kharijites: the earliest sect who separated themselves from the main body of the Muslims and declared war on all those who disagreed with them. They were of the opinion that a wrong action turns a Muslim into an unbeliever.

khutba: a speech, and in particular a standing speech given by the Imam before the *Jumu'a* prayer and after the two *'Id* prayers.

kitaba: a contract by which a slave acquires his freedom against a future payment, or payment by instalments, to his owner.

khul': a form of divorce in which a woman obtains a divorce by returning her dower, or by some other form of compensation.

kunya: a respectful but intimate way of addressing people as "the father of so-and-so" or "the mother of so-and-so."

Maghrib: the sunset prayer.

makkuk: a measure which holds 1 ½ *sa'as*.

maqsura: a box or compartment erected in the mosque for the ruler, as a means of protection, usually near the *mihrab*.

marzban: military governor of a Sasanian frontier district.

Masjid al-Haram: The Inviolable Mosque, the name of the mosque built around the Ka'ba in Makka.

mawla, pl. *mawali*: client of an Arab tribe; freed slave.

Mesopotamia: in Arabic, *al-Jazira*, the name of a district covering northeastern Syria and northern Iraq.

Mihna: the Inquisition instituted by the Abbasid khalif, al-Ma'mun, which required all important people to publicly state the belief that the Qur'an was created.

mihrab: the prayer niche, a recess in a mosque indicating the direction of *qibla*.

minbar: steps on which the Imam stands to deliver the *khutba*.

mu'adhdhin: someone who calls the *adhan*, the call to prayer.

mudd: a measure of volume, approximately a double-handed scoop.

Mufassal: the *suras* of the Qur'an starting from *Surat Qaf* (50) to the end of the Qur'an.

mufti: a specialist in Islamic law who can issue a *fatwa*. His authority derives from his reputation as a scholar.

muhaddith: someone who transmits and studies *hadith*.

Muhajirun: Companions of the Messenger of Allah who accepted Islam in Makka and made *hijra* to Madina before the Conquest of Makka in 8/630.

Muhammad ibn al-Hanafiyya: a son of 'Ali by a Hanafi woman. It was in his name that al-Mukhtar revolted in Kufa 66/685.

Muharram: the first month of the Muslim year.

mukatib: a slave who has been given a *kitaba*.

Murji'ites: the opponents of the Kharijites. They held that it is faith and not actions which is important. There is also a political posi-

Glossary

tion, held by the Murji'ites, which suspends judgement on a person guilty of major sins.

mursal: a *hadith* which a man belonging to the generation after the Companions quotes directly from the Prophet ﷺ without mentioning the Companion from whom he heard the *hadith*.

Musnad: a collection of *hadith* arranged according to the first authority in its *isnad*.

Mu'tazila: a theological ideology and political movement hostile to the Umayyads which maintained, among other things, that man has free will and that the Qur'an is created.

Mu'tazilite: a follower of the Mu'tazila school.

Qadar: lit. the Decree, used to designate the doctrine of the Qadariyya.

Qadariyya: an early sect who said that people have power (*qadar*) over their actions and hence free will in what they do.

qadi: a judge, qualified to judge all matters in accordance with the Shari'a and to dispense and enforce legal punishments.

Qadisiyya: A decisive four day battle fought against the Persians in Iraq in 15/636.

qafiz: a dry measure consisting of twelve *sa's*.

qanut: supplication in the prayer, particularly in the standing position after *ruku'* in the *Subh* prayer in the Maliki school.

qibla: the direction faced in the prayer which is towards the Ka'ba in Makka. The first *qibla* had been towards Jerusalem until it was changed, and so the early Muslims had prayed towards two *qiblas*.

qiyas: analogy, a method of arriving at a legal judgement by using something analogous.

qurra': those who did not take part in the *Ridda*, namely the *Ahl al-Qura* or people of the towns. As *qurra'* is also the plural of *qari'*, meaning Qur'an reciter, there is sometimes confusion about whom is being referred to when this term is used.

Rabi': Rabi' al-Awwal and Rabi' ath-Thani are the third and fourth months of the Muslim lunar calendar.

Rajab: the seventh month of the Muslim calendar.

rak'at: a unit of the prayer consisting of a series of standings, bowing, prostrations and sittings.

Ramadan: the month of fasting, the ninth month in the Muslim calendar.

ra'y: opinion, a legal decision based on the use of common sense and personal opinion, used where there is no explicit guidance in the Qur'an and *Sunna* and where it is not possible to use *qiyas*.

Ridda: the defection of various Arab tribes away from Islam after the death of the Prophet ﷺ which brought about the Ridda War.

329

riwaya: a reading or transmission of the Qur'an or another text.

sa': a measure of volume equal to four *mudd*s, a *mudd* being a double-handed scoop.

sadaqa: giving in the way of Allah, a gift without any ulterior motive other than giving.

Safar: the second month in the Muslim calendar.

sahur: pre-dawn meal before a day of fasting.

Sha'ban: the eighth month of the Muslim calendar

Sham: Syria.

Shari'a: The legal modality of a people based on the revelation of their Prophet. The final *Shari'a* is that of Islam.

Shawwal: the tenth month of the Muslim calendar.

Shaytan: a devil, particularly Iblis.

Shi'a: lit. party or faction, specifically the party who claim that 'Ali should have succeeded the Prophet as the first khalif and that the leadership of the Muslims rightfully belongs to his descendants.

Siffin: a ruined Roman town by the Euphrates in Syria where, in 37/657, a battle between the forces of 'Ali and Mu'awiya took place.

siwak: a toothstick.

Subh: the obligatory prayer before sunrise.

Sunna: lit. a form, the customary practice of a person or group of people. It has come to refer almost exclusively to the practice of the Messenger of Allah, may Allah bless him and grant him peace.

sutra: an object placed in front of a man praying, so that people will not pass between him and the *qibla*.

Tabi'un: the second generation of the early Muslims who did not meet the Prophet Muhammad, may Allah bless him and grant him peace, but who learned the *deen* of Islam from his Companions.

tafsir: commentary or explanation of the meanings of the *ayats* of the Noble Qur'an.

takbir: saying "*Allahu akbar*" or "Allah is greater".

takfir: to declare someone an unbeliever.

Tarwiyya: "drawing water", 8th Dhu'l-Hijja, the day before 'Arafa when the pilgrims gather water.

Tashriq: the days of the 10th, 11th, and 12th of Dhu'l-Hijja when the pilgrims sacrifice their animals and stone the *jamras* at Mina.

tawaf: circling the Ka'ba, which is done in sets of seven circuits.

tayammum: purification for prayer with dust, earth or stone when water is unavailable or would be harmful.

tharid: a dish of bread, meat and broth, reported to be a favourite dish of the Prophet, peace and blessings be upon him.

Glossary

Umm al-Mu'minin: lit. 'Mother of the Believers', an honorary title given to the wives of the Prophet.

umm walad, lit. 'mother of a child', a slave-girl who has given birth to a child by her master and hence cannot be sold and becomes free when her master dies.

'umra: the lesser pilgrimage which can be performed at any time of the year.

uqiyya, pl. of *awaq*: a measurement of silver equivalent to 40 dirhams or 123 gms of silver.

waqf: perpetual endowment for a charitable use which makes the property inalienable.

wasq, pl. *awsaq*, a measure of volume equal to sixty *sa's*.

witr: lit. odd, a single *rak'at* which makes the number of *sunna* prayers done in a day uneven.

wudu': ritual washing to be pure for the prayer.

Yarmuk: an important battle fought between the Muslims and the Byzantines in 13/ 636.

zakat: a wealth tax, one of the five pillars of Islam.

zakat al-fitr: the obligatory head tax paid by or on behalf of every Muslim at the end of Ramadan.

Zamzam: the well of the Haram of Makka.

zuhd: doing without what you do not need, and making do with little.

Index

Aban al-Muharibi 52-53
'Abbad al-'Asari 78
'Abbad ibn Shurahbil 32
'Abbad ibn Suhayb al-Kalbi 183
Al-'Abbas as-Sulami 46
Al-'Abbas ibn Mirdas 19
'Abdullah as-Sunabihi 264
'Abdullah ibn Abi'l-Hamsa' 35
'Abdullah ibn 'A'idh ath-Thumali 254
'Abdullah ibn 'Amr al-Muzani 18
'Abdullah ibn 'Amr ibn al-'As 189, 306-307
'Abdullah ibn 'Awn 114, 118, 127, 128, 129, 132, 154, 155, 161-167, 180, 181
'Abdullah ibn Burayda 101, 139, 207
'Abdullah ibn Busr al-Mazini 256
'Abdullah ibn Ghalib 104, 141
'Abdullah ibn al-Harith az-Zubaydi 308
'Abdullah ibn al-Harith b. Nawfal 60-61
'Abdullah ibn Mikhmar 280
'Abdullah ibn Mu'arrid 46
'Abdullah ibn Mu'awiya al-Ghadiri 261
'Abdullah ibn al-Mubarak 229, 230, 232
'Abdullah ibn al-Mughaffal 7-8
'Abdullah ibn Muhayriz 277, 315
'Abdullah ibn Mutarrif 99, 151
'Abdullah ibn Rawaha 242, 243
'Abdullah ibn Sa'd 310
'Abdullah ibn Sa'd ibn Abi Sarh 305, 307
'Abdullah ibn Sarjis 35
'Abdullah ibn Saydan as-Sulami 271
'Abdullah ibn Shaqiq al-'Uqayli 79
'Abdullah ibn ash-Shikhkhir 19-20
'Abdullah ibn 'Uqba ibn Lahi'a 320
'Abdullah ibn az-Zubayr *see* Ibn az-Zubayr
'Abdu'l-Mun'im ibn Idris 224
'Abdu'r-Rahman ibn Khabbab 47
'Abdu'r-Rahman ibn Qatada 258
'Abdu'r-Rahman ibn Salama 49
'Abdu'r-Rahman ibn Samura 8, 41, 82, 100, 111, 228

'Abdu'r-Rahman ibn Shibl 250
'Abdu'r-Rahman ibn Ya'mur 228
Abu 'Adhaba al-Hadrami 274
Abu'l-'Aliyya ar-Riyahi 70-73, 121
Abu'l-Asad as-Sulami 282
Abu 'Asib 36
Abu'l-Aswad ad-Du'ali 5, 59-60
Abu 'Awana 177-179, 220
Abu'l-Bakhtari the Qadi 221
Abu Bakr 12, 22, 61, 62, 122, 129, 130, 237-239, 241, 245, 246, 248, 250-252, 259, 260, 270, 273, 274, 277, 305, 308, 313, 318
Abu Bakr ibn 'Abdullah al-Ghassani 289
Abu Bakra 5, 8-9, 42, 82, 120
Abu Balj 191
Abu Barza 4, 8, 18, 82, 227
Abu Basir 247, 252
Abu'l-Bujayr 262
Abu Burda 311
Abu'd-Darda' 242-243, 274, 276, 279
Abu Dharr 17, 79, 134
Abu Fatima al-Azdi 315
Abu Hanash al-Ansari 263
Abu Hanifa 198, 204, 205, 208, 231, 232
Abu Hind ad-Dari 261
Abu Hurayra 123, 131, 140, 174
Abu'l-Jald al-Jawni 140
Abu Jandal ibn Suhayl 252
Abu'l-Jawza' ar-Rab'i 112, 140-141
Abu Jum'a 315
Abu Khayra 52
Abu Kinana al-Qurashi 82
Abu'l-Malih al-Hudhali 138
Abu Malik al-Ash'ari 248
Abu Maryam 270
Abu Maryam al-Hanafi 55
Abu Musa al-Ash'ari 42, 59, 60, 77, 79, 80, 82, 137, 248, 268, 274
Abu Mushir 292-293
Abu Muslim ad-Da'i 211, 215, 222, 229-230
Abu Muslim al-Khawlani 240, 279

Index

Abu Nadra 132
Abu Nawfal ibn Muslim 147-148
Abu Qilaba al-Jarmi 116, 118-19, 156
Abu Rafi' as-Sa'igh 77
Abu Raja' al-'Utaridi 5, 45, 87-88
Abu Rayhana al-Ansari 262
Abu Rifa'a al-'Adawi 41-42
Abu Ruhm ibn Qays al-Ash'ari 268
Abu Sa'd al-Khayr al-Anmari 311
Abu Safiyya 36
Abu Sa'id al-Mu'addib 201-202
Abu Sakhr al-Ayli 322
Abu Salama 48
Abu Salma 267
Abu's-Sawwar al-'Adawi 50, 96-97
Abu Sayyara al-Mut'i 259
Abu Shaykh al-Hunna'i 99
Abu Sufra al-'Ataki 61-62
Abu Sufyan Madluk 270
Abu Tha'laba al-Khushani 258
Abu 'Ubayd 38
Abu 'Ubayda ibn al-Jarrah 237, 239, 247, 256, 315
Abu Ubayy 249-250
Abu Umama al-Bahili 256
Abu Umayya 73-74, 171
Abu 'Uthman an-Nahdi 58-59, 195
Abu'l-Yaqzan 312
Abu Yusuf the Qadi 204, 209, 217, 221
Abu Zaynab 84
Al-'Adda' ibn Khalid 30-31
'Adi ibn 'Amira 294
'Afiyya ibn Yazid al-Awdi 215, 220
Ahmad ibn Muhammad ibn Hanbal 220
Ahmar ibn Jaz' 28
Ahl as-Suffa 254
Al-Ahnaf ibn Qays 56-58, 81
'A'idh ibn 'Amr al-Muzani 7, 18
'A'isha 56, 60, 64, 77, 103, 132, 174
Al-'Ala' ibn Ziyad al-'Adawi 143
'Ali 34, 52, 59, 71, 253, 266, 269, 288, 295, 316
'Alqama ibn Rimtha al-Balawi 310
'Amir ibn 'Abdullah ibn 'Abdu Qays 63-69

'Ammar ibn Yasir 103
'Amr ibn 'Abasa 250
'Amr ibn al-Ahtam 22
'Amr ibn Akhtab 16
'Amr ibn al-'As 244, 245, 305-307, 309, 313- 314
'Amr al-Bakali 261
'Amr ibn Malik al-'Akki 269
'Amr ibn al-Muhajir 285
'Amr ibn 'Umayr 44
'Amwas 237, 239, 240, 241, 248, 251, 252
Anas ibn Malik 9-15, 72, 75, 97, 100, 112, 116, 121-122, 130, 131, 161, 237, 239, 249, 281
Anas ibn Sirin 122, 131, 166
'Aqaba 238, 239, 240
'Arfaja ibn As'ad 26
Artaban 76
'As'as ibn Salama 98
A'sha ibn Mazin 31-32
Ashajj 'Abdu'l-Qays 50-51
Ash'ath al-Humrani 124, 158, 171-172
'Asim al-Jahdari 152
'Asim al-Laythi 48
'Asim ibn Sulayman al-Ahwal 158-159
al-Asla' 39-40
Asrim 47
Al-Aswad ibn Sari' 24-25
'Atiyya ibn 'Amr as-Sa'di 266
'Awf ibn Abi Jamila al-A'rabi 159-160, 171
'Awf ibn Malik al-Ashja'i 247
Ayyub ibn Abi Tamima as-Sakhtiyani 105, 106, 113, 118, 149, 150, 153-156, 172, 177, 179
Badr 1, 4, 15, 102, 122, 195, 237, 238, 239, 240, 241, 249, 250, 256, 278, 279
Bakkar ibn Muhammad 75, 76, 125, 129, 160, 162-167, 183, 205
Bakr ibn 'Abdullah al-Muzani 18, 73, 106, 113, 132-134
al-Bara' ibn Malik 9-10, 75
Bashir ibn 'Aqraba al-Juhani 265
Bashir ibn Zayd ad-Duba'i 46

333

Men of Madina

Bilal ibn Rabah 233-239, 250, 254, 312, 316
Bishr ibn Harb 152-153
Bishr ibn al-Harith 212
Bishr ibn al-Walid al-Kindi 237
Burayda ibn al-Husayb 3-4, 73, 227
Bushayr ibn Abi Zayd 16
Busr ibn Abi Arta' 254
Busr ibn Jahhash al-Qurashi 264
Camel, Battle of 56, 107
Ad-Dahhak ibn Qays 255
Da'ud ibn Abi Hind 158, 171
Dhu Mikhmar 264
Dirar ibn al-Khattab 253
Ditch 9, 195, 237, 239, 241, 242, 249, 250
Fadala al-Laythi 48
Fadala ibn 'Ubayd 249
Al-Fadl ibn al-'Abbas 248
Farwa ibn 'Amr al-Judhami 269, 270
Al-Fudayl ibn Zayd 84
Ghadira ibn 'Urwa 79
Ghanm ibn Sa'd 274
Gharafa ibn al-Harith al-Kindi 266
Ghazwan ibn Ghazwan 137-138
Ghudayf ibn al-Harith al-Kindi 265
Ghunaym ibn Qays al-Ka'bi 77
Ghutayf ibn al-Harith al-Kindi 275
Habib b. Maslama al-Fihri 243, 255, 276
Habis ibn Sa'd at-Ta'i 267
Hajjaj 13, 72, 78, 81, 91, 96, 100, 104-105, 128, 137, 229
Al-Hajjaj ibn Abi Mani' 293
Al-Hakam ibn 'Amr ibn Mujadda' 16-17, 227
Al-Hakam ibn al-Harith as-Sulami 46
Hamal ibn Malik al-Hudhali 19
Hammad ibn Salama 151, 158, 175
Hammad ibn Zayd 153-156, 161, 186, 176-177
Hani' al-Hamdani 270
Harim ibn Hayyan al-'Abdi 82-84
Al-Harith ibn 'Amr as-Sahmi 38-39
Al-Harith ibn Hisham 251
Al-Harith ibn Nawfal 8
Harmala al-'Anbari 19-30

Al-Harra, Battle of 16, 138
Harun ibn Ri'ab 78, 150, 151, 155
Al-Hasan al-Basri 88, 91, 94, 100-113, 114, 115, 121, 123, 124, 128, 132-133, 134, 137-138, 143, 146, 153, 154, 160, 165, 171, 172, 178, 191
Al-Hasan ibn Dinar 173
Al-Hasan ibn Musa al-Ashyab 209
Hashraj 272
Hidhyam ibn Hanifa 42-43
Hisham ad-Dastawa'i 173
Hisham ibn 'Amir 15
Hisham ibn Hubayra 96
Hudaybiyya 7, 247, 253, 307
Hudhayfa ibn al-Yaman 61-62, 195
Humayd ibn Hilal al-'Adawi 145, 154, 174
Humran ibn Aban 95
Hunayn 26, 47, 248, 250, 251, 253, 279
Hurayth ibn Hassan 34
Husayn ibn Abi'l-Hurr 78-79
Al-Husayn ibn Ibrahim ibn al-Hurr 232
Husayn ibn Muhammad al-Marwazi 209
Ibn 'Abbas 59, 71, 114, 123, 134, 141, 174
Ibn al-Ash'ath 91, 103, 104, 105, 113, 119, 141, 160
Ibn Masruh al-Habashi 9
Ibn az-Zubayr 61, 91, 131, 255, 278
Ibrahim ibn Maymun as-Sa'igh 214, 229-232
'Ikrash ibn Dhu'ayb 44-45
'Ikrima ibn Abi Jahl 61, 123, 245, 251
'Imran ibn al-Husayn 5-6, 15, 57, 92
Isma'il ibn Ibrahim ibn Miqsam 201
Isma'il ibn Muslim al-Makki 171
'Iyad ibn Ghanm 247
'Iyad ibn Hammad at-Tamim 20
Iyas ibn Mu'awiya ibn Qurra 102, 108, 115, 146-147, 175
Iyas ibn Qatada 89-90
Jabala ibn al-Azraq 267
Jabir ibn Zayd al-Azdi 114-116
Jahima ibn al-'Abbas 19
Jamajim 147, 296
Jariya ibn Qudama 33

Index

Al-Jarud 51
Jibril 36, 39
jizya 246
Jubayr ibn Nufayr al-Hadrami 273
Al-Jullah 267
Junada al-Azdi 310
Jurmuz al-Hujaymi 47
Juwayriyya ibn Asma' ibn 'Ubayd 174
Ka'b al-Ahbar 68, 249, 274-277, 279, 280
Ka'b ibn Suwar 55-56, 95
Kahmas al-Hilali 26, 50
Kathir ibn Murra al-Hadrami 278
Al-Khabt 237
Khalaf ibn Hisham al-Bazzaz 232
Khalid ibn al-Hawatiri 271
Khalid ibn Ma'dan al-Kila'i 282-283
Khalid ibn Mihran al-Hadhdha' 126, 160
Khalid ibn al-Walid 37, 45, 47, 95, 244-247, 259, 297
Kharasha ibn al-Harith 310
Kharija ibn Hudhaqa 307
Kharijites 18, 72, 73, 84, 92, 111, 115, 117, 198, 307
Al-Khashkhash ibn al-Harith 28
Khidash 48
Khilas ibn 'Amr al-Hajari 99
Khuzayma ibn Jaz' 29
kitaba 73-75, 182, 195
Kulthum ibn Hani' al-Kindi 280
Al-Layth ibn Sa'd 320
Mahmiyya ibn Jaz' 308
Makhul ad-Dimishqi 144, 238, 253, 281-282, 283
Malik ibn 'Amr 24, 269
Malik ibn Anas 121-122, 185, 214, 229
Malik ibn Hubayra as-Sulami 260
Malik ibn al-Huwayrith 26
Mansur ibn Zadhan 191
Ma'qil ibn Yasar 8, 64, 70
Marj Rahit 255, 270
Maslama ibn Makhlad ibn as-Samit 313
Maymun ibn Mihran 128, 132, 296, 299
Maymun ibn Siyah 97
Maymuna 297
Maysara al-Fajr 34

Mazin ibn Khaythama 263
Mihjan ibn al-Adra' 6
Mihna 208, 214, 220, 221, 291, 321
Mu'adh ibn Jabal 110, 239-240, 273, 274, 275
Mu'adha al-Ansariyya 85-87
Mu'awiya al-Hudhali 261
Mu'awiya ibn Abi Sufyan 9, 35, 48, 59, 60, 67-69, 71, 89, 239-250, 253, 255, 270, 276, 277, 279, 288, 295, 305, 307, 308
Mu'awiya ibn Hayda 20
Mu'awiya ibn Hudayj 311
Mu'awiya ibn Qurra 18, 139, 243
Al-Mughira ibn Shu'ba 3, 9, 77, 80, 82
Al-Muhallab ibn Abi Sufra al-'Anaki 84
Muhammad ibn 'Abdullah al-Ansari 74, 126, 160-161, 164, 182
Muhammad ibn 'Abdullah al-Kilabi 215
Muhammad ibn al-Hasan 208
Muhammad ibn Sirin 11, 14, 74, 103, 106, 110, 113, 114, 115, 121-130, 131, 154, 161-162, 164-165, 183, 241
Muhammad ibn Thabit al-'Abdi 229-230
Muhammad ibn 'Umar al-Aslami 207
Muhammad ibn Wasi' 149-150
Mujiba al-Bahiyya 49
Al-Munaqqa' ibn al-Husayn 37
Murji'ites 142, 197, 217, 231, 232
Mus'ab ibn 'Abdullah 229
Mus'ab ibn az-Zubayr 58, 297
Musaylima 55, 246, 259
Al-Musayyab ibn Darim 79-80
Muslim ibn Harith 260
Muslim ibn Kabis or Kubays 281
Muslim ibn Yasar 105, 116, 118-119
Mu'ta 245
Mutarrif ibn 'Abdullah 5, 6, 69, 75, 91-93, 105, 147, 151
Mu'tazilites 164, 168
Muwarriq ibn al-Mushmarij 73, 124, 140-142
An-Nadr ibn Anas ibn Malik 121
Nafi' ibn al-Harith 41-42
Nahik ibn Sarim as-Sakuni 262
An-Namir ibn Tawlab 23

335

Nubayh ibn Sawab al-Mahri 308-309
Nubaysha al-Hudhali 30
Numayr al-Khuza'i 36
Qabisa ibn Dhu'ayb al-Khuza'i 278
Qabisa ibn al-Mukhariq 20
Qabisa ibn Waqqas 33
Qadar 106, 111, 125, 126, 133, 143, 151, 155, 161, 164, 171, 173, 183, 282, 288, 289, 296
Qadisiyya 1, 37
Al-Qasim ibn 'Abdu'r-Rahman 279
Al-Qasim ibn Rabi'a 100
Qatada ibn Di'ama 102, 122, 126, 143-145, 170
Qays al-Judhami 264
Qays ibn 'Asim 21
Qays ibn 'Ubad al-Qaysi 82
Qubath ibn Ashyam 256
Qurra ibn Du'mus 27
Qurra ibn Iyas 18
Qutba ibn Qatada 45
Qutham ibn al-'Abbas 228
Ar-Rabi' ibn Anas 229, 235
Rabi'a ibn 'Amr al-Jurshi 271
Rabi'a ibn Kulthum 105
Rafi' ibn 'Amr 17
Raja' ibn Haywa 281
ra'y 105, 159, 168, 198, 204, 208, 209, 212, 217
Ridda 22, 51, 55, 61-62, 246, 259
Rifa'a ibn Zayd al-Judhami 269
Sa'd ibn Abi Waqqas 1-3, 298
Sa'd ibn al-Atwal 34
Sa'd ibn Ibrahim az-Zuhri 228
Sa'd ibn 'Ubada 240-241, 259
Sa'id ibn Abi 'Aruba 141, 158, 170, 206
Sa'id ibn Abi'l-Hasan 104-105, 113-114
Sa'id ibn 'Amir 247
Sa'id ibn Iyas al-Jurayri 69, 80, 136, 161, 178, 193
Sa'id ibn Musayyab 105, 108, 144, 240, 246, 276
Safwan ibn Muhriz 94
Sahl ibn al-Hanzaliyya 249
Sahm ibn 'Amr al-Ash'ari 268
Salama al-Abrash ibn al-Fadl 235

Salama al-Jarmi 53-54
Salama ibn Nufayl al-Hadrami 264-265
Salih al-Murri 175, 201
Salim ibn 'Abdullah 154
Salm ibn Salim al-Balkhi 232
Salman al-Farisi 59, 195-196
Samura ibn Jundub 29-30, 60
Sandar 314-315
Sa'sa'a ibn Mu'awiya 22
Sa'sa'a ibn Najiyya 22
Sawada ibn Rabi'a al-Jarmi 28
Sawwar ibn 'Abdullah ibn Qudama 125, 161, 164, 171, 176
Shaddad ibn Aws 249
Sharahbil ibn Aws 266-267
Sharahbil ibn as-Samt 243
Shu'ba ibn al-Hajjaj 173-174
Shurahbil ibn Hasana 243-244, 319
Shuways ibn Jabbash 80
Siffin 71, 100, 254, 256, 283, 288, 305, 307, 308, 316
Sila ibn Ashyam al-'Adawi 84-87
Sinan ibn Gharafa 261
Sinan ibn Salama al-Hudhali 78
Sirin 74-76, 129, 163
Suffa 30
Sufyan ath-Thawri 154, 165, 172, 175, 187, 202
Sufyan ibn Usayd al-Hadrami 262
Suhar ibn 'Abbas al-'Abdi 52
Suhayl ibn 'Amr 245, 251, 252
Sulaym ibn Jabir al-Hujaymi 25
Sulayman ibn al-Mughira al-Qaysi 154, 174
Sulayman ibn Tarkhan at-Taymi 114, 132, 156-157
Surraq 312
Suwayd ibn 'Abdu'l-'Aziz 290-291
Suwayd ibn Hubayra 48
Tabuk 7, 47, 258, 240, 253
Talha ibn 'Abdullah an-Nadri 30
At-Talib ibn Zayd 25
Talq ibn Habib al-'Anazi 142
Tamim ad-Dari 254
Tawba al-'Anbari 147-148
Thabit ibn Aslam al-Bunani 85, 93, 94,

Index

110, 115, 126, 129, 145-146, 148
Thabit ibn Zayd 15
Thawban 248
Thawban ibn Yamrad 263
Thawr ibn Yazid al-Kila'i 288
'Ubada ibn Qurs al-'Abasi 49
'Ubada ibn as-Samit 239, 249, 275
'Ubaydullah ibn Abi Bakra 120
'Ubaydullah ibn al-Hasan 69
'Ubaydullah ibn Ziyad 7, 18, 36, 56, 63, 293
Ubayy ibn Ka'b 24, 76, 81, 122
Uhud 9, 15, 16, 29, 132, 210, 227, 237, 238, 239, 241, 242, 250
'Ulatha ibn Shajjar 28
'Ulayya bint Isma'il 201
'Umar ibn 'Abdi'l-'Aziz 112, 117, 118, 121, 127, 128, 138, 149, 177, 227, 229, 265, 285, 295, 296, 297
'Umar ibn al-Khattab 1-3, 5, 8, 9, 11-13, 15, 23, 33, 42, 50, 55-60, 62, 71, 73-84, 100, 102, 131, 139, 150, 171, 195, 237-238, 240-241, 243, 245-248, 250-253, 260, 270, 273-277, 305, 307, 313
'Umara ibn Ahmar 43-44
'Umayr ibn 'Atiyya al-Laythi 78
'Umayr ibn Ishaq 138-139
'Umayr ibn Sa'd 250
Umayya ibn Makhshi 7
Umm Salama 103, 210
'Uqba ibn 'Abdu'l-Ghafir 104, 153
'Uqba ibn 'Amir al-Juhami 308
'Uqba ibn Malik 28
'Urayb 268
'Urwa ibn Samura 40
Usama ibn 'Umayr 26
Usayr 40
'Utba ibn 'Abd as-Sulami 266
'Utba ibn Ghazwan 1-3
'Uthman ibn Abi'l-'As 23-24
'Uthman ibn 'Affan 4, 47, 58, 67-68, 95, 100, 102, 122, 239, 243, 253, 254, 270, 305, 307, 315
'Uthman ibn Miqsam 193
'Uthman ibn Talha 244-245

'Uthman ibn 'Uthman ath-Thaqafi 260
Uways al-Qarani 83
Wahshi ibn Harb al-Habashi 259-260
Al-Walid ibn Muslim 291
Wathila ibn al-Asqa' 253-254
Yahya ibn Ma'in 235, 279
Yahya ibn Sa'id ibn Aban 154, 210
Yahya ibn Ya'mar al-Laythi 228-229
Yamama 55
Ya'qub ibn Ibrahim az-Zuhri 228
Yarmuk 237, 256, 260, 305
Yazid ibn 'Abdullah b. ash-Shikhkhir 99
Yazid ibn Abi Sufyan 253, 269
Yazid ibn Asad 265
Yazid ibn al-Asamm 296
Yazid ibn al-Aswad al-Jurashi 276
Yazid ibn Mu'awiya 4, 36, 42, 227, 255, 276, 306
Yazid ibn al-Muhallab 84, 104, 128, 138, 174
Yunus ibn 'Ubayd 154, 160-161, 170, 171
Yusuf ibn Khalid as-Samti 181
Zayd 39
Az-Zibriqan ibn Badr 21
Ziyad ibn Abi Sufyan 6, 16, 18, 31, 42, 60, 101, 120, 228
Ziyad ibn al-Harith as-Suda'i 312
Zuhayr ibn Harb ibn Ishtal 220
Zurara ibn Awfa al-Harshi 96